THE DICTIONARY OF
Global Sustainability

With Case Studies on the
Environmental, Economic, Technological,
and Social Aspects of Sustainability

Tracy Green

University of California, Los Angeles

The McGraw-Hill Companies

Mc
Graw
Hill

Connect
Learn
Succeed™

THE DICTIONARY OF GLOBAL SUSTAINABILITY: WITH CASE STUDIES ON THE
ENVIRONMENTAL, ECONOMIC, TECHNOLOGICAL, AND SOCIAL ASPECTS OF
SUSTAINABILITY

This text is published by the Contemporary Learning Series group within the McGraw-Hill Higher
Education division.

1 2 3 4 5 6 7 8 9 0 DOC/DOC 1 0 9 8 7 6 5 4 3 2

MHID: 0-07-351452-7
ISBN: 978-0-07-351452-9

Managing Editor: *Larry Loeppke*
Developmental Editor: *Debra A. Henricks*
Senior Permissions Coordinator: *Lenny J. Behnke*
Marketing Specialist: *Alice Link*
Project Manager: *Erin Melloy*
Design Coordinator: *Brenda A. Rolwes*
Cover Design: *Rick D. Noel*
Buyer: *Nicole Baumgartner*
Media Project Manager: *Sridevi Palani*

Compositor: *Laserwords Private Limited*
Cover Image: © *Design Pics Inc./Alamy RF*

Library of Congress Cataloging-in-Publication Data

Green, Tracy.
  The dictionary of global sustainability: with case studies on the environmental, economic, technological,
and social aspects of sustainability/Tracy Green.
    p. cm.
  Includes bibliographical references.
  ISBN 978-0-07-351452-9 (alk. paper)
1. Sustainable living—Dictionaries. I. Title.
  GE196.G75 2012
  338.9'2703—dc23   2011046867

www.mhhe.com

CONTENTS

Preface   vii

PART I: THE DICTIONARY OF GLOBAL SUSTAINABILITY   **1**
An A through Z listing of terms and definitions particularly useful to students and practitioners in the interdisciplinary field of sustainability.

References for Terms   **144**

PART II: CASE STUDIES ON THE ENVIRONMENTAL, ECONOMIC, TECHNOLOGICAL, AND SOCIAL ASPECTS OF SUSTAINABILITY   **145**

I. Agricultural
1. Mother Goose Farms *(South Kona, HI)*   147
2. Village Farms of Buffalo, Inc. *(Buffalo, NY)*   149

II. Commercial
3. Boyle Heights Youth Technology Center *(Los Angeles, CA)*   150
4. The Crestwood Building, Atlanta Metro Area *(Atlanta, GA)*   151
5. One Potomac Yard *(Arlington, VA)*   153
6. On the Road to Success: Rome, New York's East Rome Business Park *(Rome, NY)*   155
7. Rising from the Depths in Naugatuck Valley: The Restoration and Reuse of Idle Land *(Seymour, CT)*   157
8. 17th Street Plaza *(Denver, CO)*   159

III. Corporate/Institutional Sustainability
9. GE & Universal Studios Hollywood: The Treasure Hunt Model *(Los Angeles, CA; Globally)*   160
10. Google's Green Data Centers: Network POP Case Study *(Mountain View, CA)*   162
11. Lockheed Martin *(Manassas, VA)*   168

IV. Government
12. Greening of the White House Status Report and Accomplishments *(Washington, DC)*   172
13. Las Vegas Cleanup a Sure Thing *(Las Vegas, NV)*   177
14. Robins U.S. Air Force Base *(Warner Robins, Georgia)*   179

V. Industrial

15. A Former California Brownfield Recycled: A Construction and Demolition
Waste Reduction Success Story *(Emeryville, CA)* **182**
16. Old Town's New Look: Along the Waterfront, an Abandoned Manufacturing
Site Joins Two City Parks *(Old Town, MA)* **185**
17. Provo City Steeling Itself for Redevelopment *(Provo City, UT)* **186**

VI. Residential

18. City of Santa Monica: Annenberg Community Beach House *(Santa Monica, CA)* **187**
19. Colorado Court Project *(Santa Monica, CA)* **189**
20. Portland State University (PSU) Stephen Epler Residence Hall *(Portland, OR)* **191**
21. Sellwood House: Apartment Owners Find Value in Green Features *(Portland, OR)* **192**

VII. International

22. Charles Hostler Student Center *(Beirut, Lebanon)* **196**
23. Omicron AEC, Ltd.: Head Office Renovation *(Vancouver, BC, Canada)* **203**
24. Passive House *(Bessancourt, France)* **209**
25. Setagaya-ku Fukasawa Symbiotic Housing Complex *(Setagaya-ku, Japan)* **211**
26. Vanke Center *(Shenzhen, China)* **213**
27. Victor Civita Park *(São Paulo, Brazil)* **215**
28. WWF and Abu Dubai's Masdar Initiative Unveil Plan For World's
First Carbon-Neutral, Waste-Free, Car-Free City *(Dubai, UAE)* **217**

References for Case Studies **219**

Appendix A: Organizations **221**

Appendix B: Journals **235**

DEDICATION

To my loving husband Dwayne, and to my wonderful children, Kirk and Delisa. They all live successful and purposeful lives and are my source of joy and energy. I thank them for their love, support, and encouragement. They make me proud.
To my parents, Gerald and Linda, for their words of wisdom, encouragement, love and sacrifice.
To my siblings, Michelle and Corey, for their continuous love and encouragement.

ABOUT THE AUTHOR

Tracy Green is an independent real estate professional and adjunct instructor in UCLA's Department of Business, Management and Legal Programs. She is also an associate faculty member at Saddleback College in the Business Sciences Department and an educational consultant teaching and developing online courses for various institutions.

She earned a BA in Geography from California State University—Fullerton and an MPA (Master in Public Administration) from California State University—Dominguez Hills. Her primary research interests are sustainable development of brownfields and green building. She served as an Annual Meeting Reviewer for the Academy of Management (AOM) Green Management Matters meeting in 2009 and is a contributing author on another book. She maintains active memberships with the U.S. Green Building Council and Urban Land Institute.

PREFACE

Sustainability is defined by the American Institute of Architect's World Commission on Environment and Development as "meeting the needs of the present generation without compromising the ability of future generations to meet their own needs." An array of new concepts and terminology are consistently becoming part of the aspects of sustainability. The constant expanding vocabulary of sustainability demands a book of this nature as these terms and concepts can be ambiguous and complicated. At various times you may read or hear terms or concepts related to sustainability that are not clear to you. This book, whether you are a student, practitioner, or layperson, will prove to be a useful reference in providing a clearer understanding of the terminology. Concise definitions are provided for more than 2,500 terms that are short enough to be read quickly but clear enough for the reader to gain an understanding.

The Dictionary of Global Sustainability is intended to provide a basic collection of key sustainable terms, organizations, and journals into one source. Case studies that examine sustainability projects from around the world are also included in this book. These case studies are included to illustrate the theory and practice of environmental, economic, technological, and social aspects of sustainability. The list of more than 200 organizations and 100 scholarly and trade journals (domestic and international) include contact information and website addresses that will lead the reader to valuable research materials. The ultimate goal of this book is to serve as a quick reference guide to "green" professionals (architects, developers, realtors, and builders), corporations, industries, governments, instructors, students, and other individuals who are looking for a better understanding of sustainable concepts.

ACKNOWLEDGMENTS

Thank you to the editorial staff at McGraw Hill: Debra Henricks, Jill Meloy, Leonard Behnke, and Larry Loeppke for their efficiency and professionalism.

Thank you to Dwayne Green for assisting in advisement and research of this book.

Thank you to Michelle Burton and Kori Burton for assisting in the research and preparation of this book.

Thank you to the Academic Advisory Board for their constructive criticism and helpful suggestions during the development of this book. These members include:

Olayiwola Abegunrin, Howard University

Shamim Ahsan, Metro State College of Denver

Robert Altamura, Heald College

Mark Anderson, University of Maine

Leonard (Andy) Andres, Boston University

Tony Aponte, International Academy of Design and Technology

John Ayers, Vanderbilt University

Thomas Ayers, Barry University

Narinder Bansal, Ohlone College

Lauren Bergey, Centenary College

Thomas Bicki, Emerson College

Jennifer Biederman, Winona State University

Charles Bomar, University of Wisconsin-Stout

Lisa Bonneau, Metropolitan Community College, Blue River

Nadine Bopp, School of the Art Institute

Thomas Bowen, Philadelphia University

Shelly Brandenburger, South Dakota State University

Edwin Brands, Birmingham Southern College

Catherine Carter, Georgia Perimeter College

Daniel Cassidy, Western Michigan University

Timothy Clarey, Delta College

Patricia Cleary, University of Wisconsin, Parkside

Cliff Cockerham, Whites Creek High School

Craig Conley, New Mexico Highlands University

Angela Costanzo, Hawaii Pacific University

Jim Countryman, University of Minnesota

Raymond Coveney, University of Missouri, Kansas City

Gerard Cronin, Salem Community College

Robert East, Washington & Jefferson College

David Elliott, Louisiana College

April Ann Fong, Portland Community College

Jonathan Frye, McPherson College

Orin Gelderloos, University of Michigan, Dearborn

Ken Gembel, Northwood University

Susan Gilbertz, Montana State University, Billings

Consuelo Guayara, University of Iowa

M. Carmen Hall, Georgia Perimeter College

William Hallahan, Nazareth College

Linda Heiland, Pinnacle Career Institute

Jacob Held, University of Central Arkansas

Pablo Hernandez, Hollins University

Jason Hlebakos, Mt. San Jacinto College

Nancy Hoalst-Pullen, Kennesaw State University

James Hollenbeck, Indiana University Southeast

Yvonne Hood, Potomac College

Barbara Ikalainen, North Shore Community College

Linda Jensen-Carey, Southwestern Michigan College

Robert Johnson, Medaille College

Jean-Gabriel Jolivet, Edgewood College

Subburaj Kannan, Southwest Texas Junior College

Ali E. Kashef, University of Northern Iowa

Joseph W. Kennedy, Edward Waters College

David Keuhl, University Of Wisconsin, River Falls

Vishnu Khade, Goodwin College

Nazrul Khandaker, York College

Julie Kinzelman, University of Wisconsin, Parkside

Birthe Veno Kjellerup, Goucher College

Katherine Law, Our Lady of Holy Cross College

Kennie Leet, Broome Community College

Kurt Leuschner, College of the Desert

Zhi-Qing Lin, Southern Illinois University, Edwardsville

Steve Manis, Mississippi Gulf Coast Community College

Nilo Marin, Broward College

Julie Maxson, Metropolitan State University

Ana McClanahan, Beaufort County Community College

Charles McClaugherty, University of Mount Union

Colleen McLean, Youngstown State University

Molly Mehling, Miami University of Ohio

John F. Molina, Bronx Community College

Aaron Moody, University of North Carolina, Chapel Hill

John Moore, Drury University

Israel Msengi, Lamar University

Katherine Nashleanas, University of Nebraska

Russell Nemecek, Columbia College

Gregory O'Mullan, Queens College, CUNY

Mark A. Ouimette, Hardin-Simmons University

Firooza Pavri, University of Southern Maine

Michael Pawlish, Montclair State University

Mary Puglia, Central Arizona College

Mohammed Rabbi, Valley Forge Military College

Laura Rademacher, University of the Pacific

Usha Rao, Saint Joseph's University

Jennifer Richter, University of New Mexico

Jeanne Saint-Amour, Glendale Community College

John Salmen, The Illinois Institute of Art

Shamili Sandiford, College of DuPage

Fausto Sarmiento, University of Georgia

Wendy Scattergood, St. Norbert College

Paul Schmidt, Ball State University

Larry Schmitt, Central Community College

Tom Schrand, Philadelphia University

Amanda Senft, Bellevue College

Andrew Shella, Terra State Community College

John Shiber, KCTCS—Big Sandy Community & Technical College

Ramesh Singh, Chapman University

Nicholas J. Smith-Sebasto, Kean University

Richard Sneed, University of Central Oklahoma

Stefan Sommer, Northern Arizona University

Ravi Srinivas, University of St. Thomas

Lynn Steel, Eastern Connecticut State University

David Stern, Nassau Community College

Frederick Stoss, University at Buffalo, SUNY

Keith Summerville, Drake University

Patricia Taylor, University of Wyoming

John Theilmann, Converse College

Mike Vozick, Borough of Manhattan Community College, SUNY

Rebecca Waggett, University of Tampa

Melanie Waite-Altringer, Anoka-Ramsey Community College

Anita Walz, Marshall University

Richard Weil, Brown College

Michael Wenzel, Folsom Lake College

Van Wheat, South Texas College

Todd Yetter, University of the Cumberlands

Craig Zoellner, North Iowa Area Community College

Part I

THE
DICTIONARY
OF
GLOBAL
SUSTAINABILITY

A

abandoned well. A well that is not used or is in such a state of disrepair that it cannot be used for its original purpose.

abatement. Reducing the degree or intensity of, or eliminating, pollution.

abatement debris. Waste from remediation activities.

absorbed dose. In exposure assessment, the amount of a substance that penetrates an exposed organism's absorption barriers (e.g., skin, lung tissue, gastrointestinal tract) through physical or biological processes.

absorption. The uptake of water, other fluids, or dissolved chemicals by a cell or an organism (as tree roots absorb dissolved nutrients in soil).

absorption barrier. Any of the exchange sites of the body that permit uptake of various substances at different rates (e.g., skin, lung tissue, and gastrointestinal-tract wall)

acceptable intake (for subchronic and chronic exposure). Numbers that describe how toxic a chemical is. The numbers are derived from animal studies of the relationship between dose and noncancer effects. There are two types of acceptable exposure values: one for acute (relatively short-term) and one for chronic (longer-term) exposure.

accident site. The location of an unexpected occurrence, failure, or loss, either at a plant or along a transportation route, resulting in a release of hazardous materials.

acclimatization. The physiological and behavioral adjustments of an organism to changes in its environment.

accountability. Being answerable to all stakeholders, including any natural or social systems affected by a business such as customers, employees, and communities.

acetone. A widely used, highly volatile solvent. It is readily absorbed by breathing, ingestion or contact with the skin. Workers who have inhaled acetone have reported respiratory problems.

acid aerosol. Acidic liquid or solid particles small enough to become airborne. High concentrations can irritate the lungs and have been associated with respiratory diseases such as asthma.

acid deposition. A complex chemical and atmospheric phenomenon that occurs when emissions of sulfur and nitrogen compounds and other substances are transformed by chemical processes in the atmosphere, often far from the original sources, and then deposited on earth in either wet or dry form. The wet forms, popularly called acid rain, can fall to earth as rain, snow, or fog. The dry forms are acidic gases or particulates.

acid mine drainage. Drainage of water from areas that have been mined for coal or other mineral ores. The water has a low pH because of its contact with sulfur-bearing material and is harmful to aquatic organisms.

acid neutralizing capacity. Measure of ability of a base (e.g., water or soil) to resist changes in pH.

acid rain. Rain that is more acidic than normal; occurs when emissions of sulfur dioxide and nitrogen oxides from utilities, manufacturers, and vehicles combine with water vapor in the air.

acidic. The condition of water or soil that contains a sufficient amount of acid substances to lower the pH below 7.0.

acoustic. Having properties or characteristics affecting or connected with sound, for example, acoustic tiles.

action level. A guideline established by environmental protection agencies to identify the concentration of a substance in a particular medium (e.g., water, soil, etc.) that may present a health risk when exceeded. If contaminants are found at concentrations above their action levels, measures must be taken to decrease the contamination.

activated carbon. A highly adsorbent form of carbon used to remove odors and toxic substances from liquid or gaseous emissions. In waste treatment, it is used to remove dissolved organic matter from waste drinking water. It is also used in motor vehicle evaporative control systems.

activated sludge. Sludge that contains microorganisms that break down organic contaminants (e.g., benzene) in liquid waste streams to simpler substances such as water and carbon dioxide. It is also the product formed when raw sewage is mixed with bacteria-laden sludge, then stirred and aerated to destroy organic matter.

activation energy. Activation energy of a reaction is the amount of energy needed to start the reaction.

activator. A chemical added to a pesticide to increase its activity.

active heating system. A solar water or space-heating system that moves heated air or water using pumps or fans.

active ingredient. In any pesticide product, the component that kills, or otherwise controls, target pests. Pesticides are regulated primarily on the basis of active ingredients.

active solar heating. Mechanical or electrical systems that collect and absorb solar radiation, then transfer the solar heat to the interior space or to a storage system, from which the heat is distributed in the home.

activity (of a radioactive isotope). The number of particles or photons ejected from a radioactive substance per unit time.

activity plans. Written procedures in a school's asbestos-management plan that detail the steps a local education agency (LEA) will follow in performing the initial and additional cleaning, operation, and maintenance-program tasks; periodic surveillance; and reinspection required by the Asbestos Hazard Emergency Response Act (AHERA).

acute effect. An adverse effect on any living organism which results in severe symptoms that develop rapidly; symptoms often subside after the exposure stops.

acute exposure. A single exposure to a toxic substance that may result in severe biological harm or death. Acute exposures are usually characterized as lasting no longer than a day, as compared to longer, continuing exposure over a period of time.

acute hazards. Hazards associated with short-term exposure to relatively large amounts of toxic substances.

acute toxicity. The ability of a substance to cause severe biological harm or death soon after a single exposure or dose. Also, any poisonous effect resulting from a single short-term exposure to a toxic substance.

adapt. Change, make suitable or fit for different use, purpose, or circumstances.

adaptation. Changes in an organism's physiological structure or function or habits that allow it to survive in new surroundings.

add-on control device. An air pollution control device, such as carbon absorber or incinerator, that reduces the pollution in an exhaust gas. The control device usually does not affect the process being controlled and thus is add-on technology, as opposed to a scheme to control pollution through altering the basic process itself.

adequately wet. Asbestos-containing material that is sufficiently mixed or penetrated with liquid to prevent the release of particulates.

administered dose. In exposure assessment, the amount of a substance given to a test subject (human or animal) to determine dose–response relationships. Since exposure to chemicals is usually inadvertent, this quantity is often called a potential dose.

administrative order. A legal document signed by the EPA (Environmental Protection Agency) directing an individual, business, or other entity to take corrective action or refrain from an activity. It describes the violations and actions to be taken, and can be enforced in court. Such orders may be issued, for example, as a result of an administrative complaint whereby the respondent is ordered to pay a penalty for violations of a statute.

administrative order on consent. A legal agreement signed by EPA and an individual, business, or other entity through which the violator agrees to pay for correction of violations, take the required corrective or cleanup actions, or refrain from an activity. It describes the actions to be taken, may be subject to a comment period, applies to civil actions, and can be enforced in court.

Administrative Procedures Act. A law that spells out procedures and requirements related to the promulgation of regulations.

administrative record. All documents that the EPA considered or relied on in selecting the response action at a Superfund site, culminating in the record of decision for remedial action or, an action memorandum for removal actions.

adsorption. Removal of a pollutant from air or water by collecting the pollutant on the surface of a solid material; e.g., an advanced method of treating waste in which activated carbon removes organic matter from wastewater.

adulterants. Chemical impurities or substances that by law do not belong in a food, a pesticide.

adulterated. Any pesticide whose strength or purity falls below the quality stated on its label. A food, feed, or product that contains illegal pesticide residues.

advanced treatment. A level of wastewater treatment more stringent than secondary treatment; requires an 85 percent reduction in conventional pollutant concentration or a significant reduction in nonconventional pollutants.

advanced wastewater treatment. Any treatment of sewage that goes beyond the secondary or biological water treatment stage and includes the removal of nutrients such as phosphorus and nitrogen and a high percentage of suspended solids.

adverse effects data. Federal Insecticide, Fungicide and Rodenticide Act (FIFRA) requires a pesticide registrant to submit data to the EPA on any studies or other information regarding unreasonable adverse effects of a pesticide at any time after its registration.

adverse health effects. Effects of chemicals or other materials that impair one's health. They can range from relatively mild temporary conditions such as minor eye or throat irritation, shortness of breath or headaches to permanent and serious conditions such as cancer, birth defects, or damage to organs.

advisory. A nonregulatory document that communicates risk information to those who may have to make risk management decisions.

advisory level. The level above which an environmental protection agency suggests it is potentially harmful to be exposed to a contaminant, although no action is mandated.

aerated lagoon. A holding and/or treatment pond that speeds up the natural process of biological decomposition of organic waste by stimulating the growth and activity of bacteria that degrade organic waste.

aeration. A process that promotes biological degradation of organic matter in water. The process may be passive (as when waste is exposed to air), or active (as when a mixing or bubbling device introduces the air).

aeration tank. A chamber used to inject air into water.

aerator. The screw-on tip of the faucet that determines the flow rate. Aerators are inexpensive to replace and they can be one of the most cost-effective household water conservation measures.

aerobic. Life or processes that require, or are not destroyed by, the presence of oxygen.

aerobic treatment. Process by which microbes decompose complex organic compounds in the presence of oxygen and use the liberated energy for reproduction and growth.

aerosol. Small droplets or particles suspended in the atmosphere, typically containing sulfur. They are usually emitted naturally (e.g., in volcanic eruptions) and as the result of anthropogenic (human) activities such as burning fossil fuels. The pressurized gas used to propel substances out of a container.

aesthetics. The study of beauty, form, and taste, including the manifestations of natural beauty and nature.

affected landfill. Under the Clean Air Act, landfills that meet criteria for capacity, age, and emissions rates set by the EPA. They are required to collect and combust their gas emissions.

affected public. The people who live and/or work near a hazardous waste site. The human population adversely impacted following exposure to a toxic pollutant in food, water, air, or soil.

afterburner. In incinerator technology, a burner located so that the combustion gases are made to pass through its flame in order to remove smoke and odors. It may be attached to or be separated from the incinerator proper.

age tank. A tank used to store a chemical solution of known concentration for feed to a chemical feeder; also called a day tank.

Agenda 21. A document adopted by the United Nations Conference on Environment and Development in Rio de Janeiro, Brazil, in 1992 representing a program for the 21st century, in particular a move toward the world's goal of sustainable development.

agent. Any physical, chemical, or biological entity that can be harmful to an organism.

Agent Orange. A toxic herbicide and defoliant used in the Vietnam conflict, containing 2,4,5-trichlorophen-oxyacetic acid (2,4,5-T) and 2-4 dichlorophenoxyacetic acid (2,4-D) with trace amounts of dioxin.

agricide. Term used by organic farmers to describe the effects of conventional agriculture.

agricultural pollution. Farming wastes, including runoff and leaching of pesticides and fertilizers; erosion and dust from plowing; improper disposal of animal manure and carcasses, crop residues, and debris.

agricultural waste. Poultry and livestock manure, and residual materials in liquid or solid form generated from the production and marketing of poultry, livestock, or fur-bearing animals; also includes grain, vegetable, and fruit harvest residue.

agroecosystem. Land used for crops, pasture, and livestock; the adjacent uncultivated land that supports other vegetation and wildlife; and the associated atmosphere, the underlying soils, groundwater, and drainage networks.

AHERA designated person (ADP). A person designated by a local education agency to ensure that the Asbestos Hazard Emergency Response Act (AHERA) requirements for asbestos management and abatement are properly implemented.

air binding. Situation where air enters the filter media and harms both the filtration and backwash processes.

air changes per hour (ACH). The movement of a volume of air in a given period of time; if a house has one air change per hour, it means that the air in the house will be replaced in a one-hour period.

air cleaning. Indoor air-quality control strategy to remove various airborne particulates and/or gases from the air. Most common methods are particulate filtration, electrostatic precipitation, and gas sorption.

air contaminant. Any particulate matter, gas, or combination thereof, other than water vapor.

air curtain. A method of containing oil spills. Air bubbling through a perforated pipe causes an upward water flow that slows the spread of oil. It can also be used to stop fish from entering polluted water.

air exchange rate. The rate at which outside air replaces indoor air in a given space.

air gap. Open vertical gap or empty space that separates drinking water supply to be protected from another water system in a treatment plant or other location. The open gap protects the drinking water from contamination by backflow or back siphonage.

air handling unit. Equipment that includes a fan or blower, heating and/or cooling coils, regulator controls, condensate drain pans, and air filters.

air mass. A large volume of air with certain meteorological or polluted characteristics (e.g., a heat inversion or smogginess) while in one location. The characteristics can change as the air mass moves away.

air padding. Pumping dry air into a container to assist with the withdrawal of liquid or to force a liquefied gas such as chlorine out of the container.

air permeability. Permeability of soil with respect to air, important to the design of soil-gas surveys. Measured in darcys or centimeters-per-second.

air plenum. Any space used to convey air in a building, furnace, or structure. The space above a suspended ceiling is often used as an air plenum.

air pollutant. Any substance in air that could, in high enough concentration, harm people, animals, vegetation, or material. Pollutants can include almost any natural or artificial composition of airborne matter capable of being airborne. They can be in the form of solid particles, liquid droplets, gases, or a combination. Generally, they fall into two main groups: (1) those emitted directly from identifiable sources; and (2) those produced in the air by interaction between two or more primary pollutants, or by reaction with normal atmospheric constituents, with or without photoactivation. Exclusive of pollen, fog, and dust, which are of natural origin, about 100 contaminants have been identified. Air pollutants are often grouped in categories for ease in classification, some of which are: solids, sulfur compounds, volatile organic chemicals, particulate matter, nitrogen compounds, oxygen compounds, halogen compounds, radioactive compound, and odors.

air pollution. The presence of contaminants or pollutant substances in the air that interfere with human health or welfare, or produce other harmful environmental effects.

air pollution control device. Mechanism or equipment that cleans emissions generated by a source (e.g., an incinerator, industrial smokestack, or an automobile exhaust system) by removing pollutants that would otherwise be released to the atmosphere.

air pollution episode. A period of abnormally high concentration of air pollutants, often due to low winds and temperature inversion, that can cause illness and death.

air quality criteria. The levels of pollution and lengths of exposure from which adverse health and welfare effects can occur.

air quality standards. The level of pollutants prescribed by regulations that are not to be exceeded during a given time in a defined area.

air sparging. Injecting air or oxygen into an aquifer to strip or flush volatile contaminants as air bubbles up through the ground water and is captured by a vapor extraction system.

air stripping. A treatment system that removes volatile organic compounds (VOCs) from contaminated ground water or surface water by forcing an airstream through the water and causing the compounds to evaporate.

air stripping tower. A tank used to remove volatile organic chemicals (such as solvents) from contaminated water by causing them to evaporate. Polluted water is sprayed downward through a tower filled with packing materials while air is blown upwards through the tower. The contaminants evaporate into the air, leaving significantly reduced pollutant levels in the water. The air is treated before it is released into the atmosphere.

air toxics. Any air pollutant for which a national ambient air quality standard (NAAQS) does not exist (i.e., excluding ozone, carbon monoxide, PM-10, sulfur dioxide, nitrogen oxide) that may reasonably be anticipated to cause cancer; respiratory, cardiovascular, or developmental effects; reproductive dysfunctions, neurological disorders, heritable gene mutations; or other serious or irreversible chronic or acute health effects in humans.

air/oil table. The surface between the vadose zone and ambient oil; the pressure of oil in the porous medium is equal to atmospheric pressure.

airborne particulates. Total suspended particulate matter found in the atmosphere as solid particles or liquid droplets. Chemical composition of particulates varies widely, depending on location and time of year. Sources of airborne particulates include dust, emissions from industrial processes, combustion products from the burning of wood and coal, combustion products associated with motor vehicle or nonroad engine exhausts, and reactions to gases in the atmosphere.

airborne release. Release of any pollutant into the air.

air-conditioning. Cooling and dehumidifying the air in a building by a refrigeration unit powered by electricity or natural gas. This definition excludes fans, blowers, or evaporative cooling systems (swamp coolers) that are not connected to a refrigeration unit.

Air-conditioning and Refrigeration Institute (ARI). 320, 325, 330. ARI heat pump classifications: 320 refers to a water-source heat pump; 325 refers to a ground water-source heat pump; 330 refers to a ground-source closed-loop heat pump.

air-conditioning equipment. Either a central system, window, or wall unit that cools the air in a housing unit by a refrigeration unit powered by electricity or natural gas. This definition excludes fans, blowers, or evaporative cooling systems (swamp coolers) that are not connected to a refrigeration unit.

alachlor. A herbicide, marketed under the trade name Lasso, used mainly to control weeds in corn and soybean fields.

alar. Trade name for daminozide, a pesticide that makes apples redder, firmer, and less likely to drop off trees before growers are ready to pick them. It is also used to a lesser extent on peanuts, tart cherries, concord grapes, and other fruits.

alcohol fuels. Blend of alcohol with gasoline for use as transportation fuel. It can be produced from a wide variety of organic feedstock. The common alcohol fuels are methanol and ethanol. Methanol can be produced from coal, natural gas, wood and organic waste. Ethanol is commonly made from agricultural plants, primarily corn, containing sugar.

aldicarb. An insecticide sold under the trade name Temik. It is made from ethyl isocyanate.

algae. Simple rootless plants that grow in sunlit waters in proportion to the amount of available nutrients. They can affect water quality adversely by lowering the dissolved oxygen in the water. They are food for fish and small aquatic animals.

algal blooms. Sudden spurts of algal growth, which can affect water quality adversely and indicate potentially hazardous changes in local water chemistry.

algicide. Substance or chemical used specifically to kill or control algae.

aliquot. A measured portion of a sample taken for analysis. One or more aliquots make up a sample.

alkaline. The condition of water or soil which contains a sufficient amount of alkali substance to raise the pH above 7.0.

alkalinity. The capacity of bases to neutralize acids; for example, lime is added to lakes to decrease acidity.

allergen. A substance that causes an allergic reaction in individuals sensitive to it.

allocative efficiency, social. The flow of goods, services, resources, and funds that are likely to maximize the quality of life of society over time, as distinct from the interests of special groups or classes.

alluvial. Relating to sand deposited by flowing water.

alluvial deposit. An area of sand, clay, or other similar material that has been gradually deposited by moving water, such as along a river bed or shore of a lake.

alpha particle. A positively charged particle emitted by radioactive atoms. Alpha particles travel less than one inch in the air, and a thin sheet of paper will stop them. The main danger from alpha particles is in ingesting the atoms that emit them. Body cells next to the atom can then be irradiated over an extended period of time, which may be prolonged if the atoms are taken up in bone, for instance.

alternate method. Any method of sampling and analyzing for an air or water pollutant that is not a reference or equivalent method but that has been demonstrated in specific cases-to EPA's satisfaction-to produce results adequate for compliance monitoring.

alternating current (AC). An electric current that reverses its direction at regularly recurring intervals, usually 50 or 60 times per second.

alternative compliance. A policy that allows facilities to choose among methods for achieving emission-reduction or risk-reduction instead of command-and-control regulations that specify standards and how to meet them. Use of a theoretical emissions bubble over a facility to cap the amount of pollution emitted while allowing the company to choose where and how (within the facility) it complies.

alternative energy. Energy that is renewable and ecologically safe.

alternative fuel vehicle (AFV). A vehicle designed to operate on an alternative fuel (e.g., compressed natural gas, methane blend, electricity). The vehicle could be either a vehicle designed to operate exclusively on alternative fuel or a vehicle designed to operate on alternative fuel and/or a traditional fuel.

alternative fuels. Substitutes for traditional liquid, oil-derived motor vehicle fuels gasoline and diesel. Include mixtures of alcohol-based fuels with gasoline, methanol, ethanol, compressed natural gas, and others.

alternative remedial contract strategy contractors. Government contractors who provide project management and technical services to support remedial response activities at national priorities list sites.

alternatives. In environmental impact assessment of projects, an examination of alternative locations, methods, and techniques for the project, including considering the alternative of not proceeding.

altruism. A regard for others as a principle of action.

ambient air. Refers to the surrounding air. Generally, ambient air refers to air outside and surrounding an air pollution source location. Often used interchangeably with "outdoor air."

ambient measurement. A measurement of the concentration of a substance or pollutant within the immediate environs of an organism; taken to relate it to the amount of possible exposure.

ambient medium. Material surrounding or contacting an organism (e.g., outdoor air, indoor air, water, or soil), through which chemicals or pollutants can reach the organism.

ambient temperature. Temperature of the surrounding air or other medium.

amenity. A word that frequently appears in environmental legislation usually referring to nonmarketable benefits such as beauty and tranquility.

amorphous silicon. An alloy of silica and hydrogen, with a disordered, noncrystalline internal atomic arrangement, that can be deposited in thin layers (a few micrometers in thickness) by a number of deposition methods to produce thin-film photovoltaic cells on glass, metal, or plastic substrates.

ampere. A unit of measure for an electrical current; the amount of current that flows in a circuit at an electromotive force of one volt and at a resistance of one ohm. Abbreviated as amp.

amplified man. The concept originated by George Girodias to summarize modern man, extended by access to technology and energy, given speed to shrink and degrade the world.

amprometric titration. A way of measuring concentrations of certain substances in water using an electric current that flows during a chemical reaction.

anaerobic. A life or process that occurs in, or is not destroyed by, the absence of oxygen.

anaerobic decomposition. Reduction of the net energy level and change in chemical composition of organic matter caused by microorganisms in an oxygen-free environment.

animal dander. Tiny scales of animal skin, a common indoor air pollutant.

animal studies. Investigations using animals as surrogates for humans with the expectation that the results are pertinent to humans.

anisotropy. In hydrology, the conditions under which one or more hydraulic properties of an aquifer vary from a reference point.

annual fuel utilization efficiency (AFUE). The measure of seasonal or annual efficiency of a residential heating furnace or boiler. Specifically, it is the ratio of heat output of the furnace or boiler compared to the total energy consumed by a furnace or boiler. An AFUE of 90 percent means that 90 percent of the energy in the fuel becomes heat for the home and the other 10 percent escapes up the chimney and elsewhere.

annualized growth rates. Calculated as follows: $(xn / x1) 1 / n$.

annular space, annulus. The space between two concentric tubes or casings, or between the casing and the borehole wall.

antagonism. Interference or inhibition of the effect of one chemical by the action of another.

Antarctic 'Ozone Hole'. Refers to the seasonal depletion of ozone in the upper atmosphere above a large area of Antarctica.

anthropogenic. Made or generated by a human or caused by human activity. The term is used in the context of global climate change to refer to gaseous emissions that are the result of human activities, as well as other potentially climate-altering activities, such as deforestation.

antidegradation clause. Part of federal air quality and water quality requirements prohibiting deterioration where pollution levels are above the legal limit.

antimicrobial. An agent that kills microbes.

appliance. A piece of equipment, commonly powered by electricity, used to perform a particular energy-driven function. Examples of common appliances are refrigerators, clothes washers and dishwashers, conventional ranges/ovens and microwave ovens, humidifiers and dehumidifiers, toasters, radios, and televisions.

applicable or relevant and appropriate requirements (ARARs). Any state or federal statute that pertains to protection of human life and the environment in addressing specific conditions or use of a particular cleanup technology such as at a Superfund site.

applied dose. In exposure assessment, the amount of a substance in contact with the primary absorption boundaries of an organism (e.g., skin, lung tissue, gastrointestinal track) and available for absorption.

appreciative inquiry. A philosophy of organizational assessment and change that seeks examples of success to emulate and organizational or personal strengths to build upon, rather than focusing on fixing negative or ineffective organizational processes.

aqueous. Water-based.

aqueous solubility. The maximum concentration of a chemical that will dissolve in pure water at a reference temperature.

aquifer. An underground geological formation, or group of formations, containing water; sources of groundwater for wells and springs.

aquifer test. A test to determine hydraulic properties of an aquifer.

aquitard. Geological formation that may contain groundwater but is not capable of transmitting significant quantities of it under normal hydraulic gradients. May function as confining bed.

Aral Sea. A large saltwater lake in south-central Russia, formerly the world's largest body of inland water.

architectural coatings. Coverings such as paint and roof tar that are used on exteriors of buildings.

area of review. In the Underground Injection Control (UIC) program, the area surrounding an injection well that is reviewed during the permitting process to determine if flow between aquifers will be induced by the injection operation.

area source. Any source of air pollution that is released over a relatively small area, but which cannot be classified as a point source. Such sources can include vehicles and other small engines, small businesses and household activities, or biogenic sources such as a forest that releases hydrocarbons.

aromatics. A type of hydrocarbon, such as benzene or toluene, with a specific type of ring structure. Aromatics are sometimes added to gasoline in order to increase octane. Some aromatics are toxic.

arsenic. A gray, brittle, and highly poisonous metal. It is used as an alloy for metals, especially lead and copper, and is used in insecticides and weed killers.

arsenicals. Pesticides containing arsenic.

artesian (aquifer or well). Water held under pressure in porous rock or soil confined by impermeable geological formations.

artesian well. A well that flows up like a fountain because of the internal pressure of the aquifer.

artificial. Made by art, not natural. As artifact, a product of human art and workmanship. More usually artificial things, particularly substances, are described as human-made.

asbestos. A general name given a family of naturally occurring fibrous silicate minerals.

Asbestos fibers were used mainly for insulation and as a fire retardant material in ship and building construction and other industries, and in brake shoes and pads for automobiles. Inhaling asbestos fibers has been shown to result in lung disease (asbestosis) and in lung cancer (mesothelioma). The risk of developing mesothelioma is significantly enhanced in smokers. The EPA has banned or severely restricted its use in manufacturing and construction.

asbestos abatement. Procedures to control fiber release from asbestos-containing materials in a building or to remove them entirely, including removal, encapsulation, repair, enclosure, encasement, and operations and maintenance programs.

asbestos assessment. In the asbestos-in-schools program, the evaluation of the physical condition and potential for damage of all friable asbestos containing materials and thermal insulation systems.

asbestos-containing waste materials (ACWM). Mill tailings or any waste that contains commercial asbestos and is generated by a source covered by the Clean Air Act Asbestos NESHAPS.

asbestos program manager. A building owner or designated representative who supervises all aspects of the facility asbestos management and control program.

asbestosis. A disease associated with inhalation of asbestos fibers. The disease makes breathing progressively more difficult and can be fatal.

A-scale sound level. A measurement of sound approximating the sensitivity of the human ear, used to note the intensity or annoyance level of sounds.

ash. The mineral content of a product remaining after complete combustion.

assay. A test for a specific chemical, microbe, or effect.

assessment endpoint. In ecological risk assessment, an explicit expression of the environmental value to be protected; includes both an ecological entity and specific attributed thereof entity (e.g., salmon are a valued ecological entity; reproduction and population maintenance—the attribute—form an assessment endpoint).

assimilation. The ability of a body of water to purify itself of pollutants.

assimilative capacity. The capacity of a natural body of water to receive wastewaters or toxic materials without deleterious effects and without damage to aquatic life or humans who consume the water.

Association of Boards of Certification. An international organization representing boards that certify the operators of waterworks and wastewater facilities.

atmosphere. The gaseous envelope of air surrounding the earth, the principle constituents of which are nitrogen and oxygen, together with carbon dioxide and very small amounts of inert gases such as argon, krypton, xenon, neon, and helium.

atomic structure. The conceptualized concept of an atom, regarded as consisting of a central positively charged nucleus (protons and neutrons) and a number of negatively charged electrons revolving about in various orbits.

attainment area. An area considered to have air quality as good as or better than the national ambient air-quality standards as defined in the Clean Air Act. An area may be an attainment area for one pollutant and a nonattainment area for others.

attenuation. The process by which a compound is reduced in concentration over time, through absorption, adsorption, degradation, dilution, and/or transformation. Also be the decrease with distance of sight caused by attenuation of light by particulate pollution.

attitudinal changes. Fundamental shifts in the attitudes of a society or large part of a society over time to various issues and practices.

attractant. A chemical or agent that lures insects or other pests by stimulating their sense of smell.

attrition. Wearing or grinding down of a substance by friction. Dust from such processes contributes to air pollution.

availability session. Informal meeting at a public location where interested citizens can talk with EPA and state officials on a one-to-one basis.

available chlorine. A measure of the amount of chlorine available in chlorinated lime, hypochlorite compounds, and other materials used as a source of chlorine when compared with that of liquid or gaseous chlorines.

average. The simple arithmetic average for a population; that is, the sum of all the values in a population divided by the size of the population. Population means are estimated by computing the weighted sum of the sample values, then dividing by the sum of the sample weights.

avoided cost. The cost a utility would incur to generate the next increment of electric capacity using its own resources; many landfill gas projects' buyback rates are based on avoided costs.

B

back pressure. A pressure that can cause water to backflow into the water supply when a user's wastewater system is at a higher pressure than the public system.

backfill. Used in two contexts: to refill an excavated area with uncontaminated soils; and the material used to refill an excavated area.

backflow/back siphonage. A reverse flow condition created by a difference in water pressures that causes water to flow back into the distribution pipes of a drinking water supply from any source other than the intended one.

background concentration. Represents the average amount of toxic chemicals in the air, water, or soil to which people are routinely exposed. More than half of the background concentration of toxic air in metropolitan areas comes from automobiles, trucks, and other vehicles. The rest comes from industry and business, agricultural, and from the use of paints, solvents, and chemicals in the home.

background level. The concentration of a substance in an environmental media (air, water, or soil) that occurs naturally or is not the result of human activities. In exposure assessment the concentration of a substance in a defined control area, during a fixed period of time before, during, or after a data-gathering operation.

backwashing. Reversing the flow of water back through the filter media to remove entrapped solids.

backyard composting. Diversion of organic food waste and yard trimmings from the municipal waste stream by composting them in one's yard through controlled decomposition of organic matter by bacteria and fungi into a humuslike product. It is considered source reduction, not recycling, because the composted materials never enter the municipal waste stream.

bacteria (singular. bacterium). Microscopic living organisms that can aid in pollution control by metabolizing organic matter in sewage, oil spills, or other pollutants. However, bacteria in soil, water, or air can also cause human, animal, and plant health problems.

bactericide. A pesticide used to control or destroy bacteria, typically in the home, schools, or hospitals.

baffle. A flat board or plate, deflector, guide, or similar device constructed or placed in flowing water or slurry systems to cause more uniform flow velocities to absorb energy and to divert, guide, or agitate liquids.

baffle chamber. In incinerator design, a chamber designed to promote the settling of fly ash and coarse particulate matter by changing the direction and/or reducing the velocity of the gases produced by the combustion of the refuse or sludge.

baghouse filter. Large fabric bag, usually made of glass fibers, used to eliminate intermediate and large (greater than 20 PM in diameter) particles. This device operates like the bag of an electric vacuum cleaner, passing the air and smaller particles while entrapping the larger ones.

bailer. A pipe with a valve at the lower end, used to remove slurry from the bottom or side of a well as it is being drilled, or to collect groundwater samples from wells or open boreholes. A tube of varying length.

balance. Equilibrium, steady state; balance of nature, constancy of conditions resulting from interaction of living things; harmony of design and proportion; steady state, as keeping things in balance; power to decide, as in hold the balance.

balance of nature. In ecology, the concept of an inherent stability in most ecosystems.

baling. Compacting solid waste into blocks to reduce volume and simplify handling.

ballistic separator. A machine that sorts organic from inorganic matter for composting.

band application. The spreading of chemicals over, or next to, each row of plants in a field.

banking. A system for recording qualified air emission reductions for later use in bubble, offset, or netting transactions.

bar screen. In wastewater treatment, a device used to remove large solids.

barrel. A unit of volume equal to 42 U.S. gallons. One barrel weighs 306 pounds or 5.80 million Btu of crude oil. Barrel is abbreviated as bbl.

barrel sampler. Open-ended steel tube used to collect soil samples.

barrier coating(s). A layer of a material that obstructs or prevents passage of something through a surface that is to be protected (e.g., grout, caulk, or various sealing compounds); sometimes used with polyurethane membranes to prevent corrosion or oxidation of metal surfaces, chemical impacts on various materials, or, for example, to prevent radon infiltration through walls, cracks, or joints in a house.

barriers. Defensive mechanisms and arrangements to protect the public against adverse effects.

basal application. In pesticides, the application of a chemical on plant stems or tree trunks just above the soil line.

basalt. Consistent year-round energy use of a facility; also refers to the minimum amount of electricity supplied continually to a facility.

bases. A class of compounds that are "opposite" to acids, in that they neutralize acids. Weak bases are used in cooking (baking soda) and cleaners. Strong bases can be corrosive or caustic. Examples of strong bases that are common around the house are drain cleaners, oven cleaners, and other heavy-duty cleaning products. Strong bases can be very dangerous to tissue, especially the eyes and mouth.

battery. An energy storage device made up of one or more electrolyte cells.

bean sheet. A pesticide data package record.

bed load. Sediment particles resting on or near the channel bottom that are pushed or rolled along by the flow of water.

BEN. EPA's computer model for analyzing a violator's economic gain from not complying with the law.

bench-scale tests. Laboratory testing of potential cleanup technologies.

beneficial use. In the context of environmental planning, a use of the environment, or any element or segment of the environment, that is conducive to public benefit, welfare, safety or health, and which requires protection from the effects of waste discharges, emissions, deposits, and despoliation.

benefit-cost analysis. An economic method for assessing the benefits and costs of achieving alternative health-based standards at given levels of health protection.

benthic/benthos. An organism that feeds on the sediment at the bottom of a water body such as an ocean, lake, or river.

bentonite. A colloidal clay, expansible when moist, commonly used to provide a tight seal around a well casing.

benzene. A petroleum derivative widely used in the chemical industry. A few uses are synthesis of rubber, nylon, polystyrene, and pesticides; and production of gasoline. Benzene is a highly volatile chemical readily absorbed by breathing, ingestion, or contact with the skin. Short-term exposures to high concentrations of benzene can result in death following depression of the central nervous system or fatal disturbances of heart rhythm. Long-term, low-level exposures to benzene can result in blood disorders such as aplastic anemia and leukemia.

Berlin Climate Conference. A conference of the world's environment ministers held in March 1995, to review progress toward achieving the objects of the convention on climate change that emerged from the UN Conference on Environment and Development 1992.

berm. A curb, ledge, wall, or mound used to prevent the spread of contaminants. It can be made of various materials, even earth in certain circumstances.

beryllium. A metal hazardous to human health when inhaled as an airborne pollutant. It is discharged by machine shops, ceramic and propellant plants, and foundries.

best available control measures (BACM). A term used to refer to the most effective measures (according to EPA guidance) for controlling small or dispersed particulates and other emissions from sources such as roadway dust, soot, and ash from woodstoves and open burning of rush, timber, grasslands, or trash.

best available control technology (BACT). An emission limitation based on the maximum degree of emission reduction (considering energy, environmental, and economic impacts) achievable through application of production processes and available methods, systems, and techniques. BACT does not permit emissions in excess of those allowed under any applicable Clean Air Act provisions. Use of the BACT concept is allowable on a case-by-case basis for major new or modified emissions sources in attainment areas and applies to each regulated pollutant.

best demonstrated available technology (BDAT). As identified by EPA, the most effective commercially available means of treating specific types of hazardous waste. The BDATs may change with advances in treatment technologies.

best management practice (BMP). Methods that have been determined to be the most effective, practical means of preventing or reducing pollution from nonpoint sources.

best practicable means (BPM). A commonly used approach to pollution control requirements from industrial and other premises.

best practice. An effective, innovative solution, process, or procedure that demonstrates a business's dedication to making progress in environmental and corporate social responsibility; sometimes shared with collaborators and competitors to shape standards for an industry.

beta particles. Very high-energy particle identical to an electron, emitted by some radioactive elements. Depending on their energy, they penetrate a few centimeters of tissue.

bimetal. Beverage containers with steel bodies and aluminum tops; handled differently from pure aluminum in recycling.

bio- (from the Greek bios = [course of] human life) indicating or involving life or living organisms.

bioaccumulants. Substances that increase in concentration in living organisms as they take in contaminated air, water, or food because the substances are very slowly metabolized or excreted.

bioaccumulation. The process by which the concentrations of some toxic chemicals gradually increase in living tissue, such as in plants, fish, or people as they breathe contaminated air, drink contaminated water, or eat contaminated food.

bioassay. A test to determine the relative strength of a substance by comparing its effect on a test organism with that of a standard preparation.

bio-assimilability. Property of substance which may be readily and beneficially absorbed by living organisms. Bio-assimilability should be a feature in the design of degradable products so that they will *enhance* the *life forms* and *cycles* which *recycle* the material from which they are made.

bioavailability. Degree of ability to be absorbed and ready to interact in organism metabolism.

biocentric, biocentrism. Life-centered. Desirable *quality* of *green culture*, focus of *green philosophy. System* of belief which gives precedence to *life* and *life needs.*

biochemical oxygen demand (BOD). A measure of the amount of oxygen consumed in the biological processes that break down organic matter in water. The greater the BOD, the greater the degree of pollution.

biocide. (from the Greek bios + Latin caedere = life-destroying). Usually *artificial* (although not necessarily) chemical used to eradicate unwanted *life* forms, particularly in modern farming.

bioconcentration. The accumulation of a chemical in tissues of a fish or other organism to levels greater than in the surrounding medium.

biodegradable. Capable of decomposing under natural conditions.

biodiesel. A type of fuel made by combining animal fat or vegetable oil (such as soybean oil or used restaurant grease) with alcohol; biodiesel can be directly substituted for diesel (known as B100, for 100 percent biodiesel), or be used as an additive mixed with traditional diesel (known as B20, for 20 percent biodiesel).

biodiversity. Refers to the variety and variability among living organisms and the ecological complexes in which they occur. Diversity can be defined as the number of different items and their relative frequencies. For biological diversity, these items are organized at many levels, ranging from complete ecosystems to the biochemical structures that are the molecular basis of heredity. Thus, the term encompasses different ecosystems, species, and genes.

biodynamic. A method of gardening initiated by Rudolf Steiner in which *organic* practice is carried out in phase with seasonal, planetary, and lunar cycles.

bioenergy. Energy generated from renewable, biological sources (biomass) such as plants, to be used for heat, electricity, or vehicle fuel.

biofuel. Fuel created from renewable, biological sources such as plants or animal byproducts, but excluding biological material (such as natural gas, coal, or methane), which has been transformed by geological processes.

biogenic waste. Waste made from materials that were produced by living organisms or biological processes. *Note:* Energy Information Administration (EIA) uses the term 'biogenic' to refer only to organic nonfossil material of biological origin, such as paper or cotton.

biological contaminants. Living organisms or derivates (e.g., viruses, bacteria, fungi, and mammal and bird antigens) that can cause harmful health effects when inhaled, swallowed, or otherwise taken into the body.

biological control. In pest control, the use of animals and organisms that eat or otherwise kill or out-compete pests.

biological integrity. The ability to support and maintain balanced, integrated, functionality in the natural habitat of a given region.

Concept is applied primarily in drinking water management.

biological magnification. Refers to the process whereby certain substances such as pesticides or heavy metals move up the food chain, work their way into rivers or lakes, and are eaten by aquatic organisms such as fish, which in turn are eaten by large birds, animals, or humans. The substances become concentrated in tissues or internal organs as they move up the chain.

biological measurement. A measurement taken in a biological medium. For exposure assessment, it is related to the measurement that is taken and related to the established internal dose of a compound.

biological medium. One of the major component of an organism (e.g., blood, fatty tissue, lymph nodes or breath), in which chemicals can be stored or transformed.

biological oxidation. Decomposition of complex organic materials by microorganisms. Occurs in self-purification of water bodies and in activated sludge wastewater treatment.

biological oxygen demand (BOD). An indirect measure of the concentration of biologically degradable material present in organic wastes. It usually reflects the amount of oxygen consumed in five days by biological processes breaking down organic waste.

biological pesticides. Certain microorganism, including bacteria, fungi, viruses, and protozoa that are effective in controlling pests. These agents usually do not have toxic effects on animals and people and do not leave toxic or persistent chemical residues in the environment.

biological remediation. The use of microorganisms and nutrients to deal with hazardous-waste problems, for example, contaminated land and manufacturing sites.

biological stressors. Organisms accidentally or intentionally dropped into habitats in which they do not evolve naturally, for example, gypsy moths, Dutch elm disease, certain types of algae, and bacteria.

biological treatment. A treatment technology that uses bacteria to consume organic waste.

biologically effective dose. The amount of a deposited or absorbed compound reaching the cells or target sites where adverse effect occur, or where the chemical interacts with a membrane.

biologicals. Vaccines, cultures, and other preparations made from living organisms and their products, intended for use in diagnosing, immunizing, or treating humans or animals, or in related research.

biomass. Any organic (plant or animal) material which is available on a renewable basis, including agricultural crops and agricultural wastes and residues, wood and wood wastes and residues, animal wastes, municipal wastes, and aquatic plants.

biomass gas (biogas). A medium Btu gas containing methane and carbon dioxide, resulting from the action of microorganisms on organic materials such as a landfill.

biome. Entire community of living organisms in a single major ecological area.

biomimicry. A science that studies natural processes and models in order to imitate the designs to solve human problems, such as studying a leaf to better understand and design solar cells.

biomonitoring. 1. The use of living organisms to test the suitability of effluents for discharge into receiving waters and to test the quality of such waters downstream from the discharge. 2. Analysis of blood, urine, tissues, and the like to measure chemical exposure in humans.

bioreactor. A landfill where the waste actively decomposes rather being simply buried in a "dry tomb."

bioregion. A natural region, exhibiting diversity and stability, defined by its ecological coherence.

bioregionalism. The proposition that human ways of life should be compatible with the requirements of the diversity of bioregional communities of the planet.

bioremediation. A process that uses microorganisms to change toxic compounds into nontoxic ones. Use of living organisms to clean up oil spills or remove other pollutants from soil, water, or wastewater; use of organisms such as non-harmful insects to remove agricultural pests or counteract diseases of trees, plants, and garden soil.

biosensor. Analytical device comprising a biological recognition element (e.g., enzyme, receptor, DNA, antibody, or microorganism) in intimate contact with an electrochemical, optical, thermal, or acoustic signal transducer that together permit analyses of chemical properties or quantities. Shows potential development in some areas, including environmental monitoring.

biosolids. Residuals generated by the treatment of sewage, petroleum refining waste, and industrial chemical manufacturing wastewater with activated sludge.

biosphere. The portion of earth and its atmosphere that can support life.

biostabilizer. A machine that converts solid waste into compost by grinding and aeration.

biota. The animal and plant life of a given region.

biotechnology. Techniques that use living organisms or parts of organisms to produce a variety of products (from medicines to industrial enzymes) to improve plants or animals or to develop microorganisms to remove toxics from bodies of water, or to act as pesticides.

bioterrorism. The use of deadly bioengineered diseases and poisons by terrorists.

biotic community. A naturally occurring assemblage of plants and animals that live in the same environment and are mutually sustaining and interdependent.

biotransformation. Conversion of a substance into other compounds by organisms; includes biodegradation.

black liquor (pulping liquor). The alkaline spent liquor removed from the digesters in the process of chemically pulping wood. After evaporation, the liquor is burned as a fuel in a recovery furnace that permits the recovery of certain basic chemicals.

blackwater. Water that contains animal, human, or food waste.

blogs. Web-based journals or logs where individuals or organizations can post information, or raise controversial issues for discussion on the Internet.

blood products. Any product derived from human blood, including but not limited to blood plasma, platelets, red or white corpuscles, and derived licensed products such as interferon.

bloom. A proliferation of algae and/or higher aquatic plants in a body of water; often related to pollution, especially when pollutants accelerate growth.

blueprint. Reproduction of architectural, engineering, or other drawing, so called because early processes reproduced in blue. Now used in the wider sense for plan or strategy, or mental model or paradigm.

BOD5. The amount of dissolved oxygen consumed in five days by biological processes breaking down organic matter.

body burden. The amount of a chemical stored in the body at a given time, especially a potential toxin in the body as the result of exposure.

bog. A type of wetland that accumulates appreciable peat deposits. Bogs depend primarily on precipitation for their water source, and are usually acidic and rich in plant residue with a conspicuous mat of living green moss.

boiler. A vessel or tank where heat produced from the combustion of fuels such as natural gas, fuel oil, or coal is used to provide either hot water or steam for home heating. Steam is distributed via pipes to steam radiators, and hot water can be distributed via baseboard radiators or radiant floor systems, or can heat air via a coil.

boiling water reactor. A nuclear reactor in which water is allowed to boil in the core. The resulting steam is used to drive a turbine generating electric power.

boom. A floating device used to contain oil on a body of water. A piece of equipment used to apply pesticides from a tractor or truck.

borehole. Hole made with drilling equipment.

boring. Usually, a vertical hole drilled into the ground from which soil samples can be collected and analyzed to determine the presence of chemicals and the physical characteristics of the soil.

borrow pit. An area where soil, sand, or gravel has been dug up for use elsewhere.

botanical pesticide. A pesticide whose active ingredient is a plant-produced chemical such as nicotine or strychnine. Also called a plant-derived pesticide.

bottle bill. Proposed or enacted legislation that requires a returnable deposit on beer or soda containers and provides for retail store or other redemption. Such legislation is designed to discourage use of throwaway containers.

bottom ash. The nonairborne combustion residue from burning pulverized coal in a boiler; the material that falls to the bottom of the boiler and is removed mechanically; a concentration of noncombustible materials, which may include toxics.

bottom land hardwoods. Forested freshwater wetlands adjacent to rivers in the southeastern United States, especially valuable for wildlife breeding, nesting, and habitat.

bounding estimate. An estimate of exposure, dose, or risk that is higher than that incurred by the person in the population with the currently highest exposure, dose, or risk. Bounding estimates are useful in developing statements that exposures, doses, or risks are not greater than an estimated value.

brackish. Mixed fresh and salt water.

Brandt Commission. A commission set up in 1977 at the instigation, among others, of the World Bank; the 20 members of the Commission were drawn from rich northern industrial countries and poorer southern countries.

breakpoint chlorination. Addition of chlorine to water until the chlorine demand has been satisfied.

breakthrough. A crack or break in a filter bed that allows the passage of floc or particulate matter through a filter; will cause an increase in filter effluent turbidity.

breathing zone. Area of air in which an organism inhales.

brine mud. Waste material, often associated with well-drilling or mining, composed of mineral salts or other inorganic compounds.

British Standard 7750. A product of the British Standards Institute on environmental management systems; it is similar to the European Eco-Management and Audit Regulation (EMAR), both including elements such as the European audit.

British thermal unit (Btu). The amount of heat required to raise the temperature of one pound of water one degree Fahrenheit; equal to 252 calories.

broadcast application. The spreading of pesticides over an entire area.

brown power/energy. Electricity generated from the combustion of nonrenewable fossil fuels (coal, oil, or natural gas) which generates significant amounts of greenhouse gas.

brownfields. Abandoned, idled, or under used industrial and commercial facilities/ sites where expansion or redevelopment is complicated by real or perceived environmental contamination. They can be in urban, suburban, or rural areas.

Btu. See British thermal unit.

bubble. A system under which existing emissions sources can propose alternate means to comply with a set of emissions limitations; under the bubble concept, sources can control more than required at one emission point where control costs are relatively low in return for a comparable relaxation of controls at a second emission point where costs are higher.

buffer. A solution or liquid the chemical makeup of which minimizes changes in pH when acids or bases are added to it.

buffer strips. Strips of grass or other erosion-resisting vegetation between or below cultivated strips or fields.

buffer zone. An area of land separating land uses that are incompatible with each other, which should be of sufficient width to prevent any conflict between them.

building cooling load. The hourly amount of heat that must be removed from a building to maintain indoor comfort (measured in British thermal units [Btus]).

building envelope. Elements of the building, including all external building materials, windows, and walls, that enclose the internal space. Also called building shell.

building related illness. Diagnosable illness whose cause and symptoms can be directly attributed to a specific pollutant source within a building (e.g., Legionnaire's disease, hypersensitivity, pneumonitis).

bulk sample. A small portion (usually thumbnail size) of a suspect asbestos-containing building material collected by an asbestos inspector for laboratory analysis to determine asbestos content.

bulky waste. Large items of waste materials, such as appliances, furniture, large auto parts, trees, or stumps.

bureaucracy. Government by central administration, officials of such government being bureaucrats; system of administration characterized by rigidity, lack of imagination, inertia. A system highly resistant to change or innovation. Usually organized as a hierarchy, wherein position will take precedence over function. Remote and inefficient, bureaucracies rapidly develop their own agenda. Bureaucracies are the essential organs of terminal culture.

burial ground (graveyard). A disposal site for radioactive waste materials that uses earth or water as a shield.

buy-back center. Facility where individuals or groups bring reyclables in return for payment.

by-product. Material, other than the principal product, generated as a consequence of an industrial process or as a breakdown product in a living system.

C

cadmium (Cd). A natural element in the earth's crust, usually found as a mineral combined with other elements such as oxygen. Because all soils and rocks have some cadmium in them, it is extracted during the production of other metals like zinc, lead, and copper. Cadmium does not corrode easily and accumulates in the environment. In industry and consumer products, it is used for batteries, pigments, metal coatings, and plastics. Cadmium salts are toxic in higher concentrations.

California Environmental Quality Act (CEQA). First enacted in 1970 to provide long-term environmental protection, the law requires that governmental decision makers and public agencies study the significant environmental effects of proposed activities, and that significant avoidable damage be avoided or reduced where feasible. CEQA also requires that the public be told why the lead public agency approved the project as it did, and gives the public a way to challenge the decisions of the agency.

calorie. A unit for measuring heat energy. This unit is equal to 4.184 joules. Often used instead of joules when dealing with the energy released from food.

Calvert. An investment firm that highlights socially responsible investing and publishes an annual index of the largest U.S.

companies that represent socially responsible investments.

cancellation. Refers to Section 6(b) of the Federal Insecticide, Fungicide and Rodenticide Act (FIFRA), which authorizes cancellation of a pesticide registration if unreasonable adverse effects to the environment and public health develop when a product is used according to widespread and commonly recognized practice, or if its labeling or other material required to be submitted does not comply with FIFRA provisions.

cancer risk. A number, generally expressed in exponential form (i.e., 1×10^{-6}, which means 1 in 1 million), which describes the increased possibility of an individual developing cancer from exposure to toxic materials. Calculations producing cancer risk numbers are complex and typically include a number of assumptions that tend to cause the final estimated risk number to be conservative.

cap. A layer, such as clay or a synthetic material, used to prevent rainwater from penetrating the soil and spreading contamination.

cap and trade system. A strategy to reduce carbon emissions via financial incentives; "caps" establish emissions limits and fines for exceeding those limits, while companies operating below their carbon limits can sell or "trade" their offsets to companies that are operating above the limits.

capacity assurance plan. A statewide plan that supports a state's ability to manage the hazardous waste generated within its boundaries over a 20-year period.

capacity factor. The ratio of the electrical energy produced by a generating unit for the period of time considered to the electrical energy that could have been produced at continuous full-power operation during the same period.

capacity, gross. The full-load continuous rating of a generator, prime mover, or other electric equipment under specified conditions as designated by the manufacturer. It is usually indicated on a nameplate attached to the equipment.

capillary action. Movement of water through very small spaces owing to molecular forces called capillary forces.

capillary fringe. The porous material just above the water table which may hold water by capillarity (a property of surface tension that draws water upwards) in the smaller void spaces.

capital. One of the factors of production that may be defined as wealth used for the production of further wealth, or simply a commodity used in the production of other goods and services.

capture efficiency. The fraction of organic vapors generated by a process that is directed to an abatement or recovery device.

carbamates. A group of insecticides related to carbamic acid. They are primarily used on corn, alfalfa, tobacco, cotton, soybeans, fruits, and ornamental plants.

carbon absorber. An add-on control device that uses activated carbon to absorb volatile organic compounds from a gas stream. (The VOCs are later recovered from the carbon.)

carbon adsorption. A treatment system in which organic contaminants are removed from groundwater and surface water by forcing it through tanks containing activated carbon, a specially treated material that retains such compounds. Activated carbon is also used to purify contaminated air by adsorbing the contaminants as the air passes through it.

carbon credits. Provide a way to reduce greenhouse effect emissions on an industrial scale by capping total annual emissions and letting the market assign a monetary value to any shortfall through trading. Credits can be exchanged between businesses or bought and sold in international markets at the prevailing market price.

carbon cycle. The cycling of the element carbon from nonliving surroundings through organisms and back again.

carbon dioxide. A colorless, odorless noncombustible gas with the formula CO_2 that is present in the atmosphere. It is formed by the combustion of carbon and carbon compounds (such as fossil fuels and biomass) and by respiration, which is a slow combustion in animals and plants, and by the gradual oxidation of organic matter in the soil.

carbon footprint. The total amount of greenhouse gases emitted directly or indirectly through any human activity, typically expressed in equivalent tons of either carbon or carbon dioxide.

carbon monoxide (CO). A colorless, odorless, poisonous gas produced by incomplete fossil fuel combustion. A very poisonous, colorless, and odorless gas formed when carbon-containing matter burns incompletely, as in automobile engines or in charcoal grills used indoors without proper ventilation.

carbon tax. A tax on the consumption of fossil carbon-containing fuels in order to discourage consumption, to reduce carbon dioxide emissions, and to provide funds to promote other measures to reduce the greenhouse effect.

carbon tetrachloride (CC14). Compound consisting of one carbon atom and four chlorine atoms, once widely used as an industrial raw material, as a solvent, and in the production of CFCs. Its use as a solvent ended when it was discovered to be carcinogenic.

carbon trading. A trading system for countries, companies, and individuals designed to offset carbon emissions from one activity with another, whereby those who cannot meet their emissions goals may purchase credits from those who surpass their goals.

carboxyhemoglobin. Hemoglobin in which the iron is bound to carbon monoxide (CO) instead of oxygen.

carcinogen. Any substance that can cause or aggravate cancer.

carrier. The inert liquid or solid material in a pesticide product that serves as a delivery vehicle for the active ingredient. Carriers do not have toxic properties of their own. Any material or system that can facilitate the movement of a pollutant into the body or cells.

carrying capacity. Ecological term, the amount of life, either number of a particular species or number of species, which a region or system, such as a river or river valley, can support indefinitely; the maximum population that an ecosystem can support.

CAS registration number. A number assigned by the Chemical Abstract Service to identify a chemical.

case study. A brief fact sheet providing risk, cost, and performance information on alternative methods and other pollution prevention ideas, compliance initiatives, voluntary efforts, and the like.

cask. A thick-walled container (usually lead) used to transport radioactive material. Also called a coffin.

cast silicon. Crystalline silicon obtained by pouring pure molten silicon into a vertical mold and adjusting the temperature gradient along the mold volume during cooling to obtain slow, vertically advancing crystallization of the silicon. The polycrystalline ingot thus formed is composed of large, relatively parallel, interlocking crystals. The cast ingots are sawed into wafers for further fabrication into photovoltaic cells. Cast-silicon wafers and ribbon-silicon sheets fabricated into cells are usually referred to as polycrystalline photovoltaic cells.

catalyst. A substance that accelerates chemical change yet is not permanently affected by the reaction (e.g., platinum in an automobile catalytic converter helps change carbon monoxide to carbon dioxide).

catalytic converter. An air pollution abatement device that removes pollutants from motor vehicle exhaust, either by oxidizing them into carbon dioxide and water or reducing them to nitrogen.

catalytic cracker unit. In a petroleum refinery, the catalytic cracker unit breaks long petroleum molecules apart, or "cracks" them, during the petroleum refining process. These smaller pieces then come together to form more desirable molecules for gasoline or other products.

catalytic incinerator. A control device that oxidizes volatile organic compounds (VOCs) by using a catalyst to promote the combustion process. Catalytic incinerators require lower temperatures than conventional thermal incinerators, thus saving fuel and other costs.

catastrophe. Sudden or widespread disaster; event subverting system of things; disastrous end; ruin.

categorical exclusion. A class of actions which either individually or cumulatively would not have a significant effect on the human environment and therefore would not require preparation of an environmental assessment or environmental impact statement under the National Environmental Policy Act (NEPA).

categorical pretreatment standard. A technology-based effluent limitation for an industrial facility discharging into a municipal sewer system. Analogous in stringency to Best Availability Technology (BAT) for direct dischargers.

cathodic protection. A technique to prevent corrosion of a metal surface by making it the cathode of an electrochemical cell.

cause-related marketing. A business strategy whereby a company aligns its mission and goals to create a specific and tailored partnership with a nonprofit organization or cause.

caustic. The common name for sodium hydroxide, a strong base. Also used as an adjective to describe highly corrosive bases.

caustic scrubber. An air pollution control device in which acid gases are neutralized by contact with an alkaline solution.

cavitation. The formation and collapse of gas pockets or bubbles on the blade of an impeller or the gate of a valve; collapse of these pockets or bubbles drives water with such force that it can cause pitting of the gate or valve surface.

cells. In solid waste disposal, holes where waste is dumped, compacted, and covered with layers of dirt on a daily basis. The smallest structural part of living matter capable of functioning as an independent unit.

cementitious. Densely packed and nonfibrous friable materials.

central collection point. Location where a generator of regulated medical waste consolidates wastes originally generated at various locations in the facility. The wastes are gathered together for treatment onsite or for transportation elsewhere for treatment and/or disposal. This term could also apply to community hazardous waste collections, industrial and other waste management systems.

centre. Position at the summary of distances (or forces) from the boundary (or within) of a space (or body). Position at which properties are assumed to act.

centrifugal collector. A mechanical system using centrifugal force to remove aerosols from a gas stream or to remove water from sludge.

CERCLIS. The federal Comprehensive Environmental Response, Compensation, and Liability Information System, a database that includes all sites which have been nominated for investigation by the Superfund program.

Ceres (pronounced "series"). A national network of investors, environmental organizations, and other public interest groups working with companies and investors to address sustainability challenges such as global climate change. Ceres hosts an annual competition to highlight the best examples of sustainability reporting in North America.

CFC. Chlorofluorocarbons. Artificial substances used in the electronics industry as a cleaner, in aerosols as a propellant, in refrigeration, and in the production of plastic foams, destroying the ozone layer and assisting the greenhouse effect.

chain reaction. A self-sustaining nuclear reaction which takes place during fission. A fissionable substance (i.e., uranium) absorbs a neutron and divides, releasing additional neutrons that are absorbed by other fissionable nuclei, releasing still more neutrons.

change. Become different, often by comparison.

channelization. Straightening and deepening streams so water will move faster, a marsh-drainage tactic that can interfere with waste assimilation capacity, disturb fish and wildlife habitats, and aggravate flooding.

chaos. Formless primordial matter; utter confusion; a lack of perceptible order.

characteristic. Any one of the four categories used in defining hazardous waste: ignitability, corrosivity, reactivity, and toxicity.

characterization of ecological effects. Part of ecological risk assessment that evaluates ability of a stressor to cause adverse effects under given circumstances.

characterization of exposure. Portion of an ecological risk assessment that evaluates interaction of a stressor with one or more ecological entities.

check-valve tubing pump. Water sampling tool also referred to as a water pump.

chemical. Substance made of natural molecules, either found or produced by refining, mixing, or compounding, these processes described as chemistry.

chemical case. For purposes of review and regulation, the grouping of chemically similar pesticide active ingredients (e.g., salts and esters of the same chemical) into chemical cases.

chemical compound. A distinct and pure substance formed by the union or two or more elements in definite proportion by weight.

chemical element. A fundamental substance comprising one kind of atom; the simplest form of matter.

chemical energy. Energy stored in a substance and released during a chemical reaction such as burning wood, coal, or oil.

chemical oxygen demand (COD). A measure of the oxygen required to oxidize all compounds, both organic and inorganic, in water.

chemical stressors. Chemicals released to the environment through industrial waste, auto emissions, pesticides, and other human activity that can cause illnesses and even death in plants and animals.

chemical treatment. Any one of a variety of technologies that uses chemicals or a variety of chemical processes to treat waste.

chemiculture. Agriculture and farming which has become totally reliant on basic chemical inputs, particularly biocides, soluble fertilizers, and drugs, usually in intensive mono-crop systems.

chemnet. Mutual aid network of chemical shippers and contractors that assigns a contracted emergency response company to provide technical support if a representative of the firm whose chemicals are involved in an incident is not readily available.

chemosterilant. A chemical that controls pests by preventing reproduction.

chemtrec. The industry-sponsored Chemical Transportation Emergency Center; provides information and/or emergency assistance to emergency responders.

Chernobyl nuclear catastrophe. Occurring in April 1986, the worst accident in nuclear power station history.

chi. From Chinese; flow or flux of force or energy; a spiritual perception of the organization of energy.

chief information officer (CIO). Manager who has been entrusted with the responsibility to manage the organization's technology with its many privacy and security issues.

child labor. The practice of employing children under a specified legal minimum age as set by a country or government; more frequently exploited in developing countries in order to establish competitive labor costs.

child resistant packaging (CRP). Packaging that protects children or adults from injury or illness resulting from accidental contact with or ingestion of residential pesticides that meet or exceed specific toxicity levels. Required by FIFRA regulations. Term is also used for protective packaging of medicines.

chiller. A device that generates a cold liquid that is circulated through an air-handling unit's cooling coil to cool the air supplied to the building.

chilling effect. The lowering of the earth's temperature because of increased particles in the air blocking the sun's rays.

China syndrome. Synonym for nuclear disaster.

chisel plowing. Preparing croplands by using a special implement that avoids complete inversion of the soil as in conventional plowing. Chisel plowing can leave a protective cover or crops residues on the soil surface to help prevent erosion and improve filtration.

chlorinated herbicides. A group of plant-killing chemicals that contain chlorine, used mainly for weed control and defoliation.

chlorinated hydrocarbons. Chemicals containing only chlorine, carbon, and hydrogen. These include a class of persistent, broad-spectrum insecticides that linger in the environment and accumulate in the food chain. Among them are DDT, aldrin, dieldrin, heptachlor, chlordane, lindane, endrin, Mirex, hexachloride, and toxaphene. Other examples include TCE, used as an industrial solvent. Any chlorinated organic compounds including chlorinated solvents such as dichloromethane, trichloromethylene, chloroform.

chlorinated solvent. An organic solvent containing chlorine atoms (e.g., methylene chloride and 1,1,1-trichloromethane). Uses of chlorinated solvents include aerosol spray containers, highway paint, and dry cleaning fluids.

chlorination. The application of chlorine to drinking water, sewage, or industrial waste to disinfect or to oxidize undesirable compounds.

chlorinator. A device that adds chlorine, in gas or liquid form, to water or sewage to kill infectious bacteria.

chlorine-contact chamber. That part of a water treatment plant where effluent is disinfected by chlorine.

chlorobenzene. A volatile organic compound that is often used as a solvent and in the production of other chemicals. It is a toxic, colorless liquid with an almondlike odor.

chlorofluorocarbons (CFCs). A family of inert, nontoxic, and easily liquefied chemicals used in refrigeration, air conditioning, packaging, insulation, or as solvents and aerosol propellants. Because CFCs are not destroyed in the lower atmosphere they drift into the upper atmosphere where their chlorine components destroy ozone.

chloroform. Chloroform was once commonly used as a general anesthetic and as a flavoring agent in toothpastes, mouthwash, and cough syrups.

chlorophenoxy. A class of herbicides that can be found in domestic water supplies and cause adverse health effects.

chlorosis. Discoloration of normally green plant parts caused by disease, lack of nutrients, or various air pollutants.

cholinesterase. An enzyme found in animals that regulates nerve impulses by the inhibition of acetylcholine. Cholinesterase inhibition is associated with a variety of acute symptoms such as nausea, vomiting, blurred vision, stomach cramps, and rapid heart rate.

chromated copper arsenate. An insecticide and herbicide containing three metals: copper, chromium, and arsenic. This salt is used extensively as a wood preservative in pressure-treating operations. It is highly toxic and dissolves in water, making it a relatively mobile contaminant in the environment.

chromium. A hard, brittle, grayish heavy metal used in tanning, in paint formulation, and in plating metal for corrosion protection. It is toxic at certain levels and in its hexavalent (versus trivalent) form.

chronic effect. An adverse effect on a human or animal in which symptoms recur frequently or develop slowly over a long period of time.

chronic exposure. Repeated contact with a chemical over a period of time, often involving small amounts of toxic substance.

chronic toxicity. The capacity of a substance to cause long-term poisonous health effects in humans, animals, fish, and other organisms.

circle of influence. The circular outer edge of a depression produced in the water table by the pumping of water from a well.

circuit(s). A conductor or a system of conductors through which electric current flows.

cistern. Small tank or storage facility used to store water for a home or farm; often used to store rain water.

civilization. Living in a state of enlightenment, with an educated and refined population. Also a highly developed society, with a rich culture.

clarification. Clearing action that occurs during wastewater treatment when solids settle out. This is often aided by centrifugal action and chemically induced coagulation in wastewater.

clarifier. A tank in which solids settle to the bottom and are subsequently removed as sludge.

Class I Area. Under the Clean Air Act, an area in which visibility is protected more stringently than under the national ambient air quality standards; includes national parks, wilderness areas, monuments, and other areas of special national and cultural significance.

Class I landfill. A landfill permitted to accept hazardous wastes.

Class I substance. One of several groups of chemicals with an ozone depletion potential of 0.2 or higher, including CFCS, halons, carbon tetrachloride, and methyl chloroform (listed in the Clean Air Act), and HBFCs and ethyl bromide (added by EPA regulations).

Class II substance. A substance with an ozone depletion potential of less than 0.2. All HCFCs are currently included in this classification.

clay soil. Soil material containing more than 40 percent clay, less than 45 percent sand, and less than 40 percent silt.

Clean Air Act. Federal legislation passed in 1970 and amended in 1990 that authorizes the EPA to set national Ambient Air Quality Standards and to regulate industry in order to meet those maximum emissions levels.

clean coal technology. Any technology not in widespread use prior to the Clean Air Act Amendments of 1990. This Act will achieve significant reductions in pollutants associated with the burning of coal.

clean fuels. Blends or substitutes for gasoline fuels, including compressed natural gas, methanol, ethanol, and liquified petroleum gas.

clean production. A concept developed under the Kyoto protocol in which manufacturing processes reduce environmental impact and decrease ecological problems by minimizing energy and raw materials use, and making sure emissions and waste are as minimal and as nontoxic to environmental and human health as possible.

Clean Water Act. Federal legislation passed in 1972 and amended in 1976 that requires the EPA to set maximum pollutant levels for each known contaminant in U.S. surface waters and authorizes the EPA to regulate industrial discharge in order to meet those standards.

cleaner production. The use of environmentally friendly processes to produce environmentally friendly products, a route to sustainable development, reducing the risk to the environment of industrial activities in the most cost-effective way.

Cleaner Technologies Substitutes Assessment. A document that systematically evaluates the relative risk, performance, and cost trade-offs of technological alternatives; serves as a repository for all the technical data (including methodology and results) developed by a DfE or other pollution prevention or education project.

cleanup. Actions taken to deal with a release or threat of release of a hazardous substance that could affect humans and/or the environment. The term *cleanup* is sometimes used interchangeably with the terms *remedial action, removal action, response action,* or *corrective action.*

cleanup process. A comprehensive program for the cleanup (remediation) of a contaminated site. It involves investigation, analysis, development of a cleanup plan, and implementation of that plan.

clear cut. Harvesting all the trees in one area at one time, a practice that can encourage fast rainfall or snowmelt runoff, erosion, sedimentation of streams and lakes, and flooding, and destroys vital habitat.

clear well. A reservoir for storing filtered water of sufficient quantity to prevent the need to vary the filtration rate with variations in demand. Also used to provide chlorine contact time for disinfection.

climate. Conditions of temperature, winds, humidity, rainfall, and the like; expression of average conditions of weather for area, region, or season. It is a characteristic of planetary zone, as in tropical, temperate, arctic, and more.

climate change (also referred to as 'global climate change'). The term *climate change* is sometimes used to refer to all forms of climatic inconsistency, but because the earth's climate is never static, the term is more properly used to imply a significant change from one climatic condition to another. In some cases, *climate change* has been used synonymously with the term, *global warming;* scientists however, tend to use the term in the wider sense to also include natural changes in climate. Changes in global climate patterns (such as temperature, precipitation, or wind) that last for extended periods of time as a result of either natural processes or human activity; the contemporary concern is that human activity is now transcending natural processes in causing the most prevalent climate changes of our time.

clinical ecology. Study of allergy and food/chemical intolerance in relation to chemical pollution of food and the environment.

cloning. In biotechnology, obtaining a group of genetically identical cells from a single cell; making identical copies of a gene.

closed-loop recycling. A process of utilizing a recycled product in the manufacturing of a similar product or the remanufacturing of the same product.

closed-loop supply chain. An ideal in which a supply chain completely reuses, recycles, or composts all wastes generated during production; at minimum closed-loop supply chain indicates that the company which produces a good is also responsible for its disposal.

closure. The procedure a landfill operator must follow when a landfill reaches its legal capacity for solid ceasing acceptance of solid waste and placing a cap on the landfill site.

coagulation. Clumping of particles in wastewater to settle out impurities, often induced by chemicals such as lime, alum, and iron salts.

coal. A fossil fuel formed by the breakdown of vegetable material trapped underground without access to air.

coal cleaning technology. A precombustion process by which coal is physically or chemically treated to remove some of its sulfur so as to reduce sulfur dioxide emissions.

coal-fired power plant. A power plant that uses coal as the fuel to generate electricity.

coal gasification. Conversion of coal to a gaseous product by one of several available technologies.

coastal protection. Measures by way of planning, prior approval of works, prohibition of some activities, physical structures, and restoration efforts to protect the coastline against the ravages of nature and haphazard and unplanned developments.

coastal zone. Lands and waters adjacent to the coast that exert an influence on the uses of the sea and its ecology, or whose uses and ecology are affected by the sea.

Code of Federal Regulations (CFR). Document that codifies all rules of the executive departments and agencies of the federal government. It is divided into 50 volumes, known as titles. Title 40 of the CFR (referenced as 40 CFR) lists all environmental regulations.

coefficient of haze (COH). A measurement of visibility interference in the atmosphere.

coefficient of performance (COP). Indicates the heating efficiency of ground-source and water-source heat pumps. More specifically, it is the ratio of heat energy delivered or extracted to the work supplied to operate the equipment. The higher the COP, the more efficient the heat pump.

cofiring. The process of burning natural gas in conjunction with another fuel to reduce air pollutants.

cogeneration. The consecutive generation of useful thermal and electric energy from the same fuel source.

coke oven. An industrial process that converts coal into coke, one of the basic materials used in blast furnaces for the conversion of iron ore into iron.

cold temperature CO. A standard for automobile emissions of carbon monoxide (CO) emissions to be met at a low temperature (i.e., 20 degrees Fahrenheit). Conventional automobile catalytic converters are not efficient in cold weather until they warm up.

coliform index. A rating of the purity of water based on a count of fecal bacteria.

coliform organism. Microorganisms found in the intestinal tract of humans and animals. Their presence in water indicates fecal pollution and potentially adverse contamination by pathogens.

collector. Public or private hauler that collects nonhazardous waste and recyclable materials from residential, commercial, institutional, and industrial sources.

collector field. The area where many solar collectors are situated in a solar power plant.

collector sewers. Pipes used to collect and carry wastewater from individual sources to an interceptor sewer that will carry it to a treatment facility.

colloids. Very small, finely divided solids (that do not dissolve) that remain dispersed in a liquid for a long time owing to their small size and electrical charge.

combined cycle. An electric-generating technology in which electricity is produced from otherwise lost waste heat exiting from one or more gas (combustion) turbines. The exiting heat is routed to a conventional boiler or to a heat recovery steam generator for utilization by a steam turbine in the production of electricity. Such designs increase the efficiency of the electric generating unit.

combined heat and power (CHP) plant. A plant designed to produce both heat and electricity from a single heat source. *Note:* This term is being used in place of the term *cogenerator* that was used by EIA in the past. CHP better describes the facilities because some of the plants included do not produce heat and power in a sequential fashion and, as a result, do not meet the legal definition of cogeneration specified in the Public Utility Regulatory Policies Act (PURPA).

combined sewer overflows. Discharge of a mixture of storm water and domestic waste when the flow capacity of a sewer system is exceeded during rainstorms.

combined sewers. A sewer system that carries both sewage and storm-water runoff. Normally, its entire flow goes to a waste treatment plant, but during a heavy storm, the volume of water may be so great as to cause overflows of untreated mixtures of storm water and sewage into receiving waters. Storm-water runoff can also carry toxic chemicals from industrial areas or streets into the sewer system.

combustible vapor mixture. The composition range over which air containing vapor of an organic compound will burn or even explode when set off by a flame or spark. Outside that range the reaction does not occur, but the mixture may nevertheless be hazardous because it does not contain enough oxygen to support life, or because the vapor is toxic.

combustion. 1. Burning, or rapid oxidation, accompanied by release of energy in the form of heat and light. 2. Refers to controlled burning of waste, in which heat chemically alters organic compounds, converting into stable inorganics such as carbon dioxide and water.

combustion chamber. The actual compartment where waste is burned in an incinerator.

combustion efficiency. A measure of how effectively the heat content of a fuel in a combustion appliance (i.e., furnace or boiler) is transferred into usable heat.

combustion gases. Gases produced by burning. The composition will depend on, among other things, the fuel; the temperature of burning; and whether air, oxygen, or another oxidizer is used. In simple cases the combustion gases are carbon dioxide and water. In some other cases, nitrogen and sulfur oxides may be produced as well. Incinerators must be controlled carefully to be sure that they do not emit more than the allowable amounts of more complex, hazardous compounds. This often requires use of emission-control devices.

combustion product. Substance produced during the burning or oxidation of a material.

command and control regulation. A regulatory approach where the government "commands" companies to meet specific standards (such as amounts of particular pollutants) and "controls" the methods (such as technology) used to achieve these standards. This approach is often contrasted with market-based regulatory approaches where the government establishes general goals and allows companies to use the most cost-effective methods possible to achieve them.

command post. Facility located at a safe distance upwind from an accident site, where the on-scene coordinator, responders, and technical representatives make response decisions, deploy manpower and equipment, maintain liaison with news media, and handle communications.

command-and-control regulations. Specific requirements prescribing how to comply with specific standards defining acceptable levels of pollution.

comment period. Time provided for the public to review and comment on a proposed EPA action or rulemaking after publication in the Federal Register.

commercial sector. An energy-consuming sector that consists of service-providing facilities and equipment of businesses; federal, state, and local governments; and other private and public organizations, such as religious, social, or fraternal groups. The commercial sector includes institutional living quarters. It also includes sewage treatment facilities. Common uses of energy associated with this sector include space heating, water heating, air conditioning, lighting, refrigeration, cooking, and running a wide variety of other equipment. *Note:* This sector includes generators that produce electricity and/or useful thermal output primarily to support the activities of the above-mentioned commercial establishments.

commercial waste. All solid waste emanating from business establishments such as stores, markets, office buildings, restaurants, shopping centers, and theaters.

commercial waste management facility. A treatment, storage, disposal, or transfer facility that accepts waste from a variety of sources, as compared to a private facility which normally manages a limited waste stream generated by its own operations.

commingled recyclables. Mixed recyclables that are collected together.

comminuter. A machine that shreds or pulverizes solids to make waste treatment easier.

comminution. Mechanical shredding or pulverizing of waste. Used in both solid waste management and wastewater treatment.

Commission for Sustainable Development, UN. A body created by the United Nations in 1992 following the UN Conference on Environment and Development held in Rio de Janeiro, Brazil, earlier that year.

common property resource. Those attributes of the natural world that are valued by society but are not in individual ownership and do not enter into the processes of market exchange and the price system.

common sense initiative. Voluntary program to simplify environmental regulation to achieve cleaner, cheaper, smarter results, starting with six major industry sectors.

commons. Traditionally, an area of land on which all citizens could graze their animals without limitation. The term now refers to any shared resource, such as land, air, or water that a group of people use collectively.

community. In ecology, an assemblage of populations of different species within a specified location in space and time. Sometimes, a particular subgrouping may be specified, such as the fish community in a lake or the soil arthropod community in a forest. Organized political, social, or municipal body; body of people living in same locality, or having same religion or profession.

community relations. The EPA effort to establish two-way communication with the public to create understanding of EPA programs and related actions, to ensure public input into decision-making processes related to affected communities, and to make certain that the Agency is aware of and responsive to public concerns. Specific community relations activities are required in relation to Superfund remedial actions.

community water system. A public water system that serves at least 15 service connections used by year-round residents or regularly serves at least 25 year-round residents.

compact fluorescent lamps (CFLs). Small fluorescent light bulbs that use 75 percent less energy (electricity), and last up to 10 times longer than a traditional incandescent bulb, and can be screwed into a regular light socket. Energy Star qualified CFLs cost little up front and provide a quick return on investment. However, all CFL contain a small amount of mercury and must be handled properly and recycled when they burn out. Also called PL, CFL, Twin-Tube, or BIAX lamps.

compaction. Reduction of the bulk of solid waste by rolling and tamping.

comparative risk assessment. Process that generally uses the judgment of experts to predict effects and set priorities among a wide range of environmental problems.

competition. Ethic or value of present culture, whereby the vast majority lose, or things are chosen on the basis of exclusive qualities.

complete treatment. A method of treating water that consists of the addition of coagulant chemicals, flash mixing, coagulation-flocculation, sedimentation, and filtration. Also called conventional filtration.

compliance coal. Any coal that emits less than 1.2 pounds of sulfur dioxide per million Btu when burned. Also known as low sulfur coal.

compliance coating. A coating whose volatile organic compound content does not exceed that allowed by regulation.

compliance cycle. The 9-year calendar year cycle, beginning January 1, 1993, during which public water systems must monitor. Each cycle consists of three 3-year compliance periods.

compliance monitoring. Collection and evaluation of data, including self-monitoring reports, and verification to show whether pollutant concentrations and loads contained in permitted discharges are in compliance with the limits and conditions specified in the permit.

compliance schedule. A negotiated agreement between a pollution source and a government agency that specifies dates and procedures by which a source will reduce emissions and, thereby, comply with a regulation.

composite sample. A series of water samples taken over a given period of time and weighted by flow rate.

compost. A humus or soil-like material created from aerobic, microbial decomposition of organic materials such as food scraps, yard trimmings, and manure.

composting. The controlled biological decomposition of organic material in the presence of air to form a humuslike material. Controlled methods of composting include mechanical mixing and aerating, ventilating the materials by dropping them through a vertical series of aerated chambers, or placing the compost in piles out in the open air and mixing it or turning it periodically.

composting facilities. An offsite facility where the organic component of municipal solid waste is decomposed under controlled conditions. An aerobic process in which organic materials are ground or shredded and then decomposed to humus in windrow piles or in mechanical digesters, drums, or similar enclosures.

Comprehensive Environmental Response, Compensation and Liability Act of 1980 (CERCLA). Also known as Superfund, this federal law authorized the EPA to respond directly to releases of hazardous substances that endangered public health or the environment. The Superfund Amendments and Reauthorization Act of 1986 (SARA), amended and reauthorized CERCLA for five years at a total funding level of $8.5 billion. SARA also strengthened state involvement in the cleanup process and encouraged the use of new treatment technologies and permanent solutions. CERCLA has since been extended by other laws.

compress. Squeeze together, bring into small space.

compressed natural gas (CNG). An alternative fuel for motor vehicles; considered one of the cleanest because of low hydrocarbon emissions and its vapors are relatively non-ozone producing. However, vehicles fueled with CNG do emit a significant quantity of nitrogen oxides.

computer hackers. Individuals often with advanced technology training who, for thrill or profit, breach a business's information security system.

concentration. The relative amount of a substance mixed with another substance. An example is 5 ppm of carbon monoxide in air or 1 mg/l of iron in water.

concentrator. A reflective or refractive device that focuses incident insulation onto an area smaller than the reflective or refractive surface, resulting in increased insulation at the point of focus.

condensate return system. System that returns the heated water condensing within steam piping to the boiler and thus saves energy.

condensate. Liquid formed when warm landfill gas cools as it travels through a collection system. Water created by cooling steam or water vapor.

conditional registration. Under special circumstances, the Federal Insecticide, Fungicide, and Rodenticide Act (FIFRA) permits registration of pesticide products that is "conditional" on the submission of additional data. These special circumstances include a finding by the EPA administrator that a new product or use of an existing pesticide will not significantly increase the risk of unreasonable adverse effects. A product containing a new (previously unregistered) active ingredient may be conditionally registered only if the administrator finds that such conditional registration is in the public interest, that a reasonable time for conducting the additional studies has not elapsed, and the use of the pesticide for the period of conditional registration will not present an unreasonable risk.

conditionally exempt (CE) generators. Persons or enterprises that produce less than 220 pounds of hazardous waste per month. Exempt from most regulation, they are required merely to determine whether their waste is hazardous, notify appropriate state or local agencies, and ship it by an authorized transporter to a permitted facility for proper disposal.

conductance. A rapid method of estimating the dissolved solids content of water supply by determining the capacity of a water sample to carry an electrical current. Conductivity is a measure of the ability of a solution to carry an electrical current.

cone of depression. A depression in the water table that develops around a pumped well.

cone of influence. The depression, roughly conical in shape, produced in a water table by the pumping of water from a well.

cone penterometer testing (CPT). A direct push system used to measure lithology based on soil penetration resistance. Sensors in the tip of the cone of the digital processing (DP) rod measure tip resistance and side-wall friction, transmitting electrical signals to DP equipment on the ground surface.

confidential business information (CBI). Material that contains trade secrets or commercial or financial information that has been claimed as confidential by its source (e.g., a pesticide or new chemical formulation registrant). The EPA has special procedures for handling such information.

confidential statement of formula (CSF). A list of the ingredients in a new pesticide or chemical formulation. The list is submitted at the time of application for registration or change in formulation.

confined aquifer. An aquifer in which groundwater is confined under pressure that is significantly greater than atmospheric pressure.

confluent growth. A continuous bacterial growth covering all or part of the filtration area of a membrane filter in which the bacteria colonies are not discrete.

consent decree. A legal document, approved by a judge, that formalizes an agreement reached between EPA and potentially responsible parties (PRPs) through which PRPs will conduct all or part of a cleanup action at a Superfund site; cease or correct actions or processes that are polluting the environment; or otherwise comply with EPA initiated regulatory enforcement actions to resolve the contamination at the Superfund site involved. The consent decree describes the actions PRPs will take and may be subject to a public comment period.

conservation. Preserving and renewing, when possible, human and natural resources. The use, protection, and improvement of natural resources according to principles that will ensure their highest economic or social benefits.

conservation easement. Easement restricting a landowner to land uses that are compatible with long-term conservation and environmental values.

conserver society. Means of transition from consumer society to sustainable future; living in simple sophistication, without waste or pointless affluence and primitive status display; reducing transport needs, especially the waste of international trade; moving toward stable self-reliance and community self-sufficiency; using appropriate technology; seeking ways of life.

constituent(s) of concern. Specific chemicals that are identified for evaluation in the site assessment process.

construction and demolition (C&D) materials. Consist of the debris generated during the construction, renovation, and demolition of buildings, roads, and bridges. C&D materials often contain bulky, heavy materials such as concrete, wood, metals, glass, and salvaged building components. May contain lead, asbestos, or other hazardous substances.

construction ban. If, under the Clean Air Act, the EPA disapproves of an area's planning requirements for correcting nonattainment, the EPA can ban the construction or modification of any major stationary source of the pollutant for which the area is in nonattainment.

consume. Destroy, use up, eat or drink, spend, waste; (passive) entirely preoccupied with.

consumptive water use. Water removed from available supplies without return to a water resources system (e.g., water used in manufacturing, agriculture, and food preparation).

contact pesticide. A chemical that kills pests when it touches them, instead of by ingestion. Also, soil that contains the minute skeletons of certain algae that scratch and dehydrate waxy-coated insects.

containment. Enclosing or containing hazardous substances in a structure to prevent the migration of contaminants into the environment.

contaminant. Any physical, chemical, biological, or radiological substance or matter that has an adverse effect on air, water, or soil.

contaminated sites. Sites that present a concentration of chemical substances that are likely to pose an immediate or long-term hazard to human health or the environment.

contamination. Introduction into water, air, and soil of microorganisms, chemicals, toxic substances, wastes, or wastewater in a concentration that makes the medium unfit for its next intended use. Also applies to surfaces of objects, buildings, and various household and agricultural use products.

contamination source inventory. An inventory of contaminant sources within delineated State Water Protection Areas. Targets likely sources for further investigation.

contingency plan. A document setting out an organized, planned, and coordinated course of action to be followed in case of a fire, explosion, or other accident that releases toxic chemicals, hazardous waste, or radioactive materials that threaten human health or the environment.

continuous discharge. A routine release to the environment that occurs without interruption, except for infrequent shutdowns for maintenance, process changes, etc.

continuous sample. A flow of water, waste, or other material from a particular place in a plant to the location where samples are collected for testing. May be used to obtain grab or composite samples.

contour plowing. Soil tilling method that follows the shape of the land to discourage erosion.

contour strip farming. A kind of contour farming in which row crops are planted in strips, between alternating strips of close-growing, erosion-resistant forage crops.

contract labs. Laboratories under contract to the EPA, which analyze samples taken from waste, soil, air, and water or carry out research projects.

control technique guidelines (CTGs). EPA documents designed to assist state and local pollution authorities to achieve and maintain air quality standards for certain sources (e.g., organic emissions from solvent metal cleaning known as degreasing) through reasonably available control technologies (RACTs).

controlled reaction. A chemical reaction under temperature and pressure conditions maintained within safe limits to produce a desired product or process.

conventional hydroelectric (hydropower) plant. A plant in which all of the power is produced from natural stream flow as regulated by available storage.

conventional pollutants. Statutorily listed pollutants understood well by scientists. These may be in the form of organic waste, sediment, acid, bacteria, viruses, nutrients, oil and grease, or heat.

conventional site assessment. Assessment in which most of the sample analysis and interpretation of data is completed off-site; process usually requires repeated mobilization of equipment and staff in order to fully determine the extent of contamination.

conventional systems. Systems that have been traditionally used to collect municipal wastewater in gravity sewers and convey it to a central primary or secondary treatment plant prior to discharge to surface waters.

conventional tilling. Tillage operations considered standard for a specific location and crop and that tend to bury the crop residues; usually considered as a base for determining the cost-effectiveness of control practices.

conversion factors. A number that translates units of one measurement system into corresponding values of another measurement system.

conveyance loss. Water loss in pipes, channels, conduits, ditches by leakage, or evaporation.

cool roofs. Roofing material that has high solar reflectance, and absorbs only small amounts of heat, which can reduce heat transfer to the indoors and enhance roof life and durability.

cooling electricity use. Amount of electricity used to meet the building cooling load.

cooling tower. A structure that helps remove heat from water used as a coolant, for example, in electric power generating plants.

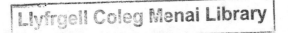

cooperative agreement. An assistance agreement whereby the EPA transfers money, property, services, or anything of value to a state, university, nonprofit, or not-for-profit organization for the accomplishment of authorized activities or tasks.

copper. Distinctively colored metal used for electric wiring, plumbing, heating, and roof and building construction, and in automobile brake linings. It is known to be toxic at certain levels.

core. The uranium-containing heart of a nuclear reactor, where energy is released.

Core Program Cooperative Agreement. An assistance agreement whereby the EPA supports states or tribal governments with funds to help defray the cost of non-item-specific administrative and training activities.

corporate citizenship. A company's responsible involvement with the wider community in which it is situated.

corporate health. The idea that companies, especially commercial businesses, have a duty to care for all of their stakeholders in all aspects of their operations.

corporate philanthropy. Dimension of social responsibility that includes charitable donations.

corporate policy. Dimension of social responsibility that refers to the position; a firm take on social and political issues.

corporate responsibility. The degree to which companies manage business practices to produce an overall positive impact on society.

corporate responsibility report. A periodically published report of a company's corporate responsibility practices, goals, and progress toward achieving those goals that may be included with the company's annual report or as a separate publication that focuses on the company's social and environmental impact; the process of creating this report is meant to uncover strengths and weaknesses as well as enhance transparency

for all company stakeholders; *see* corporate sustainability report.

corporate social initiatives. Dimension of social responsibility that includes enhanced forms of corporate philanthropy directly related to the company's competencies.

corporate social responsibility. The continuing commitment by businesses to behave ethically and contribute to economic development while improving the quality of life of the workplace as well as the local community and society at large; a company's obligation to be accountable to all of its stakeholders in all of its operations and activities (including financial stakeholders as well as suppliers, customers, and employees) with the aim of achieving sustainable development not only in the economic dimension but also in the social and environmental dimensions.

corporate sustainability report. A periodic report published by a company to outline its progress toward meeting its financial, environmental, and social sustainability goals; often published in compliance with third-party standards such as the UN Global Compact or Global Reporting Initiative; *see* corporate responsibility report.

corrective action. The EPA can require treatment, storage, and disposal (TSDF) facilities handling hazardous waste to undertake corrective actions to clean up spills resulting from failure to follow hazardous waste management procedures or other mistakes. The process includes cleanup procedures designed to guide TSDFS facilities in cleaning up after spills.

corrosion. The dissolution and wearing away of metal caused by a chemical reaction such as between water and the pipes, chemicals touching a metal surface, or contact between two metals.

corrosive. A chemical agent that reacts with the surface of a material causing it to deteriorate or wear away.

corrosivity. A characteristic of acidic and basic hazardous wastes.

cost recovery. A legal process by which potentially responsible parties who contributed to contamination at a Superfund site can be required to reimburse the Trust Fund for money spent during any cleanup actions by the federal government.

cost sharing. A publicly financed program through which society, as a beneficiary of environmental protection, shares part of the cost of pollution control with those who must actually install the controls. In a Superfund, for example, the government may pay part of the cost of a cleanup action with those responsible for the pollution paying the major share.

cost/benefit analysis. A quantitative evaluation of the costs that would have incurred by implementing an environmental regulation versus the overall benefits to society of the proposed action.

cost-effective alternative. An alternative control or corrective method identified after analysis as being the best available in terms of reliability, performance, and cost. Although costs are one important consideration, regulatory and compliance analysis does not require the EPA to choose the least expensive alternative. For example, when selecting or approving a method for cleaning up a Superfund site, the Agency balances costs with the long-term effectiveness of the methods proposed and the potential danger posed by the site.

Council of Europe. A body created in 1949 to secure a greater measure of unity between the European countries.

Council on Environment Quality, U.S.A council created by the National Environmental Policy Act 1969, the members being appointed by the U.S. president.

cover crop. A crop that provides temporary protection for delicate seedlings and/or provides a cover canopy for seasonal soil protection and improvement between normal crop production periods.

cover material. Soil used to cover compacted solid waste in a sanitary landfill.

cradle-to-cradle. A design philosophy put forth by architect William McDonough that considers the life cycle of a material or product, and ensures that the product is completely recycled at the end of its defined lifetime.

cradle-to-grave or manifest system. A procedure in which hazardous materials are identified and followed as they are produced, treated, transported, and disposed of by a series of permanent, linkable, descriptive documents (e.g., manifests), commonly referred to as the cradle-to-grave system.

create. Bring into existence.

creosotes. Chemicals used in wood preserving operations that are produced by distilling coal tar. They contain polycyclic aromatic hydrocarbons and polynuclear aromatic hydrocarbons (PAHs and PNAs). High-level, short-term exposures may cause skin ulcerations.

crisis. Turning point, especially of disease; time of danger. A decisive point in time or process, the culmination of events from which change must ensue. Hence environmental crisis, population crisis, etc.

criteria. Descriptive factors taken into account by the EPA in setting standards for various pollutants. These factors are used to determine limits on allowable concentration levels, and to limit the number of violations per year. When issued by the EPA, the criteria provide guidance to the states on how to establish their standards.

criteria pollutants. The 1970 amendments to the Clean Air Act required the EPA to set National Ambient Air Quality Standards for certain pollutants known to be hazardous to human health. EPA has identified and set standards to protect human health and welfare for six pollutants: ozone, carbon monoxide, total suspended particulates, sulfur dioxide, lead, and nitrogen oxide.

critical effect. The first adverse effect, or its known precursor, that occurs as a dose rate increases. Designation is based on evaluation of overall database.

crop consumptive use. The amount of water transpired during plant growth plus what evaporated from the soil surface and foliage in the crop area.

crop rotation. Planting a succession of different crops on the same land area as opposed to planting the same crop time after time.

cross-connection. Any actual or potential connection between a drinking water system and an unapproved water supply or other source of contamination.

cross contamination. The movement of underground contaminants from one level or area to another due to invasive subsurface activities.

crumb rubber. Ground rubber fragments the size of sand or silt used in rubber or plastic products, or processed further into reclaimed rubber or asphalt products.

cryptosporidium. A protozoan microbe associated with the disease cryptosporidiosis in people. The disease can be transmitted through the ingestion of drinking water, person-to-person contact, or other pathways, and can cause acute diarrhea, abdominal pain, vomiting, or fever, and can be fatal (e.g., as in the Milwaukee episode).

cubic feet per minute (CFM). A measure of the volume of a substance flowing through air within a fixed period of time. With regard to indoor air, CFM refers to the amount of air, in cubic feet, that is exchanged with outdoor air in a minute's time; that is, the air exchange rate.

cul-de-sac. Usually a blocked path or way with only one means of access.

cullet. Crushed glass.

cultural environment. A concept that includes: rock-art sites, ceremonial grounds, sacred sites, camp sites, and shell mounds; historical and archaeological sites such as old missions and cemeteries, historic buildings and structures, historic towns and precincts; current evidence of distinctive characteristic of communities and their ambiance; and evidence of the degree of development of the art in a society, viewed in a domestic and world setting.

cultural eutrophication. Increasing rate at which water bodies "die" by pollution from human activities.

culture. That which is cultivated.

cultures and stocks. Infectious agents and associated biologicals including cultures from medical and pathological laboratories; cultures and stocks of infectious agents from research and industrial laboratories; waste from the production of biologicals; discarded live and attenuated vaccines; and culture dishes and devices used to transfer, inoculate, and mix cultures.

cumulative ecological risk assessment. Consideration of the total ecological risk from multiple stressors to a given eco-zone.

cumulative effects. Progressive environmental degradation over time arising from a range of activities throughout an area or region, each activity considered in isolation being possibly not a significant contributor.

cumulative exposure. The sum of exposures of an organism to a pollutant over a period of time.

cumulative impact. Used in several ways as the effect of exposure to more than one compound; as the effect of exposure to emissions from more than one facility; the combined effects of a facility and surrounding facilities or projects on the environment; or some combination of these.

cumulative working level months (CWLMs). The sum of lifetime exposure to radon working levels expressed in total working level months.

curb stop. A water service shutoff valve located in a water service pipe near the curb and between the water main and the building.

curbside collection. Method of collecting recyclable materials at homes, community districts, or businesses.

cutie-pie. An instrument used to measure radiation levels.

cuttings. Spoils left by conventional drilling with hollow stem auger or rotary drilling equipment.

cyanide. A highly toxic chemical often used in metal finishing or in extraction of precious metal from ore.

cyberspace. A virtual location where information is stored, ideas are described, and communication takes place in and through an electronic network of linked systems.

cycles. Recurring series of events, operations, or states. Also a wheeled vehicle, as a bicycle, tricycle, etc.

cyclone collector. A device that uses centrifugal force to remove large particles from polluted air.

D

dam. A structure constructed to restrict the flow of tidal or river water for the purpose of hydroelectricity or irrigation, or as a means of containing industrial wastes.

data call-in. A part of the Office of Pesticide Programs (OPPs) process of developing key required test data, especially on the long-term, chronic effects of existing pesticides, in advance of scheduled registration standard reviews. Data call-in from manufacturers is an adjunct of the Registration Standards Program intended to expedite reregistration.

Data Quality Objectives (DQOs). Qualitative and quantitative statements of the overall level of uncertainty that a decision maker will accept in results or decisions based on environmental data. They provide the statistical framework for planning and managing environmental data operations consistent with user's needs.

day tank. Another name for deaerating tank.

DDT. An environmentally persistent insecticide banned for most uses by the U.S. EPA in 1972. It accumulates in fatty tissues of animals and has lead to serious environmental problems such as the thinning of shells of certain birds and their resulting die-off. It may also have toxic effects on humans upon prolonged exposure.

de minimis risk. A level of risk that the scientific and regulatory community asserts is too insignificant to regulate.

dead end. The end of a water main that is not connected to other parts of the distribution system.

deadmen. Anchors drilled or cemented into the ground to provide additional reactive mass for dP sampling rigs.

debt-for-nature swaps. The promotion of nature conservation projects out of the vast indebtedness incurred by many Third World countries during the 1980s.

decant. To draw off the upper layer of liquid after the heaviest material (a solid or another liquid) has settled.

decay products. Degraded radioactive materials, often referred to as "daughters" or "progeny"; radon decay products of most concern from a public health standpoint are polonium-214 and polonium-218.

dechlorination. Removal of chlorine from a substance.

decision. Formal judgment; considered choice, making up one's mind, means of resolution.

decomposition. The breakdown of matter by bacteria and fungi, changing the chemical makeup and physical appearance of materials.

deconstruction. The careful and systematic dismantling of a building structure to maximize the recovery of valuable building materials. Deconstruction is an environmentally friendly alternative to demolition, which produces large quantities of debris requiring disposal.

decontamination. Removal of harmful substances such as noxious chemicals, harmful bacteria or other organisms, or radioactive material from exposed individuals, rooms and furnishings in buildings, or the exterior environment.

deep ecology. The development of ecology, a branch of biology concerned with organisms' relationships to one another and their surroundings, from a descriptive minor science (now referred to as shallow ecology) to the science of the relationships of all life and its context.

deep repositories. A solution offered for high-level radioactive wastes, the idea being to put nuclear waste far out of reach, and, it is hoped, out of mind.

deep-well injection. Deposition of raw or treated, filtered hazardous waste by pumping it into deep wells, where it is contained in the pores of permeable subsurface rock.

deflocculating agent. A material added to a suspension to prevent settling.

defluoridation. The removal of excess flouride in drinking water to prevent the staining of teeth.

defoliant. An herbicide that removes leaves from trees and growing plants.

deforestation. The net removal of trees from forested land.

degasification. A water treatment that removes dissolved gases from the water.

degrease. To remove grease from machinery, tools, and the like, usually using solvents. Aqueous (water-based) cleaners are becoming popular and are required in some parts of the state.

degree-day. A rough measure used to estimate the amount of heating required in a given area; defined as the difference between the mean daily temperature and 65 degrees Fahrenheit. Degree-days are also calculated to estimate cooling requirements.

deionized water. Water that has been specifically treated to remove minerals.

delegated state. A state (or other governmental entity such as a tribal government) that has received authority to administer an environmental regulatory program in lieu of a federal counterpart. As used in connection with NPDES, UIC, and PWS programs, the term does not connote any transfer of federal authority to a state.

delist. Use of the petition process to have a facility's toxic designation rescinded.

demand management. The ways in which the character of effective demand can be influenced by pricing and other policies.

demand-side management. The implementation of policies that control or influence the demand of certain products or services.

demand-side waste management. Prices whereby consumers use purchasing decisions to communicate to product manufacturers that they prefer environmentally sound products packaged with the least amount of waste, made from recycled or recyclable materials, and containing no hazardous substances.

dematerialization. The reduction of total materials used in providing customers with products or services.

demineralization. A treatment process that removes dissolved minerals from water.

demographic transition. A fundamental change in the characteristic trends of a population, for example, a transition from high birth rates and high death rates, to low birth rates and low death rates.

denitrification. The biological reduction of nitrate to nitrogen gas by denitrifying bacteria in soil.

dense non-aqueous phase liquid (DNAPL). Non-aqueous phase liquids, such as chlorinated hydrocarbon solvents or petroleum fractions, with a specific gravity greater than 1.0 that sink through the water column until they reach a confining layer. Because they are at the bottom of aquifers instead of floating on the water table, typical monitoring wells do not indicate their presence.

density. A measure of how heavy a specific volume of a solid, liquid, or gas is in comparison to water, depending on the chemical.

density. The amount of residential development permitted on a given parcel of land, typically measured in dwelling units per acre—the larger the number of units permitted per acre, the higher the density; the fewer units permitted, the lower the density. Well-designed neighborhood density can help achieve local economic development goals, provide housing options, create walkable neighborhoods, and protect their air, water, and open space.

Department of Toxic Substances Control (DTSC). A department within the California Environmental Protection Agency charged with the regulation of hazardous waste from generation to final disposal, and for overseeing the investigation and cleanup of hazardous waste sites.

depletion curve. In hydraulics, a graphical representation of water depletion from storage-stream channels, surface soil, and groundwater. A depletion curve can be drawn for base flow, direct runoff, or total flow.

depressurization. A condition that occurs when the air pressure inside a structure is lower than the air pressure outdoors. Depressurization can occur when household appliances, such as fireplaces or furnaces, that consume or exhaust house air, are not supplied with enough makeup air. Radon may be drawn into a house more rapidly under depressurized conditions.

dermal absorption/penetration. Process by which a chemical penetrates the skin and enters the body as an internal dose.

dermal exposure. Contact between a chemical and the skin.

dermal toxicity. The ability of a pesticide or toxic chemical to poison people or animals by contact with the skin.

derrick. A frame tower that supports the drill equipment used to find oil and natural gas in the earth.

DES (diethylstilbestrol). A synthetic estrogen, diethylstilbestrol is used as a growth stimulant in food animals. Residues in meat are thought to be carcinogenic.

desalination. Removing salts from ocean or brackish water by using various technologies. Removal of salts from soil by artificial means, usually leaching.

desiccant. A chemical agent that absorbs moisture; some desiccants are capable of drying out plants or insects, causing death.

design capacity. The average daily flow that a treatment plant or other facility is designed to accommodate.

design for deconstruction. Designing buildings to facilitate future renovations and eventual dismantlement, including designing for durability and adaptability; using fewer adhesives and sealants; using fewer materials; and reuseable components.

design value. The monitored reading used by the EPA to determine an area's air quality status; e.g., for ozone, the fourth highest reading measured over the most recent three years is the design value.

designated pollutant. An air pollutant that is neither a criteria nor hazardous pollutant, as described in the Clean Air Act, but for which new source performance standards exist. The Clean Air Act requires states to control these pollutants, which include acid mist, total reduced sulfur (TRS), and fluorides.

designated uses. Those water uses identified in state water quality standards that must be achieved and maintained as required under the Clean Water Act. Uses can include cold water fisheries, public water supply, and irrigation.

designer bugs. Popular term for microbes developed through biotechnology that can degrade specific toxic chemicals at their source in toxic waste dumps or in groundwater.

destination facility. The facility to which regulated medical waste is shipped for treatment and destruction, incineration, and/or disposal.

destratification. Vertical mixing within a lake or reservoir to totally or partially eliminate separate layers of temperature, plant, or animal life.

destroyed medical waste. Regulated medical waste that has been ruined, torn apart, or mutilated through thermal treatment, melting, shredding, grinding, tearing, or breaking, so that it is no longer generally recognized as medical waste, but has not yet been treated (excludes compacted regulated medical waste).

destruction and removal efficiency (DRE). A percentage that represents the number of molecules of a compound removed or destroyed in an incinerator relative to the number of molecules entering the system (e.g., a DRE of 99.99 percent means that 9,999 molecules are destroyed for every 10,000 that enter; 99.99 percent is known as "four nines." For some pollutants, the RCRA removal requirement may be as stringent as "six nines").

destruction facility. A facility that destroys regulated medical waste; destruction or incineration system, processing waste materials into slag and gases ignited inside of a secondary combustion chamber that follows the reactor.

desulfurization. Removal of sulfur from fossil fuels to reduce pollution.

detectable leak rate. The smallest leak (from a storage tank), expressed in terms of gallons- or liters-per-hour, that a test can reliably discern with a certain probability of detection or false alarm.

detection criterion. A predetermined rule to ascertain whether a tank is leaking or not. Most volumetric tests use a threshold value as the detection criterion.

detection limit. The lowest concentration of a chemical that can reliably be distinguished from a zero concentration.

detention time. The theoretical calculated time required for a small amount of water to pass through a tank at a given rate of flow. The actual time that a small amount of water is in a settling basin, flocculating basin, or rapid-mix chamber. In storage reservoirs, the length of time water will be held before being used.

detergent. Synthetic washing agent that helps to remove dirt and oil. Some contain compounds that kill useful bacteria and encourage algae growth when they are in wastewater that reaches receiving waters.

development. The application of human, physical, natural, and financial resources to meet effective or prospective market demands and other human needs.

development effects. Adverse effects such as altered growth, structural abnormality, functional deficiency, or death observed in a developing organism.

devolution, devolve. These are de- words for which there is no apposite alternative. Re-evolution would be correct, but revolution means something else.

dewater. To remove or separate a portion of the water in a sludge or slurry to dry the sludge so it can be handled and disposed of. Also to remove or drain the water from a tank or trench.

diatomaceous earth (diatomite). A chalk-like material (fossilized diatoms) used to filter out solid waste in wastewater treatment plants; also used as an active ingredient in some powdered pesticides.

diazinon. An organophosphate insecticide. In 1986, EPA banned its use on open areas such as sod farms and golf courses because it posed a danger to migratory birds. The ban did not apply to agricultural, home lawn or commercial establishment uses.

dibenzofurans. A group of organic compounds, some of which are toxic.

dibromochloropropane (DBCP). An amber-colored liquid used in agriculture to kill pests in the soil. Inhalation of high concentrations of DBCP causes nausea and irritation of the respiratory tract. Chronic exposure results in sterility in males. Although not in use as a pesticide in this country since 1979 (until 1985 in Hawaii), it is found as a contaminant at many hazardous substances sites.

dichlorobenzene (DCB). A volatile organic compound often used as a deodorizer, and as a moth, mold, and mildew killer. It is a white solid with a strong odor of mothballs.

dichloroethane. A colorless, oily liquid having an etherlike odor. It is used to make other chemicals and to dissolve other substances such as paint and varnish, and to remove grease. In the past, this chemical was used as a surgical anesthetic, but it is no longer used for this purpose. Because 1,1-dichloroethane evaporates easily into the air, it is usually present in the environment as a vapor rather than a liquid.

dicofol. A pesticide used on citrus fruits.

dieldrin. An insecticide that was used on crops such as corn and cotton. The EPA banned its use in 1987.

diesel engine. Internal combustion engines that burn diesel oil rather than gasoline.

diesel fuel. A fuel composed of distillates obtained in petroleum refining operation or blends of such distillates with residual oil used in motor vehicles. The boiling point and specific gravity are higher for diesel fuels than for gasoline.

diffuse. Spread out, not concentrated, not concise.

diffused air. A type of aeration that forces oxygen into sewage by pumping air through perforated pipes inside a holding tank.

diffusion. The movement of suspended or dissolved particles (or molecules) from a more concentrated to a less concentrated area. The process tends to distribute the particles or molecules more uniformly.

digester. In wastewater treatment, a closed tank; in solid-waste conversion, a unit in which bacterial action is induced and accelerated in order to break down organic matter and establish the proper carbon to nitrogen ratio.

digester gas. Biogas that is produced using a digester, which is an airtight vessel or enclosure in which bacteria decomposes biomass in water to produce biogas.

digestion. The biochemical decomposition of organic matter, resulting in partial gasification, liquefaction, and mineralization of pollutants.

digital divide. The gap between those who have technology and those who do not.

Digital Millennium Copyright Act. The U.S. law that made it a crime to circumvent antipiracy measures built into most commercial software agreements between the manufacturers and their users.

dike. A low wall that can act as a barrier to prevent a spill from spreading.

diluent. Any liquid or solid material used to dilute or carry an active ingredient.

dilution ratio. The relationship between the volume of water in a stream and the volume of incoming water. It affects the ability of the stream to assimilate waste.

dimictic. Lakes and reservoirs that freeze over and normally go through two stratifications and two mixing cycles a year.

dinocap. A fungicide used primarily by apple growers to control summer diseases. The EPA proposed restrictions on its use in 1986 when laboratory tests found it caused birth defects in rabbits.

dinoseb. A herbicide that is also used as a fungicide and insecticide. It was banned by the EPA in 1986 because it posed the risk of birth defects and sterility.

dioxins. A family of chlorinated organic compounds that are undesirable by-products in the manufacture of certain classes of herbicides, disinfectants, bleaches, and other agents. Concern about them arises from their potential toxicity as contaminants in commercial products. Tests on laboratory animals indicate that it is one of the more toxic anthropogenic (human-made) compounds.

direct current (dc). An electric current that flows in only one direction through a circuit, as from a battery.

direct discharger. A municipal or industrial facility which introduces pollution through a defined conveyance or system such as outlet pipes; a point source.

direct filtration. A method of treating water that consists of the addition of coagulent chemicals, flash mixing, coagulation, minimal flocculation, and filtration. Sedimentation is not used.

direct push. Technology used for performing subsurface investigations by driving, pushing, and/or vibrating small-diameter hollow steel rods into the ground. Also known as direct drive, drive point, or push technology.

direct runoff. Water that flows over the ground surface or through the ground directly into streams, rivers, and lakes.

discharge. Flow of surface water in a stream or canal or the outflow of groundwater from a flowing artesian well, ditch, or spring. Can also apply to discharge of liquid effluent from a facility or to chemical emissions into the air through designated venting mechanisms.

disinfectant. A chemical or physical process that kills pathogenic organisms in water, air, or on surfaces. Chlorine is often used to disinfect sewage treatment effluent, water supplies, wells, and swimming pools.

disinfectant by-product. A compound formed by the reaction of a disinfectant such as chlorine with organic material in the water supply; a chemical by-product of the disinfection process.

disinfectant time. The time it takes water to move from the point of disinfectant application (or the previous point of residual disinfectant measurement) to a point before or at the point where the residual disinfectant is measured. In pipelines, the time is calculated by dividing the internal volume of the pipe by the maximum hourly flow rate; within mixing basins and storage reservoirs it is determined by tracer studies of an equivalent demonstration.

dispersant. A chemical agent used to break up concentrations of organic material such as spilled oil.

displacement savings. Saving realized by displacing purchases of natural gas or electricity from a local utility by using landfill gas for power and heat.

disposables. Consumer products, other items, and packaging used once or a few times and discarded.

disposal. Final placement or destruction of toxic, radioactive, or other wastes; surplus or banned pesticides or other chemicals; polluted soils; and drums containing hazardous materials from removal actions or accidental releases. Disposal may be accomplished through use of approved secure landfills, surface impoundments, land farming, deep-well injection, ocean dumping, or incineration.

disposal facilities. Repositories for solid waste, including landfills and combustors intended for permanent containment or destruction of waste materials. Excludes transfer stations and composting facilities.

dissolved oxygen (DO). The oxygen freely available in water, vital to fish and other aquatic life and for the prevention of odors. DO levels are considered a most important indicator of a water body's ability to support desirable aquatic life. Secondary and advanced waste treatment are generally designed to ensure adequate DO in waste-receiving waters.

dissolved solids. Disintegrated organic and inorganic material in water. Excessive amounts make water unfit to drink or use in industrial processes.

distillate fuel oil. A general classification for one of the petroleum fractions produced in conventional distillation operations. It includes diesel fuels and fuel oils. Products known as No. 1, No. 2, and No. 4 diesel fuel are used in on-highway diesel engines, such as those in trucks and automobiles, as well as off-highway engines, such as those in railroad locomotives and agricultural machinery. Products known as No. 1, No. 2, and No. 4 fuel oils are used primarily for space heating and electric power generation.

distillation. The act of purifying liquids through boiling, so that the steam or gaseous vapors condense to a pure liquid. Pollutants and contaminants may remain in a concentrated residue.

distillation unit (atmospheric). The primary distillation unit that processes crude oil (including mixtures of other hydrocarbons) at approximately atmospheric conditions. It includes a pipe still for vaporizing the crude oil and a fractionation tower for separating the vaporized hydrocarbon components in the crude oil into fractions with different boiling ranges. This is done by continuously vaporizing and condensing the components to separate higher oiling point material.

distributed generation (distributed energy resources). Refers to electricity provided by small, modular power generators (typically ranging in capacity from a few kilowatts to 50 megawatts) located at or near customer demand.

disturbance. Any event or series of events that disrupt ecosystem, community, or population structure and alters the physical environment.

diverse. Various, different, unlike in nature, appearance of qualities, qualities.

diversion. Use of part of a stream flow as water supply. Also a channel with a supporting ridge on the lower side constructed across a slope to divert water at a non-erosive velocity to sites where it can be used and disposed of.

diversion rate. The percentage of waste materials diverted from traditional disposal such as landfilling or incineration to be recycled, composted, or reused.

DNA hybridization. Use of a segment of DNA, called a DNA probe, to identify its complementary DNA; used to detect specific genes.

Dobson Unit (DU). Units of ozone level measurement. If, for example, 100 dU of ozone were brought to the earth's surface, they would form a layer 1 millimeter thick. Ozone levels vary geographically, even in the absence of ozone depletion.

domestic application. Pesticide application in and around houses, office buildings, motels, and other living or working areas.

domini social investment. An investment firm specializing exclusively in socially responsible investing, based on its own development and application of social and environmental standards.

dosage/dose. 1. The actual quantity of a chemical administered to an organism or to which it is exposed. 2. The amount of a substance that reaches a specific tissue (e.g., the liver). 3. The amount of a substance available for interaction with metabolic processes after crossing the outer boundary of an organism.

dose equivalent. The product of the absorbed dose from ionizing radiation and such factors as account for biological differences due to the type of radiation and its distribution in the body.

dose rate. In exposure assessment, dose per time unit (e.g., mg/day), sometimes also called dosage.

dose response. Shifts in toxicological responses of an individual (such as alterations in severity) or populations (such as alterations in incidence) that are related to changes in the dose of any given substance.

dose response curve. Graphical representation of the relationship between the dose of a stressor and the biological response thereto.

dose-response assessment. Estimating the potency of a chemical. In exposure assessment, the process of determining the relationship between the dose of a stressor and a specific biological response. Evaluating the quantitative relationship between dose and toxicological responses.

dose-response relationship. The quantitative relationship between the amount of exposure to a substance and the extent of toxic injury or disease produced.

dosimeter. An instrument to measure dosage; many so-called dosimeters actually measure exposure rather than dosage. Dosimetry is the process or technology of measuring and/or estimating dosage.

DOT reportable quantity. The quantity of a substance specified in a U.S. Department of Transportation regulation that triggers labeling, packaging, and other requirements related to shipping such substances.

Dow Jones Sustainability Indexes (DJSI). The first global indexes to track the financial performance of sustainability-driven companies.

downgradient. The direction in which groundwater flows.

downstream processors. Industries dependent on crop production (e.g., canneries and food processors).

dP hole. Hole in the ground made with DP equipment.

draft permit. A preliminary permit drafted and published by the EPA; subject to public review and comment before final action on the application.

draft. The act of drawing or removing water from a tank or reservoir. The water that is drawn or removed.

drainage basin. The area of land that drains water, sediment, and dissolved materials to a common outlet at some point along a stream channel.

drainage well. A well drilled to carry excess water off agricultural fields. Because they act as a funnel from the surface to the groundwater below. Drainage wells can contribute to groundwater pollution.

drainage. Improving the productivity of agricultural land by removing excess water from the soil by such means as ditches or subsurface drainage tiles.

drawdown. The drop in the water table or level of water in the ground when water is being pumped from a well. The amount of water used from a tank or reservoir. The drop in the water level of a tank or reservoir.

dredging. Removal of mud from the bottom of water bodies. This can disturb the ecosystem and causes silting that kills aquatic life. Dredging of contaminated muds can expose biota to heavy metals and other toxics. Dredging activities may be subject to regulation under Section 404 of the Clean Water Act.

drilling. The act of boring a hole (1) to determine whether minerals are present in commercially recoverable quantities and (2) to accomplish production of the minerals (including drilling to inject fluids). There are three types of drilling: exploratory—drilling to locate probable mineral deposits or to establish the nature of geological structures; such wells may not be capable of production if minerals are discovered; developmental—drilling to delineate the boundaries of a known mineral deposit to enhance the productive capacity of the producing mineral property; and directional—drilling that is deliberately made to depart significantly from the vertical.

drilling fluid. Fluid used to lubricate the bit and convey drill cuttings to the surface with rotary drilling equipment. Usually composed of bentonite slurry or muddy water. Can become contaminated, leading to cross contamination, and may require special disposal. Not used with DP methods

drinking water equivalent level. Protective level of exposure related to potentially noncarcinogenic effects of chemicals that are also known to cause cancer.

Drinking Water State Revolving Fund. The fund provides capitalization grants to states to develop drinking water revolving loan funds to help finance system infrastructure improvements, assure source-water protection, enhance operation and management of drinking-water systems, and otherwise promote local water-system compliance and protection of public health.

drinking water quality guidelines. The decade 1980–1990 devoted by the UN to bringing clean water and adequate sanitation to everyone by 1990.

drive casing. Heavy-duty steel casing driven along with the sampling tool in cased DP systems. Keeps the hole open between sampling runs and is not removed until the last sample has been collected.

drive point (DO) profiler. An exposed groundwater DP system used to collect multiple-depth discrete groundwater samples. Ports in the tip of the probe connect to an internal stainless-steel or teflon tube that extends to the surface. Samples are collected via suction or airlift methods. Deionized water is pumped down through the ports to prevent plugging while driving the tool to the next sampling depth.

drop-off. Recyclable materials collection method in which individuals bring them to a designated collection site.

drought. Insufficiency of rain for an extended period with associated water shortages, crop impairment or failure, stream-flow reduction, and depletion of groundwater and soil moisture.

dual-phase extraction. Active withdrawal of both liquid and gas phases from a well usually involving the use of a vacuum pump.

dump. A site used to dispose of solid waste without environmental controls.

duplicate. A second aliquot or sample that is treated the same as the original sample in order to determine the precision of the analytical method.

dustfall jar. An open container used to collect large particles from the air for measurement and analysis.

dynamo. A device that changes mechanical energy into electrical energy.

dynamometer. A device used to place a load on an engine and measure its performance.

dystrophic lakes. Acidic, shallow bodies of water that contain much humus and/or other organic matter; contain many plants but few fish.

E

earth. Dry land, soil, ground; the old English name for our home planet.

earthwatch. A plan for global environment assessment arising out of the UN conference on the human environment in 1972.

eco-efficiency. Occurs when businesses or societies are simultaneously economically efficient and environmentally responsible; the creation of more goods and services while using fewer resources and creating less waste and pollution.

ecofeminism. A view that androcentrism, with its associated domination of woman, ethnic minorities, and intolerance and war, stands also at the root of the domination and exploitation of nature.

ecofundamentalism. A view that environmental protection and ecologically sustainable development require fundamental changes to the structure of society; the reconstructing of the tax system to ensure much reduced disparities in the net incomes of individuals.

ecoholism. The inherent coherence of relationships within a particular environment; the dynamics of the web of life.

ecolabel. Third-party certifications that attest the characteristic of a product and its low impact on the environment; there are various ecolabels, some are single criteria (GREENGUARD, SCS for recycle content) others are multicriteria (GECA and the EU ecoflower).

eco-labeling. The certification of a product so that it meets a published specification relating to environmental performance.

ecological entity. In ecological risk assessment, a general term referring to a species, a group of species, an ecosystem function or characteristic, or a specific habitat or biome.

Ecological Environmental Impact Assessment (EEIA). An assessment of the potential ecological impacts of a proposed development.

ecological equity. The balancing of humans' appropriation of the earth's resources for their own use with the needs of all species and biological systems for self-regeneration.

ecological exposure. Exposure of a nonhuman organism to a stressor.

ecological footprint. The total amount of land, food, water, and other resources used by, or the total ecological impact of, a person or organization's subsistence; usually measured in acres or hectares of productive land.

ecological impact. The effect that a human-caused or natural activity has on living organisms and their nonliving (abiotic) environment.

ecological indicator. A characteristic of an ecosystem that is related to, or derived from, a measure of biotic or abiotic variable, that can provide quantitative information on ecological structure and function. An indicator can contribute to a measure of integrity and sustainability.

ecological integrity. A living system exhibits integrity if, when subjected to disturbance, it sustains and organizes self-correcting ability to recover toward a biomass end-state that is normal for that system. End-states other than the pristine or naturally whole may be accepted as normal and good.

ecological justice (ecojustice). The concept that all components of an ecosystem (such as plant and animal life as well as natural resources) have a right to be free from human exploitation and free from destruction, discrimination, bias, or extinction; distinct from environmental justice.

ecological risk assessment. The application of a formal framework, analytical process, or model to estimate the effects of human actions(s) on a natural resource and to interpret the significance of those effects in light of the uncertainties identified in each component of the assessment process. Such analysis includes initial hazard identification, exposure and dose-response assessments, and risk characterization.

ecological sensitivity. It characterizes those who are sensitive to the environmental issues and problems and start to activate behavior to protect the natural resources, reducing the impact in the environment with their own activity.

ecological/environmental sustainability. Maintenance of ecosystem components and functions for future generations.

ecologically sustainable organization (ESO). A business that operates in a way that is consistent with the principle of sustainable development.

ecology. The study of the relationships between organisms and their environment or the study of ecosystems.

e-commerce. Electronic business exchanges where the buying and selling of goods and services is done electronically via the Internet.

economic development. The process whereby relatively poor countries are transformed into much richer industrial economies, the changes being both qualitative and quantitative.

economic equity. The distribution of assets, resources, and tax liability among society that is considered fair and just.

economic impact assessment. Consideration of the economic implications alone of a proposed policy, plan, program project, or activity.

economic instruments. Economic or fiscal measures to influence environmental behavior.

economic poisons. Chemicals used to control pests and to defoliate cash crops such as cotton.

economic systems, functions of. To match supply to effective demand for goods and services in an efficient manner and to an acceptable quality.

economic welfare. Defined by the Cambridge economist A. C. Pigou (1877–1959) as "that part of social welfare that can be brought directly or indirectly into relation with the measuring rod of money."

economics. Practical and theoretical science of the production and distribution of wealth; application to a particular thing, as in the economics of authorship.

ecopolitics. The influence of ecological considerations, in local and national policies, expressed in policies, and programs by incumbent governments of all shades, and in the presence of "green" parties and candidates in many parliaments and councils.

ecosphere. The "bio-bubble" that contains life on earth, in surface waters, and in the air.

eco-sustainable. A service, a material, a technique, a product, or a building that has a low impact (or carbon footprint) on the environment; owing not only to the adoption of new technologies, but also because of the use of renewable materials, energy, and recycle mechanisms.

ecosystem. The complexity of living organisms, their physical environment, and their entire interrelationships within a defined unit of space, through which matter and energy flow.

ecosystem structure. Attributes related to the instantaneous physical state of an ecosystem; examples include species population density, species richness or evenness, and standing crop biomass.

ecotax. Any tax or charge, usually on goods and services, intended to influence users and consumers so that a desirable shift in use and consumption occur.

ecotone. A habitat created by the juxtaposition of distinctly different habitats; an edge habitat; or an ecological zone or boundary where two or more ecosystems meet.

efficiency. Ratio of useful work done in relation to energy expended.

effluent guidelines. Technical EPA documents which set effluent limitations for given industries and pollutants.

effluent limitation. Restrictions established by a state or the EPA on quantities, rates, and concentrations in wastewater discharges.

effluent. Wastewater, treated or untreated, that flows out of a treatment plant, sewer, or industrial outfall. Generally refers to wastes discharged into surface waters.

effluent. Wastewater—treated or untreated—that flows out of a treatment plant, sewer, or industrial outfall. Generally refers to wastes discharged into surface waters.

ejector. A device used to disperse a chemical solution into water being treated.

electric motor. A device that takes electrical energy and converts it into mechanical energy to turn a shaft.

electric power. The amount of energy produced per second; the power produced by an electric current.

electric power sector. An energy-consuming sector that consists of electricity only and combined heat and power (CHP) plants whose primary business is to sell electricity, or electricity and heat, to the public—i.e., North American Industry Classification System 22 plants.

electric utility. A corporation, person, agency, authority, or other legal entity or instrumentality aligned with distribution facilities for delivery of electric energy for use primarily by the public. Included are investor-owned electric utilities, municipal and state utilities, federal electric utilities, and rural electric cooperatives. A few entities that are tariff based and corporately aligned with companies that own distribution facilities are also included.

electric utility restructuring. The introduction of competition into at least the generation phase of electricity production, with a corresponding decrease in regulatory control.

electrical energy. The energy associated with electric charges and their movements.

electricity. A form of energy characterized by the presence and motion of elementary charged particles generated by friction, induction, or chemical change.

electricity generation. The process of producing electric energy or the amount of electric energy produced by transforming other forms of energy, commonly expressed in kilowatt hours (kWh) or megawatt hours (MWh).

electrochemistry. The branch of chemistry that deals with the chemical changes produced by electricity and the production of electricity by chemical changes.

electrodialysis. A process that uses electrical current applied to permeable membranes to remove minerals from water. Often used to desalinize salty or brackish water.

electromagnetic. Having to do with magnetism produced by an electric current.

electromagnetic energy. Energy that travels in waves, such as ultra-violet radiation. It can be thought of as a combination of electric and magnetic energy.

electromagnetic geophysical methods. Ways to measure subsurface conductivity via low-frequency electromagnetic induction.

electromagnetic waves. Radiation that consists of traveling waves of electric and magnetic disturbances. X rays, light rays, and radio waves are among the many kinds of electromagnetic waves.

electron. A subatomic particle with a negative electric charge. Electrons form part of an atom and move around its nucleus.

electronic recycling (e-cycling). The reuse of electronic devices.

electronic waste (e-waste). Commonly referred to as electronic products that are discarded by consumers. Electronic waste is any refuse created by discarding electronic products and components; materials and substances involved in the manufacturing or use of electronic products is also referred to as e-waste.

electrostatic precipitator (ESP). An air pollution control device that uses electrical charges to remove particulate matter from emission gases.

element. Any substance that cannot be separated into different substances. All matter is composed of elements.

eligible costs. The construction costs for wastewater treatment works upon which EPS grants are based.

EMAP data. Environmental monitoring data collected under the auspices of the Environmental Monitoring and Assessment Program. All EMAP data share the common attribute of being of known quality, having been collected in the context of explicit data quality objectives (DQOs), and a consistent quality assurance program.

embodied energy. The amount of energy consumed to produce a product, in this case building materials. This includes the energy needed to mine or harvest natural resources and raw materials, and manufacture and transport finished materials.

emergency (chemical). A situation created by an accidental release or spill of hazardous chemicals that poses a threat to the safety of workers, residents, the environment, or property.

emergency and hazardous chemical inventory. An annual report by facilities having one or more extremely hazardous substances or hazardous chemicals above certain weight limits.

emergency exemption. Provision in FIFRA under which the EPS can grant temporary exemption to a state or another federal agency to allow the use of a pesticide product not registered for that particular use. Such actions involve unanticipated and/or severe pest problems where there is not time or interest by a manufacturer to register the product for that use. (Registrants cannot apply for such exemptions.)

emergency removal action. Steps taken to remove contaminated materials that pose imminent threats to local residents (e.g., removal of leaking drums or the excavation of explosive waste.). The state record of such removals.

emergency response values. Concentrations of chemicals, published by various groups, defining acceptable levels for short-term exposures in emergencies.

emergency suspension. Suspension of a pesticide product registration due to an imminent hazard. The action immediately halts distribution, sale, and sometimes actual use of the pesticide involved.

emission. A discharge or something that is given off; generally used in regard to discharges into the air. Or, releases of gases to the atmosphere from some type of human activity (cooking, driving a car, etc.). In the context of global climate change, they consist of greenhouse gases (e.g., the release of carbon dioxide during fuel combustion).

emission cap. A limit designed to prevent projected growth in emissions from existing and future stationary sources from eroding any mandated reductions. Generally, such provisions require that any emission growth from facilities under the restrictions be off-set by equivalent reductions at other facilities under the same cap.

emission factor. The relationship between the amount of pollution produced and the amount of raw material processed. For example, an emission factor for a blast furnace making iron would be the number of pounds of particulates per ton of raw materials.

emission inventory. A listing, by source, of the amount of air pollutants discharged into the atmosphere of a community; used to establish emission standards.

emission standard. The maximum amount of air polluting discharge legally allowed from a single source, mobile or stationary.

emissions trading. The creation of surplus emission reductions at certain stacks, vents, or similar emissions sources and the use of this surplus to meet or redefine pollution requirements applicable to other emissions sources. This allows one source to increase emissions when another source reduces them, maintaining an overall constant emission level. Facilities that reduce emissions substantially can "bank" their "credits" or sell them to other facilities or industries.

emission trading program. An attempt to introduce some free-market principles into the use of environmental resources introduced into the United States in the early 1980s.

emulsifier. A chemical that aids in suspending one liquid in another. Usually an organic chemical in an aqueous solution.

encapsulation. The treatment of asbestos-containing material with a liquid that covers the surface with a protective coating or embeds fibers in an adhesive matrix to prevent their release into the air.

enclosure. Putting an airtight, impermeable, permanent barrier around asbestos-containing materials to prevent the release of asbestos fibers into the air.

end user. Consumer of products for the purpose of recycling; excludes products for reuse or combustion for energy recovery.

endangered species. Animals, birds, fish, plants, or other living organisms threatened with extinction by anthropogenic (human-caused) or other natural changes in their environment. Requirements for declaring a species endangered are contained in the Endangered Species Act.

endangerment assessment. A study to determine the nature and extent of contamination at a site on the National Priorities List and the risks posed to public health or the environment. EPS or the state conducts the study when a legal action is to be taken to direct potentially responsible parties to clean up a site or pay for it. An endangerment assessment supplements a remedial investigation.

end-of-the-pipe. Technologies such as scrubbers on smokestacks and catalytic convertors on automobile tailpipes that reduce emissions of pollutants after they have formed.

endosulfan. An insecticide used on vegetable crops, fruits, and nuts.

endrin. A pesticide toxic to freshwater and marine aquatic life that produces adverse health effects in domestic water supplies.

end-use product. A pesticide formulation for field or other end use. The label has instructions for use or application to control pests or regulate plant growth. The term excludes products used to formulate other pesticide products.

energy conservation. The better and more efficient use of energy with proper regard to the related costs and benefits, whether economic, social, or environmental.

energy consumption. The use of energy as a source of heat or power or as a raw material input to a manufacturing process.

energy crops. Crops grown specifically for their fuel value. These include food crops such as corn and sugarcane, and nonfood crops such as poplar trees and switchgrass. Currently, two energy crops are under development: short-rotation woody crops, which are fast-growing hardwood trees harvested in five to eight years, and herbaceous energy crops, such as perennial grasses, which are harvested annually after taking two to three years to reach full productivity.

energy efficiency. Refers to activities that are aimed at reducing the energy used by substituting technically more advanced equipment, typically without affecting the services provided. Examples include high-efficiency appliances, efficient lighting programs, high-efficiency heating, ventilating and air conditioning (HVAC) systems or control modifications, efficient building design, advanced electric motor drives, and heat recovery systems.

energy efficiency. The result of actions taken to reduce dependence on or to save fuels, i.e., selection of road vehicles with higher MPG or the use of renewable sources of power for heating and cooling.

energy management system. A control system capable of monitoring environmental and system loads and adjusting HVAC operations accordingly in order to conserve energy while maintaining comfort.

energy recovery. Obtaining energy from waste through a variety of processes (e.g. combustion).

Energy Star. A joint program of the U.S. Environmental Protection Agency and the U.S. Department of Energy helping to save money and protect the environment through the promotion of energy-efficient buildings, homes, products, and practices. ENERGY-STAR-labeled products have met federal energy efficiency standards.

energy. The ability to do work or the ability to move an object. Electrical energy is usually measured in kilowatt hours (kWh), while heat energy is usually measured in British thermal units (Btu).

energy-efficiency ratio (EER). A measure of how efficiently a cooling system (e.g., air conditioner, heat pump) operates when the outdoor temperature is at a specific level (e.g., 95°F). It represents the ratio of heat removed (Btu/hour) to the electricity required to run the system (watts). The higher the EER, the more efficient the system is.

EnergyGuide. Yellow label that manufacturers are required to display on many appliances, which shows how much energy the appliance uses, compares its energy use to similar products, and lists approximate annual operating costs. Manufacturers must use standard test procedures developed by the U.S. Department of Energy (DOE) to verify the energy use and efficiency information reported on the EnergyGuide label.

enforceable requirements. Conditions or limitations in permits issued under the Clean Water Act Section 402 or 404 that, if violated, could result in the issuance of a compliance order or initiation of a civil or criminal action under federal or applicable state laws. If a permit has not been issued, the term includes any requirement which, in the regional administrator's (RA's) judgment, would be included in the permit when issued. Where no permit applies, the term includes any requirement that the RA determines is necessary for the best practical waste treatment technology to meet applicable criteria.

enforcement. EPS, state, or local legal actions to obtain compliance with environmental laws, rules, regulations, or agreements and/or obtain penalties or criminal sanctions for violations. Enforcement procedures may vary, depending on the requirements of different environmental laws and related implementing regulations. Under CERCLA, for example, EPS will seek to require potentially responsible parties to clean up a Superfund site, or pay for the cleanup, whereas under the clean Air Act the Agency may invoke sanctions against cities failing to meet ambient air quality standards that could prevent certain types of construction or federal funding. In other situations, if investigations by EPS and state agencies uncover willful violations, criminal trials and penalties are sought.

enforcement decision document (EDD). A document that provides an explanation to the public of the EPS's selection of the cleanup alternative at enforcement sites on the National Priorities List. Similar to a record of decision.

engineered controls. Method of managing environmental and health risks by placing a barrier between the contamination and the rest of the site, thus limiting exposure pathways.

engineered wood. Products made from lumber, veneers, strands of wood, or from other small wood and sometimes recycled plastic elements that are bound together with structural resins to form lumberlike structural products. They are designed for use in the same structural applications as conventional lumber, and allow production of large-lumber substitutes from small lower-grade logs.

enhanced inspection and maintenance (I&M). An improved automobile inspection and maintenance program, aimed at reducing automobile emissions, that contains, at a minimum, more vehicle types and model years, tighter inspection, and better management practices. It may also include annual computerized or centralized inspections, under-the-hood inspection, for signs of tampering with pollution control equipment and increased repair waiver cost.

enrichment. The addition of nutrients (e.g., nitrogen, phosphorus, carbon compounds) from sewage effluent or agricultural runoff to surface water, greatly increases the growth potential for algae and other aquatic plants.

entrain. To trap bubbles in water either mechanically through turbulence or chemically through a reaction.

entropy. The loss of energy (or information) within a system owing to its circumstances; measure of the degradation or disorganized of a system.

environment. Surroundings; the physical and biological system supporting life; the place where you live, here and now.

environmental agencies. Government bodies set up to administer the environmental planning, pollution control, and nature conservation activities, which are responsibilities of that government.

environmental assessment. An environmental analysis prepared pursuant to the National Environmental Policy Act to determine whether a federal action would significantly affect the environment and thus require a more detailed environmental impact statement.

environmental audit. A systematic, documented, periodic, and objective evaluation of how well a project, organization, individual, or service is performing in terms of environmental impact, including, but not necessarily limited to, compliance with any relevant standards or regulations.

environmental certification. It is the recognition that a company can request from an outside authority to analyze and demonstrate its environmental qualities. The environmental management system is a tool through which the company can determine, analyze, and increase its own eco-sustainability.

environmental economics. A recognized field of specialization in the discipline of economics, with a number of associated academic journals.

environmental equity. Equal protection from environmental hazards for individuals, groups, or communities regardless of race, ethnicity, or economic status. This applies to the development, implementation, and enforcement of environmental laws, regulations, and policies, and implies that no population of people should be forced to shoulder a disproportionate share of negative environmental impacts of pollution or environmental hazard owing to a lack of political or economic strength levels.

environmental exposure. Human exposure to pollutants originating from facility emissions. Threshold levels are not necessarily surpassed, but low-level chronic pollutant exposure is one of the most common forms of environmental exposure.

environmental fate. The destiny of a chemical or biological pollutant after release into the environment.

environmental fate data. Data that characterize a pesticide's fate in the ecosystem, considering factors that foster its degradation (light, water, microbes), pathways and resultant products.

environmental health impact assessment (EHIA). An assessment of the effects on the environment and people of aspects of a project recognized as having potentially adverse health effects; the health component is often insufficiently addressed in environmental impact assessments (EIAs).

environmental impact. Every action creates a reaction or an impact. The environmental impact is the final outcome of every human action. Usually considered in negative terms, but it can also be a positive outcome. The analysis of the environmental impact is done every time (society, companies, or single individual) we want to determine what kind of repercussions our actions will have on the environment.

environmental impact assessment (EIA). An assessment of potential environmental effects of development projects; required by the National Environmental Policy Act (NEPA) for any proposed major federal action with significant environmental impact.

environmental impact statement (EIs). A document required of federal agencies by the National Environmental Policy Act for major projects or legislative proposals significantly affecting the environment. A tool for decision making, it describes the positive and negative effects of the undertaking and cites alternative actions.

environmental indicator. A measurement, statistic, or value that provides a proximate gauge or evidence of the effects of environmental management programs or of the state or condition of the environment.

environmental justice. The concept of equal access to environmental resources and protection from environmental hazards regardless of race, ethnicity, national origin, or income; distinct from ecological justice. The fair treatment of people of all races, cultures, incomes, and educational levels with respect to the development and enforcement of environmental laws, regulations, and policies. The efforts to prevent inequitable exposure to risk, such as from hazardous waste.

environmental lien. A charge, security, or encumbrance on a property's title to secure payment of cost or debt arising from response actions, cleanup, or other remediation of hazardous substances or petroleum products.

environmental management. A concept of care applied to localities, regions, catchments, natural resources, areas of high conservation value, cleaner processing and recycling systems, waste handling and disposal, pollution control generally, landscaping and aesthetics, and enhancement of amenities.

environmental medium. A major environmental category that surrounds or contacts humans, animals, plants, and other organisms (e.g. surface water, groundwater, soil, or air) and through which chemicals or pollutants move.

environmental monitoring for public access and community tracking. Joint EPA, NOAA, and USGS program to provide timely and effective communication of environmental data and information through improved and updated technology solutions that support timely environmental monitoring reporting, interpreting, and use of the information for the benefit of the public.

environmental partnerships. A voluntary, collaborative partnership between or among businesses, government regulators, and environmental organizations to achieve specific environmental goals.

environmental planning. The identification of desirable objectives for the physical environment, including social and economic objectives, and the creation of administrative procedures and program to meet those objectives.

environmental policy. Series of actions that an organization/company enacts in order to reduce its carbon footprint.

Environmental Product Declaration (EDP). An EPD is a standardized (ISO 14025/TR) and LCA-based tool to communicate the environmental performance of a product or system, and is applicable worldwide for all interested companies and organizations. Certified EPDs are available for all products and services. There is no evaluation of the environmental information because no predetermined environmental performance levels are set. Instead it builds on well-structured and quantitative data certified by an independent third party.

Environmental Protection Agency (EPA). The U.S. federal government agency responsible for most environmental regulation and enforcement.

environmental protection policies. Policies developed by governments, agencies, associations, communities, groups, corporations, and companies, relating to the protection of the natural environment, the control of wastes, the improvement of the human-made environment, the protection of heritage values, the declaration of natural parks and reserves, the protection of fauna and flora, the conservation of forests and landscapes, the protection of wilderness, the promotion of environmental planning, and the implementation of international conventions and agreements.

environmental response team. EPA experts located in Edison, NJ, and Cincinnati, OH, who can provide around-the-clock technical assistance to EPA regional offices and states during all types of hazardous waste site emergencies and spills of hazardous substances.

environmental risk assessment (ERA). The tracking and rating of environmental risks, such as emissions, associated with a product and its manufacturing.

environmental site assessment. The process of determining whether contamination is present on a parcel of real property.

environmental standards. Standard amounts of particular pollutants allowable by law.

environmental sustainability. Long-term maintenance of ecosystem components and functions for future generations.

environmental tobacco smoke. Mixture of smoke from the burning end of a cigarette, pipe, or cigar, and smoke exhaled by the smoker.

environmental valuation. The inclusion of environmental costs and benefits into accounting practices using such mechanisms as taxes, tax incentives, and subsidies; by quantifying environmentally related costs and revenues, better management decisions, and increased investment in environmental protection and improvement are encouraged.

environmental, social and government (ESG). The types of issues or factors considered in measuring a company's "responsible practices"; these issues or factors include the environmental effects of a company's business practices, social metrics such as fair pay and treatment of labor and community involvement, and ethical corporate governance practices that are both transparent and anticorruption.

environmental/ecological risk. The potential for adverse effects on living organisms associated with pollution of the environment by effluents, emissions, wastes, or accidental chemical releases; energy use; or the depletion of natural resources.

environmentally hazardous chemicals. Chemicals and chemical wastes that pose a threat to the environment, directly or indirectly, either in their immediate potential effects, or through long-term insidious adverse influences.

epidemiology. Study of the distribution of disease or other health-related states and events in human populations, as related to age, sex, occupation, ethnicity, and economic status in order to identify and alleviate health problems and promote better health.

epilimnion. Upper waters of a thermally stratified lake subject to wind action.

episode (pollution). An air pollution incident in a given area caused by a concentration of atmospheric pollutants under meteorological conditions that may result in a significant increase in illnesses or deaths. May also describe water pollution events or hazardous material spills.

equilibrium. in relation to radiation, the state at which the radioactivity of consecutive elements within a radioactive series is neither increasing nor decreasing.

equivalent method. Any method of sampling and analyzing for air pollution which has been demonstrated to the EPA Administrator's satisfaction to be, under specific conditions, an acceptable alternative to normally used reference methods.

erosion. The wearing away of land surface by wind or water, intensified by land-clearing practices related to farming, residential or industrial development, road building, or logging.

established treatment technologies. Technologies for which cost and performance data are readily available.

estimated environmental concentration. The estimated pesticide concentration in an ecosystem.

estuary. Areas where fresh water from rivers mixes with salt water from nearshore ocean. They include bays, mouths of rivers, salt marshes, and lagoons. These brackish water ecosystems shelter and feed marine life, birds, and wildlife.

ethanol. An alternative automotive fuel derived from grain and corn; usually blended with gasoline to form gasohol.

ethylene dibromide (EDB). A chemical used as an agricultural fumigant and in certain industrial processes; extremely toxic and found to be a carcinogen in laboratory animals, EDB has been banned for most agricultural uses in the United States.

eutrophic lakes. Shallow, murky bodies of water with concentrations of plant nutrients causing excessive production of algae.

eutrophication. The slow aging process during which a lake, estuary, or bay evolves into a bog or marsh and eventually disappears. During the later stages of eutrophication the water body is choked by abundant plant life due to higher levels of nutritive compounds such as nitrogen and phosphorus. Human activities can accelerate the process.

eutrophy. To fill up with nutrients.

evacuated tube. In a solar thermal collector, an absorber tube, which is contained in an evacuated glass cylinder, through which collector fluids flow.

evaporation ponds. Areas where sewage sludge is dumped and dried.

evo-economics. A merging of economics and Darwinian biology, resulting in the discipline of evolutionary economics.

evolution. Opening out, unfolding, developing; development of organism, process, organization, society, cosmos; emergency from simpler forms; derivation rather than of special creation.

exceedance. Violation of the pollutant levels permitted by environmental protection standards.

exclusion. In the asbestos program, one of several situations that permit a local education agency (LEA) to delete one or more of the items required by the Asbestos Hazard Emergency Response Act (AHERA); for example, records of previous asbestos sample collection and analysis may be used by the accredited inspector in lieu of AHERA bulk sampling.

exclusionary ordinance. Zoning that excludes classes of persons or businesses from a particular neighborhood or area.

exempt solvent. Specific organic compounds not subject to requirements of regulation because they are deemed by the EPA to be of negligible photochemical reactivity.

exempted aquifer. Underground bodies of water defined in the Underground Injection Control program as aquifers that are potential sources of drinking water though not being used as such, and thus exempted from regulations barring underground injection activities.

exemption. A state (with primacy) may exempt a public water system from a requirement involving a Maximum Contaminant Level (MCL), treatment technique, or both, if the system cannot comply owing to compelling economic or other factors, or because the system was in operation before the requirement or MCL was instituted; and the exemption will not create a public health risk.

exotic species. A species that is not indigenous to a region.

experimental use permit. A permit granted by the EPA that allows a producer to conduct tests of a new pesticide, product, and/or use outside the laboratory. The testing is usually done on 10 or more acres of land or water surface.

explosive limits. The amounts of vapor in the air that form explosive mixtures; limits are expressed as lower and upper limits and give the range of vapor concentrations in air that will explode if an ignition source is present.

exports. In a solid waste program, municipal solid waste and recyclables transported outside the state or locality where they originated.

exposure. The amount of radiation or pollutant present in a given environment that represents a potential health threat to living organisms.

exposure assessment. Identifying the pathways by which toxicants can reach individuals, estimating how much of a chemical an individual is likely to be exposed to, and estimating the number likely to be exposed.

exposure concentration. The concentration of a chemical or other pollutant representing a health threat in a given environment.

exposure indicator. A characteristic of the environment measured to provide evidence of the occurrence or magnitude of a response indicator's exposure to a chemical or biological stress.

exposure level. The amount (concentration) of a chemical at the absorptive surfaces of an organism.

exposure pathway. The path from sources of pollutants via soil, water, or food to humans and other species or settings.

exposure route. The way a chemical or pollutant enters an organism after contact; that is, by ingestion, inhalation, or dermal absorption.

exposure-response relationship. The relationship between exposure level and the incidence of adverse effects.

externality. A benefit or cost falling on a third party who normally cannot pay or be compensated for it through the market mechanism.

extinction. The end termination of a form of activity or life.

extraction procedure (Ep toxic). Determining toxicity by a procedure that simulates leaching; if a certain concentration of a toxic substance can be leached from a waste, that waste is considered hazardous.

extraction well. A discharge well used to remove groundwater or air.

extremely hazardous substances. Any of 406 chemicals identified by the EPA as toxic, and listed under SARA Title III. The list is subject to periodic revision.

F

fabric filter. A cloth device that catches dust particles from industrial emissions.

facilities plans. Plans and studies related to the construction of treatment works necessary to comply with the Clean Water Act or RCRA. A facilities plan investigates needs and provides information on the cost-effectiveness of alternatives, a recommended plan, an environmental assessment of the recommendations, and descriptions of the treatment works, costs, and a completion schedule.

facility emergency coordinator. Representative of a facility covered by environmental law (e.g., a chemical plant) who participates in the emergency reporting process with the local emergency planning committee (LEPC).

facultative bacteria. Bacteria that can live under aerobic or anaerobic conditions.

fair trade. An international trading partnership that seeks to help marginalized producers and workers achieve financial self-sufficiency by establishing direct lines of trade between producers and consumers, guaranteeing producers fair prices for goods, restricting exploitative labor processes, and favoring environmentally-sustainable production processes through a system of labeling products.

fauna impact statement. A specialized impact statement concerned with the possible effects and implications of a proposed policy, plan, program, project, or activity for fauna.

feasibility study. 1. Analysis of the practicability of a proposal; e.g., a description and analysis of potential cleanup alternatives for a site such as one on the National Priorities List. The feasibility study usually recommends selection of a cost-effective alternative. It usually starts as soon as the remedial

investigation is underway; together, they are commonly referred to as the "RI/FS." 2. A small-scale investigation of a problem to ascertain whether a proposed research approach is likely to provide useful data.

fecal coliform bacteria. Bacteria found in the intestinal tracts of mammals. Their presence in water or sludge is an indicator of pollution and possible contamination by pathogens.

federal energy regulatory agency (FERC). The federal government agency that regulates and oversees energy industries in the economic, environmental, and safety interests of the American public.

federal implementation plan. Under current law, a federally implemented plan to achieve attainment of air quality standards, used when a state is unable to develop an adequate plan.

federal motor vehicle control program. All federal actions aimed at controlling pollution from motor vehicles by such efforts as establishing and enforcing tailpipe and evaporative emission standards for new vehicles, testing methods development, and guidance to states operating inspection and maintenance programs. Federally designated area that is required to meet and maintain federal ambient air quality standards. May include nearby locations in the same state or nearby states that share common air pollution problems.

feedlot. A confined area for the controlled feeding of animals. Tends to concentrate large amounts of animal waste that cannot be absorbed by the soil and, hence, may be carried to nearby streams or lakes by rainfall runoff.

fen. A type of wetland that accumulates peat deposits. Fens are less acidic than bogs, deriving most of their water from groundwater rich in calcium and magnesium; *see* wetlands.

ferrous metals. Magnetic metals derived from iron or steel; products made from ferrous metals include appliances, furniture, containers, and packaging like steel drums and barrels. Recycled products include processing tin/steel cans, strapping, and metals from appliances into new products.

fertilizer. Natural or artificial materials containing chemical elements that improve the growth and productiveness of plants.

FIFRA pesticide ingredient. An ingredient of a pesticide that must be registered with the EPA under the federal Insecticide, Fungicide, and Rodenticide Act. Products making pesticide claims must register under FIFRA and may be subject to labeling and use requirements.

filament. The fine metal wire in a light bulb that glows when heated by an electric current.

fill. Human-made deposits of natural soils or rock products and waste materials.

filling. Depositing dirt, mud, or other materials into aquatic areas to create more dry land, usually for agricultural or commercial development purposes, often with ruinous ecological consequences.

filter strip. Strip or area of vegetation used for removing sediment, organic matter, and other pollutants from runoff and wastewater.

filtration. A treatment process, under the control of qualified operators, for removing solid (particulate) matter from water by means of porous media such as sand or a human-made filter; often used to remove particles that contain pathogens.

financial assurance for closure. Documentation or proof that an owner or operator of a facility such as a landfill or other waste repository is capable of paying the projected costs of closing the facility and monitoring it afterward as provided in RCRA regulations.

finding of no significant impact. A document prepared by a federal agency showing why a proposed action would not have a significant impact on the environment and thus would not require preparation of an environmental impact statement. An FNSI is based on the results of an environmental assessment.

finished water. Water is "finished" when it has passed through all the processes in a water treatment plant and is ready to be delivered to consumers.

first draw. The water that comes out when a tap is first opened, likely to have the highest level of lead contamination from plumbing materials.

first world. The industrialized Western World, where relative political freedom is combined with disproportionate consumption of resources; for example, the United States, where 2 percent of the global population consumes 25 percent of resources.

fisheries. Areas dedicated to the harvesting of fish, shellfish, and sea mammals as a commercial enterprise.

fission. The splitting apart of atoms. This splitting releases large amounts of energy and one or more neutrons. Nuclear power plants split the nuclei of uranium atoms in a process called fission.

fix a sample. A sample is "fixed" in the field by adding chemicals that prevent water quality indicators of interest in the sample from changing before laboratory measurements are made.

fixed-location monitoring. Sampling of an environmental or ambient medium for pollutant concentration at one location continuously or repeatedly.

flammable. Any material that ignites easily and will burn rapidly.

flare. A control device that burns hazardous materials to prevent their release into the environment; can operate continuously or intermittently, usually on top of a stack.

flash point. The lowest temperature at which evaporation of a substance produces sufficient vapor to form an ignitable mixture with air.

flat plate pumped. A medium-temperature solar thermal collector that typically consists of a metal frame, glazing, absorbers (usually metal), and insulation and that uses a pump liquid as the heat-transfer medium; predominant use is in water heating applications.

flat-plate solar connector. A device designed to capture the sun's energy and produce low temperature heat energy. They are commonly used as collectors in solar heating systems.

flexible manufacturing. Designing machines to do multiple tasks so that they can produce a variety of products.

floc. A clump of solids formed in sewage by biological or chemical action.

flocculation. Process by which clumps of solids in water or sewage aggregate through biological or chemical action so they can be separated from water or sewage.

floodplain. The flat or nearly flat land along a river or stream or in a tidal area that is covered by water during a flood.

floor sweep. Capture of heavier-than-air gases that collect at floor level.

flow. To move or run smoothly with unbroken continuity, as in the manner characteristic of a fluid.

flow rate. The rate, expressed in gallons or liters-per-hour, at which a fluid escapes from a hole or fissure in a tank. Such measurements are also made of liquid waste, effluent, and surface water movement.

flowable. Pesticide and other formulations in which the active ingredients are finely ground insoluble solids suspended in a liquid. They are mixed with water for application.

flowmeter. A gauge indicating the velocity of wastewater moving through a treatment plant or of any liquid moving through various industrial processes.

flue gas desulfurization. A technology that employs a sorbent, usually lime or limestone, to remove sulfur dioxide from the gases produced by burning fossil fuels. Flue gas desulfurization is current state-of-the art technology for major SO2 emitters, such as power plants.

flue gas. The air coming out of a chimney after combustion in the burner it is venting.

It can include nitrogen oxides, carbon oxides, water vapor, sulfur oxides, particles, and many chemical pollutants.

fluidized bed incinerator. An incinerator that uses a bed of hot sand or other granular material to transfer heat directly to waste. Used mainly for destroying municipal sludge.

fluidized. A mass of solid particles that is made to flow like a liquid by injection of water or gas is said to have been fluidized. In water treatment, a bed of filter media is fluidized by backwashing water through the filter.

flume. A natural or human-made channel that diverts water.

fluoridation. The addition of a chemical to increase the concentration of fluoride ions in drinking water to reduce the incidence of tooth decay.

fluorides. Gaseous, solid, or dissolved compounds containing fluorine that result from industrial processes. Excessive amounts in food can lead to fluorosis.

fluorocarbons (FCs). Any of a number of organic compounds analogous to hydrocarbons in which one or more hydrogen atoms are replaced by fluorine. Once used in the United States as a propellant for domestic aerosols, they are now found mainly in coolants and some industrial processes. FCs containing chlorine are called chlorofluorocarbons (CFCs). They are believed to be modifying the ozone layer in the stratosphere, thereby allowing more harmful solar radiation to reach the earth's surface.

flush. To force large amounts of water through a system to clean out piping or tubing, and storage or process tanks. In new homes, to flush a system means to send large volumes of water gushing through the unused pipes to remove loose particles of solder and flux.

flux. A flowing or flow; a substance used to help metals fuse together.

fly ash. Noncombustible residual particles expelled by flue gas.

fogging. Applying a pesticide by rapidly heating the liquid chemical so that it forms very fine droplets that resemble smoke or fog. Used to destroy mosquitoes, black flies, and similar pests.

food. Substances ingested that are fundamental to maintain life and growth. All animals and some plants eat other living things; something dies so that another may live.

food chain. A sequence of organisms, each of which uses the next, lower member of the sequence as a food source.

food processing waste. Food residues produced during agricultural and industrial operations.

food waste. Uneaten food and food preparation wastes from residences and commercial establishments such as grocery stores, restaurants, and produce stands, institutional cafeterias and kitchens, and industrial sources like employee lunchrooms.

food web. The feeding relationships by which energy and nutrients are transferred from one species to another.

force. Something that changes the state of rest or motion of something.

forest. Tract of land covered with trees and associated life forms; unenclosed woodlands.

forestry. The business of managing forests for commercial wood production and other forest products.

formaldehyde. A colorless, pungent, and irritating gas, CH_2O, used chiefly as a disinfectant and preservative and in synthesizing other compounds such as resins.

formulation. The substances comprising all active and inert ingredients in a pesticide.

fossil fuels. Fuels such as natural gas, coal, and petroleum, that formed from the fossilized (or geologically transformed) remains of plants and animals.

fourth world. An emerging world based on small nations, communities of self-reliance, and life on a human scale.

fracture. A break in a rock formation owing to structural stresses, such as faults, shears, joints, and planes of fracture cleavage.

free product. A petroleum hydrocarbon in the liquid-free or nonaqueous phase.

freeboard. Vertical distance from the normal water surface to the top of a confining wall. Vertical distance from the sand surface to the underside of a trough in a sand filter.

fresh water. Water that generally contains less than 1,000 milligrams-per-liter of dissolved solids.

friable. Capable of being crumbled, pulverized, or reduced to powder by hand pressure.

friable asbestos. Any material containing more than 1 percent asbestos, and that can be crumbled or reduced to powder by hand pressure. (May include previously nonfriable material which becomes broken or damaged by mechanical force.)

fuel. Any material that can be burned to make energy.

fuel cells. One or more cells capable of generating an electrical current by converting the chemical energy of a fuel directly into electrical energy. Fuel cells differ from conventional electrical cells in that the active materials such as fuel and oxygen are not contained within the cell but are supplied from outside.

fuel cycle. The entire set of stages involved in the utilization of fuel, including extraction, transformation, transportation, and combustion.

fuel economy standard. The Corporate Average Fuel Economy Standard (CAFE) effective in 1978; it enhanced the national fuel conservation effort imposing a miles-per-gallon floor for motor vehicles.

fuel efficiency. The proportion of energy released by fuel combustion that is converted into useful energy.

fuel oil. An oil that is used for fuel and that usually ignites at a higher temperature than kerosene.

fuel switching. 1. A precombustion process whereby a low-sulfur coal is used in place of a higher sulfur coal in a power plant to reduce sulfur dioxide emissions. 2. Illegally using leaded gasoline in a motor vehicle designed to use only unleaded.

fuelwood. Wood and wood products, possibly including coppices, scrubs, branches, etc., bought or gathered, and used by direct combustion.

fugitive emissions. Emissions not caught by a capture system.

fume. Tiny particles trapped in vapor in a gas stream.

fumigant. A pesticide vaporized to kill pests. Used in buildings and greenhouses.

functional equivalent. Term used to describe the EPA's decision-making process and its relationship to the environmental review conducted under the National Environmental Policy Act (NEPA). A review is considered functionally equivalent when it addresses the substantive components of a NEPA review.

fungicide. Pesticides that are used to control, deter, or destroy fungi.

fungistat. A chemical that keeps fungi from growing.

fungus (fungi). Molds, mildews, yeasts, mushrooms, and puffballs, a group of organisms lacking in chlorophyll (i.e., are not photosynthetic) and which are usually nonmobile, filamentous, and multicellular. Some grow in soil, others attach themselves to decaying trees and other plants from which they obtain nutrients. Some are pathogens; others stabilize sewage and digest composted waste.

furnace. An enclosed structure in which heat is produced for the purpose of heating a house or a building.

furrow irrigation. Irrigation method in which water travels through the field by means of small channels between each groups of rows.

fusion. When the nuclei of atoms are combined or "fused" together. The sun combines the nuclei of hydrogen atoms into helium atoms in a process called fusion. Energy from the nuclei of atoms, called nuclear energy, is released from fusion.

future liability. Refers to potentially responsible parties' obligations to pay for additional response activities beyond those specified in the Record of Decision or Consent Decree.

G

gallon. A measure of volume equal to 4 quarts (231 cubic inches). One barrel equals 42 gallons.

game fish. Species like trout, salmon, or bass, caught for sport. Many of them show more sensitivity to environmental change than "rough" fish.

garbage. Animal and vegetable waste resulting from the handling, storage, sale, preparation, cooking, and serving of foods.

gas. A nonsolid, nonliquid (as hydrogen or air) substance that has no fixed shape and tends to expand without limit. A state of matter in which the matter concerned occupies the whole of its container irrespective of its quantity. Includes natural gas, coke-oven gas, blast furnace gas, and refinery gas.

gas chromatograph/mass spectrometer. Instrument that identifies the molecular composition and concentrations of various chemicals in water and soil samples.

gas to liquids (GTLs). A process that combines the carbon and hydrogen elements in natural gas molecules to make synthetic liquid petroleum products, such as diesel fuel.

gas turbine plant. A plant in which the prime mover is a gas turbine. A gas turbine consists typically of an axial-flow air compressor and one or more combustion chambers where liquid or gaseous fuel is burned

and the hot gases are passed to the turbine and where the hot gases expand drive
the generator and are then used to run the
compressor.

gasahol. Mixture of gasoline and ethanol
derived from fermented agricultural products
containing at least 9 percent ethanol. Gasohol
emissions contain less carbon monoxide than
those from gasoline.

gasification. Conversion of solid material
such as coal into a gas for use as a fuel.

gasoline. A complex mixture of relatively
volatile hydrocarbons with or without small
quantities of additives, blended to form a fuel
suitable for use in spark-ignition engines.

gasoline volatility. The property of gasoline
whereby it evaporates into a vapor. Gasoline vapor is a mixture of volatile organic
compounds.

gene. Unit of heredity in chromosome, controlling a particular characteristic, or the
operation or timing of the function of other
genes.

general permit. A permit applicable to a
class or category of dischargers.

general reporting facility. A facility
having one or more hazardous chemicals
above the 10,000-pound threshold for planning quantities. Such facilities must file
MSDS and emergency inventory information with the SERC, LEPC, and local fire
departments.

generally recognized as safe (GRAS). Designation by the FDA that a chemical or substance (including certain pesticides) added to
food is considered safe by experts, and so is
exempted from the usual FFDCA food additive tolerance requirements.

generating capacity. The amount of electrical power a power plant can produce.

generation (electricity). The process
of producing electric energy from other
forms of energy; also, the amount of electric energy produced, expressed in watt
hours (Wh).

generator. A facility or mobile source that
emits pollutants into the air or releases hazardous waste into water or soil. Any person,
by site, whose act or process produces regulated medical waste or whose act first causes
such waste to become subject to regulation.
Where more than one person (e.g., doctors
with separate medical practices) are located
in the same building, each business entity is
a separate generator.

genetic engineering. The altering of the
natural makeup of a living organism, which
allows scientists to insert virtually any gene
into a plant and create a new crop, or an
entire new species.

genetically modified foods. Food processed
from genetically engineered crops.

genotoxic. Damaging to DNA or pertaining
to agents known to damage DNA.

geographic information system (GIS). A
computer system designed for storing,
manipulating, analyzing, and displaying data
in a geographic context.

geological log. A detailed description of all
underground features (depth, thickness, type
of formation) discovered during the drilling
of a well.

geophysical log. A record of the structure
and composition of the earth encountered
when drilling a well or similar type of test
hold or boring.

geothermal energy. The heat energy that
is produced by natural processes inside the
earth. It can be taken from hot springs, reservoirs of hot water deep below the ground, or
by breaking open the rock itself.

geothermal plant. A plant in which a
turbine is driven either from hot water or
by natural steam that derives its energy
from heat found in rocks or fluids at various depths beneath the surface of the earth.
The fluids are extracted by drilling and/or
pumping.

geothermal/ground source heat pump.
These heat pumps are underground coils to

transfer heat from the ground to the inside of a building.

germicide. Any compound that kills disease-causing microorganisms.

giardia lamblia. Protozoan in the feces of humans and animals that can cause severe gastrointestinal ailments. It is a common contaminant of surface waters.

giga. One billion.

glass containers. For recycling purposes, containers such as bottles and jars for drinks, food, cosmetics, and other products. When being recycled, container glass is generally separated into color categories for conversion into new containers, construction materials, or fiberglass insulation.

global. Worldwide, affecting the whole planet.

global dimming. When particulate material (e.g., soot and carbon products), generated from vehicle exhausts, aircraft, and industry, enters the atmosphere, less light reaches the ground.

global environmental facility. A facility to provide additional grant and concessional funding for the achievement of agreed global environmental benefits.

global reporting initiative (GRI). A reporting standard generally accepted to be the leading international standard for reporting social, environmental, and economic performance.

global warming. An increase in the near surface temperature of the earth. The gradual warming of the earth's climate, believed by some scientists to be caused by an increase in carbon dioxide and other trace gases in the earth's atmosphere resulting from human activity, mainly the burning of fossil fuels. Global warming has occurred in the distant past as the result of natural influences, but the term is most often used to refer to the warming predicted to occur as a result of increased emissions of greenhouse gases. Scientists generally agree that the earth's surface has warmed by about 1° F in the past 140 years.

The Intergovernmental Panel on Climate Change (IPCC) recently concluded that increased concentrations of greenhouse gases are causing an increase in the earth's surface temperature and that increased concentrations of sulfate aerosols have led to relative cooling in some regions, generally over and downwind of heavily industrialized areas.

global warming potential (GWP). The ratio of the warming caused by a substance to the warming caused by a similar mass of carbon dioxide. CFC-12, for example, has a GWP of 8,500, while water has a GWP of zero.

glovebag. A polyethylene or polyvinyl chloride baglike enclosure affixed around an asbestos-containing source (most often thermal system insulation) permitting the material to be removed while minimizing release of airborne fibers to the surrounding atmosphere.

gooseneck. A portion of a water service connection between the distribution system water main and a meter. Sometimes called a pigtail.

grab sample. A single sample collected at a particular time and place that represents the composition of the water, air, or soil only at that time and place.

grain loading. The rate at which particles are emitted from a pollution source. Measurement is made by the number of grains per cubic foot of gas emitted.

granular activated carbon treatment. A filtering system often used in small water systems and individual homes to remove organics. Also used by municipal water treatment plants. GAC can be highly effective in lowering elevated levels of radon in water.

grasscycling. Source reduction activities in which grass clippings are left on the lawn after mowing.

grassed waterway. Natural or constructed watercourse or outlet that is shaped or graded and established in suitable vegetation for the disposal of runoff water without erosion.

grassroots. From the bottom of society, the basic level.

gravity. The natural force of attraction of the mass of a heavenly body (as the earth) for bodies at or near its surface.

gray water. Domestic wastewater composed of wash water from kitchen, bathroom, and laundry sinks, tubs, and washers.

green accounting. The incorporation of the amount of natural resources used and pollutants expelled into conventional economic accounting in order to provide a detailed measure of all environmental consequences of any and all economic activities.

green building. A comprehensive process of design and construction that employs techniques to minimize adverse environmental impacts and reduce the energy consumption of a building, while contributing to the health and productivity of its occupants; a common metric for evaluating green buildings is the LEED (Leadership in Energy and Environmental Design) certification.

Green Building Council. A voluntary and not-for-profit organization, whose aim is to define a series of standards for the building industry. The Green Building Council worldwide has tried to favor and promote the use of sustainability, educate communities and professionals about sustainable practices and give to builders, constructors, and manufacturers a set of standard rules to follow.

green design. The design of products, services, buildings, or experiences that are sensitive to environmental issues and achieve greater efficiency and effectiveness in terms of energy and materials use.

green marketing. A concept that describes the creation, promotion, and sale of environmentally safe products and service by business.

green mortgage. Mortgages that provide benefits to homeowners who reduce their impacts on the environment and minimize household energy or transportation costs, while potentially increasing their homes' future value and selling potential.

green power. Electricity produced from renewable and nonpolluting energy resources such as solar, wind, geothermal, biogas, biomass, and low-impact small hydroelectric sources.

green pricing. In the case of renewable electricity, green pricing represents a market solution to the various problems associated with regulatory valuation of the nonmarket benefits of renewables. Green pricing programs allow electricity customers to express their willingness to pay for renewable energy development through direct payments on their monthly utility bills.

green roof. Roof of a building that is partially or completely covered with vegetation and soil, planted over a waterproofing membrane.

GREENGUARD. An ecolabel that certifies the low Volatile Organic Compound (VOC) emissions of a product. GREENGUARD has various standards depending on the final use of a material.

greenhouse effect. The warming of the earth's atmosphere attributed to a buildup of carbon dioxide or other gases; some scientists think that this buildup allows the sun's rays to heat the earth, while making the infrared radiation atmosphere opaque to infra-red radiation, thereby preventing a counterbalancing loss of heat.

greenhouse emissions. Waste gases given off by industrial and power plants, automobiles and other processes.

greenhouse gas. A gas that contributes to the natural greenhouse effect, whereby heat is trapped within the earth's atmosphere, including carbon dioxide, methane, nitrous oxide, hydrofluorocarbons, perfluorocarbons, and sulfur hexafluoride, which contributes to potential climate change.

greening of management. The process by which managers become more proactive with respect to environmental issues.

greening. Originally of specific environmental projects, e.g. planting tress and conservation.

greens. People subscribing to green values, ethos, philosophy, and the like in politics; supporters of "green" parties or policies.

greenwashing. The practice of advertising a product or process as "green" or environmentally friendly, when the product really is not, or does not achieve the advertised marketing claims. A false or misleading picture of environmental friendliness used to conceal or obscure damaging activities.

grey water. Nondrinkable water that can be reused for irrigation, flushing toilets, and other purposes.

grid. The layout of an electrical distribution system.

grinder pump. A mechanical device that shreds solids and raises sewage to a higher elevation through pressure sewers.

gross alpha/beta particle activity. The total radioactivity owing to alpha or beta particle emissions as inferred from measurements on a dry sample.

gross domestic product. The value of final goods and services produced within a nation during a specified period of time, usually one year.

gross generation. The total amount of electric energy produced by the generating units at a generating station or stations, measured at the generator terminals.

gross power-generation potential. The installed power generation capacity that landfill gas can support.

ground cover. Plants grown to keep soil from eroding.

ground-penetrating radar. A geophysical method that uses high-frequency electromagnetic waves to obtain subsurface information.

ground-source geothermal system. A type of heat pump that uses the ground, groundwater, or ponds as a heat source and heat sink, rather than outside air.

groundwater. The supply of fresh water found beneath the earth's surface, usually in aquifers, which supply wells and springs. Because groundwater is a major source of drinking water, there is growing concern over contamination from leaching agricultural or industrial pollutants or leaking underground storage tanks.

groundwater discharge. Groundwater entering near coastal waters, which has been contaminated by landfill leachate, deep well injection of hazardous wastes, septic tanks, etc.

groundwater disinfection rule. A 1996 amendment of the Safe Drinking Water Act requiring the EPA to promulgate national primary drinking water regulations requiring disinfection as for all public water systems, including surface waters and groundwater systems.

groundwater under the direct influence (UDI) of surface water. Any water beneath the surface of the ground with significant occurence of insects or other microorganisms, algae, or large-diameter pathogens; significant and relatively rapid shifts in water characteristics such as turbidity, temperature, conductivity, or ph, which closely correlate to climatological or surface water conditions. Direct influence is determined for individual sources in accordance with criteria established by a state.

growth. Increase in size or complexity; also (economics) in value.

gully erosion. Severe erosion in which trenches are cut to a depth greater than 30 centimeters (a foot). Generally, ditches deep enough to cross with farm equipment are considered gullies.

H

habitat. The place where a population (e.g., human, animal, plant, microorganism) lives and its surroundings, both living and nonliving.

habitat indicator. A physical attribute of the environment measured to characterize conditions necessary to support an organism, population, or community in the absence of pollutants; e.g. salinity of estuarine waters or substrate type in streams or lakes.

half-life. The time required for a pollutant to lose one-half of its original coconcentrationor example, the biochemical half-life of DDT in the environment is 15 years. The time required for half of the atoms of a radioactive element to undergo self-transmutation or decay (half-life of radium is 1620 years). The time required for the elimination of half a total dose from the body.

halogen. A type of incandescent lamp with higher energy efficiency than standard ones.

halon. Bromine-containing compounds with long atmospheric lifetimes whose breakdown in the stratosphere causes depletion of ozone. Halons are used in firefighting.

hammer mill. A high-speed machine that uses hammers and cutters to crush, grind, chip, or shred solid waste.

hard water. Alkaline water containing dissolved salts that interfere with some industrial processes and prevent soap from sudsing.

hardwoods. Usually broad-leaved and deciduous trees.

harmony. Agreeable effect of apt arrangement of parts. The result of positive synergy in a system; one of life's objectives within the environment.

hauler. Garbage collection company that offers complete refuse removal service; many will also collect recyclables.

hazard. Potential for radiation, a chemical or other pollutant to cause human illness or injury. In the pesticide program, the inherent toxicity of a compound. Hazard identification of a given substance is an informed judgment based on verifiable toxicity data from animal models or human studies.

hazard and risk assessment. An essential component of many environmental impact statements, embracing the potentially adverse effects of a project involving fire, heat, blast, explosion, or flood, arising from a manufacturing plant or transportation system.

hazard assessment. Evaluating the effects of a stressor or determining a margin of safety for an organism by comparing the concentration that causes toxic effects with an estimate of exposure to the organism.

hazard communication standard. An OSHA regulation that requires chemical manufacturers, suppliers, and importers to assess the hazards of the chemicals that they make, supply, or import, and to inform employers, customers, and workers of these hazards through MSDS information.

hazard evaluation. A component of risk evaluation that involves gathering and evaluating data on the types of health injuries or diseases that may be produced by a chemical and on the conditions of exposure under which such health effects are produced.

hazard identification. Determining if a chemical or a microbe can cause adverse health effects in humans and what those effects might be.

hazard quotient. The ratio of estimated site-specific exposure to a single chemical from a site over a specified period to the estimated daily exposure level, at which no adverse health effects are likely to occur.

hazard ratio. A term used to compare an animal's daily dietary intake of a pesticide to its LD 50 value. A ratio greater than 1.0 indicates that the animal is likely to consume a dose amount which would kill 50 percent of animals of the same species.

hazardous air pollutants. Air pollutants which are not covered by ambient air quality standards but which, as defined in the Clean Air Act, may present a threat of adverse human health effects or adverse environmental effects. Such pollutants include asbestos, beryllium, mercury, benzene, coke oven emissions, radionuclides, and vinyl chloride.

hazardous chemical. An EPA designation for any hazardous material requiring an MSDS under OSHA's Hazard Communication Standard. Such substances are capable of producing fires and explosions or adverse health effects like cancer and dermatitis. Hazardous chemicals are distinct from hazardous waste.

hazardous ranking system. The principal screening tool used by EPA to evaluate risks to public health and the environment associated with abandoned or uncontrolled hazardous waste sites. The HRS calculates a score based on the potential of hazardous substances spreading from the site through the air, surface water, or groundwater, and on other factors such as density and proximity of human population. This score is the primary factor in deciding if the site should be on the National Priorities List and, if so, what ranking it should have compared to other sites on the list.

hazardous substance. Any material that poses a threat to human health and/or the environment. Typical hazardous substances are toxic, corrosive, ignitable, explosive, or chemically reactive. Any substance designated by EPA to be reported if a designated quantity of the substance is spilled in the waters of the United States or is otherwise released into the environment.

hazardous waste. By-products of society that can pose a substantial or potential hazard to human health or the environment when improperly managed. Possesses at least one of four characteristics (ignitability, corrosivity, reactivity, or toxicity), or appears on special EPA lists.

hazardous waste landfill. An excavated or engineered site where hazardous waste is deposited and covered.

hazardous waste minimization. Reducing the amount of toxicity or waste produced by a facility via source reduction or environmentally sound recycling.

hazards analysis. Procedures used to (1) identify potential sources of release of hazardous materials from fixed facilities or transportation accidents; (2) determine the vulnerability of a geographical area to a release of hazardous materials; and (3) compare hazards to determine which present greater or lesser risks to a community.

hazards identification. Providing information on which facilities have extremely hazardous substances, what those chemicals are, how much there is at each facility, how the chemicals are stored, and whether they are used at high temperatures.

headspace. The vapor mixture trapped above a solid or liquid in a sealed vessel.

health. Soundness of body and/or mind.

health advisory level. A nonregulatory health-based reference level of chemical traces (usually in ppm) in drinking water at which there are no adverse health risks when ingested over various periods of time. Such levels are established for one day, 10 days, long-term and life-time exposure periods. They contain a wide margin of safety.

health assessment. An evaluation of available data on existing or potential risks to human health posed by a Superfund site. The Agency for Toxic Substances and Disease Registry (ATSDR) of the Department of Health and Human Services (DHHS) is required to perform such an assessment at every site on the National Priorities List.

heat content. The gross heat content is the number of British thermal units (Btu) produced by the combustion, of a volume of gas under certain with air of the same temperature and pressure as the gas, when the products of combustion are cooled to the initial temperature of gas and air and when the water formed by combustion is condensed to the liquid state.

heat exchanger. Any device that transfers heat from one fluid (liquid or gas) to another or to the environment.

heat island effect. Localized increase in ambient urban air temperatures resulting primarily from the replacement of vegetation with buildings, roads, and other heat-absorbing infrastructure. The heat island effect can result in significant temperature differences between rural and urban areas and contributes to global warming.

heat pump. An electric device with both heating and cooling capabilities. It extracts heat from one medium at a lower (the heat source) temperature and transfers it to another at a higher temperature (the heat sink), thereby cooling the first and warming the second.

heating equipment. Any equipment designed and/or specifically used for heating ambient air in an enclosed space. Common types of heating equipment include central warm air furnace, heat pump, plug-in or built-in room heater, boiler for steam or hot water heating system, heating stove, and fireplace.

heating seasonal performance factor. The measure of seasonal or annual efficiency of a heat pump operating in the heating mode. it takes into account the variations in temperature that can occur within a season and is the average number of Btu of heat delivered for every watt hour of electricity used by the heat pump over a heating season.

heating, ventilation, and air conditioning (HVAC) system. Controls a home's internal environment (temperature, humidity, air flow, and air filtering).

heavy metals. Metallic elements with high atomic weights (e.g., mercury, chromium, cadmium, arsenic, and lead); can damage living things at low concentrations and tend to accumulate in the food chain.

heliostat. Flat sun-tracking mirrors used to reflect and concentrate the sun's energy onto a central receiver tower.

heptachlor. An insecticide that was banned on some food products in 1975 and in all of them in 1978. It was allowed for use in seed treatment until 1983. More recently it was found in milk and other dairy products in Arkansas and Missouri where dairy cattle were illegally fed treated seed.

herbicide. A chemical pesticide designed to control or destroy plants, weeds, or grasses.

herbivore. An animal that feeds on plants.

heritage conservation. Measures adopted to restore, preserve, and maintain buildings, townscapes, structures, objects, and landscapes of heritage significance.

heterotrophic organisms. Species that are dependent on organic matter for food.

high-end exposure (dose) estimate. An estimate of exposure, or dose level received anyone in a defined population that is greater than the 90th percentile of all individuals in that population, but less than the exposure at the highest percentile in that population. A high-end risk descriptor is an estimate of the risk level for such individuals. Note that risk is based on a combination of exposure and susceptibility to the stressor.

high-intensity discharge. A generic term for mercury vapor, metal halide, and high-pressure sodium lamps and fixtures.

high-density polyethylene. A material used to make plastic bottles and other products that produce toxic fumes when burned.

highest dose tested. The highest dose of a chemical or substance tested in a study.

high-level nuclear waste facility. Plant designed to handle disposal of used nuclear fuel, high-level radioactive waste, and plutonium waste.

high-level radioactive waste (HLRW). Waste generated in core fuel of a nuclear reactor, found at nuclear reactors or by nuclear fuel reprocessing; is a serious threat to anyone who comes near the waste without shielding.

high-line jumpers. Pipes or hoses connected to fire hydrants and laid on top of the ground to provide emergency water service for an isolated portion of a distribution system.

high-risk community. A community located within the vicinity of numerous sites of facilities or other potential sources of environmental exposure/health hazards, which may result in high levels of exposure to contaminants or pollutants.

high-temperature collector. A solar thermal collector designed to operate at a temperature of 180° F or higher.

high-to-low-dose extrapolation. The process of prediction of low exposure risk to humans and animals from the measured high-exposure, high-risk data involving laboratory animals.

holding pond. A pond or reservoir, usually made of earth, built to store polluted runoff.

holding time. The maximum amount of time a sample may be stored before analysis.

hollow stem auger drilling. Conventional drilling method that uses augurs to penetrate the soil. As the augers are rotated, soil cuttings are conveyed to the ground surface via augur spirals. DP tools can be used inside the hollow augers.

home energy rating system (HERS) index. A nationally recognized energy rating system that gives homeowners, sellers, buyers, builders, mortgage lenders, and secondary lending markets a precise evaluation of home energy efficiency in the form of a score. A home built to the specifications of the International Energy Conservation Code scores a HERS index of 100, while a net zero energy home scores a HERS index of 0. The lower a home's HERS index, the more energy efficient it is.

homeowner water system. Any water system which supplies piped water to a single resident.

homogeneous area. In accordance with Asbestos Hazard and Emergency Response Act (AHERA) definitions, an area of surfacing materials, thermal surface insulation, or miscellaneous material that is uniform in color and texture.

hood capture efficiency. Ratio of the emissions captured by a hood and directed into a control or disposal device, expressed as a percent of all emissions.

horsepower. A unit for measuring the rate of work (or power) equivalent to 33,000 footpounds per minute or 746 watts.

host. 1. In genetics, the organism, typically a bacterium, into which a gene from another organism is transplanted. 2. In medicine, an animal infected or parasitized by another organism.

household hazardous waste. Hazardous products used and disposed of by residential as opposed to industrial consumers. Includes paints, stains, varnishes, solvents, pesticides, and other materials or products containing volatile chemicals that can catch fire, react or explode, or that are corrosive or toxic.

household waste (domestic waste). Solid waste, composed of garbage and rubbish, which normally originates in a private home or apartment house. Domestic waste can contain a significant amount of toxic or hazardous waste.

housing. Buildings for human habitation or shelter. One of the five basic needs.

human development index. Introduced in 1990 by the United Nations Development Program as an alternative measure of economic and social progress, gross domestic product being a poor measure of relative living standards and conditions.

human equivalent dose. A dose which, when administered to humans, produces an effect equal to that produced by a dose in animals.

human exposure evaluation. Describing the nature and size of the population exposed to a substance and the magnitude and duration of their exposure.

human genome. Strands of DNA developing a unique pattern for every human.

human health risk. The likelihood that a given exposure or series of exposures may have damaged or will damage the health of individuals.

human scale. Life and provision within the scale of people as individuals.

hydraulic conductivity. The rate at which water can move through a permeable medium (i.e., the coefficient of permeability).

hydraulic gradient. In general, the direction of groundwater flow owing to changes in the depth of the water table.

hydrocarbons (hc). Chemical compounds that consist entirely of carbon and hydrogen.

hydroelectric power plant. A power plant that uses moving water to power a turbine generator to produce electricity.

hydrogen sulfide (h₂s). Gas emitted during organic decomposition; also a by-product of oil refining and burning. Smells like rotten eggs and, in heavy concentration, can kill or cause illness.

hydrogen. A colorless, odorless, highly flammable gaseous element. It is the lightest of all gases and the most abundant element in the universe, occurring chiefly in combination with oxygen in water and also in acids, bases, alcohols, petroleum, and other hydrocarbons.

hydrogeological cycle (also hydrologic or hydrological cycle). The natural process recycling water from the atmosphere down to (and through) the earth and back to the atmosphere again.

hydrogeology. The geology of groundwater, with particular emphasis on the chemistry and movement of water.

hydrology. The science dealing with the properties, distribution, and circulation of water.

hydrolysis. The decomposition of organic compounds by interaction with water.

hydronic. A ventilation system using heated or cooled water pumped through a building.

hydrophilic. Having a strong affinity for water.

hydropneumatic. A water system, usually small, in which a water pump is automatically controlled by the pressure in a compressed air tank.

hydropower. Energy that comes from moving water.

hygiene. The science of the preservation of health and the prevention of disease.

hypersensitivity diseases. Diseases characterized by allergic responses to pollutants; diseases most clearly associated with indoor air quality are asthma, rhinitis, and pneumonic hypersensitivity.

hypolimnion. Bottom waters of a thermally stratified lake. The hypolimnion of a eutrophic lake is usually low or lacking in oxygen.

hypoxia/hypoxic waters. Waters with dissolved oxygen concentrations of less than 2 ppm, the level generally accepted as the minimum required for most marine life to survive and reproduce.

I

ice age. Any geological period during which thick ice sheets have covered vast areas of the earth; such periods may last several million years.

identification code or EPA I. D. number. The unique code assigned to each generator, transporter, and treatment, storage, or disposal facility by regulating agencies to facilitate identification and tracking of chemicals or hazardous waste.

ignitable. Capable of burning or causing a fire.

IM240. A high-tech, transient dynamometer automobile emissions test that takes up to 240 seconds.

imbalance. The loss, or change in state, of integrity in a form, system, or relationship.

imhoff cone. A clear, cone-shaped container used to measure the volume of settleable solids in a specific volume of water.

immediately dangerous to life and health (IDLH). The maximum level to which a healthy individual can be exposed to a chemical for 30 minutes and escape without suffering irreversible health effects or impairing symptoms. Used as a "level of concern."

imminent hazard. One that would likely result in unreasonable adverse effects on humans or the environment or risk unreasonable hazard to an endangered species during the time required for a pesticide registration cancellation proceeding.

imminent threat. A high probability that exposure is occurring.

immiscibility. The inability of two or more substances or liquids to readily dissolve into one another, such as soil and water.

impermeable. Not easily penetrated. The property of a material or soil that does not allow, or allows only with great difficulty, the movement or passage of water.

impervious surfaces. Surfaces such as paved streets, parking lots, and building rooftops that prevent precipitation from soaking into the ground. Different surfaces can have different degrees of imperviousness.

imports. Municipal solid waste and recyclables that have been transported to a state or locality for processing or final disposition (but that did not originate in that state or locality).

impoundment. A body of water or sludge confined by a dam, dike, floodgate, or other barrier.

in situ. In its original place; unmoved unexcavated; remaining at the site or in the subsurface.

in vitro. Testing or action outside an organism (e.g., inside a test tube or culture dish.)

in vivo. Testing or action inside an organism.

incandescent light bulb. An incandescent bulb is a type of electric light in which light is produced by a filament heated by electric current. The most common example is the type you find in most table and floor lamps. In commercial buildings, incandescent lights are used for display lights in retail stores, hotels, and motels. This includes the very small, high-intensity track lights used to display merchandise or provide spot illumination in restaurants.

incentives. Subsidies and other government actions where the government's financial assistance is indirect.

incident command post. A facility located at a safe distance from an emergency site, where the incident commander, key staff, and technical representatives can make decisions and deploy emergency manpower and equipment.

incident command system (ICS). The organizational arrangement wherein one person, normally the fire chief of the impacted district, is in charge of an integrated, comprehensive emergency response organization and the emergency incident site, backed by an emergency operations center staff with resources, information, and advice.

incineration. A treatment technology involving destruction of waste by controlled burning at high temperatures; e.g., burning sludge to remove the water and reduce the remaining residues to a safe, nonburnable ash that can be disposed of safely on land, in some waters, or in underground locations.

incineration at sea. Disposal of waste by burning at sea on specially designed incinerator ships.

incinerator. A furnace for burning waste under controlled conditions.

incompatible waste. A waste unsuitable for mixing with another waste or material because it may react to form a hazard.

indemnification. In the pesticide program, legal requirement that the EPA pay certain end users, dealers, and distributors for the cost of stock on hand at the time a pesticide registration is suspended.

independent power producer (IPP). A corporation, person, agency, authority, or other legal entity or instrumentality that owns or operates facilities for the generation of electricity for use primarily by the public, and that is not an electric utility.

indicator. 1. In biology, any biological entity or processes, or community whose characteristics show the presence of specific environmental conditions. 2. In chemistry, a substance that shows a visible change, usually of color, at a desired point in a chemical reaction. 3. A device that indicates the result of a measurement, for example, a pressure gauge or a moveable scale.

indirect discharge. The introduction of pollutants from a nondomestic source into a publicly owned waste treatment system. Indirect dischargers can be commercial or industrial facilities whose wastes enter local sewers.

indirect source. Any facility or building, property, road or parking area that attracts motor vehicle traffic and, indirectly, causes pollution.

indoor air. The breathable air inside a habitable structure or conveyance.

indoor air pollution. Chemical, physical, or biological contaminants in indoor air.

indoor air quality (IAQ). The healthiness of the air inside homes. Indoor air pollution sources that release gases or particles into the air and/or a lack or proper ventilation are the primary causes of indoor air quality problems in homes.

indoor climate. Temperature, humidity, lighting, air flow, and noise levels in a habitable structure or conveyance. Indoor climate can affect indoor air pollution.

induction. The process of producing an electrical or magnetic effect through the influence of a nearby magnet, electric current, or electrically charged body.

industrial ecology. Designing factories and distribution systems as if they were self-contained ecosystems, such as using waste from one process as raw material for another.

industrial pollution prevention. Combination of industrial source reduction and toxic chemical use substitution.

industrial process waste. Residues produced during manufacturing operations.

industrial recycle. Post-industrial recycled material is usually derived from the manufacturing process or materials recycled prior to distribution to the market.

industrial revolution. Period from the late eighteenth century to the present when the combination of fossil energy, materials technology, and innovative designs were produced by the mass society.

industrial sector. The part of the economy having to do with the production of goods. An energy-consuming sector that consists of all facilities and equipment used for producing, processing, or assembling goods. The industrial sector encompasses the following types of activity: manufacturing (NAICS codes 31–33); agriculture, forestry, and fisheries (NAICS code 11); mining, including oil and gas extraction (NAICS code 21); natural gas transmission (NAICS code 2212); and construction (NAICS code 23). Overall energy use in this sector is largely for processing heat and cooling and powering machinery, with lesser amounts used for facility heating, air conditioning, and lighting. Fossil fuels are also used as raw material inputs to manufactured products. *Note:* This sector includes generators that produce electricity and/or useful thermal output primarily to support the above-mentioned industrial activities.

industrial sludge. Semiliquid residue or slurry remaining from treatment of industrial water and wastewater.

industrial society. Mass society wherein the population is dependent on institutionalized industrial processes for its sustenance.

industrial source reduction. Practices that reduce the amount of any hazardous substance, pollutant, or contaminant entering any waste stream or otherwise released into the environment. Also reduces the threat to public health and the environment associated with such releases. Term includes equipment or technology modifications, substitution of raw materials, and improvements in housekeeping, maintenance, training, or inventory control.

industrial waste. Unwanted materials from an industrial operation; may be liquid, sludge, solid, or hazardous waste.

industrialization. The evolution of forms of production characterized by increasing capital intensity; and intensive division of labor;

increasingly complex forms of transport, and increasingly complex forms of industrial organization among other things.

industrial waste strategy. Outlines policies and procedures to be adopted for industrial waste management.

inert ingredient. Pesticide components such as solvents, carriers, dispersants, and surfactants that are not active against target pests. Not all inert ingredients are innocuous.

inertia. A property of matter by which it remains at rest or in uniform motion in the same straight line unless acted upon by some outside force.

inertial separator. A device that uses centrifugal force to separate waste particles.

infectious agent. Any organism, such as a pathogenic virus, parasite, or bacterium, that is capable of invading body tissues, multiplying, and causing disease.

infectious waste. Hazardous waste capable of causing infections in humans, including contaminated animal waste, human blood and blood products, isolation waste, pathological waste, and discarded sharps (needles, scalpels, or broken medical instruments).

infiltration gallery. A subsurface groundwater collection system, typically shallow in depth, constructed with open-jointed or perforated pipes that discharge collected water into a watertight chamber from which the water is pumped to treatment facilities and into the distribution system. Usually located close to streams or ponds.

infiltration rate. The quantity of water that can enter the soil in a specified time interval.

infiltration. 1. The penetration of water through the ground surface into subsurface soil or the penetration of water from the soil into sewer or other pipes through defective joints, connections, or manhole walls. 2. The technique of applying large volumes of wastewater to land to penetrate the surface and percolate through the underlying soil. 3. Unintended air leakage, or infiltration, occurs when outside air enters a house through cracks and

openings around doors, windows, and ducts. Properly sealing these cracks and openings in a home can significantly reduce heating and cooling costs, improve building durability, and help prevent pests from entering your home.

inflow. Entry of extraneous rainwater into a sewer system from sources other than infiltration, such as basement drains, manholes, storm drains, and street washing.

influent. Water, wastewater, or other liquid flowing into a reservoir, basin, or treatment plant.

information collection request (ICR). A description of information to be gathered in connection with rules, proposed rules, surveys, and guidance documents that contain information-gathering requirements. The ICR describes what information is needed, why it is needed, how it will be collected, and how much collecting it will cost. The ICR is submitted by the EPA to the Office of Management and Budget (OMB) for approval.

information file. In the Superfund program, a file that contains accurate, up-to-date documents on a Superfund site. The file is usually located in a public building (school, library, or city hall) convenient for local residents.

information society. The current phase of technology; emphasizes the use and transfer of knowledge and information.

inhalable particles. All dust capable of entering the human respiratory tract.

initial compliance period (water). The first full three-year compliance period which begins at least 18 months after promulgation.

injection well. A well into which fluids are injected for purposes such as waste disposal, improving the recovery of crude oil or solution mining.

injection zone. A geological formation receiving fluids through a well.

in-line filtration. Pretreatment method in which chemicals are mixed by the flowing water; commonly used in pressure filtration installations. Eliminates need for flocculation and sedimentation.

innovative technologies. New or inventive methods to treat effectively hazardous waste and reduce risks to human health and the environment.

innovative treatment technologies. Technologies whose routine use is inhibited by lack of data on performance and cost.

inoculum. 1. Bacteria or fungi injected into compost to start biological action. 2. A medium containing organisms, usually bacteria or a virus, that is introduced into cultures or living organisms.

inorganic chemicals. Chemical substances of mineral origin, not of basically carbon structure.

insecticide. A pesticide compound specifically used to kill or prevent the growth of insects.

in-situ flushing. Introduction of large volumes of water, at times supplemented with cleaning compounds, into soil, waste, or groundwater to flush hazardous contaminants from a site.

in-situ oxidation. Technology that oxidizes contaminants dissolved in groundwater, converting them into insoluble compounds.

in-situ stripping. Treatment system that removes or "strips" volatile organic compounds from contaminated ground or surface water by forcing an airstream through the water and causing the compounds to evaporate.

in-situ vitrification. Technology that treats contaminated soil in place at extremely high temperatures, at or more than 3000° F.

inspection and maintenance (I/M). 1. Activities to ensure that vehicles' emission controls work properly. 2. Also applies to wastewater treatment plants and other anti-pollution facilities and processes.

institution. Originally established (of person) in cure of souls; established law, custom, or practice; body exercising established law, custom, or the like, for charitable or public purpose.

institutional waste. Waste generated at institutions such as schools, libraries, hospitals, prisons, etc.

instream use. Water use taking place within a stream channel; e.g., hydro-electric

power generation, navigation, water quality improvement, fish propagation, recreation.

insulating concrete forms (ICF). Forms for poured concrete walls that remain part of the wall assembly, adding to the insulation of a home because of their high thermal resistance.

integrated design. A design approach where all the members of the building stakeholder community, technical planning, design, construction, and maintenance and operation teams evaluate the project objectives collectively, and make design decisions for building materials, systems, and assemblies to meet the project goals. This approach is a deviation from the typical planning and design process of relying on the expertise of specialists who work in their respective specialties somewhat isolated from each other.

integrated exposure assessment. Cumulative summation (over time) of the magnitude of exposure to a toxic chemical in all media.

integrated pest management (IPM). A mixture of chemical and other, nonpesticide, methods to control pests.

integrated pollution control. Introduced in Britain, under the Environmental Protection Act of 1990, a procedure whereby all major emission to land, air, and water are considered simultaneously and not in isolation to avoid situations in which one control measure for one medium adversely affects another.

integrated waste management. Using a variety of practices to handle municipal solid waste; can include source reduction, recycling, incineration, and landfilling

intellectual property. Ideas, concepts, and other symbolic creations of the human mind that are recognized and protected under a nation's copyright, patent, and trademark laws.

interaction matrix. One of the earlier methodologies used in the United States and elsewhere to examine the environmental impacts and effects of development projects.

interceptor sewers. Large sewer lines that, in a combined system, control the flow of sewage to the treatment plant. In a storm, they allow some of the sewage to flow directly into a receiving stream, thus keeping it from overflowing onto the streets. Also used in separate systems to collect the flows from main and trunk sewers and carry them to treatment points.

interconnectedness. Property of connection; nature of relationship.

interdependent. Things that depend upon other things; form of existence that is reliant on its source.

interface. The common boundary between two substances such as a water and a solid, water and a gas, or two liquids such as water and oil.

interfacial tension. The strength of the film separating two immiscible fluids (e.g., oil and water) measured in dynes or millidynes per centimeter.

intergenerational equity. A concept that those living today should not compromise or restrict the opportunities open to future generations.

interim (permit) status. Period during which treatment, storage, and disposal facilities coming under RCRA in 1980 are temporarily permitted to operate while awaiting a permanent permit. Permits issued under these circumstances are usually called Part A or Part B permits.

internal collector storage (ICS). A solar thermal collector in which incident solar radiation is absorbed by the storage medium.

internal dose. In exposure assessment, the amount of a substance penetrating the absorption barriers (e.g., skin, lung tissue, gastrointestinal tract) of an organism through either physical or biological processes.

internal recycle. Internal material reused during the same production cycle. It represents a virtuous behavior from the environmental point of view, resulting from shrewd management of the company waste, but in the majority of these cases there is no value in terms of the environmental certifications. For example, trend reuses its own mosaic in the production of some agglomerates.

Internet. A global communications network linking individuals and organizations.

interstate carrier water supply. A source of water for drinking and sanitary use on planes, buses, trains, and ships operating in more than one state. These sources are federally regulated.

Interstate Commerce Clause. A clause of the U.S. Constitution which reserves to the federal government the right to regulate the conduct of business across state lines. Under this clause, for example, the U.S. Supreme Court has ruled that states may not inequitably restrict the disposal of out-of-state wastes in their jurisdictions.

interstate waters. Waters that flow across or form part of state or international boundaries, such as the great Lakes, the Mississippi River, or coastal waters.

interstitial monitoring. The continuous surveillance of the space between the walls of an underground storage tank.

intractable wastes. Potentially hazardous or persistent wastes that are difficult to treat and adequately dispose of.

intragenerational equity. The concept of fairness between individuals and groups, within society, locally, regionally, nationally, and globally.

intrastate product. Pesticide products once registered by states for sale and use only in the state. All intrastate products have been converted to full federal registration or canceled.

inventory (TSCA). Inventory of chemicals produced pursuant to Section 8 (b) of the Toxic Substances Control Act.

inversion. A layer of warm air that prevents the rise of cooling air and traps pollutants beneath it; can cause an air pollution episode.

investment. Investing of money in property, etc.; provision for the future.

ion exchange treatment. A common water-softening method often found on a large scale at water purification plants that remove some organics and radium by adding calcium oxide or calcium hydroxide to increase the ph to a level where the metals will precipitate out.

ion. An electrically charged atom or group of atoms.

ionization chamber. A device that measures the intensity of ionizing radiation.

ionizing radiation. Radiation that can strip electrons from atoms; e.g. alpha, beta, and gamma radiation.

iris. The EPA's Integrated Risk Information System, an electronic database containing the Agency's latest descriptive and quantitative regulatory information on chemical constituents.

irradiated food. Food subject to brief radioactivity, usually gamma rays, to kill insects, bacteria, and mold, and to permit storage without refrigeration.

irradiation. Exposure to radiation of wavelengths shorter than those of visible light (gamma, X ray, or ultraviolet), for medical purposes, to sterilize milk or other foodstuffs, or to induce polymerization of monomers or vulcanization of rubber.

irreversible effect. Effect characterized by the inability of the body to partially or fully repair injury caused by a toxic agent.

irrigation. Applying water or wastewater to land areas to supply the water and nutrient needs of plants.

irrigation efficiency. The amount of water stored in the crop root zone compared to the amount of irrigation water applied.

irrigation return flow. Surface and subsurface water that leaves the field following application of irrigation water.

irritant. A substance that can cause irritation of the skin, eyes, or respiratory system. Effects may be acute from a single high-level exposure, or chronic from repeated low-level exposures to such compounds as chlorine, nitrogen dioxide, and nitric acid.

ISO 14000. A collection of the best practices for managing an organization's impact on the environment.

ISO 14001. International standard for environmental management in manufacturing, distribution sites. This set of standards has three stages: measuring where you are, how to improve and how to implement policies to do it, and define and implement a tracking system to measure improvements.

ISO 14025. This set of standards is set to clarify how to create procedures in order to monitor and develop new ecolabeling systems. It is aimed at creating a world-recognized standard for ecolabeling programs. ISO 14025:2006 establishes the principles and specifies the procedures for developing Type III environmental declaration programs and Type III environmental declarations. It specifically establishes the use of the ISO 14040 series of standards in the development of Type III environmental declaration programs and Type III environmental declarations. ISO 14025:2006 establishes principles for the use of environmental information, in addition to those given in ISO 14020:2000 Type III environmental declarations as described in ISO 14025:2006 are primarily intended for use in business-to-business communication, but they're use in business-to-consumer communication under certain conditions is not precluded.

isoconcentration. More than one sample point exhibiting the same isolate concentration.

isopleth. The line or area represented by an isoconcentration.

isotope. A variation of an element that has the same atomic number of protons but a different weight because of the number of neutrons. Various isotopes of the same element may have different radioactive behaviors; some are highly unstable.

isotropy. The condition in which the hydraulic or other properties of an aquifer are the same in all directions.

J

jar test. A laboratory procedure that simulates a water treatment plant's coagulation/flocculation units with differing chemical doses, mix speeds, and settling times to estimate the minimum or ideal coagulant dose required to achieve certain water quality goals.

joint and several liability. Under CERCLA, a legal concept that relates to the liability for Superfund site cleanup and other costs on the part of more than one potentially responsible party (i.e., if there were several owners or users of a site that became contaminated over the years, they could all be considered potentially liable for cleaning up the site.)

joule. A metric unit for measuring work and energy, named after James Joule. It is equal to the work done when 1 ampere current is passed through a resistance of 1 ohm for 1 second.

just-in-time (JIT) inventory control. A production process in which a minimum of inventory is kept on the premises, and parts, supplies, and other needs are delivered just in time to go on the assembly line.

K

Karst. A goelogic formation of irregular limestone deposits with sinks, underground streams, and caverns.

kerosene. A thick oil obtained from petroleum and used as a fuel and solvent.

kilowatt (kW). A unit of power, usually used for electric power or to energy consumption (use). A kilowatt equals 1,000 watts.

kilowatt hour (kWh). A measure of electricity defined as a unit of work or energy, measured as 1 kilowatt (1,000 watts) of power expended for 1 hour. One kWh is equivalent to 3,412 Btu or 3.6 million joules.

kinetic. The energy of a body which results from its motion.

kinetic energy. Energy possessed by a moving object or water body.

kinetic rate coefficient. A number that describes the rate at which a water constituent such as a biochemical oxygen demand or dissolved oxygen rises or falls, or at which an air pollutant reacts.

kinetic theory of energy. The theory that the minute particles of all matter are in constant motion and that the temperature of a substance depends on the velocity (speed) of the motion.

kinetic theory of gases. The theory that physical properties of a gas are due to the rapid motion in a straight line of its molecules, to their impacts against each other and the walls of the container, and to weak attraction of forces between the molecules.

Kyoto Protocol. An international treaty negotiated in 1997 in Kyoto, Japan, that committed its signatories to reduce emissions of greenhouse gases, such as carbon dioxide.

L

laboratory animal studies. Investigations using animals as surrogates for humans.

lagoon. A shallow pond where sunlight, bacterial action, and oxygen work to purify wastewater; also used for storage of wastewater or spent nuclear fuel rods. Shallow body of water, often separated from the sea by coral reefs or sandbars.

land. Solid part of earth's surface; ground, soil. The most basic resource, foundation of the real economy of life. Land is both a finite resource in that there is only so much of it and one capable of indefinite use in the right circumstances.

land application. Discharge of wastewater onto the ground for treatment or reuse.

land ban. Phasing out of land disposal of most untreated hazardous wastes, as mandated by the 1984 Resource Conservation and Recovery Act (RCRA) amendments.

land capability. The uses to which an area of land may be put, taking into account all the physical, economic, social, and environmental constraints.

land disposal restrictions. Rules that require hazardous wastes to be treated before disposal on land to destroy or immobilize hazardous constituents that might migrate into soil and groundwater.

land farming (of waste). A disposal process in which hazardous waste deposited on or in the soil is degraded naturally by microbes.

landfills. 1. Disposal sites for nonhazardous solid wastes spread in layers, compacted to the smallest practical volume, and covered by material applied at the end of each operating day. 2. Secure chemical landfills are disposal sites for hazardous waste, selected and designed to minimize the chance of release of hazardous substances into the environment.

landfill gas. Gas that is generated by decomposition of organic material at a landfill.

landscape. The traits, patterns, and structure of a specific geographic area, including its biological composition, its physical environment, and its anthropogenic or social patterns. An area where interacting ecosystems are grouped and repeated in similar form.

landscape characterization. Documentation of the traits and patterns of the essential elements of the landscape.

landscape ecology. The study of the distribution patterns of communities and ecosystems, the ecological processes that affect those patterns, and changes in pattern and process over time.

landscape indicator. A measurement of the landscape, calculated from mapped or remotely sensed data, used to describe spatial patterns of land use and land cover across a geographic area. Landscape indicators may be useful as measures of certain kinds of environmental degradation such as forest fragmentation.

land-use planning. Traditionally, a technical or physical approach to the segregation of incompatible activities, such as housing and industry, through systems of land-use, zoning, and development controls.

Langelier index (LI). An index reflecting the equilibrium pH of a water with respect to calcium and alkalinity; used in stabilizing water to control both corrosion and scale deposition.

large quantity generator. Person or facility generating more than 2,200 pounds of hazardous waste per month. Such generators produce about 90 percent of the nation's hazardous waste, and are subject to all RCRA requirements.

large water system. A water system that services more than 50,000 customers.

laser induced fluorescence. A method for measuring the relative amount of soil and/or groundwater with an in-situ sensor.

latency. Time from the first exposure of a chemical until the appearance of a toxic effect.

lateral sewers. Pipes that run under city streets and receive the sewage from homes and businesses, as opposed to domestic feeders and main trunk lines.

laundering weir. Sedimentation basin overflow weir.

LC 50/lethal concentration. Median-level concentration, a standard measure of toxicity. It tells how much of a substance is needed to kill half of a group of experimental organisms in a given time.

LD 50/ lethal dose. The dose of a toxicant or microbe that will kill 50 percent of the test organisms within a designated period. The lower the LD 50, the more toxic the compound.

ldlo. Lethal dose low; the lowest dose in an animal study at which lethality occurs.

leachate. Water that collects contaminants as it trickles through wastes, pesticides, or fertilizers. Leaching can occur in farming areas, feedlots, and landfills, and can result in hazardous substances entering surface water, groundwater, or soil.

leachate collection system. A system that gathers leachate and pumps it to the surface for treatment.

leaching. The process by which soluble constituents are dissolved and filtered through the soil by a percolating fluid.

lead (Pb). A heavy metal that is hazardous to health if breathed or swallowed. Its use in gasoline, paints, and plumbing compounds has been sharply restricted or eliminated by federal laws and regulations.

lead service line. A service line made of lead which connects the water to the building inlet and any lead fitting connected to it.

lean manufacturing. The production of goods using less of everything compared to mass production.

LEED certification. An acronym for Leadership in Energy and Environmental Design sponsored by the U.S. Green Building Council that creates standards for developing high-performance, sustainable buildings.

LEED (leadership in energy and environmental design). Green Building Rating System. An independent certification program that provides voluntary guidelines for developing high-performance, sustainable buildings. Created by the U.S. Green Building Council (USGBC), the program awards varying levels of certification to buildings that meet LEED rating standards in five major categories: sustainable site development, water savings, energy efficiency, materials selection, and indoor environmental quality. LEED standards exist for new construction as well as existing buildings and remodeling, and can be applied to homes, commercial facilities, and even neighborhood development. Architects, engineers, interior designers, landscape architects, and facilities managers use LEED in developing new projects.

legionella. A genus of bacteria, some species of which have caused a type of pneumonia called Legionaires Disease.

lethal concentration 50. Also referred to as LC50, a concentration of a pollutant or effluent at which 50 percent of the test organisms die; a common measure of acute toxicity.

lethal dose 50. Also referred to as LD50, the dose of a toxicant that will kill 50 percent of test organisms within a designated period of time; the lower the LD50, the more toxic the compound.

level of concern (LOC). The concentration in air of an extremely hazardous substance above which there may be serious immediate health effects to anyone exposed to it for short periods

levelized cost. The present value of the total cost of building and operating a generating plant over its economic life, converted to equal annual payments. Costs are levelized in real dollars (i.e., adjusted to remove the impact of inflation).

life. State of functional activity and continual change peculiar to organized matter; manner of existence.

life cycle analysis (LCA). A methodological study that evaluates the impact of a product on the environment during its life—from the raw materials extraction and the impact of energy, waste, pollution, to shipment for its transformation. The impact of the manufacturing process and then the impact of shipment; finally how to dispose of the material, it is a cradle-to-grave product, or how to reuse it, if it is a cradle-to-cradle.

life cycle impacts. Environmental impacts, including energy consumption, over the course of the product's lifespan from raw material harvesting, manufacture, transport, use, and maintenance, to disposal.

life cycle of a product. All stages of a product's development, from extraction of fuel for power to production, marketing, use, and disposal.

lifetime average daily dose. Figure for estimating excess lifetime cancer risk.

lifetime exposure. Total amount of exposure to a substance that a human would receive in a lifetime (usually assumed to be 70 years).

lift. In a sanitary landfill, a compacted layer of solid waste and the top layer of cover material.

light. Radiant electromagnetic energy that an observer can see.

light emitting diodes (LEDs). Small light sources that become illuminated by the movement of electrons through a semiconductor material. LED lighting is more energy efficient, durable, versatile, and longer lasting than incandescent and fluorescent lighting.

light non-aqueous phase liquid (LNAPL). A non-aqueous phase liquid with a specific gravity less than 1.0. Because the specific gravity of water is 1.0, most LNAPLs float on top of the water table. Most common petroleum hydrocarbon fuels and lubricating oils are LNAPLs.

limestone scrubbing. Use of a limestone and water solution to remove gaseous stack-pipe sulfur before it reaches the atmosphere.

limit of detection (LOD). The minimum concentration of a substance being analyzed test that has a 99 percent probability of being identified.

limited degradation. An environmental policy permitting some degradation of natural systems but terminating at a level well beneath an established health standard.

limited liability corporation (LLC). A company that limits the liability of its participants to the assets they commit to the enterprise.

limiting factor. A condition whose absence or excessive concentration is incompatible with the needs or tolerance of a species or population and which may have a negative influence on their ability to thrive.

limits to growth hypothesis. The idea that human society is now exceeding the carrying capacity of the earth's ecosystem and that unless corrective action is taken soon, catastrophic consequences will result.

limnology. The study of the physical, chemical, hydrological, and biological aspects of freshwater bodies.

lindane. A pesticide that causes adverse health effects in domestic water supplies and is toxic to freshwater fish and aquatic life.

liner. 1. A relatively impermeable barrier designed to keep leachate inside a landfill. Liner materials include plastic and dense clay. 2. An insert or sleeve for sewer pipes to prevent leakage or infiltration.

lipid solubility. The maximum concentration of a chemical that will dissolve in fatty substances. Lipid soluble substances are insoluble in water. They will very selectively disperse through the environment via uptake in living tissue.

liquefaction. Changing a solid into a liquid.

liquefied petroleum gas (LPG). A group of hydrocarbon-based gases derived from crude oil refining or natural gas fractionation. They include ethane, ethylene, propane, propylene, normal butane, butylene, isobutane, and isobutylene. For convenience of transportation, these gases are liquefied through pressurization.

liquid collector. A medium-temperature solar thermal collector, employed predominantly in water heating, which uses pumped liquid as the heat-transfer medium.

liquid injection incinerator. Commonly used system that relies on high pressure to prepare liquid wastes for incineration by breaking them up into tiny droplets to allow easier combustion.

list. Shorthand term for EPA list of violating facilities or firms debarred from obtaining government contracts because they violated certain sections of the Clean Air or Clean Water Acts. The list is maintained by the Office of Enforcement and Compliance Monitoring.

listed waste. Wastes listed as hazardous under RCRA, but which have not been subjected to the Toxic Characteristics Listing Process because the dangers they present are considered self-evident.

lithology. Mineralogy, grain size, texture, and other physical properties of granular soil, sediment, or rock.

litter. The highly visible portion of solid waste carelessly discarded outside the regular garbage and trash collection and disposal system. Leaves and twigs fallen from forest trees.

littoral zone. That portion of a body of fresh water extending from the shoreline lakeward to the limit of occupancy of rooted plants. A strip of land along the shoreline between the high and low water levels.

living, art of. Creative self-fulfillment; understanding all that we are capable of becoming; choosing to express those capabilities that add to the joy of others, experiencing the ecstasy of ecology, using abilities to add to the capacity of all life.

load. The power and energy requirements of users on the electric power system in a certain area or the amount of power delivered to a certain point.

local currency. A community-based means of exchange of goods, skills, and the like. Local currencies presently operate on the basis of the nation state.

local education agency (LEA). In the asbestos program, an educational agency at the local level that exists primarily to operate schools or to contract for educational services, including primary and secondary public and private schools. A single, unaffiliated school can be considered an LEA for AHERA purposes.

local emergency planning committee (LEPC). A committee appointed by the state emergency response commission, as required by SARA (Superfund Amendments and Reauthorization Act) Title III, to formulate a comprehensive emergency plan for its jurisdiction.

LOHAS market (lifestyles of health and sustainability). A market that consists of mindful consumers passionate about the environment, sustainability, social issues, and health.

longwall mining. An automated form of underground coal mining characterized by high recovery and extraction rates, feasible only in relatively flat-lying, thick, and uniform coalbeds. A high-powered cutting machine is passed across the exposed face of coal, shearing away broken coal, which is continuously hauled away by a floor-level conveyor system. Longwall mining extracts all machine-minable coal between the floor and ceiling within a contiguous block of coal, known as a panel, leaving no support pillars within the panel area. Panel dimensions vary over time and with mining conditions, but currently average about 900 feet wide (coal face width) and more than 8,000 feet long (the minable extent of the panel, measured in direction of mining). Longwall mining is done under movable roof supports that are advanced as the bed is cut. The roof in the mined-out area is allowed to fall as the mining advances.

Love Canal. In 1977, a crisis when it was revealed that many residents in the Love Canal area of Niagara Falls Township were suffering severe chromosome damage from toxic chemical waste buried there.

low density polyethylene (LOPE). Plastic material used for both rigid containers and plastic film applications.

low emissivity (low-E) coating. A film or thin coating applied to the surface of glass to reduce heat transfer through a window. Low-e coatings reduce solar heat gain through windows in the summer and heat loss during the winter.

low emissivity (low-E) windows. New window technology that lowers the amount of energy loss through windows by inhibiting the transmission of radiant heat while still allowing sufficient light to pass through.

low NOx Burners. One of several combustion technologies used to reduce emissions of Nitrogen Oxides (NOx.)

lower detection limit. The smallest signal above background noise an instrument can reliably detect.

lower explosive limit (LEL). The concentration of a compound in air below which the mixture will not catch on fire.

lowest acceptable daily dose. The largest quantity of a chemical that will not cause a toxic effect, as determined by animal studies.

lowest achievable emission rate. Under the Clean Air Act, the rate of emissions that reflects (1) the most stringent emission limitation in the implementation plan of any state for such source unless the owner or operator demonstrates such limitations are not achievable; or (2) the most stringent emissions limitation achieved in practice, whichever is more stringent. A proposed new or modified source may not emit pollutants in excess of existing new source standards.

lowest observed adverse effect level (LOAEL). The lowest level of a stressor that causes statistically and biologically significant differences in test samples as compared to other samples subjected to no stressor.

low-level radioactive waste (LLRW). Wastes less hazardous than most of those associated with a nuclear reactor, generated by hospitals, research laboratories, and certain industries. The Department of Energy, Nuclear Regulatory Commission, and the EPA share responsibilities for managing them.

low-temperature collectors. Metallic or nonmetallic solar thermal collectors that generally operate at temperatures below 110°F and use pumped liquid or air as the heat transfer medium. They usually contain no glazing or insulation, and they are often made of plastic or rubber, although some are made of metal.

M

macropores. Secondary soil features such as root holes or desiccation cracks that can create significant conduits for movement of NAPL and dissolved contaminants, or vapor phase contaminants.

magnet. Any piece of iron, steel, etc., that has the property of attracting iron or steel.

magnetic separation. Use of magnets to separate ferrous materials from mixed municipal waste stream.

major modification. Defines modifications of major stationary sources of emissions with respect to Prevention of Significant Deterioration and New Source Review under the Clean Air Act.

major stationary sources. Determines the applicability of Prevention of Significant Deterioration and new source regulations. In a nonattainment area, any stationary pollutant source with the potential to emit more than 100 tons per year is considered a major stationary source. In PSD areas, the cutoff level may be either 100 or 250 tons, depending upon the source.

majors. Larger publicly owned treatment works (POTWs) with flows equal to at least 1 million gallons per day (mgd) or servicing a population equivalent to 10,000 persons; certain other POTWs having significant water quality impacts.

management plan. Under the Asbestos Hazard Emergency Response Act (AHERA), a document that each local education agency is required to prepare, describing all activities planned and undertaken by a school to comply with AHERA regulations, including building inspections to identify asbestos-containing materials, response actions, and operations and maintenance programs to minimize the risk of exposure.

managerial controls. Methods of nonpoint source pollution control based on decisions about managing agricultural wastes or application times or rates for agrochemicals.

mandatory recycling. Programs which by law require consumers to separate trash so that some or all recyclable materials are recovered for recycling rather than going to landfills.

mangroves. Plant communities and trees that inhabit tidal swamps, muddy silt, and sand banks at the mouths of rivers and other low-lying areas which are regularly inundated by the sea, but which are protected from strong waves and currents.

manifest. A one-page form used by haulers transporting waste that lists EPA identification numbers, type and quantity of waste, the generator it originated from, the transporter that shipped it, and the storage or disposal facility to which it is being shipped. It includes copies for all participants in the shipping process.

manifest system. Tracking of hazardous waste from "cradle-to-grave" (generation through disposal) with accompanying documents known as manifests. (*See* cradle to grave.)

man-made (anthropogenic) beta particle and photon emitters. All radionuclides emitting beta particles and/or photons listed in Maximum Permissible Body Burdens and Maximum Permissible Concentrations of Radonuclides in Air and Water for Occupational Exposure.

manual separation. Hand-sorting of recyclable or compostable materials in waste.

manufacturer's formulation. A list of substances or component parts as described by the maker of a coating, pesticide, or other product containing chemicals or other substances.

manufacturing use product. Any product intended (labeled) for formulation or repackaging into other pesticide products.

margin of exposure (MOE). The ratio of the no-observed adverse-effect-level to the estimated exposure dose.

margin of safety. Maximum amount of exposure producing no measurable effect in animals (or studied humans) divided by the actual amount of human exposure in a population.

marginal cost. The change in cost associated with a unit change in quantity supplied or produced.

marine ecosystems. Oceans and the salt marshes, lagoons, and tidal zones that border them, as well as the diverse communities of life they support.

marine park. An area of marine and estuarine habitat set aside as an underwater park and reserve.

marine sanitation device. Any equipment or process installed onboard a vessel to receive, retain, treat, or discharge sewage.

market. Gathering of people for the purchase and sale of provisions, livestock, and the like; the demand for particular goods or services; means of giving value to things.

market-based mechanisms. A form of regulation used in environmental policy that uses market mechanisms to control corporate behavior.

marsh. A type of wetland that does not accumulate appreciable peat deposits and is dominated by herbaceous vegetation. Marshes may be either fresh or saltwater, tidal or nontidal.

mass. Coherent body of similar constituents, of matter or people; of indefinite shape; dense aggregation of objects, color, relating to large numbers of persons of things; action by large numbers; gathering into or of large numbers.

material category. In the asbestos program, broad classification of materials into thermal surfacing insulation, surfacing material, and miscellaneous material.

material safety data sheet (MSDS). A compilation of information required under the OSHA Communication Standard on the identity of hazardous chemicals, health, and physical hazards, exposure limits, and precautions. Section 311 of SARA requires facilities to submit MSDSs under certain circumstances.

material type. Classification of suspect material by its specific use or application, such as pipe insulation, fireproofing, and floor tile.

materials recovery facility (MRF). A facility that processes residentially collected mixed recyclables into new products available for market.

maximally (or most) exposed individual. The person with the highest exposure in a given population.

maximum acceptable toxic concentration. For a given ecological effects test, the range (or geometric mean) between the No Observable Adverse Effect Level and the Lowest Observable Adverse Effects Level.

maximum available control technology (MACT). The emission standard for sources of air pollution requiring the maximum reduction of hazardous emissions, taking cost and feasibility into account. Under the Clean Air Act Amendments of 1990, the MACT must not be less than the average emission level achieved by controls on the best performing 12 percent of existing sources, by category of industrial and utility sources.

maximum contaminant level goal (MCLG). Under the Safe Drinking Water Act, a nonenforceable concentration of a drinking water contaminant, set at the level at which no known or anticipated adverse effects on human health occur and which allows an adequate safety margin. The MCLG is usually the starting point for determining the regulated maximum contaminant level.

maximum contaminant level. The maximum permissible level of a contaminant in water delivered to any user of a public system. MCLs are enforceable standards.

maximum exposure range. Estimate of exposure or dose level received by an individual in a defined population that is greater than the 98th percentile dose for all individuals in that population, but less than the exposure level received by the person receiving the highest exposure level.

maximum residue level. Comparable to a U.S. tolerance level, the maximum residue level is the enforceable limit on food pesticide levels in some countries. Levels are set by the Codex Alimentarius Commission, a UN agency managed and funded jointly by the World Health Organization and the Food and Agriculture Organization.

maximum sustainable yield. The maximum possible yield or catch that can be removed repeatedly from a population without, in the long term, reducing its size.

maximum tolerated dose. The maximum dose that an animal species can tolerate for a major portion of its lifetime without significant impairment or toxic effect other than carcinogenicity.

M-commerce. Commerce conducted by using mobile or cell telephones.

measure of effect/measurement endpoint. A measurable characteristic of ecological entity that can be related to an assessment endpoint; for example, a laboratory test for eight species meeting certain requirements may serve as a measure of effect for an assessment endpoint, such as survival of fish, aquatic, invertebrate, or algal species under acute exposure.

measure of exposure. A measurable characteristic of a stressor (such as the specific amount of mercury in a body of water) used to help quantify the exposure of an ecological entity or individual organism.

mechanical aeration. Use of mechanical energy to inject air into water to cause a waste stream to absorb oxygen.

mechanical energy. The energy of motion used to perform work.

mechanical power. The power produced by motion.

mechanical separation. Using mechanical means to separate waste into various components.

mechanical turbulence. Random irregularities of fluid motion in air caused by buildings or other nonthermal, processes.

media. Specific environments—air, water, soil—which are the subject of regulatory concern and activities.

medical surveillance. A periodic comprehensive review of a worker's health status; acceptable elements of such surveillance program are listed in the Occupational Safety and Health Administration standards for asbestos.

medical waste. Any solid waste generated in the diagnosis, treatment, or immunization of human beings or animals, in research pertaining thereto, or in the production or testing of biologicals, excluding hazardous waste identified or listed under 40 CFR Part 261 or any household waste as defined in 40 CFR Subsection 261.4 (b)(1).

medium-size water system. A water system that serves 3,300 to 50,000 customers.

medium-temperature collectors. Solar thermal collectors designed to operate in the temperature range of 140 °F to 180°F, but that can also operate at a temperature as low as 110°F. The collector typically consists of a metal frame, metal absorption panels with integral flow channels (attached tubing for liquid collectors or integral ducting for air collectors), and glazing and insulation on the sides and back.

megawatt. A unit of electrical power equal to 1,000 kilowatts or 1 million watts.

Mekong River Commission. A commission established by an Agreement on Cooperation from the Sustainable Development of the Mekong River Basin that came into force in 1995.

meniscus. The curved top of a column of liquid in a small tube.

mercaptan. An organic chemical compound that has a sulfurlike odor that is added to natural gas before distribution to the consumer, to give it a distinct, unpleasant odor (like rotten eggs). This serves as a safety device by allowing it to be detected in the atmosphere, in cases where leaks occur.

mercury (Hg). Heavy metal that can accumulate in the environment and is highly toxic if breathed or swallowed.

mesotrophic. Reservoirs and lakes that contain moderate quantities of nutrients and are moderately productive in terms of aquatic animal and plant life.

metabolites. Any substances produced by biological processes, such as those from pesticides.

metalimnion. The middle layer of a thermally stratified lake or reservoir. In this layer there is a rapid decrease in temperature with depth. Also called thermocline.

metamorphosis. Change of form, nature, or character; change into new form.

meta-trend. A global and overarching force that will affect many multidimensional changes, for example, environmental impacts on business, individuals, and countries.

meteorological influences. The effect of a range of atmospheric characteristics on the disperse of pollutants.

methane. A colorless, flammable, odorless hydrocarbon gas (CH_4) which is the major component of natural gas. It is also an important source of hydrogen in various industrial processes. Methane is a greenhouse gas.

methanol. An alcohol that can be used as an alternative fuel or as a gasoline additive. It is less volatile than gasoline; when blended with gasoline it lowers the carbon monoxide emissions but increases hydrocarbon emissions. Used as pure fuel, its emissions are less ozone-forming than those from gasoline. Poisonous to humans and animals if ingested.

method 18. An EPA test method that uses gas chromatographic techniques to measure the concentration of volatile organic compounds in a gas stream.

method 24. An EPA reference method to determine density, water content, and total volatile content (water and VOC) of coatings.

method 25. An EPA reference method to determine the VOC concentration in a gas stream.

methoxychlor. Pesticide that causes adverse health effects in domestic water supplies and is toxic to freshwater and marine aquatic life.

methyl orange alkalinity. A measure of the total alkalinity in a water sample in which the color of methyl orange reflects the change in level.

microbial growth. The amplification or multiplication of microorganisms such as bacteria, algae, diatoms, plankton, and fungi.

microbial pesticide. A microorganism that is used to kill a pest but is of minimum toxicity to humans.

microclimate. 1. Localized climate conditions within an urban area or neighborhood. 2. The climate around a tree or shrub or a stand of trees.

microenvironmental method. A method for sequentially assessing exposure for a series of microenvironments that can be approximated by constant concentrations of a stressor.

microenvironments. Well-defined surroundings such as the home, office, or kitchen that can be treated as uniform in terms of stressor concentration.

miles per gallon (MPG). A measure of vehicle fuel efficiency. MPG is computed as the ratio of the total number of miles traveled by a vehicle to the total number of gallons consumed.

million gallons per day (MGD). A measure of water flow.

minimization. A comprehensive program to minimize or eliminate wastes, usually applied to wastes at their point of origin.

mining of an aquifer. Withdrawal over a period of time of groundwater that exceeds the rate of recharge of the aquifer.

mining waste. Residues resulting from the extraction of raw materials from the earth.

minor source. New emissions sources or modifications to existing emissions sources that do not exceed National Ambient Air Quality Standards (NAAQS) emission levels.

minors. Publicly owned treatment works with flows less than 1 million gallons per day.

miscellaneous ACM. Interior asbestos-containing building material or structural components, members or fixtures, such as floor and ceiling tiles; does not include surfacing materials or thermal system insulation.

miscellaneous materials. Interior building materials on structural components, such as floor or ceiling tiles.

miscible liquids. Two or more liquids that can be mixed and will remain mixed under normal conditions.

missed detection. The situation that occurs when a test indicates that a tank is "tight" when in fact it is leaking.

mist. Liquid particles measuring 40 to 500 micrometers (pm), are formed by condensation of vapor. By comparison, fog particles are smaller than 40 micrometers (pm).

mitigating measures. Physical actions taken to prevent, avoid, or minimize the actual or potential adverse effects of a project or activity.

mitigation. Measures taken to reduce adverse impacts on the environment.

mixed funding. Settlements in which potentially responsible parties and the EPA share the cost of a response action.

mixed glass. Recovered container glass not sorted into categories (e.g., color, grade).

mixed liquor. A mixture of activated sludge and water containing organic matter undergoing activated sludge treatment in an aeration tank.

mixed metals. Recovered metals not sorted into categories, such as aluminum, tin, or steel cans or ferrous or nonferrous metals.

mixed municipal waste. Solid waste that has not been sorted into specific categories (such as plastic, glass, yard trimmings, etc.)

mixed paper. Recovered paper not sorted into categories such as old magazines, old newspapers, old corrugated boxes, and the like.

mixed plastic. Recovered plastic unsorted by category.

mobile home. A trailer that is used as a permanent dwelling.

mobile incinerator systems. Hazardous waste incinerators that can be transported from one site to another.

mobile source. Any nonstationary source of air pollution, such as cars, trucks, motorcycles, buses, airplanes, and locomotives.

model plant. A hypothetical plant design used for developing economic, environmental, and energy impact analyses as support for regulations or regulatory guidelines; first step in exploring the economic impact of a potential New Source Performance Standards (NSPS).

modified bin method. Way of calculating the required heating or cooling for a building based on determining how much energy the system would use if outdoor temperatures were within a certain temperature interval and then multiplying the energy use by the time the temperature interval typically occurs.

modified source. The enlargement of a major stationary pollutant source is often referred to as modification, implying that more emissions will occur.

moisture content. 1.The amount of water lost from soil upon drying to a constant weight, expressed as the weight per unit of dry soil or as the volume of water per unit bulk volume of the soil. For a fully saturated medium, moisture content indicates the porosity. 2. Water equivalent of snow on the ground; an indicator of snowmelt flood potential.

molecule. The smallest division of a compound that still retains or exhibits all the properties of the substance. Normally consists of two or more atoms joined together. An example is a water molecule that is made up of two hydrogen atoms and one oxygen atom.

molten salt reactor. A thermal treatment unit that rapidly heats waste in a heat-conducting fluid bath of carbonate salt.

monitoring. Periodic or continuous surveillance or testing to determine the level of compliance with statutory requirements and/or pollutant levels in various media or in humans, plants, and animals.

monitoring well. A well used to obtain water quality samples or measure groundwater levels. A well drilled at a hazardous waste management facility or Superfund site to collect groundwater samples for the purpose of physical, chemical, or biological analysis to determine the amounts, types, and distribution of contaminants in the groundwater beneath the site.

monoclonal antibodies (MABs or MCAs). Human-made (anthropogenic) clones of a molecule, produced in quantity for medical or research purposes. Molecules of living organisms that selectively find and attach to other molecules to which their structure conforms exactly. This could also apply to equivalent activity by chemical molecules.

monomictic. Lakes and reservoirs that are relatively deep, do not freeze over during winter, and undergo a single stratification and mixing cycle during the year (usually in the fall).

Montreal Protocol. Treaty, signed in 1987, which governs stratospheric ozone protection and research, and the production and use of ozone-depleting substances. It provides for the end of the production of ozone-depleting substances such as CFCS. Under the Protocol, various research groups continue to assess the ozone layer. The Multilateral Fund provides resources to developing nations to promote the transition to ozone-safe technologies.

moratorium. During the negotiation process, a period of 60 to 90 days during which the EPA and potentially responsible parties may reach settlement, but no site response activities can be conducted.

morbidity. Rate of disease incidence.

morphology. Study of the form of things; in biology, study of the form of animals and plants; in philology the study of the form of words and the system of form in a language.

mortality. Death rate.

most probable number. An estimate of microbial density per unit volume of water sample, based on probability theory.

motive. Tending to initiate movement, concerned with movement; that which induces a person to act, such as fear, desire, circumstances, etc.

motor vehicle pollution. The emission of undesirable particles and gases from motor vehicle exhausts and engines contribution to visible and invisible pollution, haze, and photochemical smog.

MSW (municipal solid waste). Residential solid waste and some nonhazardous commercial, institutional, and industrial wastes.

MTBE (Methyl Tertiary Butyl Ether). A fuel oxygenate produced by reacting methanol with isobutylene.

muck soils. Earth made from decaying plant materials.

mudballs. Round material that forms in filters and gradually increases in size when not removed by backwashing.

mulch. A layer of material (wood chips, straw, leaves, etc.) placed around plants to hold moisture, prevent weed growth, and enrich or sterilize the soil.

multifamily dwellings. Apartment building and condominiums.

multimedia approach. Joint approach to several environmental media, such as air, water, and land.

multinational. Large business corporation whose activities extend across national boundaries; can include an international corporation, multinational company, or corporation, transnational company, or corporation.

multiple chemical sensitivity. A diagnostic label for people who suffer multisystem illnesses as a result of contact with, or proximity to, a variety of airborne agents and other substances.

multiple use. Use of land for more than one purpose; e.g., grazing of livestock, watershed and wildlife protection, recreation, and timber production. Also applies to use of bodies of water for recreational purposes, fishing, and water supply.

multiplier. A radio indicating the effect on total employment or on total income of a specified amount of capital investment or expenditure.

multistage remote sensing. A strategy for landscape characterization that involves gathering and analyzing information at several geographic scales, ranging from generalized levels of detail at the national level through high levels of detail at the local scale.

municipal discharge. Discharge of effluent from wastewater treatment plants, which receive wastewater from households, commercial establishments, and industries in the coastal drainage basin. Combined sewer/separate storm overflows are included in this category.

municipal sewage. Wastes (mostly liquid) originating from a community; may be composed of domestic wastewaters and/or industrial discharges.

municipal sludge. Semiliquid residue remaining from the treatment of municipal water and wastewater.

municipal solid waste. Common garbage or trash generated by industries, businesses, institutions, and homes.

mutagen/mutagenicity. An agent that causes a permanent genetic change in a cell other than that which occurs during normal growth. Mutagenicity is the capacity of a chemical or physical agent to cause such permanent changes.

N

nanotechnology. The ability to create human-made structures only a few billionths of a meter in size.

National Ambient Air Quality Standards (NAAQS). Standards established by EPA that apply for outdoor air throughout the country.

National Emissions Standards for Hazardous Air Pollutants (NESHAPS). Emissions standards set by the EPA for an air pollutant not covered by NAAQS that may cause an increase in fatalities or in serious, irreversible, or incapacitating illness. Primary standards are designed to protect human health, secondary standards to protect public welfare (e.g., building facades, visibility, crops, and domestic animals).

national environmental performance partnership agreements. System that allows states to assume greater responsibility for environmental programs based on their relative ability to execute them.

national estate. Components of the natural or cultural environment of a nation that have special value for future generations, as well as for the present community.

National Estuary Program. A program established under the Clean Water Act Amendments of 1987 to develop and implement conservation and management plans for protecting estuaries and restoring and maintaining their chemical, physical, and biological integrity, as well as controlling point and nonpoint pollution sources.

national municipal plan. A policy created in 1984 by the EPA and the states in 1984 to bring all publicly owned treatment works (POTWs) into compliance with Clean Water Act requirements.

National Oil and Hazardous Substances Contingency Plan (NOHSCP/NCP). The federal regulation that guides determination of the sites to be corrected under both the Superfund program and the program to prevent or control spills into surface waters or elsewhere.

national park. A relatively large area of land set aside by legislation for its features of predominantly unspoiled natural landscape.

National Pollutant Discharge Elimination System (NPDES). A provision of the Clean Water Act which prohibits discharge of pollutants into waters of the United States unless a special permit is issued by the EPA, a state, or, where delegated, a tribal government on an Indian reservation.

National Priorities List (NPL). EPA's list of the most serious uncontrolled or abandoned hazardous waste sites identified for possible long-term remedial action under Superfund. The list is based primarily on the score a site receives from the Hazard Ranking System. EPA is required to update the NPL at least once a year. A site must be on the NPL to receive money from the Trust Fund for remedial action.

national response center. The federal operations center that receives notifications of all releases of oil and hazardous substances into the environment; open 24 hours a day, is operated by the U.S. Coast Guard, which evaluates all reports and notifies the appropriate agency.

national response team (NRT). Representatives of 13 federal agencies that, as a team, coordinate federal responses to nationally significant incidents of pollution—an oil spill, a major chemical release, or a Superfund response action—and provide advice and technical assistance to the responding agency(ies) before and during a response action.

native plants. Plants that have evolved over thousands of years to be able to survive in a particular region, and have adapted to the geography, hydrology, and climate of that region. A community of native plants provides habitat for a variety of native wildlife species; and will be hardy and resistant to the local conditions, thereby usually requiring less maintenance when used in landscaping.

natural. Existing in or by nature, not artificial; innate, inherent; uncultivated.

natural capital. A company's environmental assets and natural resources existing in the physical environment, either owned (such as mineral, forest, or energy resources) or simply utilized in business operations (such as clean water and atmosphere); often traditional economic measures and indicators fail to take into account the development use of natural capital, although preservation of its quantity and quality and therefore its sustainable use is essential to a business's long-term survival and growth.

natural environment. A concept that includes national parks, nature reserves, and other places for protection of flora and fauna; the coastline and islands; inland water bodies, rivers, lakes, and other wetlands.

natural gas. An odorless, colorless, tasteless, nontoxic clean-burning fossil fuel. It is usually found in fossil fuel deposits and used as a fuel.

natural gas hydrates. Solid, crystalline, waxlike substances composed of water, methane, and usually a small amount of other gases, with the gases being trapped in the interstices of a water-ice lattice. They form beneath permafrost and on the ocean floor under conditions of moderately high pressure and at temperatures near the freezing point of water.

natural gas liquids (NGL). Substances that can be processed as liquids out of natural gas by absorption or condensation.

natural lighting/daylighting. The use of windows and skylights to bring more natural light into a home. Can also refer to architectural design that makes significant use of natural light.

natural resource accounting. Accounting procedures applied to the natural resources of a nation.

nature. Innate quality of things, existence; the expression of such qualities.

nature reserve. An area set aside by a government for the purpose of protecting certain fauna and flora, or both.

navigable waters. Traditionally, waters sufficiently deep and wide for navigation by all, or specified vessels; such waters in the United States come under federal jurisdiction and are protected by certain provisions of the Clean Water Act.

necrosis. Death of plant or animal cells or tissues. In plants, necrosis can discolor stems or leaves or kill a plant entirely.

need. Circumstance requiring action for fulfillment.

negotiations (under Superfund). After potentially responsible parties are identified for a site, EPA coordinates with them to reach a settlement that will result in the potentially responsible party (PRP) paying for or conducting the cleanup under EPA supervision. If negotiations fail, EPA can order the PRP to conduct the cleanup or EPA can pay for the cleanup using Superfund monies and then sue to recover the costs.

nematocide. A chemical agent that is destructive to nematodes.

nephelometric. Method of measuring turbidity in a water sample by passing light through the sample and measuring the amount of the light that is deflected.

net energy principle. Means of energy accounting in system or process. The amount of energy used or lost in making something or achieving a purpose is measured or calculated as a means of determining the most effective, that is, energy efficient, option.

net generation. Gross generation less the electric energy consumed at the generating station for station's use.

net metering. Arrangement that permits a facility (using a meter that reads inflows and outflows of electricity) to sell any excess power it generates over its load requirement back to the electrical grid to offset consumption. Net metering allows a homeowner to sell surplus electricity back to the utility.

net photovoltaic cell shipment. The difference between photovoltaic cell shipments and photovoltaic cell purchases.

net photovoltaic module shipment. The difference between photovoltaic module shipments and photovoltaic module purchases.

net summer capacity. The maximum output, commonly expressed in megawatts (MW), that generating equipment can supply to system load, as demonstrated by a multihour test, at the time of summer peak demand (period of May 1 through October 31). This output reflects a reduction in capacity owing to electricity use for station service or auxiliaries.

netting. A concept in which all emissions sources in the same area that owned or controlled by a single company are treated as one large source, thereby allowing flexibility in controlling individual sources in order to meet a single emissions standard.

network. Arrangement with intersecting lines and interstices similar to those of a net; complex interconnecting system, as of paths, roads, railways, or communications, also of people or organizations with particular interests.

neutralization. Decreasing the acidity or alkalinity of a substance by adding alkaline or acidic materials, respectively.

New Source Performance Standards (NSPS). Uniform national EPA air emission and water effluent standards which limit the amount of pollution allowed from new sources or from modified existing sources.

New Source Review (NSR). A Clean Air Act requirement that state implementation plans must include a permit review that applies to the construction and operation of new and modified stationary sources in nonattainment areas to ensure attainment of national ambient air quality standards.

new source. Any stationary source built or modified after publication of final or proposed regulations that prescribe a given standard of performance.

nitrate. A compound containing nitrogen that can exist in the atmosphere or as a dissolved gas in water and which can have harmful effects on humans and animals. Nitrates in water can cause severe illness in infants and domestic animals. A plant nutrient and inorganic fertilizer, nitrate is found in septic systems, animal feed lots, agricultural fertilizers, manure, industrial wastewaters, sanitary landfills, and garbage dumps.

nitric oxide (NO). A gas formed by combustion under high temperature and high pressure in an internal combustion engine; it is converted by sunlight and photochemical processes in ambient air to nitrogen oxide. NO is a precursor of ground-level ozone pollution, or smog.

nitrification. The process whereby ammonia in wastewater is oxidized to nitrite and then to nitrate by bacterial or chemical reactions.

nitrilotriacetic acid (NTA). A compound now replacing phosphates in detergents.

nitrite. An intermediate in the process of nitrification. Nitrous oxide salts used in food preservation.

nitrogen oxide (NOx). The result of photochemical reactions of nitric oxide in ambient air; major component of photochemical smog. Product of combustion from transportation and stationary sources and a major contributor to the formation of ozone in the troposphere and to acid deposition.

nitrogenous wastes. Animal or vegetable residues that contain significant amounts of nitrogen.

nitrophenols. Synthetic organopesticides containing carbon, hydrogen, nitrogen, and oxygen.

no further remedial action planned. Determination made by the EPA following a preliminary assessment that a site does not pose a significant risk and so requires no further activity under CERCLA.

no observable adverse effect level (NOAEL). An exposure level at which there are no statistically or biologically significant increases in the frequency or severity of adverse effects between the exposed population and its appropriate control; some effects may be produced at this level, but they are not considered as adverse or as precursors to adverse effects. In an experiment with several NOAELs, the regulatory focus is primarily on the highest one, leading to the common usage of the term NOAEL as the highest exposure without adverse effects.

no till. Planting crops without prior seedbed preparation, into an existing cover crop, sod, or crop residues, and eliminating subsequent tillage operations.

noble metal. Chemically inactive metal such as gold; does not corrode easily.

noise. 1. Product-level or product-volume changes occurring during a test that are not related to a leak but may be mistaken for one. 2. Sound that is not wanted by the recipient.

non-aqueous phase liquid (NAPL). Contaminants that remain undiluted as the original bulk liquid in the subsurface, e.g., spilled oil.

non-attainment area. Area that does not meet one or more of the National Ambient Air Quality Standards for the criteria pollutants designated in the Clean Air Act.

non-binding allocations of responsibility (NBAR). A process for the EPA to propose a way for potentially responsible parties to allocate costs among themselves.

nonbiogenic waste. Waste made from fossil materials or materials of nonbiological origin, such as plastics, and tire-derived fuels.

noncommunity water system. A public water system that is not a community water system; e.g. the water supply at a camp site or national park.

noncompliance coal. Any coal that emits greater than 3.0 pounds of sulfur dioxide per million BTU when burned. Also known as high-sulfur coal.

nonconcentrator system. A type of solar energy system that does not rely on special devices to concentrate the sun's radiation while collecting it.

noncontact cooling water. Water used for cooling which does not come into direct contact with any raw material, product, by-product, or waste.

nonconventional pollutant. Any pollutant not statutorily listed or which is poorly understood by the scientific community.

nondegradation. An environmental policy that disallows any lowering of naturally occurring quality regardless of preestablished health standards.

nondischarging treatment plant. A treatment plant that does not discharge treated wastewater into any stream or river. Most are pond systems that dispose of the total flow they receive by means of evaporation or percolation to groundwater, or facilities that dispose of their effluent by recycling or reuse (e.g., spray irrigation or groundwater discharge).

nonferrous metals. Nonmagnetic metals such as aluminum, lead, and copper. Products made all or in part from such metals include containers, packaging, appliances, furniture, electronic equipment, and aluminum foil.

nonfriable asbestos-containing materials. Any material containing more than one percent asbestos (as determined by polarized light microscopy) that, when dry, cannot be crumbled, pulverized, or reduced to powder by hand pressure.

non-governmental organization (NGO). A private, nonprofit organization that is independent of business and government, that works toward some specific social, environmental, or economic goal through research, activism, training, promotion, advocacy, lobbying, and community service.

nonhazardous industrial waste. Industrial process waste in wastewater not considered municipal solid waste or hazardous waste under Resource Conservation and Recovery Act (RARA).

non-ionizing electromagnetic radiation. 1. Radiation that does not change the structure of atoms but does heat tissue and can cause harmful biological effects. 2. Microwaves, radio waves, and low-frequency electromagnetic fields from high-voltage transmission lines.

non-methane hydrocarbon (NMHC). The sum of all hydrocarbon air pollutants except methane; significant precursors to ozone formation.

non-methane organic gases (NMOG). The sum of all organic air pollutants. Excluding methane; they account for aldehydes, ketones, alcohols, and other pollutants that are not hydrocarbons but are precursors of ozone.

nonpoint sources. Diffuse pollution sources (i.e., without a single point of origin or not introduced into a receiving stream from a specific outlet). The pollutants are generally carried off the land by storm water. Common nonpoint sources are agriculture, forestry, urban, mining, construction, dams, channels, land disposal, saltwater intrusion, and city streets.

nonpotable. Water that is unsafe or unpalatable to drink because it contains pollutants, contaminants, minerals, or infective agents.

nonrenewable. Fuels that cannot be easily made or "renewed." We can use up nonrenewable fuels. Oil, natural gas, and coal are nonrenewable fuels.

nonroad emissions. Pollutants emitted by combustion engines on farm and construction equipment, gasoline-powered lawn and garden equipment, and power boats and outboard motors.

nontransient noncommunity water system. A public water system that regularly serves at least 25 of the same nonresident persons per day for more than six months per year.

nonutility generation. Electric generation by nonutility power producers to supply electric power for industrial, commercial, and military operations, or sales to electric utilities. *See* nonutility power producer.

nonutility power producer. A corporation, person, agency, authority, or other legal entity or instrumentality that owns electric generating capacity and is not an electric utility. Nonutility power producers include qualifying cogenerators, qualifying small power producers, and other nonutility generators (including independent power producers) without a designated, franchised service area that do not file forms listed in the Code of Federal Regulations, Title 18, Part 141.

no-observed effect level (NOEL). Exposure level at which there are no statistically or biological significant differences in the frequency or severity of any effect in the exposed or control populations.

notice of deficiency. An EPA request to a facility owner or operator requesting additional information before a preliminary decision on a permit application can be made.

notice of intent to cancel. Notification sent to registrants when the EPA decides to cancel registration of a product containing a pesticide.

notice of intent to deny. Notification by EPA of its preliminary intent to deny a permit application.

notice of intent to suspend. Notification sent to a pesticide registrant when the EPA decides to suspend product sale and distribution because of failure to submit requested data in a timely and/or acceptable manner, or because of imminent hazard.

nuclear. Of, relating to, a nucleus, the central part of a thing around which others form.

nuclear energy. Energy that comes from splitting atoms of radioactive materials, such as uranium.

nuclear reactors and support facilities. Uranium mills, commercial power reactors, fuel reprocessing plants, and uranium enrichment facilities.

nuclear winter. Prediction by some scientists that smoke and debris rising from massive fires of a nuclear war could block sunlight for weeks or months, cooling the earth's surface and producing climate changes that could, for example, negatively affect world agricultural and weather patterns.

nuclide. An atom characterized by the number of protons, neturons, and energy in the nucleus.

nurture. To bring up, train, care, nourish.

nutrient pollution. Contamination of water resources by excessive inputs of nutrients. In surface waters, excess algal production is a major concern.

nutrient. Any substance assimilated by living things that promotes growth. The term is generally applied to nitrogen and phosphorus in wastewater, but is also applied to other essential and trace elements.

O

ocean discharge waiver. A variance from Clean Water Act requirements for discharge into marine waters.

ocean dumping. Historically, the use of the oceans as a dumping ground for industrial and radioactive wastes, sewage effluents, and sewage sludge.

odor threshold. The minimum odor of a water or air sample that can just be detected after successive dilutions with odorless water. Also called threshold odor.

OECD guidelines. Testing guidelines prepared by the Organization of Economic and Cooperative Development of the United Nations. They assist in preparation of protocols for studies of toxicology, environmental fate, etc.

office paper. High-grade papers such as copier paper, computer printout, and stationery almost entirely made of uncoated chemical pulp, although some ground wood is used. Such waste is also generated in homes, schools, and elsewhere.

offsets. A concept whereby emissions from proposed new or modified stationary sources are balanced by reductions from existing sources to stabilize total emissions.

offshore. The geographic area that lies seaward of the coastline. In general, the coastline is the line of ordinary low water along with that portion of the coast that is in direct contact with the open sea or the line marking the seaward limit of inland water.

offshore reserves and production. Unless otherwise dedicated, energy source reserves and production that are in either state or federal domains, located seaward of the coastline.

off-site facility. A hazardous waste treatment, storage, or disposal area that is located away from the generating site.

offstream use. Water withdrawn from surface or groundwater sources for use at another place.

ohm. The unit of resistance to the flow of an electric current.

oil. The raw material that petroleum products are made from. A black liquid fossil fuel found deep in the earth. Gasoline and most plastics are made from oil.

oil and gas waste. Gas and oil drilling muds, oil production brines, and other waste associated with exploration for, development, and production of crude oil or natural gas.

oil desulfurization. Widely used precombustion method for reducing sulfur dioxide emissions from oil-burning power plants. The oil is treated with hydrogen, which removes some of the sulfur by forming hydrogen sulfide gas.

oil fingerprinting. A method that identifies sources of oil and allows spills to be traced to their source.

oil spill. An accidental or intentional discharge of oil which reaches bodies of water. Can be controlled by chemical dispersion, combustion, mechanical containment, and/or adsorption. Spills from tanks and pipelines can also occur away from water bodies, contaminating the soil, getting into sewer systems, and threatening underground water sources.

oligotrophic lakes. Deep clear lakes with few nutrients, little organic matter, and a high dissolved-oxygen level.

onboard controls. Devices placed on vehicles to capture gasoline vapor during refueling and route it to the engines when the vehicle is starting so that it can be efficiently burned.

onconogenicity. The capacity to induce cancer.

on-demand hot water systems. Tankless or instantaneous water heaters that provide hot water only as it is needed. On-demand water heaters heat water directly without the use of a storage tank, avoiding the heat losses associated with hot water storage tanks.

one-hit model. A mathematical model based on the biological theory that a single "hit" of some minimum critical amount of a carcinogen at a cellular target such as DNA can start an irreversible series events leading to a tumor.

on-scene coordinator (OSC). The predesignated EPA, Coast Guard, or Department of Defense official who coordinates and directs

Superfund removal actions or Clean Water Act oil- or hazardous-spill response actions.

on-site facility. A hazardous waste treatment, storage, or disposal area that is located on the generating site.

opacity. The amount of light obscured by particulate pollution in the air; clear window glass has zero opacity, a brick wall is 100 percent opaque. Opacity is an indicator of changes in performance of particulate control systems.

OPEC. The Organization of Petroleum Exporting Countries organized for the purpose of negotiating with oil companies on matters of oil production, prices, and future concession rights. Current members (as of the date of writing this definition) are Algeria, Indonesia, Iran, Iraq, Kuwait, Libya, Nigeria, Qatar, Saudi Arabia, the United Arab Emirates, and Venezuela.

open burning. Uncontrolled fires in an open dump.

open dump. An uncovered site used for disposal of waste without environmental controls.

open-loop recycling. A recycling process in which materials from old products are made into new products in a manner that changes the inherent properties of the materials, often via a degradation in quality, such as recycling white writing paper into cardboard rather than more premium writing paper; often used for steel, paper, and plastic, open-loop recycling is also known as downcycling or reprocessing.

operable unit. Term for each of a number of separate activities undertaken as part of a Superfund site cleanup. A typical operable unit would be removal of drums and tanks from the surface of a site.

operating conditions. Conditions specified in a RCRA permit that dictate how an incinerator must operate as it burns different waste types. A trial burn is used to identify operating conditions needed to meet specified performance standards.

operation and maintenance (O&M) cost. Operating expenses are associated with operating a facility (i.e., supervising and engineering expenses). Maintenance expenses are that portion of expenses consisting of labor, materials, and other direct and indirect expenses incurred for preserving the operating efficiency or physical condition of utility plants that are used for power production, transmission, and distribution of energy.

operation and maintenance. 1. Activities conducted after a Superfund site action is completed to ensure that the action is effective. 2. Actions taken after construction to ensure that facilities constructed to treat wastewater will be properly operated and maintained to achieve normative efficiency levels and prescribed effluent limitations in an optimum manner. 3. Ongoing asbestos management plan in a school or other public building, including regular inspections, various methods of maintaining asbestos in place, and removal when necessary.

operator certification. Certification of operators of community and nontransient noncommunity water systems, asbestos specialists, pesticide applicators, hazardous waste transporter, and other such specialists as required by the EPA or a state agency implementing an EPA-approved environmental regulatory program.

opportunity cost. The cost of satisfying an objective, measured by the value those resources would have had in another attractive alternative use.

optimal corrosion control treatment. An erosion control treatment that minimizes the lead and copper concentrations at users' taps while also ensuring that the treatment does not cause the water system to violate any national primary drinking water regulations.

optimum value engineering (OVE). Lumber Layout and usage techniques that minimize the amount of lumber used to construct a house without compromising its structural integrity. OVE can improve a home's energy efficiency and durability, reduce construction costs, and avoid waste. In addition, optimizing the amount of lumber used to frame homes creates more space for insulation in exterior walls. Also known as advanced framing.

oral toxicity. Ability of a pesticide to cause injury when ingested.

organic. Referring to or derived from living organisms. Signifying the absence of pesticides, hormones, synthetic fertilizers, and other toxic materials in the cultivation of agricultural products; *organic* is also a food labeling term that denotes the product was produced under the authority of the Organic Foods Production Act. In chemistry, any compound containing carbon.

organic chemicals/compounds. Naturally occurring (animal, plant-produced, or synthetic) substances containing mainly carbon, hydrogen, nitrogen, and oxygen.

organic matter. Carbonaceous waste contained in plant or animal matter and originating from domestic or industrial sources.

organic waste. Waste material of animal or plant origin.

organism. Any form of animal or plant life.

organophosphates. Pesticides that contain phosphorus; short-lived, but some can be toxic when first applied.

organophyllic. A substance that easily combines with organic compounds.

organotins. Chemical compounds used in antifoulant paints to protect the hulls of boats and ships, buoys, and pilings from marine organisms such as barnacles.

original AHERA inspection/original inspection/inspection. Examination of school buildings arranged by local education agencies to identify asbestos-containing materials, evaluate their condition, and take samples of materials suspected to contain asbestos; performed by EPA-accredited inspectors.

original generation point. Where regulated medical or other material first becomes waste.

osmosis. The passage of a liquid from a weak solution to a more concentrated solution across a semipermeable membrane that allows passage of the solvent (water) but not the dissolved solids.

other biomass. This category of biomass energy includes agricultural by-products/crops (agricultural by-products, straw); other biomass gas (digester gas, methane); other biomass liquids (fish oil, liquid acetonitrite, waste, tall oil, waste alcohol); other biomass solids (medical waste, solid by-products; sludge waste and tires.

other ferrous metals. Recyclable metals from strapping, furniture, and metal found in tires and consumer electronics but does not include metals found in construction materials or cars, locomotives, and ships.

other glass. Recyclable glass from furniture, appliances, and consumer electronics. Does not include glass from transportation products (cars, trucks, or shipping containers) and construction or demolition debris.

other nonferrous metals. Recyclable nonferrous metals such as lead, copper, and zinc from appliances, consumer electronics, and nonpackaging aluminum products. Does not include nonferrous metals from industrial applications and construction and demolition debris

other paper. For recyclable paper from books, third-class mail, commercial printing, paper towels, plates and cups; and other nonpackaging paper such as posters, photographic papers, cards and games, milk cartons, folding boxes, bags, wrapping paper, and paperboard. Does not include wrapping paper or shipping cartons.

other plastics. Recyclable plastic from appliances, eating utensils, plates, containers, toys, and various kinds of equipment. Does not include heavy-duty plastics such as yielding materials.

other solid waste. Recyclable nonhazardous solid wastes, other than municipal solid waste, covered under Subtitle D of RARA.

other wood. Recyclable wood from furniture, consumer electronics cabinets, and other nonpackaging wood products. Does not include lumber and tree stumps recovered from construction and demolition activities, and industrial process waste such as shavings and sawdust.

outdoor air supply. Air brought into a building from outside.

outer continental shelf. Offshore federal domain.

outfall. The place where effluent is discharged into receiving waters.

overburden. Rock and soil cleared away before mining.

overdraft. The pumping of water from a groundwater basin or aquifer in excess of the supply flowing into the basin; results in a depletion or "mining" of the groundwater in the basin.

overfire air. Air forced into the top of an incinerator or boiler to fan the flames.

overflow rate. One of the guidelines for design of the settling tanks and clarifiers in a treatment plant; used by plant operators to determine if tanks and clarifiers are over or under-used.

overland flow. A land application technique that cleanses waste water by allowing it to flow over a sloped surface. As the water flows over the surface, contaminants are absorbed, and the water is collected at the bottom of the slope for reuse.

oversized regulated medical waste. Medical waste that is too large for plastic bags or standard containers.

overturn. One complete cycle of top to bottom mixing of previously stratified water masses. This phenomenon may occur in spring or fall, or after storms, and results in uniformity of chemical and physical properties of water at all depths.

oxidant. A collective term for some of the primary constituents of photochemical smog.

oxidation. The chemical addition of oxygen to break down pollutants or organic waste; e.g., destruction of chemicals such as cyanides, phenols, and organic sulfur compounds in sewage by bacterial and chemical means.

oxidation pond. A human-made (anthropogenic) body of water in which waste is consumed by bacteria, used most frequently with other waste-treatment processes; a sewage lagoon.

oxidation-reduction potential. The electric potential required to transfer electrons from one compound or element (the oxidant) to another compound (the reductant); used as a qualitative measure of the state of oxidation in water treatment systems.

oxygenated fuels. Gasoline that has been blended with alcohols or ethers that contain oxygen in order to reduce carbon monoxide and other emissions.

oxygenated solvent. An organic solvent containing oxygen as part of the molecular structure. Alcohols and ketones are oxygenated compounds often used as paint solvents.

ozonation/ozonator. Application of ozone to water for disinfection or for taste and odor control. The ozonator is the device that does this.

ozone. A gas composed of three bonded oxygen atoms, ozone in the lower atmosphere is a dangerous component of urban smog; ozone in the upper atmosphere provides a shield against ultraviolet light from the sun.

ozone (O_3). Found in two layers of the atmosphere, the stratosphere and the troposphere. In the stratosphere (the atmospheric layer 7 to 10 miles or more above the earth's surface) ozone is a natural form of oxygen that provides a protective layer shielding the earth from ultraviolet radiation. In the troposphere (the layer extending up 7 to 10 miles from the earth's surface), ozone is a chemical oxidant and major component of photochemical smog. It can seriously impair the respiratory system and is one of the most widespread of all the criteria pollutants for which the Clean Air Act required the EPA to set standards. Ozone in the troposphere is produced through complex chemical reactions of nitrogen oxides, which are among the primary pollutants emitted by combustion sources; hydrocarbons, released into the atmosphere through the combustion, handling and processing of petroleum products; and sunlight.

ozone depletion. Destruction of the stratospheric ozone layer which shields the earth from ultraviolet radiation harmful to life. This destruction of ozone is caused by the breakdown of certain chlorine and/or bromine containing compounds (chlorofluorocarbons or halons), which break down when they reach the stratosphere and then catalytically destroy ozone molecules.

ozone hole. A thinning break in the stratospheric ozone layer. Designation of amount of such depletion as an "ozone hole" is made when the detected amount of depletion exceeds 50%. Seasonal ozone holes have been observed over both the Antarctic and Arctic regions, part of Canada, and the extreme northeastern United States.

ozone layer. The protective layer in the atmosphere, about 15 miles above the ground, that absorbs some of the sun's ultraviolet rays, thereby reducing the amount of potentially harmful radiation that reaches the earth's surface.

P

packaging. The assembly of one or more containers and any other components necessary to ensure minimum compliance with a program's storage and shipment packaging requirements. Also, the containers and other equipment involved.

packed bed scrubber. An air pollution control device in which emissions pass through alkaline water to neutralize hydrogen chloride gas.

packed tower. A pollution control device that forces dirty air through a tower packed with crushed rock or wood chips while liquid is sprayed over the packing material. The pollutants in the air stream either dissolve or chemically react with the liquid.

packer. An inflatable gland, or balloon, used to create a temporary seal in a borehole, probe hole, well, or drive casing. It is made of rubber or nonreactive materials.

palatable water. Water, at a desirable temperature, that is free from objectionable tastes, odors, colors, and turbidity.

pandemic. A widespread epidemic throughout an area, nation, or the world.

paper. In the recycling business, refers to products and materials, including newspapers, magazines, office papers, corrugated containers, bags, and some paperboard packaging that can be recycled into new paper products.

paper pellets. Paper compressed and bound into uniform diameter pellets to be burned in a heating stove.

paper processor/plastics processor. Intermediate facility where recovered paper or plastic products and materials are sorted, decontaminated, and prepared for final recycling.

parabolic dish. A high-temperature (above 180°F) solar thermal concentrator, generally bowl-shaped, with two-axis tracking.

parabolic trough. A high-temperature (above 180°F) solar thermal concentrator with the capacity for tracking the sun using one axis of rotation.

paradigm. Example or pattern, especially of sound; inflexion.

parameter. A variable, measurable property whose value is a determinant of the characteristics of a system; for example, temperature, pressure, and density are parameters of the atmosphere.

paraquat. A standard herbicide used to kill various types of crops, including marijuana. Causes lung damage if smoke from the crop is inhaled.

parshall flume. Device used to measure the flow of water in an open channel.

participation rate. Portion of population participating in a recycling program.

particle count. Results of a microscopic examination of treated water with a special "particle counter" that classifies suspended particles by number and size.

particulate loading. The mass of particulates per unit volume of air or water.

particulates. 1. Fine liquid or solid particles such as dust, smoke, mist, fumes, or smog, found in air or emissions. 2. Very small solids suspended in water; they can vary in size, shape, density, and electrical charge and can be gathered together by coagulation and flocculation.

partition coefficient. Measure of the sorption phenomenon, whereby a pesticide is divided between the soil and water phase; also referred to as adsorption partition coefficient.

parts per billion (PPB)/parts per million (PPM). Units commonly used to express contamination ratios, as in establishing the maximum permissible amount of a contaminant in water, land, or air.

passive cooling. Cooling buildings without the use of mechanical equipment, by using natural ventilation.

passive heating system. A means of capturing, storing, and using heat from the sun.

passive smoking/secondhand smoke. Inhalation of others' tobacco smoke.

passive solar heating. Designing a home's windows, walls, and floors to collect, store, and distribute solar energy in the form of heat in the winter and reject solar heat in the summer. Unlike active solar heating systems, passive solar design doesn't involve the use of mechanical and electrical devices, such as pumps, fans, or electrical controls to move the solar heat.

passive treatment walls. Technology in which a chemical reaction takes place when contaminated groundwater comes in contact with a barrier such as limestone or a wall containing iron filings.

pathogens. Microorganisms (e.g., bacteria, viruses, or parasites) that can cause disease in humans, animals, and plants.

pathway. The physical course a chemical or pollutant takes from its source to the exposed organism.

pay-as-you-throw/unit-based pricing. Systems under which residents pay for municipal waste management and disposal services by weight or volume collected, not a fixed fee.

peak electricity demand. The maximum electricity used to meet the cooling load of a building or buildings in a given area.

peak levels. Levels of airborne pollutant contaminants much higher than average or occurring for short periods of time in response to sudden releases.

peak load plant. A plant usually housing old, low-efficiency steam units, gas turbines, diesels, or pumped-storage hydroelectric equipment normally used during the peak-load periods.

peak watt. A manufacturer's unit indicating the amount of power a photovoltaic cell or module will produce at standard test conditions (normally 1,000 watts per square meter and 25°C).

peat. Partially decomposed plant debris. It is considered an early stage in the development of coal. Peat is distinguished from lignite by the presence of free cellulose and a high moisture content (exceeding 70 percent). The heat content of air-dried peat (about 50 percent moisture) is about 9 million Btu per ton. Most U.S. peat is used as a soil conditioner. The first U.S. electric power plant fueled by peat began operation in Maine in 1990.

penstock. A large pipe that carries moving water from the reservoir to a turbine generator in a hydropower plant.

people, planet, profit. The expanded set of values for companies and individuals to use in measuring organizational and societal success, specifically economic, environmental, and social values; "people, planet, profit" are also referred to as the components of the "triple bottom line."

percent saturation. The amount of a substance that is dissolved in a solution compared to the amount that could be dissolved in it.

perched water. Zone of unpressurized water held above the water table by impermeable rock or sediment.

percolating water. Water that passes through rocks or soil under the force of gravity.

percolation. 1. The movement of water downward and radially through subsurface soil layers, usually continuing downward to groundwater. Can also involve upward movement of water. 2. Slow seepage of water through a filter.

performance bond. Cash or securities deposited before a landfill operating permit is issued, which are held to ensure that all requirements for operating and subsequently closing the landfill are faithfully performed. The money is returned to the owner after proper closure of the landfill is completed. If contamination or other problems appear at any time during operation, or upon closure, and are not addressed, the owner must forfeit all or part of the bond which is then used to cover cleanup costs.

performance data (for incinerators). Information collected, during a trial burn, on concentrations of designated organic compounds and pollutants found in incinerator emissions. Data analysis must show that the incinerator meets performance standards under operating conditions specified in the RCRA permit.

performance standards. 1. Regulatory requirements limiting the concentrations of designated organic compounds, particulate matter, and hydrogen chloride in emissions from incinerators. 2. Operating standards established by EPA for various permitted pollution control systems, asbestos inspections, and various program operations and maintenance requirements.

periodic table. Table of all known elements in a meaningful pattern.

periphyton. Microscopic underwater plants and animals that are firmly attached to solid surfaces such as rocks, logs, and pilings.

permaculture. An integrated system of perennial agriculture, designed to enrich rather than destroy local ecosystems, which is as far as possible self-sufficient in energy needs.

permeability. The rate at which liquids pass through soil or other materials in a specified direction.

permissible dose. The dose of a chemical that may be received by an individual without the expectation of a significantly harmful result.

permissible exposure limit (PEL). Federal limits for workplace exposure to contaminants as established by OSHA.

permit. An authorization, license, or equivalent control document issued by the EPA or an approved state agency to implement the requirements of an environmental regulation, for example, a permit to operate a wastewater treatment plant or to operate a facility that may generate harmful emissions.

persistence. Refers to the length of time a compound stays in the environment, once introduced. A compound may persist for less than a second or indefinitely.

persistent pesticides. Pesticides that do not break down chemically or break down very slowly and remain in the environment after a growing season.

personal air samples. Air samples taken with a pump that is directly attached to the worker with the collecting filter and cassette placed in the worker's breathing zone (required under OSHA asbestos standards and EPA worker protection rule).

personal measurement. A measurement collected from an individual's immediate environment.

personal protective equipment. Clothing and equipment worn by pesticide mixers, loaders and applicators and reentry workers, hazmat emergency responders, workers cleaning up Superfund sites, and so on, which is worn to reduce their exposure to potentially hazardous chemicals and other pollutants.

pervious surface. Porous surface with spaces in the material, such as landscaping, gravel, and alternative pavers. Pervious surfaces allow rainwater or snowmelt to pass through into the ground, thereby reducing runoff and filtering pollutants.

pest. An insect, rodent, nematode, fungus, weed, or other form of terrestrial or aquatic plant or animal life that is injurious to health or the environment.

pest control operator. Person or company that applies pesticides as a business (e.g., exterminator); usually describes household services, not agricultural applications.

pesticide. Substances or mixture intended for preventing, destroying, repelling, or mitigating any pest. Also, any substance or mixture intended for use as a plant regulator, defoliant, or desiccant.

pesticide regulation notice. Formal notice to pesticide registrants about important changes in regulatory policy, procedures, regulations.

pesticide tolerance. The amount of pesticide residue allowed by law to remain in or on a harvested crop. EPA sets these levels well below the point where the compounds might be harmful to consumers.

PETE (polyethylene terepthalate). Thermoplastic material used in plastic soft drink and rigid containers.

petrochemicals. Organic and inorganic petroleum compounds and mixtures that include but are not limited to organic chemicals, cyclic intermediates, plastics and resins, synthetic fibers, elastomers, organic dyes, organic pigments, detergents, surface active agents, carbon black, and ammonia.

petroleum. Generally refers to crude oil or the refined products obtained from the processing of crude oil (gasoline, diesel fuel, heating oil, etc.) Petroleum also includes lease condensate, unfinished oils, and natural gas plant liquids.

petroleum derivatives. Chemicals formed when gasoline breaks down in contact with groundwater.

petroleum. Crude oil or any fraction thereof that is liquid under normal conditions of temperature and pressure. The term includes petroleum-based substances comprising a complex blend of hydrocarbons derived from crude oil through the process of separation, conversion, upgrading, and finishing, such as motor fuel, jet oil, lubricants, petroleum solvents, and used oil.

pH. An expression of the intensity of the basic or acid condition of a liquid; may range from 0 to 14, where 0 is the most acid and 7 is neutral. Natural waters usually have a pH between 6.5 and 8.5.

pharmacokinetics. The study of the way that drugs move through the body after they are swallowed or injected.

phenolphthalein alkalinity. The alkalinity in a water sample measured by the amount of standard acid needed to lower the pH to a level of 8.3 as indicated by the change of color of the phenolphthalein from pink to clear.

phenols. Organic compounds that are by-products of petroleum refining, tanning, and textile, dye, and resin manufacturing. Low concentrations cause taste and odor problems in water; higher concentrations can kill aquatic life and humans.

phishing. The practice of duping computer users into revealing their passwords or other private data under false pretenses.

phosphates. Certain chemical compounds containing phosphorus.

phosphogypsum piles (stacks). Principal by-product generated in production of phosphoric acid from phosphate rock. These piles may generate radioactive radon gas.

phosphorus. An essential chemical food element that can contribute to the eutrophication of lakes and other water bodies. Increased phosphorus levels result from discharge of phosphorus-containing materials into surface waters.

phosphorus plants. Facilities using electric furnaces to produce elemental phosphorous for commercial use, such as high-grade phosphoric acid, phosphate-based detergent, and organic chemicals use.

photochemical oxidants. Air pollutants formed by the action of sunlight on oxides of nitrogen and hydrocarbons.

photochemical smog. A type of smog first observed and named in Los Angeles, California, shortly after the Second World War. Photochemical smog has since been identified in many cities, most notably Tokyo.

photochemical smog. Air pollution caused by chemical reactions of various pollutants emitted from different sources.

photon. A particle of light that acts as an individual unit of energy.

photosynthesis. The process by which green plants make food (carbohydrates) from water and carbon dioxide, using the energy in sunlight.

photovoltaic (PV). A system that converts sunlight directly into electricity using cells made of silicon or other conductive materials. When sunlight hits the cells, a chemical reaction occurs, resulting in the release of electricity. Solar panels are an example of a photovoltaic system.

photovoltaic cells. A device, usually made from silicon, which converts some of the energy from light (radiant energy) into electrical energy. Another name for a solar cell.

photovoltaic conversion. The process by which radiant (light) energy is changed into electrical energy.

Photovoltaic (PV) Module. An integrated assembly of interconnected photovoltaic cells designed to deliver a selected level of working voltage and current at its output terminals, packaged for protection against environment degradation, and suited for incorporation in photovoltaic power systems.

physical and chemical treatment. Processes generally used in large-scale wastewater treatment facilities. Physical processes may include air-stripping or filtration. Chemical treatment includes coagulation, chlorination, or ozonation. The term can also refer to treatment of toxic materials in surface and groundwaters, oil spills, and some methods of dealing with hazardous materials on or in the ground.

phytoplankton. That portion of the plankton community comprised of tiny plants, e.g., algae, diatoms.

phytoremediation. Low-cost remediation option for sites with widely dispersed contamination at low concentrations.

phytotoxic. Harmful to plants.

phytotreatment. The cultivation of specialized plants that absorb specific contaminants from the soil through their roots or foliage. This reduces the concentration of contaminants in the soil, but incorporates them into biomasses that may be released back into the environment when the plant dies or is harvested.

picocuries per liter pCi/L). A unit of measure for levels of radon gas; becquerels per cubic meter is metric equivalent.

piezometer. A nonpumping well, generally of small diameter, for measuring the elevation of a water table.

pilot tests. Testing a cleanup technology under actual site conditions to identify potential problems prior to full-scale implementation.

pipeline, distribution. A pipeline that conveys gas from a transmission pipeline to its ultimate consumer.

plankton. Tiny plants and animals that live in water.

plasma. A high-temperature, ionized gas composed of electrons and positive ions in such number that it is electrically neutral.

plasma arc reactors. Devices that use an electric arc to thermally decompose organic and inorganic materials at ultra-high temperatures into gases and a vitrified slag residue.

plasmid. A circular piece of DNA that exists apart from the chromosome and replicates independently of it. Bacterial plasmids carry information that renders the bacteria resistant to antibiotics. Plasmids are often used in genetic engineering to carry desired genes into organisms.

plastics. Nonmetallic chemoreactive compounds molded into rigid or pliable construction materials, fabrics, and the like.

plate tower scrubber. An air pollution control device that neutralizes hydrogen chloride gas by bubbling alkaline water through holes in a series of metal plates.

plug flow. Type of flow the occurs in tanks, basins, or reactors when a slug of water moves through without ever dispersing or mixing with the rest of the water flowing through.

plugging. Act or process of stopping the flow of water, oil, or gas into or out of a formation through a borehole or well penetrating that formation.

plume. 1. A visible or measurable discharge of a contaminant from a given point of origin. Can be visible or thermal in water, or visible in the air as, for example, a plume of smoke. 2. The area of radiation leaking from a damaged reactor. 3. Area downwind within which a release could be dangerous for those exposed to leaking fumes.

plutonium. A radioactive metallic element chemically similar to uranium.

PM-10/PM-2.5. PM 10 is measure of particles in the atmosphere with a diameter of less than 10 or equal to a nominal 10 micrometers. PM-2.5 is a measure of smaller particles in the air. PM-10 has been the pollutant particulate level standard against which EPA has been measuring Clean Air Act compliance. On the basis of newer scientific findings, the Agency is considering regulations that will make PM-2.5 the new "standard."

pneumoconiosis. Health conditions characterized by permanent deposition of substantial amounts of particulate matter in the lungs and by the tissue reaction to its presence; can range from relatively harmless forms of sclerosis to the destructive fibrotic effect of silicosis.

point-of-contact measurement of exposure. Estimating exposure by measuring concentrations over time (while the exposure is taking place) at or near the place where it is occurring.

point-of-disinfectant application. The point where disinfectant is applied and water downstream of that point is not subject to recontamination by surface water runoff.

point-of-use treatment device. Treatment device applied to a single tap to reduce contaminants in the drinking water at the one faucet.

point source. A stationary location or fixed facility from which pollutants are discharged; any single identifiable source of pollution, such as a pipe, ditch, ship, ore pit, or factory smokestack.

pollen. The fertilizing element of flowering plants; background air pollutant.

pollutant. Generally, any substance introduced into the environment that adversely affects the usefulness of a resource or the health of humans, animals, or ecosystems.

pollutant pathways. Avenues for distribution of pollutants. In most buildings, for example, HVAC systems are the primary pathways although all building components can interact to affect how air movement distributes pollutants.

pollutant standard index (PSI). Indicator of one or more pollutants that may be used to inform the public about the potential for adverse health effects from air pollution in major cities.

pollute. Destroy the purity or integrity of environment.

polluter-pays-principle. A principle that equates the price charged for the use of environmental resources with the cost of damage inflicted on society by using them.

pollution. Generally, the presence of a substance in the environment that because of its chemical composition or quantity prevents the functioning of natural processes and produces undesirable environmental and health effects. Under the Clean Water Act, for example, the term has been defined as the human-made or human-induced alteration of the physical, biological, chemical, and radiological integrity of water and other media.

pollution-control strategy. Measures adopted to combat pollution both at its source and after release.

pollution prevention. 1. Identifying areas, processes, and activities which create excessive waste products or pollutants in order to reduce or prevent them through, alteration, or eliminating a process. Such activities, consistent with the Pollution Prevention Act of 1990, are conducted across all EPA programs and can involve cooperative efforts with such agencies as the Departments of Agriculture and Energy. 2. EPA has initiated a number of voluntary programs in which industrial, or commercial or "partners" join with EPA in promoting activities that conserve energy, conserve and protect water supply, reduce emissions or find ways of utilizing them as energy resources, and reduce the waste stream. Among these are Agstar, to reduce methane emissions through manure management; Climate Wise, to lower industrial greenhouse-gas emissions and energy costs; Coalbed Methane Outreach, to boost methane recovery at coal mines; Design for the Environment, to foster including environmental considerations in product design and processes; Energy Star programs, to promote energy efficiency in commercial and residential buildings, office equipment, transformers, computers, office equipment, and home appliances; Environmental Accounting, to help businesses identify environmental costs and factor them into management decision making; Green Chemistry, to promote and recognize cost-effective breakthroughs in chemistry that prevent pollution. Green Lights, to spread the use of energy-efficient lighting technologies; Indoor Environments, to reduce risks from indoor-air pollution; Landfill Methane Outreach, to develop landfill gas-to-energy projects; Natural Gas Star, to reduce methane emissions from the natural gas industry; Ruminant Livestock Methane, to reduce methane emissions from ruminant livestock; Transportation Partners, to reduce carbon dioxide emissions from the transportation sector; Voluntary Aluminum Industrial Partnership, to reduce perfluorocarbon emissions from the primary aluminum industry; WAVE, to promote efficient water use in the lodging industry; Wastewi$e, to reduce business-generated solid waste through prevention, reuse, and recycling.

polonium. A radioactive element that occurs in pitchblende and other uranium-containing ores.

polychlorinated biphenyls. A group of toxic, persistent chemicals used in electrical transformers and capacitors for insulating purposes, and in gas pipeline systems as lubricant. The sale and new use of these chemicals, also known as PCBs, were banned by law in 1979.

polyelectrolytes. Synthetic chemicals that help solids to clump during sewage treatment.

polymer. A natural or synthetic chemical structure where two or more like molecules are joined to form a more complex molecular structure (e.g., polyethylene in plastic).

polyvinyl chloride (PVC). A tough, environmentally indestructible plastic that releases hydrochloric acid when burned.

population. A group of interbreeding organisms occupying a particular space; the number of humans or other living creatures in a designated area.

population at risk. A population subgroup that is more likely to be exposed to a chemical, or is more sensitive to the chemical, than is the general population.

porosity. Degree to which soil, gravel, sediment, or rock is permeated with pores or cavities through which water or air can move.

porous pavement. Special type of pavement that allows rain and snowmelt to pass through it, thereby reducing the runoff from a site and surrounding areas. In addition, well-maintained porous pavement filters pollutants from runoff.

portal-of-entry effect. A local effect produced in the tissue or organ of first contact between a toxicant and the biological system.

post-chlorination. Addition of chlorine to plant effluent for disinfectant purposes after the effluent has been treated.

postclosure. The time period following the shutdown of a waste management or manufacturing facility; for monitoring purposes, often considered to be 30 years.

postconsumer content. Material from products that were used by consumers and would otherwise be discarded as waste. These materials are recovered through consumer recycling and include items such as newspapers, cardboard, aluminum, glass, and plastics.

postconsumer materials/waste. Materials or finished products that have served their intended use and have been diverted or recovered from waste destined for disposal, having completed their lives as consumer items. Postconsumer materials are part of the broader category of recovered materials.

postconsumer recycled glass. Glass discarded by final consumers that has been collected, cleaned, and divided, and it can be utilized in the production of new products.

postconsumer recycling. Use of materials generated from residential and consumer waste for new or similar purposes, such as converting wastepaper from offices into corrugated boxes or newsprint.

postindustrial future. The concept of an emerging society that is not dominated by dependence upon, and the needs of, manufacturing industry.

potable water. Water that is safe for drinking and cooking.

potential dose. The amount of a compound contained in material swallowed, breathed, or applied to the skin.

potentially responsible party (PRP). Any individual or company—including owners, operators, transporters or generators—potentially responsible for, or contributing to a spill or other contamination at a Superfund site. Whenever possible, through administrative and legal actions, EPA requires PRPs to clean up hazardous sites they have contaminated.

potentiation. The ability of one chemical to increase the effect of another chemical.

potentiometric surface. The surface to which water in an aquifer can rise by hydrostatic pressure.

power. The rate at which energy is transferred. Electrical energy is usually measured in watts. Also used for a measurement of capacity.

power degradation. The loss of power when electricity is sent over long distances.

power-generating efficiency. The percentage of the total energy content of a power plant's fuel, which is converted into electric energy. The remaining energy is lost to the environment as heat.

power plant. A facility where power, especially electricity, is generated.

Precautionary Principle. A principle adopted by the UN Conference on Environment and Development (the Earth Summit) 1992, that in order to protect the environment, a precautionary approach should be widely applied. When information about potential risks is incomplete, basing decisions about the best ways to manage or reduce risks on a preference for avoiding unnecessary health risks instead of on unnecessary economic expenditures.

prechlorination. The addition of chlorine at the headworks of a treatment plant prior to other treatment processes. Done mainly for disinfection and control of tastes, odors, and aquatic growths, and to aid in coagulation and settling.

precipitate. A substance separated from a solution or suspension by chemical or physical change.

precipitation. Removal of hazardous solids from liquid waste to permit safe disposal; removal of particles from airborne emissions as in rain (e.g., acid precipitation).

precipitator. Pollution control device that collects particles from an air stream.

preconsumer content. Excess by-products, or damaged materials, generated during manufacturing processes that are recovered and used as inputs in a manufacturing process, for instance, rejected materials or packaging trimmings.

preconsumer materials/waste. Materials generated in manufacturing and converting processes such as manufacturing scrap and trimmings and cuttings. Includes print overruns, overissue publications, and obsolete inventories.

precursor. In photochemistry, a compound antecedent to a pollutant. For example, volatile organic compounds (VOCs) and nitric oxides of nitrogen react in sunlight to form ozone or other photochemical oxidants. As such, VOCs and oxides of nitrogen are precursors.

preharvest interval. The time between the last pesticide application and harvest of the treated crops.

preliminary assessment. The process of collecting and reviewing available information about a known or suspected waste site or release.

prescriptive. Water rights, which are acquired by diverting water and putting it to use in accordance with specified procedures, for example, filing a request with a state agency to use unused water in a stream, river, or lake.

pressed wood products. Materials used in building and furniture construction that are made from wood veneers, particles, or fibers bonded together with an adhesive under heat and pressure.

pressure sewers. A system of pipes in which water, wastewater, or other liquid is pumped to a higher elevation.

pressure, static. In flowing air, the total pressure minus velocity pressure, pushing equally in all directions.

pressure, total. In flowing air, the sum of the static and velocity pressures.

pressure, velocity. In flowing air, the pressure due to velocity and density of air.

pressurized water reactor. A reactor in which water, heated by nuclear energy, is kept at high pressure to prevent the water from boiling. Steam is then generated in a secondary coolant loop.

pretreatment. Processes used to reduce, eliminate, or alter the nature of wastewater pollutants from nondomestic sources before they are discharged into publicly owned treatment works (POTWs).

prevalent levels. Levels of airborne contaminant occurring under normal conditions.

prevalent level samples. Air samples taken under normal conditions (also known as ambient background samples).

prevention of significant deterioration (PSD). EPA program in which state and/or federal permits are required in order to restrict emissions from new or modified sources in places where air quality already meets or exceeds primary and secondary ambient air quality standards.

primacy. Having the primary responsibility for administering and enforcing regulations.

primary drinking water regulation. Applies to public water systems and specifies a contaminant level, which, in the judgment of the EPA administrator, will not adversely affect human health.

primary effect. An effect where the stressor acts directly on the ecological component of interest, not on other parts of the ecosystem.

primary standards. National ambient air quality standards designed to protect human health with an adequate margin for safety.

primary treatment. First stage of wastewater treatment in which solids are removed by screening and settling.

primary waste treatment. First steps in wastewater treatment; screens and sedimentation tanks are used to remove most materials that float or will settle. Primary treatment removes about 30 percent of carbonaceous biochemical oxygen demand from domestic sewage.

prime mover. The engine, turbine, water wheel, or similar machine that drives an electric generator; or, for reporting purposes, a device that converts energy to electricity directly (e.g., photovoltaic solar and fuel cells).

principal organic hazardous constituents (POHCs). Hazardous compounds monitored during an incinerator's trial burn, selected for high concentration in the waste feed and difficulty of combustion.

prions. Microscopic particles made of protein that can cause disease.

prior appropriation. A doctrine of water law that allocates the rights to use water on a first-come, first-served basis.

privacy policy. Business policies that explain what use of the company's technology is permissible and how the business will monitor employee activities.

probability of detection. The likelihood, expressed as a percentage, that a test method will correctly identify a leaking tank.

process. Course of action, proceeding, especially of a series of operations in manufacture or production.

process heating. The direct-process end use in which energy is used to raise the temperature of substances involved in the manufacturing process.

process variable. A physical or chemical quantity that is usually measured and controlled in the operation of a water treatment plant or industrial plant.

process verification. Verifying that process raw materials, water usage, waste treatment processes, production rate, and other facts relative to quantity and quality of pollutants contained in discharges are substantially described in the permit application and the issued permit.

process wastewater. Any water that comes into contact with any raw material, product, by-product, or waste.

process weight. Total weight of all materials, including fuel, used in a manufacturing process; used to calculate the allowable particulate emission rate.

producers. Plants that perform photosynthesis and provide food to consumers.

product level. The level of a product in a storage tank.

product water. Water that has passed through a water treatment plant and is ready to be delivered to consumers.

production tax credit (PTC). An inflation-adjusted 1.5 cents per kilowatt hour payment for electricity produced using qualifying renewable energy sources.

production, oil and gas. The lifting of oil and gas to the surface and gathering, treating, field processing (as in the case of processing gas to extract liquid hydrocarbons), and field storage.

products of incomplete combustion (PICs). Organic compounds formed by combustion. Usually generated in small amounts and sometimes toxic, PICs are heat-altered versions of the original material fed into the incinerator (e.g., charcoal is a PIC from burning wood).

program impact statements. The adoption of Environmental Impact Assessment procedures in respect to complete programs, or in respect of the broader task of policy formulations.

progress. Move forward, onward, further; advance or develop. It is usually implied that progress leads to something better, bigger or more, or to another state or form.

project XL. An EPA initiative to give states and the regulated community the flexibility to develop comprehensive strategies as alternatives to multiple current regulatory requirements in order to exceed compliance and increase overall environmental benefits.

propane (C^3H^8). A normally gaseous straight-chain hydrocarbon. It is a colorless paraffinic gas that boils at a temperature of $-43.67°F$. It is extracted from natural gas or refinery gas streams.

propellant. Liquid in a self-pressurized pesticide product that expels the active ingredient from its container.

proportionate mortality ratio (PMR). The number of deaths from a specific cause in a specific period of time per 100 deaths from all causes in the same time period.

proposed plan. A plan for a site cleanup that is available to the public for comment.

proteins. Complex nitrogenous organic compounds of high molecular weight made of amino acids; essential for growth and repair of animal tissue. Many, but not all, proteins are enzymes.

protocol. A series of formal steps for conducting a test.

protoplast. A membrane-bound cell from which the outer wall has been partially or completely removed. The term often is applied to plant cells.

protozoa. One-celled animals that are larger and more complex than bacteria. May cause disease.

public comment period. The time allowed for the public to express its views and concerns regarding an action by EPA (e.g., a Federal Register Notice of proposed rulemaking, a public notice of a draft permit, or a Notice of Intent to Deny).

public health approach. Regulatory and voluntary focus on effective and feasible risk management actions at the national and community level to reduce human exposures and risks, with priority given to reducing exposures with the biggest impacts in terms of the number affected and severity of effect.

public health. The art and science of preventing disease, prolonging life, and promoting health and well-being through public administration and community efforts.

public health context. The incidence, prevalence, and severity of diseases in communities or populations and the factors that account for them, including infections, exposure to pollutants, and other exposures or activities.

public hearing. A formal meeting wherein EPA officials hear the public's views and concerns about an EPA action or proposal. The EPA is required to consider such comments when evaluating its actions. Public hearings must be held upon request during the public comment period.

public notice. Notification by the EPA informing the public of agency actions such as the issuance of a draft permit or scheduling of a hearing. The EPA is required to ensure proper public notice, including publication in newspapers and broadcast over radio and television stations. In the safe drinking water program, water suppliers are required to publish and broadcast notices when pollution problems are discovered.

public utility regulatory policies act of 1978 (PURPA). One part of the National Energy Act, PURPA contains measures designed to encourage the conservation of energy, more efficient use of resources, and equitable rates. Principal among these were suggested retail rate reforms and new incentives for production of electricity by cogenerators and users of renewable resources.

public water system. A system that provides piped water for human consumption to at least 15 service connections or regularly serves 25 individuals.

publicly owned treatment works (POTWs). A waste-treatment works owned by a state, unit of local government, or Indian tribe, usually designed to treat domestic wastewaters.

pumped storage. A method of storing and producing electricity to supply high peak demands by moving water between reservoirs at different elevations.

pumped-storage hydroelectric plant. A plant that usually generates electric energy during peak load periods by using water previously pumped into an elevated storage reservoir during off-peak periods when excess generating capacity is available to do so. When additional generating capacity is needed, the water can be released from the reservoir through a conduit to turbine generators located in a power plant at a lower level.

pumping station. Mechanical device installed in a sewer or water system or other liquid-carrying pipelines to move the liquids to a higher level.

pumping test. A test conducted to determine aquifer or well characteristics.

purging. Removing stagnant air or water from sampling zone or equipment prior to sample collection.

putrefaction. Biological decomposition of organic matter; associated with anaerobic conditions.

putrescible. Able to rot quickly enough to cause odors and attract flies.

pyrolysis. The decomposition of biomass at very high temperatures. It results in a mixture of solids (char), liquids (oxygenated oils), and gases (methane, carbon monoxide, and carbon dioxide).

pyrolysis. Decomposition of a chemical by extreme heat.

Q

quadrillion btu. One quadrillion (10^{15} = 10 to the 15th power) British thermal units (Btu).

qualifying (or qualified) facility (QF). A cogeneration or small power production facility that meets certain ownership, operating, and efficiency criteria established by the Federal Energy Regulatory Commission (FERC) pursuant to the Public Utility Regulatory Policies Act of 1978 (PURPA).

qualitative use assessment. Report summarizing the major uses of a pesticide including percentage of crop treated, and amount of pesticide used on a site.

quality assurance/quality control. A system of procedures, checks, audits, and corrective actions to ensure that all EPA research design and performance, environmental monitoring and sampling, and other technical and reporting activities are of the highest achievable quality.

quality of life. A concept embracing a miscellany of desirable things not always recognized, or adequately recognized, in the marketplace.

quench tank. A water-filled tank used to cool incinerator residues or hot materials during industrial processes.

R

radiant energy. Any form of energy radiating from a source in waves.

radiation. Any high-speed transmission of energy in the form of particles or electromagnetic waves. Also known as radiant energy.

radiation standards. Regulations that set maximum exposure limits for protection of the public from radioactive materials.

radioactive decay. Spontaneous change in an atom by emission of charged particles and/or gamma rays; also known as radioactive disintegration and radioactivity.

radioactive element. An element whose atoms have unstable nuclei that stabilizes itself by giving off radiation.

radioactive substances. Substances that emit ionizing radiation.

radioactive waste. Any waste that emits energy as rays, waves, streams or energetic particles. Radioactive materials are often mixed with hazardous waste, from nuclear reactors, research institutions, or hospitals.

radioactivity. The property possessed by some elements, such as uranium, of giving off alpha, beta, or gamma rays.

radioisotopes. Chemical variants of radioactive elements with potentially oncogenic, teratogenic, and mutagenic effects on the human body.

radionuclide. Radioactive particle, human-made (anthropogenic) or natural, with a distinct atomic weight number. Can have a long life as soil or water pollutant.

radius of influence. The radial distance from the center of a wellbore to the point where there is no lowering of the water table or potentiometric surface (the edge of the cone of depression); the radial distance from an extraction well that has adequate airflow for effective removal of contaminants when a vacuum is applied to the extraction well.

radius of vulnerability zone. The maximum distance from the point of release of a hazardous substance in which the airborne concentration could reach the level of concern under specified weather conditions.

radon. A colorless, odorless, naturally occurring, radioactive, inert, gaseous element formed by radioactive decay of radium atoms. Radon typically moves up through the ground to the air above and into a home through cracks and other holes in the foundation. Radon testing is recommended for most homes because radon is the second-leading cause of lung cancer.

radon daughters/radon progeny. Short-lived radioactive decay products of radon that decay into longer-lived lead isotopes that can attach themselves to airborne dust and other particles and, if inhaled, damage the linings of the lungs.

radon decay products. A term used to refer collectively to the immediate products of the radon decay chain. These include Po-218, Pb-214, Bi-214, and Po-214, which have an average combined half-life of about 30 minutes.

rain barrel. Mosquito-proof container used to collect and store rainwater that would otherwise wind up in storm drains and streams. The rain collected provides free "soft water" to homeowners—containing no chlorine, lime, or calcium—that can be used to water gardens and houseplants, or for car and window washing.

rain garden. A planted depression that allows rainwater runoff from impervious urban areas such as roofs, driveways, walkways, and compacted lawn areas the opportunity to be absorbed. This reduces rain runoff by allowing stormwater to soak into the ground (as opposed to flowing into storm drains and surface waters which causes erosion, water pollution, flooding, and diminished groundwater). Native plants are recommended for rain gardens because they generally don't require fertilizer and are more tolerant of the local climate, soil, and water conditions.

rainbow report. Comprehensive document giving the status of all pesticides now or ever in registration or special reviews. Known as the "rainbow report" because chapters are printed on different colors of paper.

rainforest. A dense, luxuriant, closed mesomorphic community; a global vegetation type containing many tree species associated with high rainfall and humidity.

rasp. A machine that grinds waste into a manageable material and helps prevent odor.

raw agricultural commodity. An unprocessed human food or animal feed crop (e.g., raw carrots, apples, corn, or eggs.)

raw sewage. Untreated wastewater and its contents.

raw water. Intake water prior to any treatment or use.

reactivity. Refers to those hazardous wastes that are normally unstable and readily undergo violent chemical change but do not explode.

reactor core. Part of a nuclear power station, the structure inside in which fission occurs in millions of atomic nuclei, producing huge amounts of heat energy.

reaeration. Introduction of air into the lower layers of a reservoir. As the air bubbles form and rise through the water, the oxygen dissolves into the water and replenishes the dissolved oxygen. The rising bubbles also cause the lower waters to rise to the surface where they take on oxygen from the atmosphere.

real-time monitoring. Monitoring and measuring environmental developments with technology and communications systems that provide time-relevant information to the public in an easily understood format people can use in day-to-day decision making about their health and the environment.

reasonable further progress. Annual incremental reductions in air pollutant emissions as reflected in a state implementation plan that the EPA deems sufficient to provide for the attainment of the applicable national ambient air quality standards by the statutory deadline.

reasonable maximum exposure. The maximum exposure reasonably expected to occur in a population.

reasonable worst case. An estimate of the individual dose, exposure, or risk level received by an individual in a defined population that is greater than the 90th percentile but less than that received by anyone in the 98th percentile in the same population.

reasonably available control measures (RACM). A broadly defined term referring to technological and other measures for pollution control.

reasonably available control technology (RACT). Control technology that is reasonably available, and both technologically and economically feasible. Usually applied to existing sources in nonattainment areas; in most cases is less stringent than new source performance standards.

recarbonization. Process in which carbon dioxide is bubbled into water being treated to lower the pH.

receiver panel (solar). A panel that contains a battery of solar cells.

receiving waters. A river, lake, ocean, stream, or other watercourse into which wastewater or treated effluent is discharged.

receptor. Ecological entity exposed to a stressor.

recharge area. A land area in which water reaches the zone of saturation from surface infiltration, such as where rainwater soaks through the earth to reach an aquifer.

recharge rate. The quantity of water per unit of time that replenishes or refills an aquifer.

recharge. The process by which water is added to a zone of saturation, usually by percolation from the soil surface, for example, the recharge of an aquifer.

reclaimed materials. Waste materials and by-products that have been recovered or diverted from the waste stream for reuse.

reclaimed water. Treated wastewater that can be used for beneficial purposes, such as irrigating certain plants.

reclamation. (In recycling) Restoration of materials found in the waste stream to a beneficial use, which may be for purposes other than the original use.

recombinant bacteria. A microorganism whose genetic makeup has been altered by deliberate introduction of new genetic elements. The offspring of these altered bacteria also contain these new genetic elements, that is, they "breed true."

recombinant DNA. The new DNA that is formed by combining pieces of DNA from different organisms or cells.

recommended maximum contaminant level (RMCL). The maximum level of a contaminant in drinking water at which no known or anticipated adverse effect on human health would occur and that includes an adequate margin of safety. Recommended levels are nonenforceable health goals.

reconstructed source. Facility in which components are replaced to such an extent that the fixed capital cost of the new components exceeds 50 percent of the capital cost of constructing a comparable brand-new facility. New-source performance standards may be applied to sources reconstructed after the proposal of the standard if it is technologically and economically feasible to meet the standards.

reconstruction of dose. Estimating exposure after it has occurred by using evidence within an organism such as chemical levels in tissue or fluids.

record of decision (ROD). A public document that explains which cleanup alternative(s) will be used at National Priorities List sites where, under CERCLA, trust funds pay for the cleanup.

recovery rate. Percentage of usable recycled materials that have been removed from the total amount of municipal solid waste generated in a specific area or by a specific business.

recycle/reuse. Minimizing waste generation by recovering and reprocessing usable products that might otherwise become waste (i.e., recycling of aluminum cans, paper, and bottles, etc.).

recycled-content materials. Materials that contain pre- or post-consumer recycled content. Purchasing recycled products creates markets for the recovered materials, conserves natural resources and energy, and reduces waste.

recycling. The process of converting materials that are no longer useful as designed or intended into a new product.

recycling and reuse business assistance centers. Located in state solid-waste or economic-development agencies, these centers provide recycling businesses with customized and targeted assistance.

recycling economic development advocates. Individuals hired by state or tribal economic development offices to focus financial, marketing, and permitting resources on creating recycling businesses.

recycling mill. Facility where recovered materials are remanufactured into new products.

recycling technical assistance partnership national network. A national information-sharing resource designed to help businesses and manufacturers increase their use of recovered materials.

red border. An EPA document undergoing review before being submitted for final management decision making.

red tide. A proliferation of a marine plankton, toxic and often fatal to fish, perhaps stimulated by the addition of nutrients. A tide can be red, green, or brown, depending on the coloration of the plankton.

redemption program. Program in which consumers are monetarily compensated for the collection of recyclable materials, generally through prepaid deposits or taxes on beverage containers. In some states or localities, legislation has enacted redemption programs to help prevent roadside litter.

reduction. The addition of hydrogen, removal of oxygen, or addition of electrons to an element or compound.

reductionism. Analysis of complex things into simpler constituents; view that a system can be fully understood in terms of its isolated parts; an idea in terms of simple concepts.

reentry interval. The period of time immediately following the application of a pesticide during which unprotected workers should not enter a field.

reentry. (In indoor air program) Refers to air exhausted from a building that is immediately brought back into the system through the air intake and other openings.

reference dose (RfD). The RfD is a numerical estimate of a daily oral exposure to the human population, including sensitive subgroups such as children, that is not likely to cause harmful effects during a lifetime. RfDs are generally used for health effects that are thought to have a threshold or low-dose limit for producing effects.

refine. Purify, clarify; make elegant or cultured, imbue with delicacy of feeling or taste.

refined petroleum products. Refined petroleum products include but are not limited to gasoline, kerosene, distillates (including No. 2 fuel oil), liquefied petroleum gas, asphalt, lubricating oils, diesel fuels, and residual fuels.

refinery. An industrial plant that heats crude oil (petroleum) so that it separates into chemical components, which are then made into more useful substances.

reformulated gasoline. Gasoline with a different composition from conventional gasoline (e.g., lower aromatics content) that cuts air pollutants.

refrigeration. To make or keep food cold or cool by using a refrigerator.

refueling emissions. Emissions released during vehicle refueling.

refuse reclamation. Conversion of solid waste into useful products, for example, composting organic wastes to make soil conditioners or separating aluminum and other metals for recycling.

regeneration. Manipulation of cells to cause them to develop into whole plants.

regional response team (RRT). Representatives of federal, local, and state agencies who may assist in coordination of activities at the request of the on-scene coordinator before and during a significant pollution incident such as an oil spill, major chemical release, or Superfund response.

registrant. Any manufacturer or formulator who obtains registration for a pesticide active ingredient or product.

registration. Formal listing with the EPA of a new pesticide before it can be sold or

distributed. Under the Federal Insecticide, Fungicide, and Rodenticide Act, the EPA is responsible for registration (premarket licensing) of pesticides on the basis of data demonstrating no unreasonable adverse effects on human health or the environment when applied according to approved label directions.

registration standards. Published documents that include summary reviews of the data available on a pesticide's active ingredient, data gaps, and the Agency's existing regulatory position on the pesticide.

regularity impact statement. As distinct from an environmental impact statement, an assessment of the likely costs and benefits of regulations created under a wide range of legislation.

regulated asbestos-containing material (RACM). Friable asbestos material or nonfriable ACM that will be or has been subjected to sanding, grinding, cutting, or abrading or has crumbled, or been pulverized or reduced to powder in the course of demolition or renovation operations.

regulated medical waste. Under the Medical Waste Tracking Act of 1988, any solid waste generated in the diagnosis, treatment, or immunization of human beings or animals, in research pertaining thereto, or in the production or testing of biologicals. Included are cultures and stocks of infectious agents; human blood and blood products; human pathological body wastes from surgery and autopsy; contaminated animal carcasses from medical research; waste from patients with communicable diseases; and all used sharp implements, such as needles and scalpels, and certain unused sharps.

relationship. The connection(s) between things.

relative ecological sustainability. Ability of an ecosystem to maintain relative ecological integrity indefinitely.

relative permeability. The permeability of a rock to gas, NAPL (Non-Aqueous Phase Liquid), or water, when any two or more are present.

relative risk assessment. Estimating the risks associated with different stressors or management actions.

release. Any spilling, leaking, pumping, pouring, emitting, emptying, discharging, injecting, escaping, leaching, dumping, or disposing into the environment of a hazardous or toxic chemical or extremely hazardous substance.

remedial action (RA). The actual construction or implementation phase of a Superfund site cleanup that follows remedial design.

remedial design. A phase of remedial action that follows the remedial investigation/feasibility study and includes development of engineering drawings and specifications for a site cleanup.

remedial investigation. An in-depth study designed to gather data needed to determine the nature and extent of contamination at a Superfund site; establish site cleanup criteria; identify preliminary alternatives for remedial action; and support technical and cost analyses of alternatives. The remedial investigation is usually done with the feasibility study. Together they are usually referred to as the RI/FS.

remedial project manager (RPM). The EPA or state official responsible for overseeing on-site remedial action.

remedial response. Long-term action that stops or substantially reduces a release or threat of a release of hazardous substances that is serious but not an immediate threat to public health.

remediation. Cleanup or other methods used to remove or contain a toxic spill or hazardous materials from a Superfund site; for the Asbestos Hazard Emergency Response program, abatement methods including evaluation, repair, enclosure, encapsulation, or removal of greater than 3 linear feet or square feet of asbestos-containing materials from a building.

remote sensing. The use of satellite sensors to provide data on many of the Earth's features such as topography, soil type, vegetation, surface water, coastal resources, the oceans, atmospheric conditions, and pollution.

removal action. Short-term immediate actions taken to address releases of hazardous substances that require expedited response; remove sulfur, ash, silicone, and other substances; usually briquetted and coated with a sealant made from coal.

renewable. Used to describe cyclic resources.

renewable energy. Energy derived from nonfossil fuel resources (such as solar, wind, or geothermal energy) that can be replenished in full without a loss of quality; separate from sustainable energy because of emissions or other unsustainable impacts of the process of creating renewable energy.

renewable energy production incentive (REPI). Incentive established by the Energy Policy Act available to renewable energy power projects owned by a state or local government or nonprofit electric cooperative.

renewable energy resources. Energy resources that are naturally replenishing but flow-limited. They are virtually inexhaustible in duration but limited in the amount of energy that is available per unit of time. Renewable energy resources include, biomass, hydro, geothermal, solar, wind, ocean thermal, wave action, and tidal action.

renewable energy sources. Fuels that can be easily made or "renewed." We can never use up renewable fuels. Types of renewable fuels are hydropower (water), solar, wind, geothermal, and biomass.

renewable portfolio standard (RPS). A mandate requiring that renewable energy provide a certain percentage of total energy generation or consumption.

renewable resource. Those resources with short cycling times, that is, the length of time required to replace a given quantity of a resource that has been used with an equivalent quantity in a similar form.

repeat compliance period. Any subsequent compliance period after the initial one.

reportable quantity (RQ). Quantity of a hazardous substance that triggers reports under CERCLA. If a substance exceeds its RQ, the release must be reported to the National Response Center, the SERC, and community emergency coordinators for areas likely to be affected.

repowering. Rebuilding and replacing major components of a power plant instead of building a new one.

representative sample. A portion of material or water that is as nearly identical in content and consistency as possible to that in the larger body of material or water being sampled.

reregistration. The reevaluation and relicensing of existing pesticides originally registered prior to current scientific and regulatory standards. EPA reregisters pesticides through its Registration Standards Program.

reserve capacity. Extra treatment capacity built into solid waste and wastewater treatment plants and interceptor sewers to accommodate flow increases due to future population growth.

reservoir. Any natural or artificial holding area used to store, regulate, or control water.

residential sector. An energy-consuming sector of the economy that consists of living quarters for private households. Common uses of energy associated with this sector include space heating, water heating, air-conditioning, lighting, refrigeration, cooking, and running a variety of other appliances. The residential sector is made up of homes, apartments, condominiums, etc. The residential sector excludes institutional living quarters.

residential use. Pesticide application in and around houses, office buildings, apartment buildings, motels, and other living or working areas.

residential waste. Waste generated in single and multifamily homes, including newspapers, clothing, disposable tableware, food packaging, cans, bottles, food scraps, and yard trimmings other than those that are diverted to backyard composting.

residual. Amount of a pollutant remaining in the environment after a natural or technological process has taken place; such as, the sludge remaining after initial wastewater treatment, or particulates remaining in air after it passes through a scrubbing or other process.

residual risk. The extent of health risk from air pollutants remaining after application of the Maximum Achievable Control Technology (MACT).

residual saturation. Saturation level below which fluid drainage will not occur.

residue. The dry solids remaining after the evaporation of a sample of water or sludge.

resistance. For plants and animals, the ability to withstand poor environmental conditions or attacks by chemicals or disease. May be inborn or acquired.

resource. Anything that can be used to provide the means to satisfy human needs and wants.

resource conservation. Conserving natural resources and energy use by managing materials more efficiently. Three primary strategies for effectively managing materials and waste are to reduce, reuse, and recycle.

resource recovery. The process of obtaining matter or energy from materials formerly discarded.

response action. 1. Generic term for actions taken in response to actual or potential health-threatening environmental events such as spills, sudden releases, and asbestos abatement/management problems. A CERCLA-authorized action involving either a short-term removal action or a long-term removal response. This may include but is not limited to removing hazardous materials from a site to an EPA-approved hazardous waste facility for treatment; containment or treating the waste on-site; identifying and removing the sources of groundwater contamination and halting further migration of contaminants. Any of the following actions taken in school buildings in response to AHERA to reduce the risk of exposure to asbestos. removal, encapsulation, enclosure, repair, and operations and maintenance.

responsible practices. Business practices that exemplify corporate responsibility.

responsiveness summary. A summary of oral and/or written public comments received by EPA during a comment period on key EPA documents, and EPA's response to those comments.

restoration. Give back (attempt to) bring back to original state, to former state or condition.

restricted entry interval. The time after a pesticide application during which entry into the treated area is restricted.

restricted use. A pesticide may be classified (under FIFRA regulations) for restricted use if it requires special handling because of its toxicity, and, if so, it may be applied only by trained, certified applicators or those under their direct supervision.

restriction enzymes. Enzymes that recognize specific regions of a long DNA molecule and cut it at those points.

retrofit. Addition of a pollution control device on an existing facility without making major changes to the generating plant. Also called backfit.

retrospective innovation. The retrieval from the past of better ways of doing things, such as the use of renewable resources, organic farming, low-energy, self-reliance, and the like.

reuse. Using a product or component of municipal solid waste in its original form more than once, such as refilling a glass bottle that has been returned or using a coffee can to hold nuts and bolts.

reverse osmosis. A treatment process used in water systems by adding pressure to force water through a semi-permeable membrane. Reverse osmosis removes most drinking water contaminants. Also used in wastewater treatment. Large-scale reverse osmosis plants are being developed.

reversible effect. An effect that is not permanent, especially adverse effects which diminish when exposure to a toxic chemical stops.

review of environmental factors. An approach often adopted when the environmental impact of a proposal is readily shown to be minor.

ribbon silicon. Single-crystal silicon derived by means of fabricating processes that produce sheets or ribbons of single-crystal silicon. These processes include edge-defined film-fed growth, dendritic web growth, and ribbon-to-ribbon growth.

ribonucleic acid (RNA). A molecule that carries the genetic message from DNA to a cellular protein-producing mechanism.

rill. A small channel eroded into the soil by surface runoff; can be easily smoothed out or obliterated by normal tillage.

Ringlemann chart. A series of shaded illustrations used to measure the opacity of air pollution emissions, ranging from light gray through black; used to set and enforce emissions standards.

riparian habitat. Areas adjacent to rivers and streams with a differing density, diversity, and productivity of plant and animal species relative to nearby uplands.

riparian rights. Entitlement of a land owner to certain uses of water on or bordering the property, including the right to prevent diversion or misuse of upstream waters. Generally a matter of state law.

risk. A measure of the probability that damage to life, health, property, and/or the environment will occur as a result of a given hazard.

risk (adverse) for endangered species. Risk to aquatic species if anticipated pesticide residue levels equal one-fifth of LD10 or one-tenth of LC50; risk to terrestrial species if anticipated pesticide residue levels equal one-fifth of LC10 or one-tenth of LC50.

risk assessment. Qualitative and quantitative evaluation of the risk posed to human health and/or the environment by the actual or potential presence and/or use of specific pollutants.

risk characterization. The last phase of the risk assessment process that estimates the potential for adverse health or ecological effects to occur from exposure to a stressor and evaluates the uncertainty involved.

risk communication. The exchange of information about health or environmental risks among risk assessors and managers, the general public, news media, interest groups, and more.

risk estimate. A description of the probability that organisms exposed to a specific dose of a chemical or other pollutant will develop an adverse response, such as cancer.

risk factor. Characteristics (e.g., race, sex, age, obesity) or variables (e.g., smoking, occupational exposure level) associated with increased probability of a toxic effect.

risk for nonendangered species. Risk to species if anticipated pesticide residue levels are equal to or greater than LC50.

risk management. The process of evaluating and selecting alternative regulatory and nonregulatory responses to risk. The selection process necessarily requires the consideration of legal, economic, and behavioral factors.

risk-based targeting. The direction of resources to those areas that have been identified as having the highest potential or actual adverse effect on human health and/or the environment.

risk-specific dose. The dose associated with a specified risk level.

river basin. The land area drained by a river and its tributaries.

rodenticide. A chemical or agent used to destroy rats or other rodent pests, or to prevent them from damaging food and crops.

rotary kiln incinerator. An incinerator with a rotating combustion chamber that keeps waste moving, thereby allowing it to vaporize for easier burning.

rough fish. Fish not prized for sport or eating, such as gar and suckers. Most are more tolerant of changing environmental conditions than are game or food species.

roundwood. Wood cut specifically for use as a fuel.

route of exposure. The avenue by which a chemical comes into contact with an organism, such as inhalation, ingestion, dermal contact, injection.

rubbish. Waste material, debris, refuse, litter; worthless material or article, trash.

running losses. Evaporation of motor vehicle fuel from the fuel tank while the vehicle is in use.

run-off. That part of precipitation, snow melt, or irrigation water that runs off the land into streams or other surface water. It can carry pollutants from the air and land into receiving waters.

R-value. A measure of insulation. The higher the R-value, the better walls and roofs will resist the transfer of heat.

S

sacrifical anode. An easily corroded material deliberately installed in a pipe or intake to give it up (sacrifice it) to corrosion while the rest of the water supply facility remains relatively corrosion free.

safe. Condition of exposure under which there is a practical certainty that no harm will result to exposed individuals.

safe water. Water that does not contain harmful bacteria, toxic materials, or chemicals, and is considered safe for drinking even if it may have taste, odor, color, and certain mineral problems.

safe yield. The annual amount of water that can be taken from a source of supply over a period of years without depleting that source beyond its ability to be replenished naturally in "wet years."

safener. A chemical added to a pesticide to keep it from injuring plants.

salinity. The percentage of salt in water.

salt water intrusion. The invasion of fresh surface or groundwater by salt water. If it comes from the ocean it may be called sea water intrusion.

salts. Minerals that water picks up as it passes through the air, over and under the ground, or from households and industry.

salvage. The utilization of waste materials.

sampling frequency. The interval between the collection of successive samples.

sanctions. Actions taken by the federal government for failure to provide or implement a state implementation plan (SIP). Such action may include withholding of highway funds and a ban on construction of new sources of potential pollution.

sand filters. Devices that remove some suspended solids from sewage. Air and bacteria decompose additional wastes filtering through the sand so that cleaner water drains from the bed.

sanitary sewers. Underground pipes that carry off only domestic or industrial waste, not storm water.

sanitary survey. An on-site review of the water sources, facilities, equipment, operation and maintenance of a public water system to evaluate the adequacy of those elements for producing and distributing safe drinking water.

sanitary water (also known as gray water). Water discharged from sinks, showers, kitchens, or other nonindustrial operations, but not from toilets.

sanitation. An important health-related branch of development embracing drainage and sewerage, sewage and sullage treatment and effluent disposal, safe and adequate domestic water supplies, avoidance of public nuisance and uncontrolled tipping, and drainage facilities for floodwater and surface run off.

saprolite. A soft, clay-rich, thoroughly decomposed rock formed in place by chemical weathering of igneous or metamorphic rock. Forms in humid, tropical, or subtropical climates.

saprophytes. Organisms living on dead or decaying organic matter that help natural decomposition of organic matter in water.

saturated zone. The area below the water table where all open spaces are filled with water under pressure equal to or greater than that of the atmosphere.

saturation. The condition of a liquid when it has taken into solution the maximum possible quantity of a given substance at a given temperature and pressure.

science advisory board (SAB). A group of external scientists who advise the EPA on science and policy.

scrap. Materials discarded from manufacturing operations that may be suitable for reprocessing.

scrap metal processor. Intermediate operating facility where recovered metal is sorted, cleaned of contaminants, and prepared for recycling.

screening. Use of screens to remove coarse floating and suspended solids from sewage.

screening risk assessment. A risk assessment performed with few data and many assumptions to identify exposures that should be evaluated more carefully for potential risk.

scrubber. An air pollution device that uses a spray of water or reactant or a dry process to trap pollutants in emissions.

seasonal energy efficiency ratio (SEER). A measure of seasonal or annual efficiency of a central air-conditioner or air conditioning heat pump. It takes into account the variations in temperature that can occur within a season, rather than a single temperature, and is the average number of Btus of cooling delivered for every watt hour of electricity. The higher the SEER, the more energy efficient the system.

secondary drinking water regulations. Nonenforceable regulations applying to public water systems and specifying the maximum contamination levels that, in the judgment of the EPA, are required to protect the public welfare. These regulations apply to any contaminants that may adversely affect the odor or appearance of such water and consequently may cause people served by the system to discontinue its use.

secondary effect. Action of a stressor on supporting components of the ecosystem, which in turn impact the ecological component of concern.

secondary materials. Materials that have been manufactured and used at least once and are to be used again.

secondary standards. National ambient air quality standards designed to protect welfare, including effects on soils, water, crops, vegetation, human-made (anthropogenic) materials, animals, wildlife, weather, visibility, and climate; damage to property; transportation hazards; economic values, and personal comfort and well-being.

secondary treatment. The second step in most publicly owned waste treatment systems in which bacteria consume the organic parts of the waste. It is accomplished by bringing together waste, bacteria, and oxygen in trickling filters or in the activated sludge process. This treatment removes floating and settleable solids and about 90 percent of the oxygen-demanding substances and suspended solids. Disinfection is the final stage of secondary treatment

secure maximum contaminant level. Maximum permissible level of a contaminant in water delivered to the free-flowing outlet of the ultimate user, or of contamination resulting from corrosion of piping and plumbing caused by water quality.

sediment. Soil, sand, and minerals washed from land into water, usually after rain. They pile up in reservoirs, rivers and harbors, destroying fish and wildlife habitat, and clouding the water so that sunlight cannot reach aquatic plants. Careless farming, mining, and building activities will expose sediment materials, allowing them to wash off the land after rainfall.

sediment yield. The quantity of sediment arriving at a specific location.

sedimentation. Letting solids settle out of wastewater by gravity during treatment.

sedimentation tanks. Wastewater tanks in which floating wastes are skimmed off and settled solids are removed for disposal.

seed protectant. A chemical applied before planting to protect seeds and seedlings from disease or insects.

seepage. Percolation of water through the soil from unlined canals, ditches, laterals, watercourses, or water storage facilities.

selective pesticide. A chemical designed to affect only certain types of pests, leaving other plants and animals unharmed.

semiconductor. Any material that has a limited capacity for conducting an electric current. Semiconductors are crystalline solids, such as silicon, that have an electrical conductivity between that of a conductor and an insulator.

semiconfined aquifer. An aquifer partially confined by soil layers of low permeability through which recharge and discharge can still occur.

semivolatile organic compounds. Organic compounds that volatilize slowly at standard temperature (20°C and 1 atm pressure).

senescence. The aging process. Sometimes used to describe lakes or other bodies of water in advanced stages of eutrophication. Also used to describe plants and animals.

septic system. An on-site system designed to treat and dispose of domestic sewage. A typical septic system consists of tank that receives waste from a residence or business and a system of tile lines or a pit for disposal of the liquid effluent (sludge) that remains after decomposition of the solids by bacteria in the tank and must be pumped out periodically.

septic tank. An underground storage tank for wastes from homes not connected to a sewer line. Waste goes directly from the home to the tank.

service connector. The pipe that carries tap water from a public water main to a building.

service line sample. A one-liter sample of water that has been standing for at least 6 hours in a service pipeline and is collected according to federal regulations.

service pipe. The pipeline extending from the water main to the building served or to the consumer's system.

set-back. Setting a thermometer to a lower temperature when the building is unoccupied to reduce consumption of heating energy. Also refers to setting the thermometer to a higher temperature during unoccupied periods in the cooling season.

settleable solids. Material heavy enough to sink to the bottom of a wastewater treatment tank.

settling chamber. A series of screens placed in the way of flue gases to slow the stream of air, thus helping gravity to pull particles into a collection device.

settling tank. A holding area for wastewater, where heavier particles sink to the bottom for removal and disposal.

sewage. The waste and wastewater produced by residential and commercial sources and discharged into sewers.

sewage sludge. Sludge produced at a publicly owned treatment works, the disposal of which is regulated under the Clean Water Act.

sewer. A channel or conduit that carries wastewater and storm-water runoff from the source to a treatment plant or receiving stream. "Sanitary" sewers carry household, industrial, and commercial waste. "Storm" sewers carry runoff from rain or snow. "Combined" sewers handle both.

sewerage. The entire system of sewage collection, treatment, and disposal.

shading coefficient. The amount of the sun's heat transmitted through a given window compared with that of a standard 1/8-inch-thick single pane of glass under the same conditions.

shaft mine. A mine that reaches the coal bed by means of a vertical shaft.

shareholder resolution. A corporate policy recommendation proposed by a shareholder holding at least $2,000 market value or 1 percent of the company's voting shares presented for a vote by other shareholders at the company's annual meeting; an increasing number of shareholder resolutions request a company and/or its board of directors to carry out responsible business practices, especially regarding social, environmental, and human rights issues.

sharps. Hypodermic needles, syringes (with or without the attached needle), Pasteur pipettes, scalpel blades, blood vials, needles with attached tubing, and culture dishes used in animal or human patient care or treatment, or in medical, research or industrial laboratories. Also included are other types of broken or unbroken glassware that were in contact with infectious agents, such as used slides and cover slips, and unused hypodermic and suture needles, syringes, and scalpel blades.

shock load. The arrival at a water treatment plant of raw water containing unusual amounts of algae, colloidal matter, color, suspended solids, turbidity, or other pollutants.

short-circuiting. When some of the water in tanks or basins flows faster than the rest; may result in shorter contact, reaction, or settling times than calculated or presumed.

short ton. A unit of weight equal to 2,000 pounds, often used to measure coal.

sick building syndrome. Building whose occupants experience acute health and/or comfort effects that appear to be linked to time spent therein, but where no specific illness or cause can be identified. Complaints can be localized in a particular room or zone, or may spread throughout the building.

signal. The volume or product-level change produced by a leak in a tank.

signal words. The words used on a pesticide label—Danger, Warning, Caution—to indicate level of toxicity.

significant deterioration. Pollution resulting from a new source in previously "clean" areas.

significant municipal facilities. Those publicly owned sewage treatment plants that discharge a million gallons per day or more and are therefore considered by states to have the potential to substantially affect the quality of receiving waters.

significant potential source of contamination. A facility or activity that stores, uses, or produces compounds with potential for significant contaminating impact if released into the source water of a public water supply.

significant violations. Violations by point source dischargers of sufficient magnitude or duration to be a regulatory priority.

silicon. A semiconductor material made from silica, purified for photovoltaic applications.

silt. Sedimentary materials composed of fine or intermediate-sized mineral particles.

silviculture. Management of forest land for timber.

single-crystal silicon (Czochralski). An extremely pure form of crystalline silicon produced by the Czochralski method of dipping a single-crystal seed into a pool of molten silicon under high vacuum conditions and slowly withdrawing a solidifying single-crystal boule rod of silicon. The boule is sawed into thin wafers and fabricated into single-crystal photovoltaic cells.

single-breath canister. Small 1 liter canister designed to capture a single breath.

sink. Place in the environment where a compound or material collects.

sinking. Controlling oil spills by using an agent to trap the oil and sink it to the bottom of the body of water where the agent and the oil are biodegraded.

sip call. EPA action requiring a state to resubmit all or part of its state implementation plan to demonstrate attainment of the required national ambient air quality standards within the statutory deadline. A SIP revision is a revision of a SIP altered at the request of EPA or on a state's initiative.

site. An area or place within the jurisdiction of the EPA and/or a state.

site assessment program. A means of evaluating hazardous waste sites through preliminary assessments and site inspections to develop a hazard ranking system score.

site inspection. The collection of information from a Superfund site to determine the extent and severity of hazards posed by the site. It follows and is more extensive than a preliminary assessment. The purpose is to gather information necessary to score the site, using the hazard ranking system, and to determine if it presents an immediate threat requiring prompt removal.

site safety plan. A crucial element in all removal actions, it includes information on equipment being used, precautions to be taken, and steps to take in the event of an on-site emergency.

siting. The process of choosing a location for a facility.

skimming. Using a machine to remove oil or scum from the surface of the water.

slow sand filtration. Passage of raw water through a bed of sand at low velocity, resulting in substantial removal of chemical and biological contaminants.

sludge. A dense, slushy, liquid-to-semifluid product that accumulates as an end result of an industrial or technological process designed to purify a substance. Industrial sludges are produced from the processing of energy-related raw materials, chemical products, water, mined ores, sewerage, and other natural and human-made products. Sludges can also form from natural processes, such as the runoff produced by rainfall, and accumulate on the bottom of bogs, streams, lakes, and tidelands.

sludge digester. Tank in which complex organic substances such as sewage sludges are biologically dredged. During these reactions, energy is released and much of the sewage is converted to methane, carbon dioxide, and water.

slurry. A watery mixture of insoluble matter resulting from some pollution control techniques.

small quantity generator (SQG-sometimes referred to as "squeegee"). Persons or enterprises that produce 220-2,200 pounds per month of hazardous waste; they are required to keep more records than conditionally exempt generators. The largest category of hazardous waste generators, SQGs, include automotive shops, dry cleaners, photographic developers, and many other small businesses. (*See* conditionally exempt generators.)

smart growth. Development, transportation, and conservation strategies that help protect the natural environment and make communities more attractive, economically stronger, and more socially diverse.

smelter. A facility that melts or fuses ore, often with an accompanying chemical change, to separate its metal content. Emissions cause pollution. "Smelting" is the process involved.

smog. Air pollution typically associated with oxidants. (*See* photochemical smog.)

smoke. Particles suspended in air after incomplete combustion.

social. Living in groups or organized communities; gregarious.

social audit. A systematic evaluation of an organization's progress toward implementing programs that are socially responsible and responsive.

social entrepreneurship. An entrepreneurial endeavor that focuses on sustainable social change, rather than merely the generation of profit.

social equity. The just, fair, and equitable distribution of resources in the operation and formation of communities.

social evolution. As distinct from biological evolution, the evolution of human society with languages, laws, customs, histories, and settlements; such evolution is comparatively short, records extending back only a few thousand years, there being no trace of humans prior to the quaternary period.

social impact assessment. A subset of environmental impact assessment, an appraisal of the effect on people of major policies, plans, programs, activities, and developments.

social return on investment (SROI). A monetary measure of the social value for a community or society yielded by a specific investment.

socially responsible investing (SRI). An investment practice that gives preference to companies that value social and environmental impacts in addition to financial gain; socially responsible investments, also known as "ethical investments," involve companies and practices that cause little or no depletion of natural assets or environmental degradation, and that do not infringe on the rights of workers, women, indigenous people, children, or animals.

soft detergents. Cleaning agents that break down in nature.

soft water. Any water that does not contain a significant amount of dissolved minerals such as salts of calcium or magnesium.

software piracy. The illegal copying of copyrighted software.

soil. The thin veneer of comparatively unconsolidated material covering large areas of the earth's surface; soil is a dynamic medium in which occur many physical, chemical, and biological processes

soil adsorption field. A subsurface area containing a trench or bed with clean stones and a system of piping through which treated sewage may seep into the surrounding soil for further treatment and disposal.

soil and water conservation practices. Control measures consisting of managerial, vegetative, and structural practices to reduce the loss of soil and water.

soil conditioner. An organic material like humus or compost that helps soil absorb water, build a bacterial community, and take up mineral nutrients.

soil erodibility. An indicator of a soil's susceptibility to raindrop impact, runoff, and other erosive processes.

soil gas. Gaseous elements and compounds in the small spaces between particles of the earth and soil. Such gases can be moved or driven out under pressure.

soil moisture. The water contained in the pore space of the unsaturated zone.

soil sterilant. A chemical that temporarily or permanently prevents the growth of all plants and animals.

solar cell. An electric cell that changes radiant energy from the sun into electrical energy by the photovoltaic process.

solar dish. A device that receives radiation collected by motorized collectors which track the sun. The collectors focus the radiation the energy at a focal point of the dish.

solar energy. The radiant energy of the sun, which can be converted into other forms of energy, such as heat or electricity.

solar power tower. The conceptual method of producing electrical energy from solar rays. It involved the focusing of a large number of solar rays on a single source (boiler), usually located on an elevated tower, to produce high temperatures. A fluid located in or passed through the source changes into steam and is used in a turbine generator to produce electrical energy.

solar spectrum. The total distribution of electromagnetic radiation emanating from the sun.

solar thermal collector. A device designed to receive solar radiation and convert it into thermal energy. Normally, a solar thermal collector includes a frame, glazing, and an absorber, together with the appropriate insulation. The heat collected by the solar thermal collector may be used immediately or stored for later use.

solar thermal heating system. Systems using concentrating collectors to focus the sun's radiant energy onto or into receivers to produce heat.

solder. Metallic compound used to seal joints between pipes. Until recently, most solder contained 50 percent lead. Use of solder containing more than 0.2 percent lead in pipes carrying drinking water is now prohibited.

sole-source aquifer. An aquifer that supplies 50 percent or more of the drinking water of an area.

solid waste. Nonliquid, nonsoluble materials ranging from municipal garbage to industrial wastes that contain complex and sometimes hazardous substances. Solid wastes also include sewage sludge, agricultural refuse, demolition wastes, and mining residues. Technically, solid waste also refers to liquids and gases in containers.

solid waste disposal. The final placement of refuse that is not salvaged or recycled.

solid waste management. The purposeful, systematic control of the generation, storage, collection, transport, separation, processing, recycling, recovery, and disposal of solid wastes in a sanitary, aesthetically acceptable, and economical manner.

solidification and stabilization. Removal of wastewater from a waste or changing it chemically to make it less permeable and susceptible to transport by water.

solubility. The amount of mass of a compound that will dissolve in a unit volume of solution. Aqueous solubility is the maximum concentration of a chemical that will dissolve in pure water at a reference temperature.

soot. Carbon dust formed by incomplete combustion.

sorption. The action of soaking up or attracting substances; process used in many pollution control systems.

source area. The location of liquid hydrocarbons or the zone of highest soil or groundwater concentrations, or both, of the chemical of concern.

source characterization measurements. Measurements made to estimate the rate of release of pollutants into the environment from a source such as an incinerator, landfill, or the like.

source reduction. Reducing the amount of materials entering the waste stream from a specific source by redesigning products or patterns of production or consumption (e.g., using returnable beverage containers).

source separation. Segregating various wastes at the point of generation (e.g., separation of paper, metal, and glass from other wastes to make recycling simpler and more efficient).

source-water protection area. The area delineated by a state for a public water supply or including numerous such suppliers, whether the source is groundwater or surface water or both.

space heating. The use of energy to generate heat for warmth in housing units using space-heating equipment. The equipment could be the main space-heating equipment or secondary space-heating equipment.

spam. Unsolicited e-mails (or junk e-mails) sent in bulk to valid e-mail accounts.

sparge or sparging. Injection of air below the water table to strip dissolved volatile organic compounds and/or oxygenate groundwater to facilitate aerobic biodegradation of organic compounds.

special local-needs (SLN) registration. Registration of a pesticide product by a state agency for a specific use that is not federally registered. However, the active ingredient must be federally registered for other uses. The special use is specific to that state and is often minor, thus may not warrant the additional cost of a full federal registration process. SLN registration cannot be issued for new active ingredients, food-use active ingredients without tolerances, or for a canceled registration. The products cannot be shipped across state lines.

special review. Formerly known as rebuttable presumption against registration (RPAR), this is the regulatory process through which existing pesticides suspected of posing unreasonable risks to human health, nontarget organisms, or the environment are referred for review by EPA. Such review requires an intensive risk/benefit analysis with opportunity for public comment. If risk is found to outweigh social and economic benefits, regulatory actions can be initiated, ranging from label revisions and use-restriction to cancellation or suspended registration.

special waste. Items such as household hazardous waste, bulky wastes (refrigerators, pieces of furniture, etc.) tires, and used oil.

species. A reproductively isolated aggregate of interbreeding organisms having common attributes and usually designated by a common name. An organism belonging to belonging to such a category.

specific conductance. Rapid method of estimating the dissolved solid content of a water supply by testing its capacity to carry an electrical current.

specific yield. The amount of water a unit volume of saturated permeable rock will yield when drained by gravity.

spectrum of electromagnetic radiation. The name that scientists give to a bunch of types of radiation when they want to talk about them as a group. The types of radiation include the full range of frequencies, from radio waves to gamma waves, which characterize light.

spent fuel. Irradiated fuel that is permanently discharged from a nuclear reactor.

Except for possible reprocessing, this fuel must eventually be removed from its temporary storage location at the reactor site and placed in a permanent repository. Spent fuel is typically measured either in metric tons of heavy metal (i.e., only the heavy metal content of the spent fuel is considered) or in metric tons of initial heavy metal (essentially, the initial mass of the fuel before irradiation). The difference between these two quantities is the weight of the fission products.

spent liquor. The liquid residue left after an industrial process; can be a component of waste materials used as fuel.

spent sulfite liquor. End product of pulp and paper manufacturing processes that contains lignins and has a high moisture content; often reused in recovery boilers. Similar to black liquor.

spill prevention, containment, and countermeasures plan (SPCP). Plan covering the release of hazardous substances as defined in the Clean Water Act.

spoil. Dirt or rock removed from its original location—destroying the composition of the soil in the process—as in strip-mining, dredging, or construction.

spontaneous. Acting, done, occurring, without external cause. That which emerges from within, inherent, instinctive or intuitive, without obvious motive.

sprawl. Unplanned development of open land.

spray tower scrubber. A device that sprays alkaline water into a chamber where acid gases are present to aid in neutralizing the gas.

spring. Groundwater seeping out of the earth where the water table intersects the ground surface.

spring melt/thaw. The process whereby warm temperatures melt winter snow and ice. Because various forms of acid deposition may have been stored in the frozen water, the melt can result in abnormally large amounts

of acidity entering streams and rivers, sometimes causing fish kills.

stabilization. Conversion of the active organic matter in sludge into inert, harmless material.

stable air. A motionless mass of air that holds, instead of dispersing, pollutants.

stack. A chimney, smokestack, or vertical pipe that discharges used air.

stack effect. Flow of air resulting from warm air rising, creating a positive pressure area at the top of a building and negative pressure area at the bottom. This effect can overpower the mechanical system and disrupt building ventilation and air circulation.

stage II controls. Systems placed on service station gasoline pumps to control and capture gasoline vapors during refueling.

stagnation. Lack of motion in a mass of air or water that holds pollutants in place.

stakeholder. An individual or group potentially affected by the activities of a company or organization; in sustainable business models the term includes financial shareholders as well as those affected by environmental or social factors such as suppliers, consumers, employees, the local community, and the natural environment; any organization, governmental entity, or individual that has a stake in or may be impacted by a given approach to environmental regulation, pollution prevention, energy conservation, and the like.

stakeholder engagement. The ongoing process of soliciting feedback regarding a company's business practices or major decisions from financial shareholders, as well as individuals or groups affected by corporate environmental or social practices such as suppliers, consumers, employees, and the local community.

standard industrial classification code. Also known as SIC codes, a method of grouping industries with similar products or services and assigning codes to these groups.

standard sample. The part of finished drinking water that is examined for the presence of coliform bacteria.

standards. Government or privately created lists of social and environmental criteria used to regulate or evaluate the corporate responsibility of various companies; examples include the Global Reporting Initiative and UN Global Compact as well as indexes used by socially responsible investment firms such as CERES, Calvert, and Domini.

start of a response action. The point in time when there is a guarantee or set-aside of funding by EPA, other federal agencies, states or Principal Responsible Parties in order to begin response actions at a Superfund site.

state emergency response commission (SERC). Commission appointed by each state governor according to the requirements of SARA Title III. The SERCs designate emergency planning districts, appoint local emergency planning committees, and supervise and coordinate their activities.

state environmental goals and indication project. Program to assist state environmental agencies by providing technical and financial assistance in the development of environmental goals and indicators.

state implementation plans (SIP). EPA-approved state plans for the establishment, regulation, and enforcement of air pollution standards.

state management plan. Under FIFRA, a state management plan required by EPA to allow states, tribes, and U.S. territories the flexibility to design and implement ways to protect groundwater from the use of certain pesticides.

state of environment reports. Reports prepared by government departments or agencies on the state of the environment with their respective geographical jurisdictions.

static water depth. The vertical distance from the centerline of the pump discharge down to the surface level of the free pool while no water is being drawn from the pool or water table.

static water level. Elevation or level of the water table in a well when the pump is not operating. The level or elevation to which water would rise in a tube connected to an artesian aquifer or basin in a conduit under pressure.

stationary source. A fixed-site producer of pollution, mainly power plants and other facilities using industrial combustion processes. (*See* point source.)

status quo. Status is social position, rank relative to others; position of affairs; quo is in which, so unchanged, previous. "The way things are."

steam. Water in vapor form; used as the working fluid in steam turbines and heating systems.

steam generator. A generator in which the prime movers (turbines) are powered by steam.

stem-cell research. Research on nonspecialized cells that have the capacity to self-renew and to differentiate into more mature cells.

sterilization. The removal or destruction of all microorganisms, including pathogenic and other bacteria, vegetative forms, and spores.

sterilizer. One of three groups of antimicrobials registered by the EPA for public health uses. The EPA considers an antimicrobial to be a sterilizer when it destroys or eliminates all forms of bacteria, viruses, and fungi and their spores. Because spores are considered the most difficult form of microorganism to destroy, the EPA considers the term sporicide to be synonymous with sterilizer.

stewardship. Function of trust and care over property of others, as in a great house or estate.

storage. Temporary holding of waste pending treatment or disposal, as in containers, tanks, waste piles, and surface impoundments.

storm sewer. A system of pipes (separate from sanitary sewers) that carries water runoff from buildings and land surfaces.

stormwater. Water from precipitation and snowmelt events. Stormwater runoff is generated when precipitation flows over land or impervious surfaces and does not percolate into the ground. In the process of flowing over the land or impervious surfaces, stormwater can accumulate debris, chemicals, sediment, or other pollutants that can adversely affect water quality if the runoff is discharged into streams or lakes untreated.

strategic environmental impact assessment (EIA). The application not only to individual projects, but also to policies, plans, programs, activities, and regional land-use objectives.

strategic philanthropy. A corporate philanthropy or community giving program that maximizes positive impact in the community as well as for the company, including bolstered employee recruitment, retention, and a stronger company brand.

stratification. Separating into layers.

stratigraphy. Study of the formation, composition, and sequence of sediments, whether consolidated or not.

stratosphere. The portion of the atmosphere 10-to-25 miles above the earth's surface.

streaming. A customized, on-demand radio service developed by music distributors to protect their copyrights to music.

stressors. Physical, chemical, or biological entities that can induce adverse effects on ecosystems or human health.

strip cropping. Growing crops in a systematic arrangement of strips or bands that serve as barriers to wind and water erosion.

strip mining. A process that uses machines to scrape soil or rock away from mineral deposits just under the earth's surface.

structural deformation. Distortion in walls of a tank after liquid has been added or removed.

structurally insulated panels (SIPs). Prefabricated insulated structural elements for use in home walls, ceilings, floors, and roofs, which provide enhanced insulation compared to more traditional construction methods.

subchronic. Of intermediate duration, usually used to describe studies or periods of exposure lasting between 5 and 90 days.

subchronic exposure. Multiple or continuous exposures lasting for approximately 10 percent of an experimental specie's lifetime, usually over a three-month period.

submerged aquatic vegetation. Vegetation that lives at or below the water surface; an important habitat for young fish and other aquatic organisms.

subsidy. Financial assistance granted by the government to firms and individuals.

subwatershed. Topographic perimeter of the catchment area of a stream tributary.

sulfur dioxide (SO2). A pungent, colorless, gas formed primarily by the combustion of fossil fuels; becomes a pollutant when present in large amounts.

sump. A pit or tank that catches liquid runoff for drainage or disposal.

superchlorination. Chlorination with doses that are deliberately selected to produce water free of combined residuals so large as to require dechlorination.

superconductivity. The abrupt and large increase in electrical conductivity exhibited by some metals as the temperature approaches absolute zero.

supercritical water. A type of thermal treatment using moderate temperatures and high pressures to enhance the ability of water to break down large organic molecules into smaller, less toxic ones. Oxygen injected during this process combines with simple organic compounds to form carbon dioxide and water.

superfund (CERCLA). A U.S. law, passed in 1980, designated to clean up hazardous or toxic waste sites. The law established a fund, supported mainly by taxes on petrochemical companies, to pay for the cleanup.

superfund innovative technology evaluation (SITE) program. EPA program to promote development and use of innovative treatment and site characterization technologies in Superfund site cleanups.

supplemental registration. An arrangement whereby a registrant licenses another company to market its pesticide product under the second company's registration.

supplier of water. Any person who owns or operates a public water supply.

supply-side economics. The use of policies such as tax cuts and business incentives to control the supply of certain goods or services.

surface impoundment. Treatment, storage, or disposal of liquid hazardous wastes in ponds.

surface mine. A coal-producing mine that is usually within a few hundred feet of the surface. Earth above or around the coal (overburden) is removed to expose the coal bed, which is then mined with surface excavation equipment, such as draglines, power shovels, bulldozers, loaders, and augers. It may also be known as an area, contour, open-pit, strip, or auger mine.

surface runoff. Precipitation, snow melt, or irrigation water in excess of what can infiltrate the soil surface and be stored in small surface depressions; a major transporter of nonpoint source pollutants in rivers, streams, and lakes.

surface uranium mines. Strip-mining operations for removal of uranium-bearing ore.

surface water. All water naturally open to the atmosphere (rivers, lakes, reservoirs, ponds, streams, impoundments, seas, estuaries, etc.)

surface water treatment rule. Rule that specifies maximum contaminant level goals for Giardia lamblia, viruses, and Legionella and promulgates filtration and disinfection requirements for public water systems using surface-water or groundwater sources under the direct influence of surface water. The regulations also specify water quality, treatment, and watershed protection criteria under which filtration may be avoided.

surfacing ACM. Asbestos-containing material that is sprayed or troweled on or otherwise applied to surfaces, such as acoustical plaster on ceilings and fireproofing materials on structural members.

surfacing material. Material sprayed or troweled onto structural members (beams, columns, or decking) for fire protection; or on ceilings or walls for fireproofing, acoustical, or decorative purposes. Includes textured plaster, and other textured wall and ceiling surfaces.

surfactant. A detergent compound that promotes lathering.

surrogate data. Data from studies of test organisms or a test substance that are used to estimate the characteristics or effects on another organism or substance.

surveillance system. A series of monitoring devices designed to check on environmental conditions.

survival. Continuing to live or exist in spite of adverse circumstances. All life evolves by the differential survival of replicating entities.

susceptibility analysis. An analysis to determine whether a public water supply is subject to significant pollution from known potential sources.

suspect material. Building material suspected of containing asbestos, such as surfacing material, floor tile, ceiling tile, thermal system insulation.

suspended loads. Specific sediment particles maintained in the water column by turbulence and carried with the flow of water.

suspended solids. Small particles of solid pollutants that float on the surface of, or are suspended in, sewage or other liquids. They resist removal by conventional means.

suspension. Suspending the use of a pesticide when the EPA deems it necessary to prevent an imminent hazard resulting from its continued use. An emergency suspension takes effect immediately; under an ordinary suspension a registrant can request a hearing before the suspension goes into effect. Such a hearing process might take six months.

suspension culture. Cells growing in a liquid nutrient medium.

sustain. Endure without giving way, stand, and continue indefinitely.

sustainability. The successful meeting of present social, economic, and environmental needs without compromising the ability of future generation to meet their own needs; derived from the most common definition of sustainability, created in 1987 at the World Commission on Environment and Development.

sustainability report. A single report integrating a business's social, economic, and economic results.

sustainable design. A process of product, service, or organizational design that complies with the principles of social, economic, and environmental sustainability.

sustainable development. Development that utilizes tools, supplies, and strategies that protect and enhance the earth's natural resources and diverse eco-systems so as to meet the social and economic needs of the present without compromising the ability to meet the needs of the future.

sustainable energy. Energy produced both from renewable resources or by use of clean production technology.

sustainable yield. The use of living resources at levels of harvesting and in ways that allow those resources to supply products and services indefinitely.

swamp. A type of wetland dominated by woody vegetation but without appreciable peat deposits. Swamps may be fresh or salt water and tidal or nontidal. (*See* wetlands.)

symbiosis. Association of two different organisms living attached or in close proximity to each other.

synchronicity. Existing or occurring at the same time. Hence, synchronicity, the occurrences of things at the same time without apparent causal link.

synergism. An interaction of two or more chemicals that results in an effect greater than the sum of their separate effects.

synergistic. The ability of things to potentiate other things. Events or processes are said to feed off each other.

synthesis. Combination, composition, putting together; building up of separate elements, components, facts, propositions, etc, into a coherent whole, especially of theory or system. Opposite of analysis.

synthetic organic chemicals (SOCs). Human-made (anthropogenic) organic chemicals. Some SOCs are volatile; others tend to stay dissolved in water instead of evaporating.

system benefits charge (SBC). A non-bypassable fee on transmission interconnection; funds are allocated among public purposes, including the development and demonstration of renewable energy technologies.

system(s). Complex whole, set of connected things or parts; organized body of things, material or other; the established political, social, or economic order.

system with a single service connection. A system that supplies drinking water to consumers via a single service line.

systemic pesticide. A chemical absorbed by an organism that interacts with the organism and makes the organism toxic to pests.

T

tail water. The runoff of irrigation water from the lower end of an irrigated field.

tailings. Residue of raw material or waste separated out during the processing of crops or mineral ores.

tailpipe standards. Emissions limitations applicable to mobile source engine exhausts.

tall oil. The oily mixture of rosin acids, fatty acids, and other materials obtained by acid treatment of the alkaline liquors from the digesting (pulping) of pine wood.

tampering. Adjusting, negating, or removing pollution control equipment on a motor vehicle.

tank far. An installation used by trunk and gathering pipeline companies, crude oil producers, and terminal operators (except refineries) to store crude oil.

tanker and barge. Vessels that transport crude oil or petroleum products.

technical assistance grant (TAG). As part of the Superfund program, Technical Assistance Grants of up to $50,000 are provided to citizens' groups to obtain assistance in interpreting information related to clean-ups at Superfund sites or those proposed for the National Priorities List. Grants are used by such groups to hire technical advisors to help them understand the site-related technical information for the duration of response activities.

technical-grade active ingredient (TGA). A pesticide chemical in pure form as it is manufactured prior to being formulated into an end-use product (e.g., wettable powders, granules, emulsifiable concentrates). Registered manufactured products composed of such chemicals are known as technical grade products.

technological change. Change in a whole system of scientific and technical knowledge, to simply change in technique; change involving fundamental scientific discoveries coupled with innovative application and far-reaching economic, social, and environmental consequences.

technological effects. Effects that alter the total production possibilities or the total welfare opportunities for consumers within an economy.

technology. A broad term dealing with the use and knowledge of humanity's tools and crafts.

technology-based limitations. Industry-specific effluent limitations based on best-available preventive technology applied to a discharge when it will not cause a violation of water quality standards at low stream flows. Usually applied to discharges into large rivers.

technology-based standards. Industry-specific effluent limitations applicable to direct and indirect sources which are developed on a category-by-category basis using statutory factors, not including water quality effects.

technology transfer. The transfer of development and design work.

telecommunications. The transmission of information over great distances via electromagnetic signals.

teratogen. A substance capable of causing birth defects.

teratogenesis. The introduction of nonhereditary birth defects in a developing fetus by exogenous factors such as physical or chemical agents acting in the womb to interfere with normal embryonic development.

terracing. Dikes built along the contour of sloping farm land that hold runoff and sediment to reduce erosion.

tertiary treatment. Advanced cleaning of wastewater that goes beyond the secondary or biological stage, removing nutrients such as phosphorus, nitrogen, and most BOD and suspended solids.

theoretical maximum residue contribution (TRMC). The theoretical maximum amount of a pesticide in the daily diet of an average person. It assumes that the diet is composed of all food items for which there are tolerance-level residues of the pesticide. The TMRC is expressed as milligrams of pesticide/kilograms of body weight/day.

therapeutic index. The ratio of the dose required to produce toxic or lethal effects to the dose required to produce nonadverse or therapeutic response.

therm. A unit of heat containing 100,000 British thermal units (Btu).

thermal energy. The total potential and kinetic energy associated with the random motions of the molecules of a material.

thermal mass materials. Materials that retain or store heat produced by sunlight or other sources. These are typically dense materials such as stone, concrete, or metal, and are often an important component of solar heating systems and other high-efficiency systems.

thermal pollution. Discharge of heated water from industrial processes that can kill or injure aquatic organisms.

thermal stratification. The formation of layers of different temperatures in a lake or reservoir.

thermal system insulation (TSI). Asbestos-containing material applied to pipes, fittings, boilers, breeching, tanks, ducts, or other interior structural components to prevent heat loss or gain or water condensation.

thermal treatment. Use of elevated temperatures to treat hazardous wastes.

thermocline. The middle layer of a thermally stratified lake or reservoir. In this layer, there is a rapid decrease in temperatures in a lake or reservoir.

thermosiphon system. A solar collector system for water heating in which circulation of the collection fluid through the storage loop is provided solely by the temperature and density difference between the hot and cold fluids.

thermostat. A device that adjusts the amount of heating and cooling produced and/or distributed by automatically responding to the temperature in the environment.

thin-film silicon. A technology in which amorphous or polycrystalline material is used to make photovoltaic (PV) cells.

third world. The peoples, populations, nations that are deprived of or lack the basic needs of life.

threshold. The lowest dose of a chemical at which a specified measurable effect is observed and below which it is not observed.

threshold level. Time-weighted average pollutant concentration values, exposure beyond which is likely to adversely affect human health.

threshold limit value (TLV). The concentration of an airborne substance to which an average person can be repeatedly exposed without adverse effects. TLVs may be expressed in three ways. (1) TLV-TWA—Time-weighted average, based on an allowable exposure averaged over a normal 8-hour workday or 40-hour work week; (2) TLV-STEL—Short-term exposure limit or maximum concentration for a brief specified period of time, depending on a specific chemical (TWA must still be met); and (3) TLV-C—Ceiling Exposure Limit or maximum exposure concentration not to be exceeded under any circumstances. (TWA must still be met.)

threshold planning quantity. A quantity designated for each chemical on the list of extremely hazardous substances that triggers notification by facilities to the State Emergency Response Commission that such facilities are subject to emergency planning requirements under SARA Title III.

thropic levels. A functional classification of species that is based on feeding relationships (e.g., generally aquatic and terrestrial green plants comprise the first thropic level, and herbivores comprise the second).

tidal marsh. Low, flat marshlands traversed by channels and tidal hollows, subject to tidal inundation; normally, the only vegetation present is salt-tolerant bushes and grasses.

tillage. Plowing, seedbed preparation, and cultivation practices.

time. Nonspatial continuum in which process takes place and events occur.

times beach. An example of the consequences of environmentally hazardous chemicals, in this case dioxin.

time-weighted average (TWA). In air sampling, the average air concentration of contaminants during a given period.

tire processor. Intermediate operating facility where recovered tires are processed in preparation for recycling.

tires. As used in recycling, passenger car and truck tires (excluding airplane, bus, motorcycle and special service military, agricultural, off-the-road and slow-speed industrial tires). Car and truck tires are recycled into rubber products such as trash cans, storage containers, rubberized asphalt or used whole for playground and reef construction.

tissue engineering. The rejuvenation or replication of healthy cells or tissues to replace failing human organs and aging cells.

tolerance petition. A formal request to establish a new tolerance or modify an existing one.

tolerances. Permissible residue levels for pesticides in raw agricultural produce and processed foods. Whenever a pesticide is registered for use on a food or a feed crop, a tolerance (or exemption from the tolerance requirement) must be established. The EPA establishes the tolerance levels, which are enforced by the Food and Drug Administration and the Department of Agriculture.

tonnage. The amount of waste that a landfill accepts, usually expressed in tons per month. The rate at which a landfill accepts waste is limited by the landfill's permit.

topography. The physical features of a surface area including relative elevations and the position of natural and man-made (anthropogenic) features.

total dissolved phosphorous. The total phosphorous content of all material that will pass through a filter, which is determined as orthophosphate without prior digestion or hydrolysis. Also called soluble P. or ortho P.

total dissolved solids (TDS). All material that passes the standard glass river filter; now called total filtrable residue. Term is used to reflect salinity.

total maximum daily load (TMDL). A calculation of the highest amount of a pollutant that a water body can receive and safely meet water quality standards set by the state, territory, or authorized tribe.

total petroleum hydrocarbons (TPH). Measure of the concentration or mass of petroleum hydrocarbon constituents present in a given amount of soil or water. The word *total* is a misnomer—few, if any, of the procedures for quantifying hydrocarbons can measure all of them in a given sample. Volatile ones are usually lost in the process and not quantified and nonpetroleum hydrocarbons sometimes appear in the analysis.

total recovered petroleum hydrocarbon. A method for measuring petroleum hydrocarbons in samples of soil or water.

total suspended particles (TSP). A method of monitoring airborne particulate matter by total weight.

total suspended solids (TSS). A measure of the suspended solids in wastewater, effluent, or water bodies, determined by tests for "total suspended nonfilterable solids."

toxaphene. Chemical that causes adverse health effects in domestic water supplies and is toxic to fresh water and marine aquatic life.

toxic chemical. Any chemical listed in EPA rules as "Toxic Chemicals Subject to Section 313 of the Emergency Planning and Community Right-to-Know Act of 1986."

toxic chemical release form. Information form required of facilities that manufacture, process, or use (in quantities above a specific amount) chemicals listed under SARA Title III.

toxic chemical use substitution. Replacing toxic chemicals with less harmful chemicals in industrial processes.

toxic cloud. Airborne plume of gases, vapors, fumes, or aerosols containing toxic materials.

toxic concentration. The concentration at which a substance produces a toxic effect.

toxic dose. The dose level at which a substance produces a toxic effect.

toxic pollutants. Materials that cause death, disease, or birth defects in organisms that ingest or absorb them. The quantities and exposures necessary to cause these effects can vary widely.

toxic release inventory. Database of toxic releases in the United States compiled from SARA Title III Section 313 reports.

toxic substance. A chemical or mixture that may present an unreasonable risk of injury to health or the environment.

toxic, toxin. Of poison, poisonous; poison especially of animal or plant origin, also of poison formed in body by pathogen.

toxic waste. A waste that can produce injury if inhaled, swallowed, or absorbed through the skin.

toxicant. A harmful substance or agent that can injure an exposed organism.

toxicity assessment. Characterization of the toxicological properties and effects of a chemical, with special emphasis on establishment of dose-response characteristics.

toxicity testing. Biological testing (usually with an invertebrate, fish, or small mammal) to determine the adverse effects of a compound or effluent.

toxicity. The degree to which a substance or mixture of substances can harm humans or animals. *Acute toxicity* involves harmful effects in an organism through a single or short-term exposure. *Chronic toxicity* is the ability of a substance or mixture of substances to cause harmful effects over an extended period, usually upon repeated or continuous exposure sometimes lasting for the entire life of the exposed organism. *Subchronic toxicity* is the ability of the substance to cause effects for more than one year but less than the lifetime of the exposed organism.

toxicological profile. An examination, summary, and interpretation of a hazardous substance to determine levels of exposure and associated health effects.

trade wastes. Wastes of organic or inorganic origin discharged by industrial and commercial enterprises.

tragedy of the commons. The inherent conflict between individual interests and the common good, based on the assumption that an individual uses a public good without considering the impact of his or her use on the availability of that good, therefore resulting in the over-exploitation of a public resource; the concept is explored in a 1968 essay written by Garrett Hardin.

transboundary pollutants. Air pollution that travels from one jurisdiction to another, often crossing state or international boundaries. Also applies to water pollution.

transfer station. Facility where solid waste is transferred from collection vehicles to larger trucks or rail cars for longer distance transport.

transformer. A device that converts the generator's low-voltage electricity to higher-voltage levels for transmission to the load center, such as a city or factory.

transient water system. A noncommunity water system that does not serve 25 of the same nonresidents per day for more than six months per year.

transmaterialization. The process of substituting a service for a product in order to meet customer needs while reducing the use of materials and natural resources.

transmission (electric). The movement or transfer of electric energy over an interconnected group of lines and associated equipment between points of supply and points at which it is transformed for delivery to consumers or is delivered to other electric systems. Transmission is considered to end when the *energy is transformed for distribution to the consumer.*

transmission line. A set of conductors, insulators, supporting structures, and associated equipment used to move large quantities of power at high voltage, usually over long distances between a generating or receiving point and major substations or delivery points.

transmission system (electric). An interconnected group of electric transmission lines and associated equipment for moving or transferring electric energy in bulk between points of supply and points at which it is transformed for delivery over the distribution system lines to consumers or is delivered to other electric systems.

transmissivity. The ability of an aquifer to transmit water.

transparency. A measure of increased accountability and decreased corruption in which a business reports on its ethics and performance results through accessible publication of the business's practices and behavior; there is a strong movement to increase the transparency of business processes via independently verified corporate responsibility reporting.

transpiration. The process by which water vapor is lost to the atmosphere from living plants. The term can also be applied to the quantity of water thus dissipated.

transport. Move things, goods, people, from one place to another; means of moving things.

transportation control measures (TCMS). Steps taken by a locality to reduce vehicular emission and improve air quality by reducing or changing the flow of traffic; may include bus and HOV lanes, carpooling, and other forms of ride-shairing, public transit, bicycle lanes.

transportation sector. An energy-consuming sector that consists of all vehicles whose primary purpose is transporting people and/or goods from one physical location to another. Included are automobiles; trucks; buses; motorcycles; trains, subways, and other rail vehicles; aircraft; and ships, barges, and other waterborne vehicles. Vehicles whose primary purpose is not transportation (e.g., construction cranes and bulldozers, farming vehicles, and warehouse tractors and forklifts) are classified in the sector of their primary use.

transporter. Hauling firm that picks up properly packaged and labeled hazardous waste from generators and transports it to designated facilities for treatment, storage, or disposal. Transporters are subject to EPA and DOT hazardous waste regulations.

trash. Material considered worthless or offensive that is thrown away. Generally defined as dry waste material, but in common usage it is a synonym for garbage, rubbish, or refuse.

trash-to-energy plan. Burning trash to produce energy.

treatability studies. Tests of potential cleanup technologies conducted in a laboratory.

treated regulated medical waste. Medical waste treated to substantially reduce or eliminate its pathogenicity, but that has not yet been destroyed.

treated wastewater. Wastewater that has been subjected to one or more physical, chemical, and biological processes to reduce its potential of being health hazard.

treatment plant. A structure built to treat wastewater before discharging it into the environment.

treatment, storage, and disposal (TSD) facility. Site where a hazardous substance is treated, stored, or disposed of. TSD facilities are regulated by the EPA and states under RCRA.

treatment. (1) Any method, technique, or process designed to remove solids and/or pollutants from solid waste, waste streams, effluents, and air emissions. (2) Methods used to change the biological character or composition of any regulated medical waste so as to substantially reduce or eliminate its potential for causing disease.

tremie. Device used to place concrete or grout under water.

trial burn. An incinerator test in which emissions are monitored for the presence of specific organic compounds, particulates, and hydrogen chloride.

trichloroethylene (TCE). A stable, low boiling-point colorless liquid, toxic if inhaled.

Used as a solvent or metal degreasing agent, and in other industrial applications.

trickle irrigation. Method in which water drips to the soil from perforated tubes or emitters.

trickling filter. A coarse treatment system in which wastewater is trickled over a bed of stones or other material covered with bacteria that break down the organic waste and produce clean water.

trihalomethane (THM). One of a family of organic compounds named as derivative of methane. THMs are generally by-products of chlorination of drinking water that contains organic material.

triple top line. A company's improved top-line financial performance over the long term due to sustainable business practices, including less capital investment and increased revenues.

troposhpere. The layer of the atmosphere closest to the earth's surface.

trust fund (CERCLA). A fund set up under the Comprehensive Environmental Response, Compensation and Liability Act (CERCLA) to help pay for cleanup of hazardous waste sites and for legal action to force those responsible for the sites to clean them up.

tube settler. Device using bundles of tubes to let solids in water settle to the bottom for removal by conventional sludge collection means; sometimes used in sedimentation basins and clarifiers to improve particle removal.

tuberculation. Development or formation of small mounds of corrosion products on the inside of iron pipe. These tubercules roughen the inside of the pipe, increasing its resistance to water flow.

tundra. A type of treeless ecosystem dominated by lichens, mosses, grasses, and woody plants. Tundra is found at high latitudes (arctic tundra) and high altitudes (alpine tundra). Arctic tundra is underlain by permafrost and is usually water saturated.

turbidimeter. A device that measures the cloudiness of suspended solids in a liquid; a measure of the quantity of suspended solids.

turbidity. 1. Haziness in air caused by the presence of particles and pollutants. 2. A cloudy condition in water due to suspended silt or organic matter.

turbine. A machine for generating rotary mechanical power from the energy of a stream of fluid (such as water, steam, or hot gas). Turbines convert the kinetic energy of fluids to mechanical energy through the principles of impulse and reaction, or a mixture of the two.

U

U-factor. Measures the heat transfer through a window, door, or skylight and tells you how well the product insulates. The lower the U-factor, the greater resistance to heat flow (in and out) and the better its insulation value.

ultraviolet (UV) rays. Radiation from the sun that can be useful or potentially harmful. UV rays from one part of the spectrum (UV-A) enhance plant life. UV rays from other parts of the spectrum (UV-B) can cause skin cancer or other tissue damage. The ozone layer in the atmosphere partly shields us from ultraviolet rays reaching the earth's surface.

UN conferences. An international conference with representatives from some 113 governments and agencies held in Stockholm, Sweden, in 1972.

UN environment program (UNEP). Created by the UN Conference on the Human Environment, 1972, UNEP has been charged with implementing its recommendations and those of subsequent environmental conference.

uncertainty factor. One of several factors used in calculating the reference dose from experimental data. UFs are intended to account for (1) the variation in sensitivity among humans; (2) the uncertainty in extrapolating animal data to humans; (3) the uncertainty in extrapolating data obtained in a study that covers less than the full life of the exposed animal or human; and (4) the uncertainty in using LOAEL data rather than NOAEL data.

unconfined aquifer. An aquifer containing water that is not under pressure; the water level in a well is the same as the water table outside the well.

underground injection control (UIC). The program under the Safe Drinking Water Act that regulates the use of wells to pump fluids into the ground.

underground injection wells. Steel- and concrete-encased shafts into which hazardous waste is deposited by force and under pressure.

underground mine. A mine where coal is produced by tunneling into the earth to the coal bed, which is then mined with underground mining equipment such as cutting machines and continuous, long wall, and short wall mining machines. Underground mines are classified according to the type of opening used to reach the coal, that is, drift (level tunnel), slope (inclined tunnel), or shaft (vertical tunnel).

underground sources of drinking water. Aquifers currently being used as a source of drinking water or those capable of supplying a public water system. They have a total dissolved solids content of 10,000 milligrams per liter or less, and are not "exempted aquifers." (See exempted aquifer.)

underground storage tank (UST). A tank located at least partially underground and designed to hold gasoline or other petroleum products or chemicals.

united nations global compact. An international initiative that seeks to bring businesses together voluntarily in order to promote socially and environmentally responsible practices; signatories pledge to uphold the Compact's 10 Principles.

united states business council on sustainable development (USBESD). A nonprofit organization promoting sustainable development by establishing networks and partnerships between American companies and government entities; the USBCSD provides a voice for industry and is the U.S. branch of the World Business Council of Sustainable Development.

unreasonable risk. Under the Federal Insecticide, Fungicide, and Rodenticide Act (FIFRA), "unreasonable adverse effects" means any unreasonable risk to humans or the environment, taking into account the medical, economic, social, and environmental costs and benefits of any pesticide.

unsaturated zone. The area above the water table where soil pores are not fully saturated, although some water may be present.

upper detection limit. The largest concentration that an instrument can reliably detect.

uranium. A heavy, naturally occurring, radioactive element.

uranium fuel cycle. The series of steps involved in supplying fuel for nuclear power reactors. It includes mining, refining, the making of fuel elements, their use in a reactor, chemical processing to recover spent (used) fuel, reenrichment of the fuel material, and remaking into new fuel elements.

uranium mill tailings piles. Former uranium ore processing sites that contain leftover radioactive materials (wastes), including radium and unrecovered uranium.

urban runoff. Storm water from city streets and adjacent domestic or commercial properties that carries pollutants of various kinds into the sewer systems and receiving waters.

urea-formaldehyde foam insulation. A material once used to conserve energy by sealing crawl spaces, attics, and the like; no longer used because emissions were found to be a health hazard.

use cluster. A set of competing chemicals, processes, and/or technologies that can substitute for one another in performing a particular function.

used oil. Spent motor oil from passenger cars and trucks collected at specified locations for recycling (not included in the category of municipal solid waste).

useful thermal output. The thermal energy made available for use in any industrial or commercial process or used in any heating or cooling application, that is, total thermal energy made available for processes and applications other than electrical generation.

utility. Usefulness, made or serving practical purpose.

utility generation. Generation by electric systems engaged in selling electric energy to the public.

utility load. The total electricity demand for a utility district.

utopia. Imaginary place with perfect social and political system; ideally perfect place or state of things.

V

vadose zone. The zone between land surface and the water table within which the moisture content is less than saturation (except in the capillary fringe) and pressure is less than atmospheric. Soil pore space also typically contains air or other gases. The capillary fringe is included in the vadose zone. (*See* Unsaturated Zone.)

valued environmental attributes/components. Those aspects (components/processes/functions) of ecosystems, human health, and environmental welfare considered to be important and potentially at risk from human activity or natural hazards. Similar to the term *valued environmental components* used in environmental impact assessment.

vapor. The gas given off by substances that are solids or liquids at ordinary atmospheric pressure and temperatures.

vapor capture system. Any combination of hoods and ventilation system that captures or contains organic vapors so they may be directed to an abatement or recovery device.

vapor dispersion. The movement of vapor clouds in air due to wind, thermal action, gravity spreading, and mixing.

vapor plumes. Flue gases visible because they contain water droplets.

vapor pressure. A measure of a substance's propensity to evaporate, vapor pressure is the force per unit area exerted by vapor in an equilibrium state with surroundings at a given pressure. It increases exponentially with an increase in temperature. A relative measure of chemical volatility, vapor pressure is used to calculate water partition coefficients and volatilization rate constants.

vapor recovery system. A system by which the volatile gases from gasoline are captured instead of being released into the atmosphere.

variance. Government permission for a delay or exception in the application of a given law, ordinance, or regulation.

vector. 1. An organism, often an insect or rodent, that carries disease. 2. Plasmids, viruses, or bacteria used to transport genes into a host cell. A gene is placed in the vector; the vector then "infects" the bacterium.

vegan. A person who eats no animal products whatsoever.

vegetarian. A person who does not eat meat, poultry or fish. Many vegetarians do consume animal products, such as milk, eggs, cheese, and honey.

vegetative controls. Non-point source pollution control practices that involve vegetative cover to reduce erosion and minimize loss of pollutants.

vehicle fuel consumption. Vehicle fuel consumption is computed as the vehicle miles traveled divided by the fuel efficiency reported in miles per gallon (MPG). Vehicle fuel consumption is derived from the actual vehicle mileage collected and the assigned

MPGs obtained from EPA certification files adjusted for on-road driving. The quantity of fuel used by vehicles.

vehicle miles traveled (VMT). A measure of the extent of motor vehicle operation; the total number of vehicle miles travelled within a specific geographic area over a given period of time.

ventilation rate. The rate at which indoor air enters and leaves a building. Expressed as the number of changes of outdoor air per unit of time; air changes per hour (ACH), or the rate at which a volume of outdoor air enters in cubic feet per minute (CFM).

ventilation/suction. The act of admitting fresh air into a space in order to replace stale or contaminated air; achieved by blowing air into the space. Similarly, suction represents the admission of fresh air into an interior space by lowering the pressure outside of the space, thereby drawing the contaminated air outward.

ventilation. The intentional exchange of indoor air with outdoor air to reduce indoor pollutants, moisture, and odors.

venture philanthropy. A charitable giving model that bridges venture capital strategies with philanthropic giving, creating strategic relationships among individuals and non-profit organizations.

venturi scrubbers. Air pollution control devices that use water to remove particulate matter from emissions.

vinyl chloride. A chemical compound, used in producing some plastics, that is believed to be oncogenic.

virgin materials. Resources extracted from nature in their raw form, such as timber or metal ore.

viscosity. The molecular friction within a fluid that produces flow resistance.

visual pollution. Visual squalor in an environment, including items such as; overhead wirescape, litter and unauthorized rubbish, abandoned cars, and large items or equipment.

vital. Concerned with or essential to life; essential to existence of a thing, or to the matter in hand.

vlogs. Video Web logs produced by a digital camera that captures moving images which are then transferred to the Internet.

volatile liquids. Liquids that easily vaporize or evaporate at room temperature.

volatile organic compound (VOC). Organic chemical compounds that have high enough vapor pressures under normal conditions to significantly vaporize and enter the atmosphere. A wide range of carbon-based molecules, such as aldehydes, ketones, and other light hydrocarbons are VOCs. The term often is used in a legal or regulatory context and in such cases the precise definition is a matter of law. The term may refer both to well characterized organic compounds and to mixtures of variable composition.

volatile solids. Those solids in water or other liquids that are lost on ignition of the dry solids at 550°C.

volatile synthetic organic chemicals. Chemicals that tend to volatilize or evaporate.

volatile. Any substance that evaporates readily.

volcanic energy. Energy produced from volcanic action.

volt (v). The International System of Units (SI) measure of electric potential or electromotive force. A potential of one volt appears across a resistance of one ohm when a current of one ampere flows through that resistance. Reduced to SI base units, $1 \text{ V} = 1$ kg times m2 times s-3 times A-1 (kilogram meter squared per second cubed per ampere).

voltage. The difference in electrical potential between any two conductors or between a conductor and ground. It is a measure of the electric energy per electron that electrons can acquire and/or give up as they move between the two conductors.

voltaic electricity. Electricity produced by chemical action.

volume reduction. Processing waste materials to decrease the amount of space they occupy, usually by compacting, shredding, incineration, or composting.

volumetric tank test. One of several tests to determine the physical integrity of a storage tank; the volume of fluid in the tank is measured directly or calculated from product-level changes. A marked drop in volume indicates a leak.

vulnerability analysis. Assessment of elements in the community that are susceptible to damage if hazardous materials are released.

vulnerable zone. An area over which the airborne concentration of a chemical accidentally released could reach the level of concern.

W

waste. Unwanted materials left over from a manufacturing process. Refuse from places of human or animal habitation. Municipal solid waste, landfill gas, methane, digester gas, liquid acetonitrile waste, tall oil, waste alcohol, medical waste, paper pellets, sludge waste, solid by-products tires, agricultural byproducts, closed loop biomass, fish oil, and straw.

waste characterization. Identification of chemical and microbiological constituents of a waste material.

waste energy. Municipal solid waste, landfill gas, methane, digester gas, liquid acetonitrile waste, tall oil, waste alcohol, medical waste, paper pellets, sludge waste, solid byproducts, tires, agricultural byproducts, closed loop biomass, fish oil, and straw used as fuel.

waste exchange. Arrangement in which companies exchange their wastes for the benefit of both parties.

waste feed. The continuous or intermittent flow of wastes into an incinerator.

waste generation. The weight or volume of materials and products that enter the waste stream before recycling, composting, landfilling, or combustion takes place. Also can represent the amount of waste generated by a given source or category of sources.

waste load allocation. The maximum load of pollutants each discharger of waste is allowed to release into a particular waterway. Discharge limits are usually required for each specific water quality criterion being, or expected to be, violated. The portion of a stream's total assimilative capacity assigned to an individual discharge.

waste management. A comprehensive, integrated, and rational systems approach toward the achievement and maintenance of acceptable environmental quality and the support of sustainable development.

waste minimization. Measures or techniques that reduce the amount of wastes generated during industrial production processes; also applies to recycling and other efforts to reduce the amount of waste going into the waste stream.

waste piles. Noncontainerized, lined, or unlined accumulations of solid, nonflowing waste.

waste reduction. Using source reduction, recycling, or composting to prevent or reduce waste generation.

waste stream. The total flow of solid waste from homes, businesses, institutions, and manufacturing plants that is recycled, burned, or disposed of in landfills, or segments thereof such as the "residential waste stream" or the "recyclable waste stream."

waste treatment lagoon. Impoundment made by excavation or earth fill for biological treatment of wastewater.

waste treatment plant. A facility containing a series of tanks, screens, filters, and other processes by which pollutants are removed from water.

waste treatment stream. The continuous movement of waste from generator to treater and disposer.

waste heat recovery. Recovering heat discharged as a by-product of one process to provide heat needed by a second process.

waste-to-energy facility/municipal-waste combustor. Facility where recovered municipal solid waste is converted into a usable form of energy, usually via combustion.

waste to energy. A recovery process in which waste is incinerated or otherwise turned into steam or electricity, and used to generate heat, light, or power through the process of combustion.

waste to profit. The process of using one company's waste or by-product as the input or raw material for another company, thereby increasing business profits and decreasing waste; also referred to as by-product synergy.

wastewater. The spent or used water from a home, community, farm, or industry that contains dissolved or suspended matter.

wastewater infrastructure. The plan or network for the collection, treatment, and disposal of sewage in a community. The level of treatment will depend on the size of the community, the type of discharge, and/or the designated use of the receiving water.

wastewater operations and maintenance. Actions taken after construction to ensure that facilities constructed to treat wastewater will be operated, maintained, and managed to reach prescribed effluent levels in an optimum manner.

wastewater treatment plan. A facility containing a series of tanks, screens, filters, and other processes by which pollutants are removed from water. Most treatments include chlorination to attain safe drinking water standards.

water cycle. Water constantly moves through a vast global cycle, in which it evaporates from lakes and oceans, forms clouds, precipitates as rain or snow, then flows back to the ocean. The energy of this water cycle, which is driven by the sun, is tapped most efficiently with hydropower.

water factor. The number of gallons per cycle per cubic foot that a clothes washer uses.

water heater. An automatically controlled, thermally insulated vessel designed for heating water and storing heated water at temperatures less than 180°F.

water pollution. The presence in water of enough harmful or objectionable material to damage the water's quality.

water purveyor. A public utility, mutual water company, county water district, or municipality that delivers drinking water to customers.

water quality criteria. Levels of water quality expected to render a body of water suitable for its designated use. Criteria are based on specific levels of pollutants that would make the water harmful if used for drinking, swimming, farming, fish production, or industrial processes.

water quality standards. State-adopted and EPA-approved ambient standards for water bodies. The standards prescribe the use of the water body and establish the water quality criteria that must be met to protect designated uses.

water quality-based limitations. Effluent limitations applied to dischargers when mere technology-based limitations would cause violations of water quality standards. Usually applied to discharges into small streams.

water quality-based permit. A permit with an effluent limit more stringent than one based on technology performance. Such limits may be necessary to protect the designated use of receiving waters (e.g., recreation, irrigation, industry, or water supply).

water solubility. The maximum possible concentration of a chemical compound dissolved in water. If a substance is water soluble it can very readily disperse through the environment.

water storage pond. An impound for liquid wastes designed to accomplish some degree of biochemical treatment.

water supplier. One who owns or operates a public water system.

water supply system. The collection, treatment, storage, and distribution of potable water from source to consumer.

water table. The level of groundwater.

water treatment lagoon. An impound for liquid wastes designed to accomplish some degree of biochemical treatment.

water turbine. A turbine that uses water pressure to rotate its blades. Primarily used to power an electric generator.

water well. An excavation where the intended use is for location, acquisition, development, or artificial recharge of groundwater.

waterborne disease outbreak. The significant occurrence of acute illness associated with drinking water from a public water system that is deficient in treatment, as determined by appropriate local or state agencies.

watershed approach. A coordinated framework for environmental management that focuses public and private efforts on the highest priority problems within hydrologically defined geographic areas taking into consideration both ground and surface water flow.

watershed area. A topographic area within a line drawn connecting the highest points uphill of a drinking water intake into which overland flow drains.

watershed. The land area that drains into a stream; the watershed for a major river may encompass a number of smaller watersheds that ultimately combine at a common point.

water-soluble packaging. Packaging that dissolves in water; used to reduce exposure risks to pesticide mixers and loaders.

water-source heat pump. Heat pump that uses wells or heat exchangers to transfer heat from water to the inside of a building. Most such units use groundwater.

watt. The rate of energy transfer equivalent to one ampere under an electrical pressure of one volt. One watt equals 1/746 horsepower, or one joule per second. The amount of light, or the energy output, of light bulbs is measured, in part, in watts. The higher the wattage level, the more energy is output and consumed.

watt hour (Wh). The electrical energy unit of measure equal to 1 watt of power supplied to, or taken from, an electric circuit steadily for 1 hour.

wavelength. The distance, measured in the direction of progression of a wave, from any given point to the next point in the same phase.

weatherization. Energy efficiency improvement measures for homes, including a wide variety of measures that encompass the building envelope, its heating and cooling systems, its electrical system, and electricity consuming appliances. Examples of weatherization include adding insulation, storm windows, or weatherstripping to your home.

web. Woven fabric, thing connected in two or three dimensions.

weight of scientific evidence. Considerations in assessing the interpretation of published information about toxicity—quality of testing methods, size, and power of study design, consistency of results across studies, and biological plausibility of exposure-response relationships and statistical associations.

weir. 1. A wall or plate placed in an open channel to measure the flow of water. 2. A wall or obstruction used to control flow from settling tanks and clarifiers to ensure a uniform flow rate and avoid short-circuiting.

well. A hole drilled in the earth for the purpose of finding or producing crude oil or natural gas; or producing services related to the production of crude or natural gas.

well field. Area containing one or more wells that produce usable amounts of water or oil.

well injection. The subsurface emplacement of fluids into a well.

well monitoring. Measurement by on-site instruments or laboratory methods of well water quality.

well plug. A watertight, gastight seal installed in a bore hole or well to prevent movement of fluids.

well point. A hollow vertical tube, rod, or pipe terminating in a perforated pointed shoe and fitted with a fine-mesh screen.

wellhead. The point at which the crude (and/or natural gas) exits the ground.

wellhead protection area. A protected surface and subsurface zone surrounding a well or well field supplying a public water system to keep contaminants from reaching the well water.

wetlands. An area that is saturated by surface or groundwater with vegetation adapted for life under those soil conditions, as swamps, bogs, fens, marshes, and estuaries.

wettability. The relative degree to which a fluid will spread into or coat a solid surface in the presence of other immiscible fluids.

wettable powder. Dry formulation that must be mixed with water or other liquid before it is applied.

wheeling. The transmission of electricity owned by one entity through the facilities owned by another (usually a utility).

whole. Whole, unadulterated, although not necessarily organic, staple, unrefined, and minimally processed foods.

whole-effluent-toxicity tests. Tests to determine the toxicity levels of the total effluent from a single source as opposed to a series of tests for individual contaminants.

wholefoods. Whole, unadulterated, although not necessarily organic, staple, unrefined and minimally processed foods.

wildlife refuge. An area designated for the protection of wild animals, within which hunting and fishing are either prohibited or strictly controlled.

wind. Any natural movement of air in the atmosphere. A renewable source of energy used to turn turbines to generate electricity.

wind energy. Energy present in wind motion that can be converted to mechanical energy for driving pumps, mills, and electric power generators. Wind pushes against sails, vanes, or blades radiating from a central rotating shaft.

wind machine. Devices powered by the wind that produce mechanical or electrical power.

wind power plant. A group of wind turbines interconnected to a common utility system through a system of transformers, distribution lines, and (usually) one substation. Operation, control, and maintenance functions are often centralized through a network of computerized monitoring systems, supplemented by visual inspection. This is a term commonly used in the United States. In Europe, it is called a generating station.

wind tower. Devices, some as tall as 120 feet, which lift wind turbine blades high above the ground to catch stronger wind currents.

wire-to-wire efficiency. The efficiency of a pump and motor together.

wood and waste (as used at electric utilities). Wood energy, garbage, bagasse (sugarcane residue), sewerage gas, and other industrial, agricultural, and urban refuse used to generate electricity for distribution.

wood energy. Wood and wood products used as fuel, including round wood (cord wood), limb wood, wood chips, bark, sawdust, forest residues, charcoal, pulp waste, and spent pulping liquor.

wood packaging. Wood products such as pallets, crates, and barrels.

wood pellets. Sawdust compressed into uniform diameter pellets to be burned in a heating stove.

wood treatment facility. An industrial facility that treats lumber and other wood products for outdoor use. The process employs chromated copper arsenate, which is regulated as a hazardous material.

wood/wood waste. This category of biomass energy includes black liquor wood/wood waste liquids (red liquor, sludge wood, spent sulfite liquor) wood/wood waste solids (peat, paper pellets, railroad ties, utility poles, wood/wood waste).

wood-burning-stove pollution. Air pollution caused by emissions of particulate matter, carbon monoxide, total suspended particulates, and polycyclic organic matter from wood-burning stoves.

working level (WL). A unit of measure for documenting exposure to radon decay products, the so-called "daughters." One working level is equal to approximately 200 picocuries per liter.

working level month (WLM). A unit of measure used to determine cumulative exposure to radon.

world bank. An agency of the United Nations, the World Bank comprises the International Bank for Reconstruction and Development and its affiliates, the International Development Association, the International Finance Corporation, and the Multilateral Investment Guarantee Agency.

world business council on sustainable development (WBCSD). An association of 170 international companies that provides business leadership with support to operate, innovate, and grow through sustainable development initiatives that incorporate the "three pillars of economic growth:" environmental protection, social development, and economic growth.

world commission on environment and development. A commission created by the UN General Assembly in 1983 for the purpose of examining potential conflicts between environment protection and economic growth.

world conservation strategy. In 1980, a strategy prepared by the World Conservation Union, the UN Environment Program, and the World Wide Fund for Nature.

world health organization (WHO). An agency of the United Nations, WHO came into being in 1948.

world heritage list. A list created by the Convention for the Protection of the World Cultural and Natural Heritage (the Paris convention) and administered by the UN Educational, Scientific, and Cultural Organization (UNESCO).

world population. An issue of crucial importance in relation to the possibilities of sustainable development.

X

xenobiota. Any biotum displaced from its normal habitat; a chemical foreign to a biological system.

xenobiotic. (foreign to life) Artificial substances, especially those which pollute, or distort, life structures.

Y

yard waste. The part of solid waste composed of grass clippings, leaves, twigs, branches, and other garden refuse.

yellow-boy. Iron oxide flocculant (clumps of solids in waste or water); usually observed as orange-yellow deposits in surface streams with excess iron content.

yellowcake. A natural uranium concentrate that takes its name from its color and texture. Yellowcake typically contains 70 to 90 percent U_3O_8 (uranium oxide) by weight. It is used as feedstock for uranium fuel enrichment and fuel pellet fabrication.

yield. The quantity of water (expressed as a rate of flow or total quantity per year) that can be collected for a given use from surface or groundwater sources.

Z

zero air. Atmospheric air purified to contain less than 0.1 ppm total hydrocarbons.

zero-net energy home/net-zero energy home. A home that produces, on average, as much energy as it uses. Zero net energy use is achieved through a combination of energy efficiency measures to reduce the overall energy load of the house (i.e., super-insulated building envelope, passive solar strategies, efficient heating/cooling systems) along with renewable energy (i.e., solar power, wind power), that offsets any nonrenewable energy consumed.

zero population growth. The idea that human population must be stabilized. If the human population is not contained and returned to sustainable levels, as far as any worthwhile future is concerned it will simply be the end.

zero waste. A production system aiming to eliminate the volume and toxicity of waste and materials by conserving or recovering all resources.

zone of saturation. The layer beneath the surface of the land containing openings that may fill with water.

zooplankton. Small (often microscopic) free-floating aquatic plants or animals.

REFERENCES FOR TERMS

California Department of Toxic Substances Control. (2011). Glossary. Retrieved on January 21, 2011, from http://www.dtsc.ca.gov/InformationResources/Glossary_of_Environmental_Terms.cfm#Y

Cleveland Carbon Fund. (2011). Sustainability Dictionary. Retrieved on January 21, 2011, from http://www.clevelandcarbonfund.org/resources/sustainability-dictionary/

Gilpin, Alan. (1996). *Dictionary of Environment and Sustainable Development*. West Sussex, England: John Wiley & Sons.

Johnson, Colin. (1991). *Green Dictionary*. London: McDonald & Company.

Lawrence, A. T. and Weber, J. (2008). *Business & Society*. New York, NY: McGraw-Hill.

Nickel, W., McHugh, J., and McHugh, S. (2008). *Understanding Business*. New York, NY: McGraw Hill.

Trend USA. (2010). "Do You Speak Green?" Retrieved on January 21, 2011, from http://www.trendingreen.com/en-us/green-dictionary.php

United States Department of Energy. (2011). "Renewable Energy Annual: Glossary." Retrieved on January 21, 2011, from http://www.eia.gov/cneaf/solar.renewables/page/rea_data/gl.html

United States Energy Information Association. (2011). Glossary. Retrieved January 23, 2011, from http://www.eia.gov/tools/glossary/index.cfm

United States Environmental Protection Agency. (2011). "Terms of Environment: Glossary, Abbreviations, and Acronyms." Retrieved on January 21, 2011, from http://www.epa.gov/OCEPAterms/aterms.htm

United States Environmental Protection Agency. (2010). "Top Green Home Terms." Retrieved on January 21, 2011, from http://www.epa.gov/greenhomes/TopGreenHomeTerms.htm

Part II

CASE STUDIES ON THE

ENVIRONMENTAL, ECONOMIC, TECHNOLOGICAL, AND SOCIAL ASPECTS OF SUSTAINABILITY

CASE 1

MOTHER GOOSE FARMS

Overview

- **Location:** Honomalino, South Kona Soil and Water Conservation District, Hawaii
- **Farmed Acres:** 7 (2 locations—see site description)
- **Enterprises:** Sheep, Pigs, Coffee

Site Description

John and Vicki Swift own Mother Goose Farms, a 5-acre coffee orchard in South Kona, Hawaii. They own two additional acres of land where they live and raise a few pigs and process the coffee they grow. John also manages 77 acres of macadamia nut orchards for absentee owners. He has 50 breeding ewes, which he grazes under the macadamia nuts to control groundcover. Mother Goose Farms has been a certified organic coffee orchard since 1992. Requirements for organic certification vary by state, but in all cases, use of synthetic pesticides and inorganic nitrogen fertilizers is prohibited.

The farm is located at an elevation of approximately 2,000 ft above sea level. The climate in South Kona is very mild. Temperatures fluctuate little, but rainfall varies widely. Normal annual rainfall is 40 inches, but the past 3 years have been unusually dry with annual rainfall varying only from 13–21 inches. Acid rainfall is common due to the activity of nearby Kilauea Volcano. Except for the unpredictable rainfall, the climate in South Kona is ideally suited to coffee growing.

The farm lies on very young, shallow, rocky organic soils.

Environmental Quality and Ecological Function

Erosion: All of the soils on this part of Hawaii are shallow and sloping, making erosion control a major concern. However, erosion is extremely low on Mother Goose Farms, since the land is never tilled and remains in permanent cover crop throughout the year. The cover crop provides an added benefit of protecting the soil from baking, a concern with bare soils in Hawaii.

Coffee Cultural Requirements: In many parts of the world coffee is planted in shade to protect it against drought, erosion and wind. In South Kona, where cloud cover is not as reliable as in the northern part of the island, additional protection may be helpful. With assistance from NRCS District Conservationist, Steve Skipper, and the NRCS Plant Materials Center on Molokai, John and Vicki Swift have recently started an intercropping trial with the fast growing, leguminous tropical tree, *Gliricidia sepium*. They expect this tree to provide protection for the coffee, add nitrogen to the soil, and provide additional food for their geese (see **Weed Pressures** section). Tree cuttings and seeds were provided by the NRCS Plant Materials Center. If the trial plantings prove successful, John and Vicki plan to intercrop more of their orchard, perhaps experimenting with other tree species.

U.S. Department of Agriculture.

Weed Pressures: Weeds are a serious problem for both coffee and macadamia nuts in Hawaii. Traditionally weeds are sprayed several times each year with herbicides. In 1989, the Swifts decided to try controlling the weeds in their coffee by non-chemical means (a necessary requirement for organic certification). Desmodium *(Desmodium* spp.), a trailing climbing perennial forage legume, immediately took over the orchard, and weed trimming soon became prohibitively expensive. The Swifts began experimenting with geese for weed control in 1991. First they fenced the orchard to keep out dogs and other potential predators. They bought 25 geese, which they raised on desmodium from four days of age. Once the feathers were developed (6–8 weeks), the Swifts moved the geese to the orchard. They immediately began eating the desmodium in the field and have been controlling its height to the point that it is now an acceptable nitrogen fixing cover crop. The Swifts currently have 60 geese that they move around in the orchard weekly using portable electric poultry netting. The Swifts estimate they save $5,000 annually on weed control, as well as the energy and time saved by letting the geese do the work.

The use of sheep to maintain groundcover under macadamia nuts is a proven practice in Kona. However, John is using katahidn hair sheep, a breed not previously used for this purpose. These sheep were bred strictly for meat. They produce no wool, which has eliminated many of the typical problems associated with sheep in a warm climate. The katahidn sheep are maintaining the groundcover effectively.

Insect Pests: The insect pests of greatest concern on Mother Goose Farms are ants and scale, which can lead to sooty mold, another pest of coffee. Ants have increased in the orchard since the irrigation system was installed. Still, Steve Skipper feels that the problem is not as severe as on many farms in the area, since the geese provide some insect as well as groundcover control. Some farms in the area have experienced problems with aphids and mites. These have not been a problem for John and Vicki. To control the scale on which the ants feed, the Swifts apply an ultra fine dormant oil.

Socioeconomic Viability

Uncertain Yields, Volatile Markets: John and Vicki Swift have taken several steps to sustain their operations in the face of uncertain yields and volatile markets. First, their coffee farm is organically certified. They are able to capture a niche market that is less volatile than the open market. Second, they process their coffee in-house and market directly to local consumers for a competitive price, thereby avoiding middle costs associated with conventional markets and saving transportation and processing costs. To date, marketing of Mother Goose Farms coffee has been primarily by word of mouth; however, Vicki is exploring more aggressive marketing strategies (though still focusing on a local niche market) as coffee yields increase. Third, they have a somewhat diversified operation with both sheep and pigs that can offset losses when coffee yields are low. The sheep are sold directly to a local restaurant. As the herd grows, more aggressive marketing will be needed. Pigs are grown primarily for family consumption. Excess pigs are sold to neighbors. District Conservationist Steve Skipper thinks there may be a commercial market for the weed eating geese. To date, however, they are not consumed. Fourth, John works as a fireman outside the farm, providing additional cash flow.

When they started the coffee orchard 6 years ago, John and Vicki assumed it would take approximately 5 years to turn a profit. Coffee yields have increased steadily since they first began transplanting the trees, and costs for weed control have dropped dramatically. Last year was a profitable one and the Swifts anticipate even better profits in the future.

CASE 2

VILLAGE FARMS OF BUFFALO, INC.

Move over Buffalo wings! A new taste treat—hydroponic tomatoes, will soon be growing in Buffalo thanks in part to the Brownfields Pilot program. This innovative greenhouse facility is a major part of Buffalo's efforts in finding new uses for abandoned industrial properties. A site that once produced millions of tons of steel will soon be producing millions of pounds of tomatoes thanks to a public/private partnership to redevelop the south side of the city.

The project included an $800,000 site cleanup. This was accomplished through a cooperative effort on the part of LTV, the former owners of the steel plant, and state and federal agencies including the EPA and NYSDEC. A specific voluntary cleanup plan for the site was worked out. Cleanup tasks were completed in about three months. Since the site is within a New York State Economic Development Zone and a Federal Enterprise Zone, tax incentives were able to be applied to help the economic viability of the project.

A "topping-off" ceremony was held September 7, 1997 and construction of the $15 Million greenhouse complex on South Park Avenue is underway. The 17-acre facility includes a 763,000 square foot greenhouse and a 42,000 square foot packing, mechanical, and administrative building. Plans include installation of 750,000 feet of heating and irrigation piping. The climate controlled facility will grow tomatoes 11 1/2 months a year, and a new crop will be planted during the other two weeks. Construction completion is expected in December, and the first harvest from 175,000 tomatoes is anticipated in March. The facility will be operated by Village Farms of Buffalo, a subsidiary of Agro Power Development.

Most importantly, the project provides jobs for 175 workers to grow the 8 million pounds of greenhouse tomatoes a year. This project will help spur the cleanup and redevelopment of hundreds of acres on the other side of South Park Avenue. The overall strategic plan deals with 1,500 acres of which 1,000 will be developed and the other 500 acres used for habitat, a golf course, and greenspace.

Environmental Protection Agency.

CASE 3

BOYLE HEIGHTS YOUTH TECHNOLOGY CENTER

The design intent for the Boyle Heights Youth Technology Center was to provide an educational and recreational environment for the Boyle Heights community.

The newly constructed two-story building occupies approximately 200,000 square feet with a total construction cost of $7,300,000. The facility was opened to the public in September, 2006.

The project was designed by the City of Los Angeles, Bureau of Engineering, which also provided construction management. The building is organized on two levels: reception, waiting area, counseling and administrative offices on the lower; four computer training rooms on the upper. The north-south clerestory orientation exploits daylight and provided visual and auditory serenity from the two interior landscaped courtyards. Administrative offices and meeting rooms buffer noisy traffic and visual distractions from Fourth Street, and open to an interior cloister that physically connects administrative functions with reception, recreation and a multi-purpose training area. A community computer training classroom and the recreation center are located on the lower-level, both feature glass walls which face each other and are connected by an open-landscape courtyard. As an independent pavilion, the recreation area creates two courtyards. The lower courtyard, adjacent to the entry, is a tranquil intimate space that provides a visual introduction into the nature of the facility and a calm private setting for the required counseling spaces. To the east the upper courtyard provides a secure outdoor space adjacent to the recreation room and multi-purpose training area. The organization of the building is based on the intention of creating a nurturing learning, working and social environment that also incorporates high environmental standards for design and construction.

This facility has been registered with the United States Green Building Council (USGBC), the certifying organization that sets the standards for green building design, for certification under their Leadership in Energy and Environmental Design (LEED) standards. The building design incorporates thoughtful site orientation for sun control; efficient mechanical and electrical systems; low-e double plate glass for all windows; photovoltaic panels for green energy generation; water efficient design for landscape and plumbing systems; and a reduction in the use of finish materials.

Built over an abandoned apartment building and liquor store, the facility has made a positive impact on the Boyle Height community. It revitalizes the area by introducing a safe learning area for at-risk youth and the housing community in the neighborhood. Every student at the center has a computer. Public transportation provides easy access to the facility which is also within walking distance of the public housing complex. Bureau of Engineering worked closely with the Community Development Department to ensure that the community participated in the design and construction process.

Bureau of Engineering, Los Angeles Department of Public Works.

CASE 4

THE CRESTWOOD BUILDING, ATLANTA METRO AREA

Georgia's first LEED-EB certified office building, the Crestwood Building is a five-story, 93,554-square-foot building set on a 5.6-acre lot outside of Atlanta. The Crestwood demonstrates how incremental and modest green building improvements can culminate in LEED certification and market differentiation.

Originally built in 1986, the Crestwood was purchased by Melaver, Inc. in 1998 for $9.4 million. Based in Savannah, Georgia, Melaver holds a predominantly green building real estate portfolio and in 2002 committed itself to pursue LEED certification on all its new developments. (Melaver created the first LEED-certified shopping center in the country in 2006, Abercorn Common in Savannah.) The Crestwood building, however, presented Melaver with its first viable opportunity to green an existing building.

Before initiating the LEED-EB certification process for the Crestwood in 2004, Melaver first assessed the building's ENERGY STAR rating. The Crestwood required window film coating and upgrades to its lighting and HVAC systems to achieve an ENERGY STAR label. Crestwood's ENERGY STAR upgrades cost $63,000, representing slightly under half of the total expenditures required to achieve LEED-EB certification.

Once the ENERGY STAR efficiency measures were addressed, Melaver's internal project team evaluated each LEED-EB credit category to identify the most feasible, cost-effective green building improvements for the Crestwood. The following strategies illustrate the various ways in which the Crestwood project team amassed 35 total LEED-EB 2.0 points to achieve basic Certified status:

- *Green site.* Contracted with a landscape architect and contractor to capitalize on the property's existing tree shade cover by strategically placing additional canopy trees to meet the 30 percent shading requirement for heat island reduction
- *HVAC improvements.* Rebuilt the building's chiller for $15,420 to improve indoor air quality and to reduce energy use.
- *Reduced water use.* Renovated the building's six bathrooms and reconfigured the landscape watering to achieve a 30 percent reduction in overall water consumption.
- *Reduced electricity use.* Utility costs increased by 25 to 40 percent in Atlanta after Hurricane Katrina in 2005. The Crestwood absorbed these increases and actually saved an estimated $26,000 from 2005 to 2008 as a result of installing new high-efficiency fluorescent lamps, photocell-based light sensors, motion-detector lighting, and energy-efficient vending machines.
- *Comprehensive recycling program.* Supplied recycling bins, collected and stored recyclable metals, plastics, glass, batteries, paper, cell phones, toner cartridges, and light bulbs until pickup for an annual recycling cost of $2,860.
- *Low-impact cleaning policy.* Applied Melaver's internal *Mark of a Difference: Interior Care* standards that include daytime janitorial cleaning and the use of sustainable, Green Seal-approved cleaning products.
- *Entryway systems.* Installed a durable metal entry grate/footmat at the building's front entry to reduce the debris, dirt, and pollutants occupants track into the building.

From Green Existing Buildings by Jerry Yudelson (McGraw-Hill Companies, 2010). Copyright © 2010 by McGraw-Hill Companies. Reprinted by permission.

All in all, Melaver invested $137,121 to obtain an ENERGY STAR label and LEED-EB Certified rating for the Crestwood. Over the investment period, Melaver has experienced an above-market occupancy rate of 92 percent, compared to 81 percent within its submarket. Although the Crestwood's higher occupancy cannot be attributed solely to its green upgrades, Melaver estimates the building's higher occupancy increases the property's net income by $109,000 (and probably adds about $2 million to its market value).

References

The Green Building Bottom Line, pp. 167–193.
www.abercorncommon.com, retrieved May 29, 2009.

CASE 5

ONE POTOMAC YARD (ARLINGTON, VIRGINIA)

One Potomac Yard illustrates the relatively quick progression new buildings can experience from LEED certification for New Construction (LEED-NC) to LEED-EB. The 654,000-square-foot office complex features two 12-story buildings and is owned by JP Morgan Asset Management and managed by Jones Lang LaSalle.

In 2004, Potomac Yard was initially designed as a speculative office building without any green specifications. The original developer, Crescent Resources LLC, effectively repositioned Potomac Yard as a LEED-certified building in order to meet the lease requirements of its anchor tenant, the U.S. Environmental Protection Agency (EPA). After achieving a LEED-NC Gold certification in 2006, Potomac Yard received a LEED-EB Gold certification in 2008.

The project team included representatives from Crescent Resources and the EPA as well as an environmental building consultant and a commissioning authority. This project incorporated the following green strategies, many of which originated in the LEED-NC certified project and also met LEED-EB version 2.0 criteria:

- *Roofing materials.* Used highly reflective and ENERGY STAR-compliant roof materials to reduce the building's solar heat gain and to decrease related cooling demand and energy use.
- *Green roofing.* An elevated patio with benches made of recycled plastic lumber and a 1711-square-foot green roof with sedum plants connects the two office towers.
- *Brownfield site remediation.* Prior to construction, the developer removed soil contaminants, including cinder ballast, arsenic, and benzo(A)pyrene.
- *On-site stormwater treatment.* Below grade sand filters treat stormwater runoff from each building before it flows into the Potomac River. The treatment system is expected to reduce total suspended solids (silt) by 80 percent and total phosphorous by 40 percent.
- *Environmentally responsible commuting.* The project provides on-site bicycle parking for 53 bikes, shower facilities, and close proximity to existing Metrorail lines, Metro buses, and EPA shuttle-bus routes.
- *Low-flow plumbing fixtures.* The project reduced water use by 41 percent through installation of dual-flush toilets, ultra-low-flush urinals, low-flow showerheads, and ultra-low-flow lavatory faucets.
- *No permanent irrigation.* The project landscaping has drought-resistant and local plants that can survive without a permanent irrigation system.
- *ENERGY STAR-efficient lighting strategies.* Installed glass panel insets in the systems, furniture, glass doors, and sidelights for conference rooms and offices that extend natural daylighting well into the occupied space.
- *Green power.* The building purchased green power to meet 68 percent of its electrical energy needs for two years.
- *Sustainably harvested wood.* FSC-certified wood-based materials constituted 83 percent of the value of all wood used in the building.
- *Low-VOC adhesives, paints, sealants, and caulks.* Tenant and public areas used low-volatile-organic-compound (VOC) materials and finishes to ensure high indoor air quality (IAQ).

From Green Existing Buildings by Jerry Yudelson (McGraw-Hill Companies, 2010). Copyright © 2010 by McGraw-Hill Companies. Reprinted by permission.

- *Green cleaning and pest management.* The building managers adopted sustainable best practices for cleaning, pest management, and landscaping.
- *Sustainable workstation furniture.* The building management procured furniture with 35 to 40 percent recycled material content as required under the federal government's Comprehensive Procurement Guidelines (CPG) program. The furniture was also Greenguard certified for air emissions.
- *Local materials.* The project received an innovation credit for exemplary performance in sourcing local materials, because 62.8 percent of the total materials by cost were manufactured within 500 miles.
- *Occupant education program.* Another innovation credit was achieved because the building used signage to inform occupants and visitors about the sustainable features and operations of the facility.

References

Potomac Yards I and 2/EPA, U.S. General Service Administration Case Study, Retrieved June 3, 2009, from http://www.gsa.gov.portal.gsa./eplcontentView.do?contentType=GSA BASIC&contentId=21865

Sustainable Facilities and EPA: One and Two Potomac Yard, U.S. Environmental Protection Agency-Fact Sheet. Retrieved May 31, 2009, from http://www.epa.gov/greeningepa/documents/py_factshtJ08.pdf

CASE 6

ON THE ROAD TO SUCCESS: ROME, NEW YORK'S EAST ROME BUSINESS PARK

Overview

- Leveraged more than $4 million in assessment, cleanup and redevelopment funding.
- Leveraged a $2.8 million cleanup of 17-acre brownfield site.

What began as a $200,000 Brownfields Assessment Pilot in Rome, New York, has become a successful redevelopment project that has leveraged more than $4 million in assessment, cleanup, and redevelopment funding and may lead to as many as 300 new jobs. A new access road through the East Rome Business Park has already been completed, and a 17-acre core property in Rome has been subdivided into six parcels ready for development. Prospects look bright for this site that once carried the stigma of a contaminated brownfield.

The East Rome Business Park lies within the heart of what was once Rome's historically industrial zone and has long been referred to by the community as the old General Cable complex. Many years ago, the site was home to a metals processing plant. Since the departure of General Cable in the mid-1960s, the vacant and abandoned buildings, combined with the site's vague reputation as "contaminated," have scared off potential developers. Community residents also suffered from fears of contamination, as well as from the blight caused by this abandoned property.

The bleak outlook for this stretch of land improved dramatically in June 1996, when EPA selected the city to receive funding under its Brownfields Pilot program. The investigative results that came out of the Pilot program, along with the planning work and community outreach efforts, provided the tools necessary to further the brownfields initiative.

The Pilot leveraged further assistance from the State of New York, which provided funding for $200,000 worth of follow-up assessments on the property and granted $1.8 million for cleanup through Governor Pataki's 1996 Clean Water/Clean Air Bond Act. The cleanup project occurred in two stages. The first was an above-ground operation to demolish a number of buildings on the site and remove asbestos. The second stage went below ground to remove six underground storage tanks, clean up numerous soil "hot spots," and clean up various tunnels and utility lines. In addition to the assessment and cleanup funds leveraged from the state, the property owner invested nearly $1 million of his own money in demolition and cleanup. The City of Rome also received nearly $1 million from the New York Department of Transportation's Industrial Access Program to build an access road through the business park, and the city leveraged $300,000 from the Empire State Development Corporation for modernization of utilities along the new access road.

With cleanup and infrastructure improvements completed, the site is now ready to welcome new business to the East Rome Business Park. The property owner has subdivided the property into six parcels, one of which is a city right-of-way for the access road. The Canterbury Printing Complex, located on the border of the neighboring industrial area, is planning to expand into the new park. Other businesses are in negotiations to relocate into the area. Some of those businesses had been waiting for the access road to be completed before proceeding.

Environmental Protection Agency.

Although the Brownfields Pilot officially ended in 1998, the progress it enabled in the East Rome Business Park continues to benefit the city. Enthusiasm for this redevelopment effort has been tremendous, particularly from neighboring residential areas plagued by high poverty and unemployment rates for decades. Estimates for employment within the finished industrial park reach as high as 300 new jobs. Resulting expansion and new business will also add significantly to the city's tax base.

CASE 7

RISING FROM THE DEPTHS IN NAUGATUCK VALLEY: THE RESTORATION AND REUSE OF IDLE LAND

Overview

- Covering only 10 percent of the state's land area, the 45-mile Naugatuck Valley includes an estimated 20 percent of the state's brownfields.
- In the City of Beacon Falls, the owners of a former manufacturing facility paid more than $500,000 in back taxes following assessment proposals by the Brownfields Pilot.
- In the City of Derby, a former mixed-use is being assessed by the Pilot using more than $180,000 in leveraged funds.

A former landfill in Seymour, Connecticut, dormant for 20 years, avoided by investors and developers alike, now has a future. Soon, the old Silvermine Landfill will be the new home of the Haynes Construction Company. In the neighboring cities of Thomaston and Beacon Falls, the owners of former commercial and industrial sites are finally making arrangements to pay long-overdue property taxes, fattening up city tax rolls by more than $500,000. And in nearby Ansonia, the charred remains of an abandoned building were removed to make room for a park enjoyed by residents of an adjacent senior citizen's center.

These four cities, along with Derby, Naugatuck, Oxford, Waterbury, and Watertown are encompassed not only by the Naugatuck Valley but by EPA's Naugatuck Valley Brownfields Pilot. Awarded in October 1996, the Pilot was designed to help remove contamination uncertainties regarding former commercial and industrial properties, or brownfields. Covering, only 10 percent of the state's land area, the 45-mile Naugatuck Valley includes an estimated 20 percent of the state's brownfields.

In addition to providing the assessment funding needed to remove potential developers' fear of the unknown, the Brownfields Pilot is helping to form partnerships between developers, local environmentalists, property owners, and city officials. In Thomaston, the Pilot worked with a local community group to develop a reuse plan for the former Plume & Atwood Brass Mill, idle since 1992. The Pilot's assessments prompted the site's owner to negotiate with the city for payment of more than $81,000 in back taxes, rather than risk losing the property to foreclosure. A cleanup plan has been approved by the city, and the owners have agreed to provide public access to the site along the Naugatuck River, where a new park and museum are among the planned reuses. Similarly, in Beacon Falls, the owners of a 60,000-square-foot former manufacturing facility paid more than $500,000 in back taxes to the city, following assessment proposals by the Brownfields Pilot.

Restoration of Naugatuck Valley's brownfields has extended beyond the activities of the Brownfields Pilot as well. A portion of the former Seymour Specialty Wire Company site was purchased by the Stop & Shop company, which conducted environmental assessments, is performing the necessary cleanup, and is building a new supermarket that will bring new jobs to the area, meeting a critical community need. The City of Seymour has since asked the

Environmental Protection Agency.

Pilot to conduct assessments on another portion of the site, which the city hopes to redevelop into a new police station. In the City of Derby, Home Depot will occupy a 10-acre former industrial site where the previous owner funded assessments. Home Depot is now conducting cleanup prior to redevelopment. Meanwhile, just across the street, a former mixed-use property is being assessed by the Pilot using more than $180,000 in leveraged funding—$100,000 in U.S. Department of Housing and Urban Development Community Development Block Grant (CDBG) funds, $50,000 from the Community Foundation for Greater New Haven, and $30,000 from EPA Region 1.

At the confluence of the Naugatuck and Housatonic Rivers lies O'Sullivan's Island, part of the City of Derby. Local environmentalists and citizens' groups see cleanup and restoration of this island and its riverbanks as a top priority, and the Brownfields Pilot adopted the island as its primary target. More than 90 drums of pollutants were taken off the island during an emergency removal action in 1985. The Brownfields Pilot performed assessments on the island in March 1999, and is now working with EPA Region 1 to determine the feasability of phytoremediation—an innovative technology that uses plants or trees to extract contaminants from soil—to further prepare the site for redevelopment. Eventually, the riverbanks surrounding O'Sullivan's Island will be restored to pristine condition, and residents will enjoy a new park, a marina, and pedestrian and bicycle paths.

CASE 8

17TH STREET PLAZA (DENVER, COLORADO)

In 2000, JP Morgan Asset Management purchased 17th Street Plaza, a 32-story Class A office building in Denver's central business district. Built in 1982, this 666,000-square-foot office tower was placed under the management of Jones Lang LaSalle (JLL). Chief engineer Curt Godes led an ongoing, eight-year effort to improve the building's performance and sustainability. Between 2000 and 2008, the property team spent $1,222,084 in capital projects, resulting in annual average electricity savings of $202,000 (from saving 4 million kilowatt-hours) and water savings of $15,630. When JP Morgan encouraged Godes' team to pursue LEED-EB certification in 2007, minimal additional work was required to achieve the building's LEED Gold rating in 2009.

Prior to pursuing LEED certification, the 17th Street Plaza building managers employed the following performance and sustainability strategies:

- *Utility rebate program.* Used the demand side management (DSM) utility rebate program developed by one of the building's lead tenant, Xcel Energy, to help pay for demand-reduction projects.
- *ENERGY STAR rating.* In 2001, the building earned its ENERGY STAR label with a score of 77 and has since improved its score. In 2008, the building scored 94 to rank among the top 6 percent of all office buildings in energy efficiency.
- *Low-mercury lighting.* JLL replaced standard fluorescent lamps with comparably priced low-mercury lamps that met the LEED-EB criteria.
- *Recycling program.* Established a recycling program that redirected 219 tons of waste from landfills and induced the building's largest tenant, Xcel Energy, to implement the same program throughout its 350,000-square-foot Denver portfolio.

Having already implemented many sustainable building practices and achieved an ENERGY STAR rating, the building team used the LEED certification process primarily to communicate with tenants and verify the building's market leadership in performance and sustainability. To achieve LEED certification, the project team's modest building improvements included the following water conservation upgrades:

- *Toilet and urinal flush valve kits.* Spent $1252 to install low-flow flush valve kits on toilets and urinals, resulting in annual water savings of $5336.
- *Lavatory aerators.* Installed 0.5-gallon-per-minute aerators on restroom faucets and 1.5-gallon-per-minute aerators on kitchen faucets at a cost of $300.
- *Weather satellite-controlled landscape irrigation.* Installed Weather TRAK-ET irrigation controllers for a cost $3800. The system has reduced irrigation water costs by $5894 in the first year of operation and is estimated to reduce annual irrigation water usage by 20 percent.

References

Building Sustainable Value at 17th Street Plaza, Jones Lang LaSalle Case Study. Retrieved May 31, 2009, from http://newyork.uli.org/Events/Past7c20Events/Content/-/media/DC/NewVo2}YorWNY%o2jDocs%o2}2lYLG%o2jRetofitVo2OHandout.ashx
Jones Lang LaSalle, 17th Street Plaza Property Details, from http://www.costar.com/costar-connect/MasterPage/main.aspx. SiteID=20865&Checksum=87669&Demo=0&RtnURL&LogRedirect=1

CASE 9

GE & UNIVERSAL STUDIOS HOLLYWOOD: THE TREASURE HUNT MODEL

Overview

- GE has conducted well over 200 treasure hunts globally with a combined emissions reduction of over 250,000 metric tons of GHGs
- Seen over $14 billion dollars in revenue from ecomagination products and services

GE & Universal Studios Hollywood

General Electric (GE) applies Lean manufacturing methods in its businesses—both manufacturing processes and transactional situations. Recently, greenhouse gas (GHG) emissions became a major target for some of the lean activities undertaken by the company.

NBC Universal, which is 80% owned by GE, is one of the world's leading entertainment companies and is involved in the development, production and marketing of various entertainment ventures throughout the world. Universal Studios Hollywood (USH) is a leading tourist destination in the Los Angeles area and hosts millions of guests each year.

The Treasure Hunt System

The purpose of GE's Energy Treasure Hunt system is to identify areas of potential savings. Based on Lean manufacturing techniques, the process allows teams to identify and more importantly quantify opportunities to improve energy efficiency. To date, GE has conducted well over 200 treasure hunts globally with a combined emissions reduction of over 250,000 metric tons of GHGs.

A critical element in the success of these events is cross-functional teamwork. Incorporating people from all aspects of the businesses allows representatives from all levels backgrounds to offer opinions and bring their vision to the process. The event highlighted below had representatives from Universal Studios, NBC, GE Energy, GE Motors, Utility Companies, Government and various vendors and contractors. Specialists were also called in to offer advice on engineering, machining, lighting and other aspects of operations.

Energy Savings on the Lot

A Treasure Hunt lasts three days (plus pre-hunt training) and allows the participants to view the processes and equipment during non-productive time, start up, productive time and breaks. The time frame covered therefore lets the Treasure Hunt Teams see the site during all stages of equipment readiness. This provides maximum opportunity for kaizen.

Environmental Protection Agency.

The ultimate goals of the event at USH in March, 2008, were to: Reduce energy consumption *by 20% - $1.4M;* Instill Energy Savings as Part of the Culture; Deploy Technologies to Eliminate Waste; and Generate a Strategic Energy Plan. These aligned with GE's overarching corporate strategy of energy reduction across the board. Ten teams focused on different aspects of operations. Electricity, water, natural gas, steam, compressed air, wastewater and chilled water were all focal points of the hunt. Although only 12% of the theme park operations were reviewed as part of this event, the most critical energy & water processes were included, and the teams identified projects which are easily leveragable to other parts of the complex. Theme park utility spend is nearly $6MM per year. Teams visited sites around the park to assess utility consumption. Some of the areas examined were prep kitchens, office buildings, rides such as Jurassic Park and The Mummy, and attractions such as the Terminator show. Each area had unique problems and associated with utility usage. Some actions were essential to a special effect or a safety, but over the three day period, participants in the event identified almost two million dollars in potential savings with less than a year's payback on any investments!

Looking Toward the Future

Through the 200 hunts conducted by GE thus far, more than 5,000 actual energy saving projects have been identified. Not all projects are implemented immediately, but as energy costs continue to rise, there is a suite of potential projects waiting on the horizon.

On May 28, 2008, GE announced that they are committed to reduce their global water usage by 20% by 2012. They have seen over $14 billion dollars in revenue from ecomagination products and services. As a global corporation, GE strives to keep a competitive edge while remaining at the forefront of environmentally conscious business operations.

CASE 10

GOOGLE'S GREEN DATA CENTERS: NETWORK POP CASE STUDY

Introduction

Every year, Google saves millions of dollars and avoids emitting tens of thousands of tons of carbon dioxide thanks to our data center sustainability efforts. In fact, our facilities use half the energy of a typical data center. This case study is intended to show you how you can apply some of the cost-saving measures we employ at Google to your own data centers and networking rooms.

At Google, we run many large proprietary data centers, but we also maintain several smaller networking rooms, called POPs or "Points of Presence". POPs are similar to millions of small and medium-sized data centers around the world. This case study describes the retrofit of one of these smaller rooms, describing best practices and simple changes that you can make to save thousands of dollars each year.

For this retrofit, Google spent a total of $25,000 to optimize this room's airflow and reduce air conditioner use. A $25,000 investment in plastic curtains, air return extensions, and a new air conditioner controller returned a savings of $67,000/year. This retrofit was performed without any operational downtime.

Best Practices: Measuring Performance, Optimizing Air Flow, and Turning Up the Thermostat

Best Practice #1—Measuring performance

The first step to managing efficiency in a POP or data center is to continuously measure energy usage focusing on two values:

- **IT equipment energy:** IT equipment energy is the energy consumed by servers, storage and networking devices—the machines that perform IT work.
- **Facility overhead energy:** The facility overhead energy is the energy used by everything else, including power distribution, cooling and lighting.

Power Usage Efficiency, or PUE, is the measurement used to compare these two types of energy. In other words, PUE is a measure for how efficiently a building delivers energy to the IT equipment inside. The ideal PUE is 1.0, meaning there's no facility overhead energy—every watt of power going into the building is going straight to the computers and nowhere else.

$$PUE = \frac{IT\ Equipment\ Energy + Facility\ Overhead\ Energy}{IT\ Equipment\ Energy}$$

PUE must be measured over a long period of time for it to prove useful. At Google we look at both quarterly and trailing twelve-month performances. Snapshots of only a few hours are not helpful to make meaningful reductions in energy use.

Best practice #2—Optimizing air flow

In a typical data center, the IT equipment is organized into rows, usually with a "cold aisle" in front where cold air enters the equipment racks and a "hot aisle" in back where hot air is exhausted. Computer room air conditioners, called CRACs, push cold air into the cold aisle, which flows through computer and network equipment into the hot aisle, where it returns to the CRAC. Cooling is the largest contributor to facility overhead energy.

The most important step in optimizing air flow is preventing hot and cold air from mixing. There is no single right way to do this. Being creative and finding simple ways to block and redirect air can greatly reduce the amount of cooling required. This includes simple things like installing blanking panels in empty rack slots and tightly sealing gaps in and around machine rows. It's very similar to weatherizing your home

It's also important to eliminate any hot spots in order to achieve a more uniform thermal 'profile.' Localized hot spots are problematic for machines and trigger CRACs to turn on unnecessarily. Proper placement of temperature monitors and using computer modeling helps to quickly identify and eliminate hot spots.

Best practice #3—Turning up the thermostat

It has long been believed that IT equipment needs to run at low temperatures—between 15°C/60°F and 21°C/70°F. However, the American Society of Heating, Refrigerating and Air Conditioning Engineers (ASHRAE) recommends cold aisle temperatures of up to 27°C/81°F, which we've found to have no detrimental effect on equipment. Most IT equipment manufacturers spec machines at 32°C/90°F or higher, so there is plenty of margin. In addition, most CRACs are set to dehumidify the air down to 40% relative humidity and to reheat air if the return air is too cold. Raising the temperature and turning off dehumidifying and reheating provides significant energy savings.

An elevated cold aisle temperature allows CRACs to operate more efficiently at higher intake temperatures. Also, it allows for more days of "free cooling"—days where mechanical cooling doesn't need to run—if the facility has air- or water-side economization.

The simple act of raising the temperature from 22°C/72°F to 27°C/81°F in a single 200kW networking room could save tens of thousands of dollars annually in energy costs.

Introducing the POP

When retrofitting our POP, we had to work with what was already in the room. This meant no large-scale capital improvements and the room had to stay operational throughout the retrofit. We had to get creative and focus on maximizing the efficiency of the equipment that was already in place. With a few minor tweaks and some careful measurements, we were able to find significant savings.

Our starting point was a typical Tier III + computing room with the following configuration:

- **Power:** Double-conversion uninterrupted power supplies (UPSs) with a designed IT load of 250kW.
- **Cooling:** Four 111 kW computer room air conditioners (CRACs) with direct expansion evaporative cooling coil and remote air cooled condensers.
- **Racks:** Populated with commercially available third-party equipment, including optical switches, network routers, power supplies and load balancers.

We looked at the settings on the CRACs and noticed their thermostats were set to 22°C/71°F at 40% relative humidity. The IT load for the room was only 85kW at the time, yet it was designed to hold 250kW of computer and network equipment. There were no attempts to optimize air flow. In this configuration, the room was overpowered, overcooled and underused.

When we took an initial measurement of PUE, **we found a high PUE of 2.4.**[1]

Immediate Improvements

We first made simple changes before moving on to larger-scale improvements. In addition to PUE, we needed to measure cooling. Our hope was to improve cooling to the point that we could shut off a few CRACs.

After installing temperature monitors and examining airflow, we created thermal models using computational fluid dynamics (CFD) to run airflow simulations. Most of the cold air bypasses the machines, coming up through the floor vents in the cold aisle, going over the machines, and plunging straight into the hot aisle.

Temperature sensors also identified hot spots in the POP. Racks with high-power machines consumed about 5.6kWs per rack and produced more heat than racks with low-power or less densely populated machines. Since all the high-power racks were located in one area, that side of the room was significantly hotter than the other side of the room.

To optimize cooling and reduce energy usage, we took these immediate steps:

Step 1: Established critical monitoring points (CMPs)

In order to effectively measure temperature changes in our POP, we determined critical monitoring points (CMPs) where we needed accurate readings of temperature. These points included the room's UPS system, which specified a temperature below 25°C/77°F, and the input and output temperatures from the room's air conditioners.

Step 2: Optimized air vent tiles

We moved air vent tiles from the side with low power racks to the side with high power racks, matching airflow with IT power and significantly reducing the large hot spot on that side. Using our critical monitoring points, we were able to find the most efficient arrangement of vent tiles.

Step 3: Increased temperature and relative humidity settings

The original settings on the CRACs were a dry and chilly 22°C/71°F at a relative humidity of 40%. We implemented the latest ASHRAE recommended temperature range of 27°C/81°F max and increased the recommended humidity range to accept 20%-80% relative humidity.

Step 4: Contained UPS

The UPS required a temperature less than 25°C/77°F. However, the cold aisle air from the CRACs was now allowed to be a few degrees warmer than that. To prevent our UPS from getting too warm, we set up containment curtains (NFPA 701 compliant) to isolate the UPS. These containment curtains are similar to the plastic curtains used in commercial refrigerators.

---

1. Measuring PUE for our sites is described at: http://www.google.com/corporate/datacenter/efficiency-measurements.html.

Step 5: Improved CRAC unit controller

Since we couldn't replace the air conditioners entirely, we decided to adjust the CRAC unit controllers to act smarter. We changed the settings on the CRACs' controllers to decrease their sensitivity to temperature changes and relative humidity, preventing the CRACs from turning on unnecessarily. We also disabled dehumidification and reheating functions and increased the amount of time required to activate cooling.

After implementing these changes, **we were happy to see a drop in PUE from 2.4 to 2.2.**

Cold Aisle Containment

Our original goal was to try to make our cooling efficient enough to shut off a few CRACs and save energy. In order to get there, we'd have to increase the efficiency of cold air entering the cold aisle air by raising the temperature difference between the cold and hot aisle so that only the hottest air is being returned to the CRACs.

To increase our cold aisle efficiency, we investigated a few ways to seal off the cold aisles from the hot aisles. Our first design involved creating a full containment unit that included putting a lid over the cold aisle. Unfortunately, that involved modifying the sprinkler system in order to comply with local fire codes.

Instead, we sealed the cold aisles by using blanking plates on the backs of empty rack space and adding refrigerator door curtains to the ends of cold aisles. We also added refrigerator curtains every 3 meters along the length of the cold aisle to better direct air flow.

After sealing off the cold aisle, **we saw another 0.2 drop in PUE to 2.0.**

Crac Air Return Extensions

A CFD simulation revealed that we had two specific issues with the CRAC hot air return:

- Hot air from a densely populated rack flowed directly into the CRAC air return, giving a falsely elevated temperature reading of the hot aisle. The false reading of an elevated temperature energized this CRAC more often than necessary.
- At a different CRAC, cold and hot air mixed directly at the CRAC air return, again reducing CRAC efficiency.

The simplest solution was to add sheet metal boxes that increased the height of the air returns by 1.2m/48in, leading to improvements in return air flow and the creation of a more uniform return air temperature to the CRAC.

By evening out the temperature in the hot aisle, we also prevented hot spots from building up. In particular, a hot spot above one of the high power racks was triggering a temperature sensor to turn on the compressor unnecessarily.

With these optimizations, we reduced the number of CRACs from 4 to 2 while maintaining our desired cold aisle temperature. The cold aisle is cooler and the warm aisle is about the same—this is with the thermostat turned up and only half the number of air conditioners turned on.

We also installed motion sensors to turn off the overhead lights when the room was unoccupied, which further reduced the electrical power. With these changes in place, **the PUE dropped from 2.0 to 1.7.**

Adding a Central CRAC Controller

We next considered ways to dynamically control the number of CRACs turned on at any given time. If we only needed one air conditioner, we'd just turn on one. If we needed three, we could turn on three. If one suddenly stopped working, we could automatically turn on another to replace it.

Setting this up required a central CRAC controller tied to the temperature monitors in the room. We purchased this controller from a third party and connected it to the CRACs using the existing building management system. Now, we could turn on the air conditioning based on the load of the room and still maintain the required 2N redundancy. Even though at 85kW the room remained underused, the central CRAC controller made the cooling of the room more energy proportional.

Installing this system increased efficiency, reduced maintenance and increased cooling system redundancy. Now we were only using as many CRACs as needed, usually between 1 and 2. With less use, each air conditioner lasts longer and requires less maintenance. The new setup also allows for redundancy—if one of the CRACs fails, another instantly turns on in its place.

We decided not to disable the local controllers on each of the CRACs. If the new CRAC controller we installed happens to fail, the air conditioning in the room would continue to operate on the old controllers. Taking a final PUE reading for our POP, **we had a PUE of 1.5.**

Final Outcome: Energy Savings and ROI

Energy savings

We've brought the facility overhead energy usage down from 1.4 to 0.5 per watt of IT computer energy, reducing it to a third of its original value. We managed to do this without any operational disruptions or causing any major temperature fluctuations within our POP.

The list of changes we made to the original space is fairly short:

1. Added temperature monitoring
2. Optimized air vent tiles
3. Increased temperature and relative humidity settings on CRACs
4. Blocked off the ends of cold aisles with curtains
5. Put blanking plates and side panels to block cold air passing through empty rack spaces
6. Added 48" extensions to all CRAC air returns
7. Added a new CRAC controller

Upon analyzing the airflow for our final setup, we can see a fairly efficient network room with far more air flowing through machines instead of bypassing them.

Having made changes to one POP, we applied the same changes to others, recording improvements each step of the way. PUE was checked using data collected every second over an 18 month period, and each PUE value contains an average of 86,400 data points. The results are consistent for every POP in which we implemented these efficiency improvements.

PUE IMPROVEMENTS FOR FIVE POPS					
	POP 1	POP 2	POP 3	POP 4	POP 5
Starting point	2.4	2.2	2.2	2.4	2.4
After immediate improvements	2.2	2.0	2.0	2.2	2.0
After cold aisle containment	2.0	1.8	1.8	2.0	1.9
After adding CRAC air return extensions	1.7	1.7	1.7	1.7	1.7
After adding new CRAC controller	1.5	1.5	(Still collecting data)	1.6	(Still collecting data)

ROI analysis

Data center energy efficiency retrofits are a good example of where smart business and environmental stewardship coexist. In the POP in our case study, a capital investment of $25,000 led to a yearly energy savings of over 670MWh, saving $67,000 in yearly energy expenses. In addition, each improvement paid for itself in less than a year and will save hundreds of thousands of dollars throughout the lifetime of the equipment.

The best practices described in this case study form the key elements of Google's power optimization strategies. Internet services have assumed a central role in daily life, driving demand for centralized networking and data centers. The energy demand created by this growth highlights the need for data center owners and operators to focus on power optimization as both an operational expense reduction and an environmental imperative.

ROI FOR POP 1 IMPROVEMENTS					
For POP 1	PUE	Capital investment	PUE improvement	Savings/ month	ROI (months)
Starting point	2.4	—	—	—	—
After immediate improvements	2.2	—	0.2	$1,238	0
After cold aisle containment	2.0	12,000	0.2	$1,238	9.7
After adding CRAC air return extensions	1.7	5,000	0.3	$1,858	2.7
After adding new CRAC controller	1.5	8,000	0.2	$1,238	6.5

CASE 11
LOCKHEED MARTIN

Background

Lockheed Martin Corporation, the world's largest defense contractor, has been implementing lean production techniques corporate-wide since the late 1990s. Lockheed Martin's "LM21 Operating Excellence" initiative provides a common management and operating system for implementing lean and Six Sigma tools throughout Lockheed Martin business units and facilities. As stated in March 2004 by Lockheed Martin Chairman and CEO Vance Coffman, "LM 21 acts as a catalyst for facilitating improvements in every aspect of the design and manufacturing process. At last count, the LM21 process was responsible for more than $5 Billion in net savings across our corporation. Those savings not only hold down costs—which, by the way, are mostly passed through to our customers—but they also accrue over time, resulting in streamlined operations, reduced overhead, better quality, less rework, improved productivity and enhanced overall performance." While initial implementation of LeanSigma focused on manufacturing operations (e.g., airplanes, missiles), application of "lean thinking" has expanded to research and development operations as well as to administrative and support activities. The status of LeanSigma implementation varies by both business unit and facility. Lockheed Martin participates in MIT's Lean Aerospace Initiative.

Primary drivers for LeanSigma implementation at Lockheed Martin include business competitiveness, customer expectations (U.S. military interest in lean), and the desire for a standard, continuous improvement quality management and operating system and toolbox throughout diverse business units. Competitive pressures have intensified in the U.S. defense sector since 1990, as federal defense budgets contracted and defense contractors consolidated through mergers. The post-1990 period has been marked by strong pressures from the U.S. Congress and the Pentagon for contractors to cut costs, to increase the reliability of current military assets, and to phase in some new technologies on delayed schedules.

Lockheed Martin's Manassas, Virginia, plant belongs to the Maritime Systems and Sensors business unit and manufactures sonar systems for defense applications. Lockheed Martin acquired a portion of the Manassas facility (one semiconductor facility and light manufacturing operations) from Loral in May 1996, with the other semiconductor facility at the site purchased by BAE Systems Inc. The acquisition reduced significantly the business scope of facility operations (manufacturing scope was reduced by 80 percent), creating limitations on staff, space, and spending.

The Manassas facility has been applying LeanSigma and the LM21 Operating Excellence system to non-traditional manufacturing, research, and support activities since its acquisition by Lockheed Martin, drawing on support from corporate LeanSigma experts. In February 1995, managers began applying "lean thinking" to restructure Chemical, Environmental, Safety, and Health (CESH) operations. As part of the process streamlining, five departments at the facility-Operations, Engineering, Chemical Management, Environmental, Health and Safety, and Industrial Hygiene-were consolidated into one department. The facility is ISO

Environmental Protection Agency.

9001/14001 certified. CESH personnel often participate in or serve as a reviewer of 6S events conducted throughout the Manassas facility.

Lean-Environment Integration

Lockheed Martin's Manassas, VA plant has primarily approached lean-environment integration by applying LeanSigma tools to improve internal environmental management business processes. In addition, the facility relies on knowledge-based expertise through the occasional involvement of personnel with environmental expertise in Lean Sigma events that have an important environmental dimension. Two employees at the facility have both Six Sigma training and environmental management backgrounds.

Case Examples: Lean Projects and Results

Leaning Chemical and Hazardous Waste Management

In 1995, the Lockheed Martin Manassas Plant's CESH department conducted improvement events to apply lean thinking to its chemical and waste management activities. The key drivers for this initiative were to significantly reduce the cost, space, and staffing needed to support chemical and waste management activities at the plant. These were critical needs since Lockheed Martin divested themselves from one of two semiconductor manufacturing operations at the Manassas plant to a single one. The one finally kept is smaller in scope, and it focuses on research and development rather than production. In their light manufacturing operations, semiconductors needed for production are purchased from off-site suppliers.

Before Lean: Prior to the lean event, chemical management at the facility focused around a chemical storage warehouse (64,000 square feet) containing a large buffer inventory of chemicals to ensure 100 percent availability. Chemicals were typically ordered quarterly in larger volumes under a blanket purchase agreement. Chemicals were stored in the warehouse until withdrawn by operations. Lockheed Martin found that a significant portion of warehoused chemicals were going directly to the hazardous waste stream without ever being used, when they expired on-shelf or when they were no longer required for research or production. Prior to the lean event, hazardous waste management activities at the plant were governed by a RCRA Part B permit.

What Was Done: The lean event aimed to move toward a just-in-time chemical management system, where chemicals are delivered three times each week in "right-sized" containers to meet real-time demand (influenced by prior week consumption rates). The objective was to dramatically reduce chemical inventories, except for selected specialty chemicals with longer lead times for acquisition and delivery. Several lean principles guided the events: (1) optimize performance for the entire system even if per unit chemical purchase or waste disposal costs increase, (2) focus on actual needs, not worse-case contingencies, and (3) focus on smooth flow of materials through the facility.

The new system also eliminated the chemical warehouse, replacing it with point-of-use storage (POUS) cabinets and right-sized containers of chemical supplies. Lockheed Martin has contracted with 5-6 suppliers (multi-year agreements) to deliver the chemicals to the facility's chemical handling dock. CESH staff then transport the chemicals from there to the POUS cabinets. Lockheed Martin has shifted its relationship with chemical suppliers to more of a partnership model, with provisions and incentives for ensuring prompt delivery and chemical availability, while limiting on-site inventory. The facility's Chemical Challenge Program poses questions up-front, at the product and process design stage, which explore opportunities to minimize chemical usage and risk.

The lean event also sought to reduce the total waste management system cost by eliminating on-site treatment and the need for the RCRA permit and shifting to regular hazardous waste pick-up by a waste management vendor. By switching from a practice that purchased and stored onsite quantities of chemicals based on estimates for the upcoming production to a purchasing practice that is driven primarily by purchasing chemicals just when needed (Just in Time; Point of Use (POUS); and rightsizing chemicals) they managed to slash significantly the quantities of wastes generated at the facility. They are now a 90 days RCRA -Subtitle C - Large Quantity Generator. In fact, they have several 90 days satellite storage areas. This is because they use chemicals and generate hazardous wastes at other parts of the facility in addition to the one they leaned out of a Part B permit.

Results: A summary table is provided below that compares the prior and current methods for chemical and waste management at the Manassas plant. The lean events achieved the following business results related to the chemical and hazardous waste management processes at the Manassas facility:

- chemical inventories were dramatically reduced, freeing capital tied up in inventory;
- chemical inventory turns dramatically increased;
- chemical utilization rates increased dramatically, virtually eliminating chemicals expiring on the shelf or being mixed in larger quantities than needed;
- chemical warehouse was eliminated, reducing chemical storage space from 64,000 square feet to 1,200 square feet; and
- despite increased unit cost for hazardous waste disposal/treatment, significant system savings have resulted from elimination of RCRA Part B permit and associated regulatory requirements.

These business results from the lean events also produced several environmental benefits:

- reduction in chemical inventories reduces likelihood of chemical-related spills and accidents;
- virtually eliminated hazardous waste caused by chemicals expiring on shelf and from excess chemicals mixed in quantities larger than needed;
- chemical authorization process and chemical challenge program tightened screening of chemical choices and increased attentiveness to chemical use and risk reduction opportunities; and
- energy savings resulted from the significant reduction in warehouse space required for chemical storage.

SUMMARY OF LEAN INITIATIVE RESULTS			
Activity	**Prior Method**	**Current Method**	**Benefits & Concerns**
Scope	Two Semiconductor Facilities and Light Manufacturing	One Semiconductor Facility and Light Manufacturing	Remaining mfg is 20% of prior scope
Total Facility Size	1,650,000 Square Feet	1,100,000 Square Feet	Several buildings sold but added four small facilities in other states (NY, CA, FL).
Basis for Chemical Purchases	Support staff estimate based on prior use with buffer to ensure 100% availability	Order as needed based on prior week consumption and lead time for specialty items	No extra chemicals ordered. Virtually eliminated waste caused by expired shelf life and unused chemical waste.
Contract with Supply	Multi-year agreements	Multi-year agreements with delivery and availability addressed	Supplier more of a partner. Minimal inventory storage shifted to supplier.
Hazardous Waste	RCRA Part B Permit	Large quantity generator	Went to pick up by vendor on a schedule. Minor increased unit cost, significant savings by eliminating permit requirements.
Chemical Storage	64,000 Square Feet	1,200 Square Feet	Significant cost savings but minimal room for future growth
Staffing	64	17	Reduced work scope and elimination of unneeded work. No backup support.
Departments	5	1	Consolidated engineering, operations, chemical, health, safety, environmental, industrial hygiene.

CASE 12

GREENING OF THE WHITE HOUSE STATUS REPORT AND ACCOMPLISHMENTS

Introduction

The White House complex comprises the Executive Residence, the East and West Wings, and the Old Executive Office Building. The White House was designed in 1792 and was first occupied in 1800. It serves many functions; it is a residence, an office complex, and the setting for special events, dinners, and other state functions and ceremonial occasions.

The White House grounds also contain recreational areas, which include a swimming pool and a running track made of recycled materials as well as gardens and lawns. It has often been at the forefront of technological advances. For example, when plumbing was first installed in the 1830s, it was one of the first houses in the country to have running water. Later, in the early 1900s, a central air-conditioning system was installed that ultimately didn't work. Today, the White House complex's east-west orientation permits the use of daylighting and passive solar heating, among other energy-efficient measures.

The Old Executive Office Building was completed in 1888. It has more than 550 offices in 600,000 square feet of space. It was originally designed to make use of daylighting, and it had an intricate system permitting natural ventilation. The ventilation system is no longer operating, but the skylights have been returned to their original function. Renovations of the Old Executive Office Building began in 1981, managed by the Office of Administration of the Executive Office of the President in cooperation with the General Services Administration (GSA). Townhouse offices on Jackson Place were added to the Greening of the White House project in 1998. During the 19th century, they were used as residences; they were converted to offices in the early 20th century.

Context of the Project

The Greening of the White House project began during the Clinton Administration. And on May 3, 2001, President George W. Bush announced that the Chief of Staff would again review energy usage in the White House. "Since I've asked other agencies to review their policy, I'm going to ask the White House to do the same. We want to be good, efficient users of energy in the White House," the President said. The purpose of the project is to demonstrate to the nation numerous energy-efficient measures that can be adopted by millions of Americans in their homes and offices. The White House context has affected this greening project in several ways. First, the historic character of the buildings has to be preserved, so visible modifications to the exterior and the interior have to be limited. Second, security is always an important consideration. Third, some energy-efficient strategies, although cost-effective from a life-cycle perspective, might have appeared extravagant because of their initial costs, so they were not implemented. Fourth, a significant amount of energy that is associated with the building's operations cannot be controlled by White House staff; these include the extensive press operations on the lawn and in the press offices. Fifth, several agencies are involved

The White House.

in managing the White House complex, including the Office of the President, the GSA, and the National Park Service (NPS); this requires a considerable amount of coordination and cooperation. Finally, the White House is exempt from Federal procurement regulations, so procurements can move more quickly and include new technologies more easily than they can in many other facilities

The Design and Decision Process

The Greening of the White House initiative was announced by President Clinton in 1993 to make the complex "a model for efficiency and waste reduction." The initiative resulted in an action plan that contained strategies in five areas: energy efficiency; building ecology; air, water, and landscape; materials, waste, and resource management; and managerial and human factors. Three major activities were carried out in the year following the announcement. First, an energy audit was conducted by the Department of Energy (DOE), with support from Lawrence Berkeley National Laboratory, the National Renewable Energy Laboratory (NREL), and the Rocky Mountain Institute. This audit examined the major systems that affect energy use: building shell, lighting, plug loads, and heating, ventilation, and air-conditioning (HVAC); it also addressed water use and efficiency.

The second major activity was an environmental audit. The team was led by the Environmental Protection Agency (EPA), with support from the District of Columbia and the Institute for Environmental Auditing. This audit examined compliance with applicable regulations as well as opportunities for pollution prevention.

Finally, a feasibility study was sponsored by the American Institute of Architects (AIA). The AIA organized a design charrette (a highly focused, interactive brainstorming session for the design team) involving more than 90 experts in architecture, interior design, engineering, building operations, and environmental concerns. The charrette produced short-term and long-term recommendations for improving energy efficiency and environmental performance. The recommendations emphasized actions that were cost-effective and that used commercially available, "off-the-shelf" technologies.

The initiative produced a *Phase 1 Action Plan* on March 11, 1994. DOE issued a follow-up Six-Year Report in November 1999.

Responsibility for greening activities has been spread across several agencies. Within the Executive Residence, the White House Ushers Office has oversight responsibility. The GSA has responsibility for the East and West Wings of the White House and the Old Executive Office Building. The NPS maintains the grounds and the guard stations.

Highlights of Environmental Strategies and Accomplishments

Several people involved in these activities have said that the greening process has been very beneficial, both in highlighting potential measures and strategies and also in stimulating action by providing a mandate and visibility for those activities.

During the greening initiative process, recommendations were developed in several areas. Highlights of activities at the Executive Residence, the East and West Wings, and the Old Executive Office Building follow.

Building Envelope

Improvements to the building envelope include a new roof for the Executive Residence and replacement of 98% of the windows in the Old Executive Office Building with double-paned, low-emissivity window units.

Lighting

Incandescent lamps were replaced by compact fluorescents in table lamps and corridors for an energy savings of 350,000 kilowatt-hours (kWh) per year and $22,815 in energy costs. A few historic fixtures could not accommodate the compact fluorescent bulbs, so the incandescent bulbs were retained. Fluorescent fixtures were retrofitted with T-8 tubes and electronic ballasts for a savings of more than $100,000 per year. In addition, the original skylights in the Old Executive Office Building were rehabilitated to provide light to stairwells and corridors.

Plug Loads

A superefficient "Golden Carrot" refrigerator was installed in the Executive Residence. Since 1995, 99% of the office equipment purchased has been Energy Star®-rated (by the DOE/EPA program for efficient appliances and consumer electronics), and staff are required to turn off computers after work.

Both high-voltage and low-voltage electrical equipment in the Executive Residence were upgraded from the transformers, switchgear, main switchboards, and distribution panelboards that had been installed during the 1948–1950 renovation.

HVAC

A new HVAC system was installed in the Residence; this system saves 400,000 kWh and $32,000 per year and uses HFC-134 rather than CFC coolant. Other systems have been upgraded, including window air-conditioning units (with timers and with some new units having an energy-efficiency rating [EER] beyond 9.5), the chiller system, pipe insulation, steam radiators, and steam traps. The use of renewable energy resources was discouraged by the higher first cost of a system, which might have made it appear to be an extravagance.

HVAC Alternatives for South Side Barriers

The South Side entry and exit booths are currently designed with a split-system air-cooled heat pump, including a ceiling-mounted indoor fan coil unit and an outdoor, pad-mounted condensing unit. NREL has recommended a ground-source heat pump as an alternative system. The ground-source heat pump includes a ceiling-mounted, indoor water-to-air heat pump unit, somewhat larger than the existing fan coil unit design, but the exterior system does not have above-ground components. A small fractional horsepower pump above the ceiling circulates water between the indoor fan coil unit and an outdoor underground array of high-density polyethylene piping. The water continuously circulates in this closed-loop system, transferring heat from the indoor unit to the ground when in an air-conditioning mode and extracting heat from the ground when in a heating mode. The International Ground Source Heat Pump Association has published procedures and guidelines for the design and installation of ground source heat pumps. This organization also facilitates training in designing and installing the systems. It also maintains an informative Web site at http://www.igshpa.okstate.edu/.

Materials

Purchasing agents use green buying standards to acquire building materials, cleaning supplies, inks for printing, and the like.

Indoor Environmental Quality: Air

A nonsmoking policy is in effect. From 1995 to 2000, 60% of the rooms in the Old Executive Office Building had been painted using paints with low levels of volatile organic compounds (VOCs); the remaining rooms are painted with oil-based paints because of historic considerations.

Indoor Environmental Quality: Daylighting

Skylights that had been blocked out in the Old Executive Office Building were returned to their original condition, providing daylight to the interior of the building.

Water

Water-conserving fixtures and devices have been installed in restrooms, kitchens, and other areas. A chiller was modified to recirculate cooling water.

Landscaping

The use of fertilizer has been reduced by one-third, and pesticide use has been reduced by 80%. Native plants have been emphasized since 1995. Watering was switched to early morning hours, which saved 1,500 gallons in one year. Trimmings and yard waste are composted off site.

Solid Waste Management/Source Reduction and Recycling

Documents are copied on both sides of recycled paper containing 30% post-consumer waste. Most documents are shredded into fibers too small for recycling, so this material is composted with yard waste.

Hazardous Waste/Toxic Substances Management

Several steps were taken to ensure the proper management, handling, and storage of hazardous materials. These steps included making agreements on procedures, consolidating hazardous waste storage, improving recordkeeping, and ensuring that transformers do not contain polychorinated biphenyls (PCBs).

Managerial and Human Factors

A team was established to create an environmental management program. Currently, several "champions" of the greening efforts continue to lead their organizations.

The buildings on Jackson Place were not part of the original greening design charrette, but were added in 1998. Energy and indoor air quality audits were conducted to identify needed improvements. Greening activities include the following:

- Replace all the windows with double-glazed windows
- Install weatherstripping, at an estimated savings of $13,000 per year
- Finish conversion of T-12 to T-8 fixtures and electronic ballasts
- Replace incandescent bulbs in table lamps with compact fluorescents
- Install motion sensors in areas with sporadic activity and maintain constant light levels in rooms with dimmable lighting systems, at an estimated savings of $3,000 per year
- Install ceiling fans, at an estimated savings of $2,300, based on lower thermostat settings
- Correct problems with makeup air systems
- Investigate HVAC upgrades such as high-pressure HVAC lines
- Improve labeling of recycling containers
- Work with EPA to establish a collection system to recycle nickel-cadmium batteries.

CASE 13
LAS VEGAS CLEANUP A SURE THING

> *Overview*
>
> - A 3.6-acre former National Guard Armory, used by the Nevada National Guard from 1948 to 1997, was returned to the city in late 1997.
> - A Brownfields Assessment Pilot grant from EPA enabled the city to conduct soil and groundwater sampling at the former Armory site.
> - In May 1999, the City of Las Vegas was selected as a BCRLF Pilot by EPA and awarded $500,000, a portion of which was used to clean up the former Armory site.

In Las Vegas, Nevada, a former National Guard Armory has the distinction of being the country's first site cleaned up under EPA's Brownfields Cleanup Revolving Loan Fund (BCRLF) Pilot Program. The $50,000 cleanup involved the removal of more than 600 cubic yards of soil contaminated with hazardous waste and petroleum hydrocarbons. A community center, cultural center, retail stores, and a small business incubator are now planned for the site.

"The Brownfields Cleanup Revolving Loan Fund helps local governments sweep away the last obstacle to redevelopment of abandoned industrial properties contamination," explains Felicia Marcus, EPA's Region 9 Administrator. "This project demonstrates EPA's and the City of Las Vegas' commitment to getting Brownfields sites in the downtown Las Vegas area cleaned up and ready for reuse. We applaud Las Vegas for getting the job done so quickly."

To date, EPA has awarded 68 BCRLF Pilots. The purpose of these Pilots is to enable states, cities, and Native American tribes to make low-interest loans to promote the cleanup and redevelopment of brownfields properties. The program has already leveraged more than $50 million in redevelopment funding from the BCRLF loans issued to date. The City of Las Vegas was selected as a BCRLF Pilot in May 1999 and received $500,000; the city loaned $50,000 to the Las Vegas Redevelopment Agency to enable cleanup of the Armory site. Covering a two-year period, the loan has an annual interest rate of only two percent.

The 3.6-acre former National Guard Armory was used by the Nevada National Guard from 1948 to 1997 for vehicle maintenance, chemical and supply storage, and general operations. The property was returned to the city in late 1997. The neighborhoods in the immediate vicinity of the Armory site are predominantly Hispanic, with high unemployment and poverty rates. Las Vegas City Councilman Gary Reese stated, "We at the City of Las Vegas firmly believe in providing clean and safe neighborhoods, free of contaminants and pollutants, for our residents. Through a shared vision and strong partnership with EPA, the city was able to fast track our efforts to become the first in the nation to clean up a brownfields site under the BCRLF program." Through the site's small business incubation center, the city hopes to provide opportunities for new community-based enterprises, as well as a community meeting place and cultural center.

EPA's partnership with the City of Las Vegas began in May 1998 when the city was awarded a $200,000 Brownfields Demonstration Assessment Pilot grant. This assessment

---

Environmental Protection Agency.

funding allowed the city to conduct soil and groundwater sampling at the Armory site. The sampling revealed that the contamination, diesel fuel and waste oil, was confined to about 600 cubic yards of soil located near where a hydraulic lift had been. The assessments also indicated that the groundwater was not contaminated. The results of these Phase I and II environmental assessments allowed the city and the Nevada Division of Environmental Protection to develop the recently completed cleanup plan.

The BCRLF bridged the gap between the environmental assessment and the eventual development of the Armory property by providing the city with the capital necessary to clean up the site.

CASE 14
ROBINS U.S. AIR FORCE BASE

Robins Air Force Base (AFB)—the largest industrial complex in Georgia—is home to the Warner Robins Air Logistics Center, a major depot for repairing aircraft and producing spare parts for the U.S. Air Force. The Air Logistics Center is responsible for depot-level repairs for the Air Force's F-15 fighter aircraft and the C-5 and C-130 transport aircraft. It provides support for 11 types of cargo and utility aircraft, four series of helicopters, three types of remotely piloted vehicles, and eight missile systems. Robins AFB is also a technology repair center for airborne electronics, gyroscopes, and life support systems for the Air Force.

I. Lean Initiative Background

Robins AFB started to implement lean in May 1999 with pilot projects in the F-15 avionics and wing shops, after being faced with base closures, outsourcing of military repair and maintenance operations, and growing national pressures to delay purchasing new aircraft while relying, instead, on those in service. By September 2002, Robins AFB had extended lean to all of its depot repair processes and had begun applying lean outside of maintenance operations, including administrative processes. Robins AFB uses external consultants as well as internal lean "change agents" to guide its lean efforts.

Robins AFB uses the following lean methods, among others:

- 6S (Straighten, Sort, Shine, Standardize, Sustain, and Safety)
- Value stream mapping
- Rapid improvement events (i.e., kaizen events)
- Standard work
- Point-of-use (POU) storage
- Cellular manufacturing / one-piece flow
- Strategy alignment and deployment (i.e., policy deployment or hoshin kanri)

II. Lean and Environmental Management Integration

Robins AFB has taken a variety of steps to integrate its lean and environmental management efforts. Initially, these efforts focused on ensuring that process changes resulting from lean events were regulatory compliant. More recently, Robins AFB has applied lean techniques to its own administrative and environmental, safety, and occupational health (ESOH) processes and has adapted its pollution prevention methodology to closely align it with lean process improvement events.

To foster lean-environmental integration, ESOH staff engages lean practitioners by:

- Verifying upcoming lean events weekly
- Participating in lean events to identify environmental improvement and pollution prevention (P2) opportunities that also meet lean operational goals
- Training lean facilitators in areas where environmental assistance may be needed

---

Environmental Protection Agency.

- Developing lean event checklists to help lean facilitators to identify potential areas of ESOH concern
- Sponsoring ESOH-led lean events to reduce major environmental impacts in repair and maintenance operations
- Embedding points of ESOH interest—including compliance and liability concerns and environmental data reporting streams—in lean value-stream maps

III. Examples: Lean Projects and Results

Chemical Point-of-Use Cabinets and Waste Collection

Robins AFB instituted lean, point-of-use (POU) cabinet systems for hazardous materials used on the shop floor to reduce the time and distance that workers travel to retrieve hazardous materials. These chemical POU storage cabinets have initial accumulation points associated with them for collecting hazardous wastes from work cells. Robins AFB designed and implemented these POU systems using lean rapid process improvement events, 6S, and visual controls. In addition, Robins AFB has developed a POU request form that allows ESOH personnel to review proposals for POU cabinets and ensure that the applicable requirements will be met for each chemical included in the cabinets. Installing POU cabinets has reduced travel time, saved 1,500 miles of worker travel, and decreased hazardous materials use and hazardous waste generation by 20 percent on the flight line, even while production was increasing. In one shop, hazardous materials use and hazardous waste generation decreased by 50 percent.

Applying Lean to Hazardous Waste Management Processes

Robins AFB applied lean techniques—such as Value-Stream Mapping, standard work, and 6S—to its hazardous waste management processes to reduce the lead time for collecting and hauling away hazardous wastes. After examining the non-value added time in its process, Robins AFB instituted a new system for collecting and transporting hazardous wastes; this system eliminated process steps, saved 1,500 hours of time handling wastes, and reduced the frequency that waste drums were handled (decreasing the number of times waste drums were touched by workers by 70 percent). Robins AFB also reorganized its hazardous waste management facility using 6S and visual controls to control inventory and work in process as well as improve flow. This made it easier to monitor the waste management processes and reduced the likelihood of accidents and spills.

Other Lean Projects and Results

Robins AFB has implemented a variety of other lean projects that have had environmental implications, such as the following examples.

- C-5 Maintenance Shop: Lean improvements in the C-5 cargo plane shop reduced "flow days" from 360 to 220 days, improved resource productivity by 30–50 percent, and saved $8 million in the first year alone. These improvements reduced raw material consumption, hazardous chemicals use, and waste associated with the C-5 maintenance processes.

- C-130 Aircraft Paint Shop: Robins AFB used 6S techniques to improve its paint system for the C-130 Hercules airplanes. Through a series of lean events, Robins AFB reduced flow days, increased production, improved worker safety, and reduced volatile organic compound (VOC) emissions, chemical use, and storage space.

IV. Summary of Environmental Results

Chemical Point-of-Use Storage and Waste Collection:

- Decreased hazardous materials use and hazardous waste generation by 20 percent on the flight line—and as high as 50 percent in one shop—while overall production increased

Lean Improvements in the Hazardous Waste Management Process:

- Reduced the potential for spills and eliminated excess waste drums

Lean Improvements in the C-5 Shop:

- Improved productivity ranging from 30 to 50 percent
- Reduced:
- Use of hazardous chemicals
- Raw material consumption
- Waste generation
- Facility space needed for operations
- Overall number of planes in repair

Lean Improvements in the C-130 Hercules Aircraft Paint Shop:

- Reduced:
- Excess tools, materials, and equipment by 39 percent
- Emitted volatile organic compounds (VOCs)
- Number of chemicals used from nine to three, as well as the overall volume of chemicals used

CASE 15

A FORMER CALIFORNIA BROWNFIELD RECYCLED: A CONSTRUCTION AND DEMOLITION WASTE REDUCTION SUCCESS STORY

Project Highlights

In July 2003, the City of Emeryville provided $1,175,000 in Environmental Protection Agency (EPA) Brownfields Revolving Loan Funds to GreenCity LLC to assist with cleanup costs associated with the GreenCity Lofts property, a former paint factory. The GreenCity Lofts project team completed cleanup of the 0.9-acre property in December 2004 and 62 condominiums were constructed in 2005. Demolition of the former paint factory and warehouse buildings was necessary before construction of the lofts could begin. The project team employed C&D waste recycling practices including deconstructing (hand dismantling) the buildings on the former industrial property as an alternative to traditional demolition. As a result, 94.6 percent of the demolition waste was recycled, exceeding the nearby City of Oakland's legal requirement by 45 percent. In addition, 21,569 tons of excavated soil were diverted from disposal and used as Beneficial Cover at a local Class II Landfill reducing project cost by an estimated $496,708 in eliminated tipping fees.

Background

The GreenCity Lofts property is on the border of Emeryville and Oakland, in the San Francisco Bay Area. The property was used for paint manufacturing from 1923 through 1991 and then as a warehouse from 1991 through 2000. The soil was contaminated with petroleum hydrocarbons due to its former use as a paint factory. The property's ground water was also contaminated with petroleum hydrocarbons due to a neighboring paint factory. The Bay Area city of Emeryville, like many other urban centers, is experiencing a major population growth. As a result, demand for housing is exerting tremendous pressure to develop remaining open space which contributes to urban sprawl. The increasing housing demand and lack of available land are driving the redevelopment of abandoned industrial land. In 2000, former Oakland Mayor Jerry Brown challenged developers to build projects that would revitalize city neighborhoods and set a new sustainable standard. Responding to the Mayor's challenge, GreenCity Development Group envisioned reclaiming the abandoned 80-year old paint factory property for construction of "green" high-density housing. However, environmental cleanup costs presented a substantial barrier to reclaiming the abandoned industrial land.

Environmental Protection Agency.

Process

To offset the costs associated with the environmental cleanup, the City of Emeryville provided $1,175,000 in EPA Brownfields Revolving Loan Funds (RLF) to GreenCity LLC in July 2003. Cleanup of the GreenCity Lofts property was subsequently completed in December 2004. As part of the building permit process, GreenCity LLC submitted a Waste Reduction & Recycling Plan (WRRP) to the City of Oakland. The WRRP documents show how the developer will meet the city's goal of reducing the quantity of construction C&D debris disposed of at landfills by 50 percent or greater.

Consistent with the approved WRRP, project contractors implemented onsite source separation of demolition materials and segregated recycling for the deconstruction and new construction phases of the project. Onsite co-mingling of C&D waste with an off-site waste segregation method was used for the final (traditional) phase of demolition. According to an Emeryville city official, C&D debris recycling strategies can increase project cost due to the need for skilled labor. Fortunately, the terms (i.e., two-year interest free grace period, 3.5-years to pay thereafter, and two percent interest rate) of the EPA Brownfields RLF loan helped to reduce the developer's C&D recycling costs.

Results

The GreenCity Lofts project recycled a record 94.6 percent of its demolition wastes; exceeding Oakland's legal requirement of 50 percent by 45 percent. The high rate of C&D recycling was achieved in large part due to the deconstruction demolition process implemented. Deconstruction versus traditional demolition allowed large quantities of market-valued materials (i.e., plumbing and electrical fixtures, lumber, windows, and steel) to be salvaged and recycled. During construction of the lofts, 21,569 tons of excavated soil were diverted from disposal and used as Beneficial Cover at a local Class II Landfill. This reduced project cost by an estimated $496,708 in eliminated tipping fees. Emeryville's RLF grant leveraged the cleanup and reuse of an 80-year old abandoned industrial property for much needed housing. The project was proclaimed "the greenest multifamily development" by former Oakland Mayor Jerry Brown. From the inception to the finished product, sustainable practices were implemented throughout the life cycle of the project:

Deconstruction of the buildings resulted in demolition waste being diverted conserving landfill space, and easing the environmental impacts and costs of processing, shipping, and extracting raw materials.

- Lofts were built following U.S. Green Building Leadership in Energy and Environmental Design (LEED) principles using recycled building materials and local/regional materials.
- Project maximized the use of energy/water efficient technologies, such as collecting water runoff for use in landscape irrigation and providing wiring in the parking garage to accommodate electric motor vehicles.
- Housing project complied with Emeryville's affordable housing goal by providing six affordable housing units.

By implementing C&D materials recycling along with other sustainable reuse practices during the redevelopment of former brownfields, key EPA Brownfields Program goals were met and creation of a potential future brownfields was avoided.

Key Benefits *(construction crew collecting demolition debris for recycling)*

- Diverted 94.6 percent of demolition wastes from disposal thus, conserving space in existing landfills.
- Reduced overall building project expenses by avoiding C&D debris disposal costs (estimated $496,708 in tipping fees).
- Allowed for the maximum recovery of waste material such as plumbing and electrical fixtures, salvageable lumber, and various metals.
- Reduced the financial and environmental impact associated with extracting, processing, and transporting raw materials.
- Generated revenue from the sale of market value materials recovered as a result of innovative demolition.
- Qualified for a significant tax rebate offered by the City of Oakland Public Works Agency.
- Strengthened the local economy by supporting local markets for recyclables and the local work force.

Construction and Demolition Debris

Construction and demolition (C&D) debris is produced during new construction, renovation, and demolition of buildings and structures. C&D debris includes bricks, concrete, masonry, soil, rocks, lumber, paving materials, shingles, glass, plastics, aluminum (including siding), steel, drywall, insulation, asphalt roofing materials, electrical materials, plumbing fixtures, vinyl siding, corrugated cardboard, and tree stumps. C&D materials can be recovered through reuse and recycling. In order for materials to be reusable, contractors generally must remove them intact (e.g., windows and frames, plumbing fixtures, floor and ceiling tiles) or in large pieces (e.g., drywall, lumber). In order to be recyclable, materials must be separated from contaminants (e.g., trash, nails, and broken glass).

CASE 16

OLD TOWN'S NEW LOOK: ALONG THE WATERFRONT, AN ABANDONED MANUFACTURING SITE JOINS TWO CITY PARKS

On the banks of the Penobscot River in Old Town, Maine, three acres of contaminated property once home to a paper plate and cup manufacturer will soon be a recreational area with a playground, a bandstand, paths for running and biking, and a winter skating rink. In spite of its prime location between two City parks, the former Lily-Tulip Company site had little to offer residents of Old Town for the past seventeen years. The site's building had been used as a warehouse since 1981, until the City arranged to purchase the property in a settlement with the previous owner for unpaid taxes. The City found eighteen transformers on the site containing polychlorinated biphenyls (PCBs), though it remained uncertain whether PCB contamination had spread to the surrounding soil. "We weren't sure what kind of liability we were looking at," explains Charles Heinonen, City Engineer. "If even one of the transformers had leaked PCB contaminated oil, the City might have been faced with a very expensive cleanup project."

Old Town's concern for the Lily-Tulip site was relieved in late 1996, when EPA determined the true extent of contamination as part of the Agency's Targeted Brownfields Assessment (TBA) program. Intended to minimize uncertainties surrounding properties with real or suspected contamination, TBAs have been helping cities like Old Town move forward in cleaning up and redeveloping their brownfields. EPA Region 1 (which covers Connecticut, Maine, Massachusetts, New Hampshire, Rhode Island, and Vermont) has received $1,100,000 in TBA funding so far. "Old Town had contacted EPA earlier, requesting assistance on the Lily-Tulip site," explains Bob Cianciarulo, Brownfields Site Assessor with EPA Region 1. "When the TBA program was initiated soon afterward, it seemed like a perfect fit." Seventeen properties throughout Region 1 are currently targeted for TBAs, and the Agency expects to target as many as six more by the end of 1998. At a cost of approximately $20,000 (the average TBA cost is $50,000), EPA's assessment of the former Lily-Tulip property revealed much lower levels of PCB contamination than originally feared. Following the assessment, the site's abandoned structures were demolished and underground storage tanks removed Petroleum-contaminated soil and PCBladen transformers were hauled away. With EPA's assistance, the City reached an agreement with two prior owners of the property to defray a significant portion of cleanup costs. Cleanup is now complete. In January 1998, the City held a public hearing at which a detailed plan to transform the site into a large, open recreational area was unveiled. In addition to a new bandstand and running and biking paths, the site's "Central Lawn" will be flooded every winter to create a skating pond. Old Town also expects to see an economic return on the redeveloped site, through planned construction of two small commercial/retail buildings and a new restaurant. Explains Ron Singel, City Manager, "Because this property is part of the downtown area, we want to see economic growth be a part of the site's development, along with recreational use." At subsequent public meetings, suggestions from local residents contributed to what would become the master plan for Old Town's new recreational and commercial area. A site redevelopment fund containing more than $100,000 has already been established, which may be used for landscaping or other beautification projects.

Environmental Protection Agency.

CASE 17

PROVO CITY STEELING ITSELF FOR REDEVELOPMENT

The 338-acre Ironton steel plant site in Provo City, Utah, is the largest underutilized tract of land in the city. The site, which has been vacant for more than thirty years, was once an industrial powerhouse for this city of 110,000. The site's derelict condition has lowered area property values and depleted Provo's tax base by an estimated $130,000 a year. Now, in partnership with Brigham Young University (BYU), the Utah Department of Environmental Quality (DEQ), steel manufacturer USX, and EPA, Provo City has taken an active role in bringing the site back to life through assessment, cleanup, and redevelopment.

From 1923 to 1962, the site was home to a steel plant that included coke ovens, blast furnaces, and other steel production facilities. The plant was operated by Columbia Steel until just prior to World War II, when Columbia Steel became a wholly owned subsidiary of U.S. Steel (now USX). In 1962, U.S. Steel closed the facility and donated the land to BYU. In the years following, the university sold the property to several developers, including the Ironton Development Corporation, whose attempts at redevelopment were blocked by environmental liabilities associated with the property. To remove potential cleanup and redevelopment complications regarding private-sector ownership, the city purchased 58 acres of the site in 1978, and optioned 149 additional acres in 1991.

In 1996, Provo was selected as an EPA Brownfields Assessment Pilot and awarded a $200,000 grant. The Pilot's funding helped the city oversee USX-funded assessments on the Ironton site, and forged valuable partnerships with USX, BYU, and the DEQ. Under the aegis of the Pilot, Econsulting, an organization run by BYU students, completed a study of the property and recommended steps necessary to return the site to productive use. The Pilot also coordinated outreach activities to keep the surrounding community informed of the project, and developed detailed plans to manage the site during its cleanup and reuse.

The influence of the city, the Brownfields Pilot, and the other partners intent on restoring the Ironton site prompted USX to enter into a Voluntary Remediation Agreement under the state's voluntary cleanup law. Under the Pilot's three-phase plan for the property, USX will clean up the site in accordance with a risk-based industrial standard agreed upon between USX and the Utah DEQ. After cleanup is complete, the city will reimburse USX with funds from the property's sale once the city's development costs are met. Potential re-uses for the site include a commercial/industrial business park that could create hundreds of new jobs.

In 1999, the city purchased the 149 acres it had optioned. Cleanup of the Ironton site, begun in September 1998, is now nearly finished, with completion scheduled for December 1999. The city estimates that once returned to active use, the site will generate more than $400,000 in annual tax revenues.

Environmental Protection Agency.

CASE 18

CITY OF SANTA MONICA: ANNENBERG COMMUNITY BEACH HOUSE

Overview

Project Owner: City of Santa Monica
Architect: Frederick Fisher and Partners Architects
Landscape Architect: Mia Lehrer & Associates
MEP Engineer: Air-Tec Air Conditioning Contractors; Angeles Electric Co.;
DK Mechanical Contractors Inc.
Structural Engineer: KPFF Consulting Engineers
Contractor: Charles Pankow Builders, Ltd.
LEED Consultant: Davis Langdon
Commissioning Mgr: EEI Consulting
Completion Date: April 2009
Construction Cost: $34.6 million
Size: 5.5 Acres; 101,869 sf (including parking)
Occupancy: 587 (total between 4 buildings)

Project Description:

The original Beach House was developed in the 1920s by William Randolph Hearst and Marion Davies. It featured a mansion with more than 100 rooms, a guest house and a marble swimming pool. After Davies sold the property in 1947, it was converted into OceanHouse, a luxury hotel and the Sand & Sea Club. In 1956 the main mansion was demolished, and in 1959 the property sold to the State of California. The 1994 Northridge Earthquake severely damaged all structures on site. The City of Santa Monica set forth a plan to re-envision the facility as an important community resource. The project sat on hold due to funding until the Annenberg Foundation, at the recommendation of Wallis Annenberg, awarded a $27.5 million grant to preserve the site for public use. Rehabilitation efforts revitalized the historic Marion Davies Guest House and pool, and new construction created recreation and event spaces. In total there are 4 buildings with parking lots to the north, south and east.

Sustainable Features:

- Project team remediated a brownfield site
- 106 bicycle racks and 14 preferred parking spaces for alternative fuel vehicles
- Water efficiency and conservation: large retention basins reduce 90% dry and stormwater runoff; drip irrigation reduces water needs by 50%; native and drought tolerant plants; low-flow shower heads; waterless urinals and dual-flush toilets

City of Santa Monica Office of Sustainability and the Environment.

- Solar thermal system to provide domestic hot water and pool heating
- Cool roof (reflective roof) to reduce air conditioning needs, and to reduce urban heat island effect
- Full cutoff lamps to prevent light pollution
- Green power purchased from local utility to reduce greenhouse gas emissions
- High performance windows with solar reflective glazing
- Smart Building automation to improve energy efficiency and user comfort
- Low-VOC (Volatile Organic Compounds) paints and coatings to improve indoor air quality by preventing paint offgassing
- High diversion rate (recycling rate) for construction waste; post-consumer content recycled building materials; recycled decking and siding
- Ozone-friendly (CFC-free) refrigerants
- Insulation made from recycled denim
- Carbon dioxide monitors to improve fresh air ventilation

CASE 19

COLORADO COURT PROJECT

Program: *The program for this single resident occupancy housing project includes:*

- 44 single resident occupancy units (375 square feet max per unit)
- Community Room
- Mail Room
- Outdoor common courtyard spaces @ ground level and 2nd level
- On-grade covered parking for 20 cars
- Bike Storage

Colorado Court will be one of the first buildings of its type in the United States that is 100% energy independent. Colorado Court distinguishes itself from most conventionally developed projects in that it incorporates energy efficient measures that exceed standard practice, optimize building performance, and ensure reduced energy use during all phases of construction and occupancy. The planning and design of Colorado Court emerged from close consideration and employment of passive solar design strategies. These strategies include: locating and orienting the building to control solar cooling loads; shaping and orienting the building for exposure to prevailing winds; shaping the building to induce buoyancy for natural ventilation; designing windows to maximize daylighting; shading south facing windows and minimizing west-facing glazing; designing windows to maximize natural ventilation; shaping and planning the interior to enhance daylight and natural air flow distribution.

Colorado Court features several state of the art technologies that distinguish it as a model demonstration building of sustainable energy supply and utilization. These technologies include a natural gas powered turbine/heat recovery system that will generate the base electrical load and hot water demands for the building and a solar electric panel system integrated into the facade and roof of the building that will supply most of the peak load electricity demand. The co-generation system will convert utility natural gas to electricity to meet the base load power needs of the building and will capture waste heat to produce hot water for the building throughout the year as well as space heating needs in the winter. This system will have a conversion efficiency of natural gas in excess of 70% compared to a less than 30% conversion efficiency of primary energy delivered by the utility grid at the building site. The solar photovoltaic system will produce green electricity at the building site that releases no pollutants to the environment. The panels are integral to the building envelope and unused solar electricity will be delivered to the grid during the daytime and retrieved from the grid at night as needed. These systems will pay for themselves in less than ten years and annual savings in electricity and natural gas bills are estimated to be in excess of $6000. Recipient of "The Westside Prize" presented by the westside urban forum.

City of Santa Monica Office of Sustainability and the Environment

Project Funding

This project was funded by:
The City of Santa Monica
State of California, Housing and Community Development
Regional Energy Efficiency Initiative
Affordable Housing Program
Bank of America
Location of Project: 502 Colorado Avenue, Santa Monica, California
Client/Owner: Community Corporation of Santa Monica
Total Square Footage: 30,150sf
Costs: $4,200,000.00

CASE 20

PORTLAND STATE UNIVERSITY (PSU) STEPHEN EPLER RESIDENCE HALL

Summary:

Portland State University's (PSU) Stephen Epler Residence Hall was sited and built to be an active participant in the University District's student housing neighborhood. From the hustle and bustle of vivacious students to the animated conveyance of the building's rainwater run-off, Epler was designed to benefit both humans and nature alike. The new residence hall is the first mixed-use LEED certified building in Portland and includes features ranging from toilet exhaust heat recovery to an engaging rainwater harvesting system that is used for onsite irrigation and toilet flushing.

Most notably, Epler Hall demonstrates that going green can be easy. The building couples smart technology with climate responsive design to take advantage of all potential resources to the building and its occupants- rainwater from the sky; light from the sun; heat from toilets, computers, and lights; and breezes from the outdoors significantly assist the building's operation. This greatly reduces reliance upon mechanical and electrical systems to light, heat, and cool the building. Furthermore, the building's relationship to the natural environment creates a more pleasant living and working space. Epler Hall is simple in design, yet effective in performance.

Project Highlights:

- Climate responsive envelope design
- Rainwater harvesting for toilet flushing and irrigation
- "Stack" ventilation
- Heat recovery
- Pre-demolition salvage
- Alternative transportation
- C&D waste recycling
- Energy efficiency via integrated design

City of Portland Bureau of Planning and Sustainability.

CASE 21

SELLWOOD HOUSE: APARTMENT OWNERS FIND VALUE IN GREEN FEATURES

> Bamboo floors and dual flush toilets. Marmoleum in the kitchen and nontoxic paint on the walls. Historical details attractively restored with salvaged wood.

Sound more like a Hawthorne bungalow than a Sellwood apartment building? Not to Jim, Judy and Jill Lyon. The family just may have hit upon a novel solution to the eternal dilemma of property management: how to keep operating costs low, while increasing property value and tenant retention. The Lyons recently completed a "green" remodel of the Sellwood House, an 11-unit historic building in southeast Portland. Instead of taking a traditional remodeling approach, they decided to create a unique rental property using many green building materials. Their risk paid off. Nearly two years after remodeling they have increased the rent by 30 percent, experienced minimal tenant turnover (only two units have turned), and are continually reminded by tenants that the Sellwood House is filling a much desired niche in the Portland rental housing market.

The Lyons had two project goals—increase property value and increase desirability of units, prompting a decrease in tenant turnover.

Their strategy to provide a green multifamily rental property more than fulfilled their project goals. According to property manager and project coordinator Jill Lyon (daughter of owners Jim and Judy), "there is definitely a market for green rental properties. Potential tenants sought us out because we were advertising it as a green property. Once rented, our tenants have created a strong community among themselves." This project was so successful, the owners are currently financing a remodel.

Project Highlights

The Lyon family has a long history of owning and managing multifamily properties in Oregon. In 2002 they purchased the Sellwood House, originally designed and built as the schoolhouse adjacent to Sacred Heart Church in SE Portland. The building had been a low-rent property for some time. Badly in need of remodeling, it was ripe for reinvestment and reinvigoration.

The driving force behind this successful remodeling project was the question, "How healthy and environmentally friendly can we make the units, while still making a profit and increasing property value?" The owners researched products and ran numbers keeping this question in mind. Decisions were made based on the initial investment price for various measures as well as the pay back time. The following products and materials reflect their final choices.

Caramelized Bamboo Flooring

A more attractive and long-lasting flooring option One of the most notable features of the Sellwood House apartments is their commercially rated, pre-finished, carbon roasted bamboo

City of Portland Bureau of Planning and Sustainability.

flooring. According to Jill Lyon, "this particular flooring has a number of desirable attributes for rental units. The color is warm; it's darker tone hides dirt; installation was relatively simple; it can be refinished; it wears well; and turnover maintenance is very fast and easy." In addition, the manufacturer, uses an exceptionally durable, solvent-free coating and the binding adhesive is virtually formaldehyde free, so installers and future tenants won't breathe the off-gassing typical of other pre-finished flooring. The flooring company, Teregren, is located in Washington State. The Lyons were pleased to support a product manufactured in the Pacific Northwest.

The cost installed was $6.75/sf. Typical 5-year carpet cost is $4–6/sf installed. Therefore, carpet and Teregren cost the same at 15 years if no additional refinishing is required. When the increased rent potential is factored in, the value of choosing bamboo over carpet is seen remarkably sooner.

Marmoleum

Durability and beauty with all-natural linoleum Marmoleum is a biodegradable natural flooring made of linseed oil, woodflour, pine rosin, jute and ground limestone. It was used in place of sheet vinyl flooring on the kitchen and bathroom floors, as well as in the bathroom as a back splash. Benefits of using marmoleum are primarily health and environmental related. Some find it more esthetically pleasing as well. Jill reports it has been very resilient and easy to maintain. Payback on the flooring is five years.

Dual-Flush Toilets, Showerheads and Faucet Aerators

Reduce costs and save water Installers removed existing five-gallon toilet tanks and installed Caroma brand dual flush low-flow toilets. Dual flush toilets operate with either 2 buttons or a specialized handle for flushing, using a full flush for solids or a half flush for liquids. Jill says the installers loved these toilets because they were exceptionally easy to install, an important feature for the cramped quarters typical of bathrooms in historic buildings.

Before installing the dual flush toilets, daily water usage was approximately .67 CCF/ day. After the toilets were installed, water usage decreased to .42–.45 CCF/ day. Annually, dual flush toilets save over 3,400 gallons of water over typical low flush toilets. Tasman toilets by Caroma cost $75 more than the typical lowbudget toilet found in apartments. Based solely on noted water savings, it would take about four years to pay off the toilets. Simplified installation cut that cost in half. In addition, the parts are warranted for life. Engineering virtually eliminates all clogs, which equates to greatly diminished maintenance calls. A 2.5 year payback period was calculated for the toilets based on 1/2 cost installation, water savings, and reduced maintenance. Low flow showerheads and faucet aerators were installed to conserve additional water. These low cost measures can save hundreds of dollars on water and sewer charges. Only some tenants have commented on these measures, indicating satisfaction with their performance.

Low-VOC (Volatile Organic Compound) Interior Paint

Tenants breathe easier The Lyons chose Miller Paint's Acro line because it is a low odor, low solvent, eco-friendly paint that contains no offgassing VOCs. VOCs are found in many common household products and can have negative health effects ranging from eye, nose and throat irritation to damage to the liver, kidneys and central nervous system. Jill Lyon reports,

"The paint from locally-owned Miller Paint was great to work with from start to finish, often covering in one coat". The price of Miller's Acro paint is comparable to conventional non zero-VOC products at just under $19 per gallon. Other companies carry low and no-VOC paints as well.

Tax Credits and Incentives Pay Half the Cost of Energy Efficiency Upgrades

The owners took advantage of a free service offered through the Office of Sustainable Development's Multifamily program. By making one phone call, providing a contractor's bid and signing a few application papers, the Lyons received approximately 50% return in cash and tax credits on their window and insulation replacement project costs.

They replaced fifty-six double-hung wood windows with wood frame and vinyl windows. In addition, they insulated 2,100 square feet of attic with cellulose insulation. Cellulose insulation is made from recycled fiber, primarily newspaper. To save on cost, they purchased it from a wholesale retailer and self installed it with a blower. As a final energy savings measure, the Multifamily Home Energy Savings program delivered and installed compact fluorescent light bulbs (CFLs) in all units. The Lyons have seen a noticeable downward trend in electric bills as a result of these measures.

Finishing Materials Don't Show

This project included other green materials rarely noticed by tenants. These finishing materials contributed to the overall goal of offering the healthiest living spaces available while still turning a profit. These products include:

- Elmer's solvent-free/water-based wood putty,
- Clean-Via vegetable-based degreaser for lightweight cleaning of all surfaces,
- DAP shrinkless, paintable, solvent-free caulking,
- Forest Stewardship Council (FSC) certified plywood for subfloors,
- Formaldehyde-free wheatboard in lieu of particle board,
- Salvaged lumber and trim, and
- Wood blinds instead of vinyl or plastic.

Results

Remodeling an investment property requires a different set of decision-making criteria than those used for remodeling a personal home. The Lyons' project shows that employing green building materials and techniques can be a profitable investment decision for multifamily property owners. Jill Lyon speaks of what happens when she places a rental ad: "the response tends to be swift, of great number, inquisitive, friendly, and aware of the limited availability. Additionally, referrals have been quite common."

According to Jill, "green retrofitting requires a shift in thinking about property investment. Payback on these units will not come in the first 12 months", but a greater return on investment is realized in other immediate benefits. These include tenant retention, decreased maintenance and less time spent on marketing.

Their well-defined goals helped the Lyons overcome some challenges involved in a green remodel. The project took longer than a traditional project, and Jill warns that tenants do require more direction when they move in. Many are unfamiliar with how to maintain bamboo floors, marmoleum and how to flush dual flow toilets.

However, once tenants understand the basic care and operation, they love the unique characteristics of the units. Both tenants and guests notice the novel and beautiful bamboo flooring right away, and even the low flow toilets are a discussion topic. Tenants actually give tours of their rental units. They consider the green materials and thoughtful details value-added features. They are willing to pay higher rent and stay longer in part because of these features.

CASE 22
CHARLES HOSTLER STUDENT CENTER

Overview

- Location: Beirut, Lebanon
- Building type(s): Campus, Recreation, Assembly, Other, Restaurant, Higher education
- New construction
- 104,000 ft2 (9,690 m2)
- Project scope: a single building
- Urban setting
- Completed February 2008

The Charles Hostler Student Center on the campus of the American University of Beirut provides a model for environmentally responsive design that meets the social needs of the campus and the larger region. Situated on Beirut's seafront and main public thoroughfare, the new 204,000 ft2 facility houses competitive and recreational athletic facilities for swimming, basketball, handball, volleyball, squash, exercise and weight training. The space also includes an auditorium with associated meeting rooms, cafeteria with study space, and underground parking for 200 cars.

Responding to the scale of the campus' existing buildings and outdoor spaces, the team challenged the University's original plan for a single large-scale building and similarly scaled open plaza. Instead, they proposed multiple building volumes connecting a continuous field of habitable space with gardens on multiple levels. These building volumes are further organized around a network of radial "streets," oriented toward the sea and woven together by a series of courtyards, circulation paths, and spectator areas, negotiating the elevation change from the upper campus to the seafront. To preserve the significant existing landscape, buildings were sited to maintain existing trees. The design for the new Hostler Center synthesizes architecture and landscape to create a set of richly varied and environmentally diverse spaces where people may gather throughout the day and into the evening.

This project was chosen as an AIA Committee on the Environment Top Ten Green Project for 2009. It was submitted by VJAA in Minneapolis, Minnesota. Additional project team members are listed on the "Process" screen.

Environmental Aspects

In traditional Mediterranean cities, the use of urban and architectural space is closely calibrated with the natural environment. Daily human migration throughout the urban environment allows social activities to "condense" at various locations as spaces are exploited for their microclimates–sun or shade, thermal mass with radiant surfaces, and natural ventilation.

Many of the sustainable design strategies used in the project couple these traditional techniques with contemporary technologies. While intended to increase social interaction, all of the strategies also focus on reducing the requirements for energy and water consumption.

The program is organized as a cluster of interior and exterior spaces rather than a single building, allowing the building forms themselves to redistribute air, activity and shade. The east-west orientation of the building forms helps to shade exterior courtyards, reducing the amount of southern exposure. The orientation also directs nighttime breezes and daytime sea breezes to cool outdoor spaces.

Green spaces on the rooftops allow for a more pleasing physical and visual integration with the upper campus, providing usable rooftop areas for activities and reducing the amount of exposure to the sun. Usable program area on the site is increased through shading and ventilation of outdoor spaces.

Owner & Occupancy

- Owned and occupied by American University of Beirut, Corporation, nonprofit
- Typically occupied by 50 people, 40 hours per person per week; and 3,500 visitors per week, 18 hours per visitor per week

The 204,000 ft2 Charles Hostler Student Center includes 100,000 ft2 of unconditioned, underground parking area.

Land Use & Community

Located on a dense 73-acre urban campus at the edge of the Mediterranean Sea, the American University of Beirut (AUB) has been described as the "Garden of Beirut" because the landscape contrasts sharply with much of the city. The design for the Hostler Center extends the lushly planted upper campus into the lower campus and connects it with Beirut's public Corniche seafront boulevard.

Unlike the high-rise condominium developments beginning to line the Corniche, the scale and massing of the buildings and landscaped spaces of the Hostler Center relate to the existing campus buildings and traditional development in the area. The design also negotiates the significant elevation drop from the upper campus to the Corniche for pedestrian use through paths, ramps, and stairways.

Beirut has lacked a significant public transportation system since the Civil War, creating high demand for parking spaces and a situation in which parking lots are maintained for the significant income they generate, often to the detriment of urban infill development. As this was the previous site of AUB's seafront surface parking lot, those parking spaces needed to be maintained, but were provided in the form of underground parking below the Hostler Center complex. No additional parking for the facility was added.

Green Strategies

- **Responsible Planning**
  - Ensure that development fits within a responsible local and regional planning framework
  - Carry out mixed-use development
- **Support for Appropriate Transportation**
  - Design development to have pedestrian emphasis rather than automobile emphasis

- **Property Selection Opportunities**
  - Look for opportunities for infill development
  - Select already-developed sites for new development
  - Look for a property where infrastructure needs can be combined

Site Description

The planned movement of air and people throughout the project are analogous. Like the pedestrian circulation paths, wind naturally flows between the upper campus and the Corniche below. The steep hillside topography of the AUB campus faces north and is densely planted, offering an unusual microclimate. Air cooled by these shaded portions of the campus drops toward the sea during the day, creating a constant cooling and flushing of the air. At night, the site's prevailing winds are redirected toward the land by its proximity to the Mediterranean Sea.

The building volumes and circulation are woven together by a series of intimate social spaces emphasizing lush and aromatic foliage, cool shade, and the sound of moving water. The Hostler Center uses rooftop gardens (green roofs) for social gathering at night. The theater, café, and gymnasium/squash court connect directly to primary rooftop gardens and an amphitheater for evening concerts. In addition to conserving as many existing native trees as possible, new native plantings were added throughout the complex. Some non-native plant species were removed and replaced with sea- and drought-tolerant species.

- Lot size: 349,700 ft2
- Previously developed land

Water Conservation and Use

The original surface parking lot diverted storm water from the upper campus down bituminous pathways directly into the sea. The Hostler Center design collects storm water through appropriately placed site drains and rooftop landscape surfaces to be reused for irrigation and flushing toilets. Even with this ready source of non-potable water for irrigation, plant materials were still chosen for their drought resistance. Excess storm water is now piped into the municipality's storm water system.

Water is a scarce resource in Beirut. With the municipal potable water supply limited and unreliable, the team elected to incorporate a potable water storage system into the Hostler Center design. Potable tap water is dedicated for indoor use only—kitchen, lavatories, and showers. Used graywater from showers and lavatories is collected within a separate piping network and treated in a graywater plant. Toilets are flushed using clarified gray water and the waste goes to the municipal sewer system. Finally, since heat rejection uses seawater, leaving no demand for cooling tower make-up water, preparations have been made for future onsite production of potable water through use of these seawater wells. The desalination process will be either reverse osmosis or thermal desalination using the large array of solar thermal collectors on the pool and gymnasium rooftops.

Water Data

Design Case water use

- Indoor potable water use: 548,000 gal/yr (2,070,000 liters/yr)
- Outdoor potable water use: 183,000 gal/yr (691,000 liters/yr)

- Total potable water use: 730,000 gal/yr (2,760,000 liters/yr)
- Potable water use per unit area: 7 gal/sq ft (285 liters/sq meter)

Green Strategies

- **Runoff Reduction**
  - Design a green roof system
- **Landscape Plantings**
  - Landscape with indigenous vegetation
- **Rainwater Collection**
  - Collect and store rainwater for domestic uses
  - Collect and store rainwater for landscape irrigation
- **Demand for Irrigation**
  - Select plants for drought tolerance
- **Wastewater and Graywater Recycling**
  - Design buildings to use treated wastewater for non-potable uses
  - Plumb building to accommodate graywater separation
- **Integration with Site Resources**
  - Use light-colored pavement to reduce heat island effect
- **Irrigation Systems**
  - Recycle graywater for landscape irrigation
- **Siting Analysis**
  - Investigate microclimate (specific variations from regional climatic conditions)

Energy

Beirut is rebuilding after years of civil war and lacks the robust municipal infrastructure that would be taken for granted in the United States. During summer months, rolling blackouts occur regularly as peak power demands exceed generating capacity. Additionally, political instability can disrupt the public utilities for extended periods of time. To address these issues, it was necessary to integrate backup systems for water and power supply into the project. Many of the sustainable systems in the project are used to provide this backup in a dependable, efficient, and optimized manner.

In addition to emphasizing air movement, the design incorporates radiant cooling for select areas of the buildings where larger gatherings occur on a regular basis, such as the gymnasium, pool, theater, squash courts, and café. Evaporative and radiant cooling are also used in the outdoor courtyard water-walls. Conversely, the project's solar panels heat water for the pool and for other uses. Floor piping directs the water into the pool area to warm the floor surfaces. During the summer, the excess thermal energy can be used for chilled water production.

The Hostler Center uses excess steam produced by AUB to provide additional heating. The ventilation system uses displacement cooling. Large concrete-slab integrated heat exchangers satisfy a major portion of the cooling load. The additional air system provides dehumidified, fresh air. Compared to an all-air system, this system reduces consumption significantly.

An advanced water-cooled centrifugal and absorption chiller provides chilled water, heat rejection is through an onsite seawater well and heat exchanger. A Building Management System (BMS) operates lighting controls and temperature and humidity controls according to outdoor conditions.

Bioclimatic Design

In Beirut, the spring, summer (with the exception of August), and fall are typically hot and dry. Winter brings cooler temperatures and rain, mostly during December and January. The regional climate could be described as semi-arid and strongly influenced by the Mediterranean Sea. Average daily temperature ranges are narrow and humidity varies between 60%–72% over the year. The interaction of topography, local urban form, and prevailing wind patterns significantly affect the AUB campus and cause very specific environmental conditions.

AUB's Master Plan recommended that buildings follow the standard east-west orientation to minimize surfaces oriented toward the sun. A more careful analysis of the shading properties of rectangular volumes demonstrated that north-south courtyards actually provided 40% more shade throughout the year at a latitude of 33 degrees. This enables the courtyards to open up to prevailing sea breezes. By reorienting the buildings on their north-south axis with the primary masonry facades facing east and west, the fanning nature of the plan places the buildings in close proximity to one another, achieving a substantial degree of self-shading while shading adjacent spaces. A highly insulated envelope and solar control windows provide comfortable interior conditions without any heating and cooling in shoulder seasons.

Energy

Beirut is rebuilding after years of civil war and lacks the robust municipal infrastructure that would be taken for granted in the United States. During summer months, rolling blackouts occur regularly as peak power demands exceed generating capacity. Additionally, political instability can disrupt the public utilities for extended periods of time. To address these issues, it was necessary to integrate backup systems for water and power supply into the project. Many of the sustainable systems in the project are used to provide this backup in a dependable, efficient, and optimized manner.

In addition to emphasizing air movement, the design incorporates radiant cooling for select areas of the buildings where larger gatherings occur on a regular basis, such as the gymnasium, pool, theater, squash courts, and café. Evaporative and radiant cooling are also used in the outdoor courtyard water-walls. Conversely, the project's solar panels heat water for the pool and for other uses. Floor piping directs the water into the pool area to warm the floor surfaces. During the summer, the excess thermal energy can be used for chilled water production.

The Hostler Center uses excess steam produced by AUB to provide additional heating. The ventilation system uses displacement cooling. Large concrete-slab integrated heat exchangers satisfy a major portion of the cooling load. The additional air system provides dehumidified, fresh air. Compared to an all-air system, this system reduces consumption significantly.

An advanced water-cooled centrifugal and absorption chiller provides chilled water, heat rejection is through an onsite seawater well and heat exchanger. A Building Management System (BMS) operates lighting controls and temperature and humidity controls according to outdoor conditions.

Data Sources & Reliability

Reliability Energy data is based on 104,329 ft2 of conditioned building space (excluding approximately 100,000 ft2 of unconditioned underground parking area) out of 204,000 ft2 total project area.

Green Strategies

- **Ground-coupled Systems**
  - Use deep well water as a sink for direct cooling
- **Solar Cooling Loads**
  - Shade south windows with exterior louvers, awnings, or trellises
- **Non-Solar Cooling Loads**
  - Use siting and topography to enhance summer breezes
  - Provide an open floor plan and openings located to catch prevailing breezes
- **Water Heaters**
  - Use waste heat from mechanical systems to heat water
- **Cooling Systems**
  - Use centrifugal chillers
  - Use water-cooled mechanical cooling equipment
  - Use evaporative cooling
  - Use night sky radiative cooling
- **Heating Systems**
  - Use hot water heat distribution
- **Other Energy Sources**
  - Consider a cogeneration system to provide heat and electricity
- **Ventilation Systems**
  - Use displacement ventilation

Materials & Resources

The materials selection process prioritized longevity and local availability. The building's systems take advantage of local building technologies and materials, including in-situ concrete, stone masonry, terrazzo flooring, and interior plaster.

The traditional Lebanese wall construction technique is a single wythe of hollow bricks covered by plaster. The U-value of this system is 2.5 W/m^2K. To achieve the required U-value of .7 W/m^2K, a double-shelled stone and concrete cavity wall was used. The new high-quality building envelope has three inches of insulation in cavity walls, eight inches of roof insulation and solar control windows. The superstructure is an economical concrete post-and-beam construction with post-tensioned long-span beams. Exterior walls are sandstone-clad, masonry-cavity wall construction emphasizing regional stone and masonry techniques. Interior surfaces are covered in plaster.

A variety of shading and ventilating wall systems were deployed in strategic locations throughout the project. Aluminum louver systems shade each building to the south, and precast louvers on the east and west walls provide shading for windows and doors. These sun-shading devices incorporate locally fabricated metal and precast concrete.

Design for Adaptability to Future Uses

Given the University's desire to build efficient spaces that minimized energy usage, the design process focused on efficient program organization and finding opportunities for mixed-use spaces. Expansion spaces and breakout spaces were defined in courtyard areas, rooftops, and circulation spaces. Although athletic competition guidelines and University standards required specifically sized spaces for sporting events, the flexibility afforded by the courtyard and circulation areas allow the design to accommodate a wide range of events and visitors. For example, a slightly larger gymnasium allowed for team handball to be played.

Spatial diversity is the key to this environmental strategy. People occupy and adapt to spaces in an ongoing cycle of interaction with daily and seasonal change. Spaces are designed for specific programs and for a range of flexible uses. All are designed for longevity and durability.

Green Strategies

- **Transportation of Materials**
  - Prefer materials that are sourced and manufactured within the local area

Indoor Environment

Responding to changing patterns of sun shading and air movement, social activity shifts among various locations throughout the day and night. Primary building volumes were organized so that the most heavily used daytime spaces—the swimming pool, the gymnasium, and the café—have strong daylighting and natural ventilation. Sixty-seven percent of interior spaces are daylit, and the large areas of glazing provide significant views of the campus, sea, and mountains beyond. Both competition and spectator areas exit directly onto exterior courtyards.

The plan for the Hostler Center orients each programmed building to follow the north-south prevailing winds and local airflow conditions. The cycle of onshore breezes during the day and offshore breezes at night provides constant air movement to cool and ventilate the interior spaces. The end walls facing north and south allow maximum air circulation through the buildings. Multiple openings in the east-west walls facilitate cross-ventilation in the summer months. Sixty percent of the spaces are naturally ventilated, either through building management system-controlled openings in the pool and gymnasium or individually controlled in the offices, cafeteria, and fitness areas.

Green Strategies

- **Visual Comfort and The Building Envelope**
  - Use large exterior windows and high ceilings to increase daylighting
- **Acoustics and Occupant Noise**
  - Use moving water to create a pleasant acoustic environment
- **Building Commissioning for IEQ**
  - Commission the mechanical and electrical systems prior to occupancy
  - Use a comprehensive commissioning process to ensure that design intent is realized

CASE 23
OMICRON AEC, LTD.: HEAD OFFICE RENOVATION

Overview

- Location: Vancouver, BC, Canada
- Building type(s): Commercial office
- Renovation of a 1974 building
- 15,400 ft2 (1,430 m2)
- Project scope: 3% of a building
- Urban setting
- Completed December 2004
  Because Omicron was taking over an entire floor with multiple tenants, the renovation was done in two phases to accommodate tenants with later lease-end dates.
- Rating: U.S. Green Building Council LEED-CI Pilot—Level: Gold (35 points)

The new Omicron office occupies the entire fifth floor of the 32-storey Bentall Tower Three in central Vancouver. The office integrates Omicron's architectural, engineering, construction, and interior design teams in one open-plan space, encouraging discussion across disciplines. Employees are grouped by project team rather than discipline. Discreet pavilions house meeting rooms and other support spaces.

The original building was constructed in the early 1970s, and the individual floors have undergone multiple renovations as tenancies have changed. The circulation core, envelope, and structure of the building, however, have remained the same throughout the building's history.

Environmental Aspects

As an integrated design and construction firm, Omicron had a strong desire to outwardly express its commitment to environmental responsibility. As such, the project team incorporated innovative green products and practices and showcased these strategies to test their broader applicability to future projects.

Waterless urinals and low-flow fixtures reduce the project's water consumption by 40%. Radiant ceiling panels provide heating and cooling. Redundant task lighting was eliminated, and occupancy sensors and a programmed timer reduce energy waste. Energy Star office equipment and appliances were used throughout the project.

More than 25% of all building materials were salvaged from Omicron's previous office location. About 60% of all new materials, by cost, include recycled content; 56% were manufactured within 500 miles of the project site; and 15% include rapidly renewable content. In addition, 98% of all wood-based products were certified according to Forest Stewardship Council (FSC) standards. More than 70% of all construction waste, by weight, was diverted from the landfill.

The project team specified low-emitting materials for all paints, carpets, composite woods, furniture, and insulation. Private offices were eliminated in favor of workstations with low dividers, allowing all employees to have access to a view and daylight.

Owner & Occupancy

- Owned and occupied by Omicron AEC, Ltd., Corporation, for-profit
- Typically occupied by 84 people, 45 hours per person per week; and 80 visitors per week, 1 hour per visitor per week

Building Programs

Indoor Spaces: Office (55%), Conference (13%), Circulation (13%), Other (10%), Lobby/reception (4%), Restrooms (2%)

Land Use & Community

The site selection process began with a list of requirements that included a long-term lease commitment, the opportunity for expansion, bike storage for employees, access to public transit, and location within the downtown core.

The selected site is located atop one of two primary downtown transit hubs and linked to a network of bicycle paths. A station for Skytrain, Vancouver's rapid-transit system, is located across the street from the new office, and the Bentall Centre itself is a bus hub with more than 25 routes originating from this location.

More than 90% of the parking at the project is underground or covered. In addition, the building site features landscaping on 29% of the nonroof surface. These strategies greatly reduce the project's contribution to the urban heat-island effect.

Green Strategies

- **Property Evaluation**
  - Assess property for integration with local community and regional transportation corridors
- **Responsible Planning**
  - Ensure that development fits within a responsible local and regional planning framework
- **Properties with Excessive Impacts**
  - Avoid contributing to sprawl
- **Support for Appropriate Transportation**
  - Provide storage area for bicycles
  - Provide access to public transportation
  - Provide incentives for non-automobile commuting options
- **Property Selection Opportunities**
  - Select already-developed sites for new development

Site Description

- Lot size: 5.03 acres
- Building footprint: 17,200 sq ft (1,600 sq meters)
- Previously developed land

Water Conservation and Use

Low-flow fixtures, including waterless urinals, reduce water consumption by almost 40%, compared with a conventional project.

Water Data

Water Use

- Indoor potable water use: 89,000 gal/yr (337,000 liters/yr)
- Outdoor potable water use: 0 gal/yr (0 liters/yr)
- Total potable water use: 89,000 gal/yr (337,000 liters/yr)
- Potable water use per occupant: 922 gal/person/yr (3,490 liters/person/yr)
- Potable water use per unit area: 5.78 gal/sq ft (235 liters/sq meter)

Green Strategies

- **Development Impacts**
  - Limit parking area
- **Waterless Fixtures**
  - Specify waterless urinals
- **Water Conservation Education**
  - Educate residents about water conservation
- **Low-Water-Use Fixtures**
  - Retrofit faucet aerators or flow-regulators onto lavatory sinks

Energy

The Omicron office renovation features several measures to reduce its energy consumption.

A radiant ceiling panel was selected instead of an air-based heating and cooling system. This system saves energy while providing heating and cooling without drafts. Air-side economizers utilize free cooling. The mechanical system supplies entirely outside air when the temperature and humidity allow, up to 80% of the time in Vancouver.

Redundant task lighting was eliminated, and occupancy sensors and a centralized, programmed timer ensure that lights are turned off when they are unneeded. The project's installed lighting power is 38% below that prescribed by ASHRAE Standard 90.1-1999.

The office features Energy Star appliances and office equipment throughout. The project achieved a connected appliance load of 0.745 watts per ft2 at peak load times; this includes all computers, office equipment, and appliances. The average connected appliance load throughout the week is 0.145 watts per ft2.

Green Strategies

- **Daylighting for Energy Efficiency**
  - Design an open floor plan to allow exterior daylighting to penetrate the interior
  - Use low partitions near the exterior glazing to promote daylight penetration
  - Use large interior windows to increase daylighting penetration
- **Interior Design for Light**
  - Use light colors for surfaces and finishes
- **Light Levels**
  - Design for no more than 1.0 watts/square foot
- **Light Sources**
  - Use high-efficacy T-5 fluorescent lamps
- **Lamp Ballasts**
  - Use high-efficiency electronic fluorescent lamp ballasts
- **Luminaires**
  - Use high-efficiency luminaires
  - Use luminaires that accommodate compact fluorescent lamps
- **Lighting Controls**
  - Use occupancy sensors
  - Use timers to control lighting
- **HVAC Controls and Zoning**
  - Use seven-day programmable thermostats
- **Computers and Office Equipment**
  - Use Energy Star copiers and fax machines
  - Use Energy Star computer equipment
  - Use laptop computers
- **Refrigerators and Freezers**
  - Use Energy Star-rated refrigerators and freezers
- **Other Energy-Efficient Appliances**
  - Use Energy Star dishwashers
  - Use dishwasher with energy-saving features
  - Use microwave or convection ovens

Materials & Resources

The disassembly and reinstallation of materials from the previous office location resulted in the reuse of 27% of the total project materials.

When possible, new materials were selected for their recycled content, local manufacturing, or rapidly renewable content. As a result, 61% of the materials, by cost, include recycled content; 56% were manufactured within 500 miles of the site; and 15% include rapidly renewable content. In addition, 98% of wood-based products were certified according to Forest Stewardship Council (FSC) standards.

Diversion of Construction & Demolition Waste

The reuse and recycling of construction waste diverted 73% of construction waste, by weight, from the landfill.

Green Products Used

- Recyclable Office Chair
- Recycled-Content, Formaldehyde-Free Fiberglass Insulation
- Recycled-Content Carpet Tile
- Recycled-Rubber Athletic Flooring
- Recycled-Wood Fiberboard and Particleboard

Design for Adaptability to Future Uses

The project's open plan should allow for future growth and flexibility in future uses.

Green Strategies

- **Building Deconstruction**
  - Investigate local markets for salvage and recycling
  - Recycle materials to be discarded from existing structure
- **Design for Materials Use Reduction**
  - Consider exposing structural materials as finished surfaces
- **Recyclable Materials**
  - Select products that manufacturers will take back for recycling
- **Job Site Recycling**
  - Require a waste management plan from the contractor
- **Toxic Upstream or Downstream Burdens**
  - Specify natural fiber carpets
- **Ozone Depleting Substances**
  - Replace chiller with new one using ozone-safe refrigerant
- **Pre-Consumer Recycled Materials**
  - Use recycled-content rubber flooring
- **Salvaged Materials**
  - Use salvaged wood for finish carpentry
- **Transportation of Materials**
  - Prefer materials that are sourced and manufactured within the local area

Indoor Environment

Private offices were eliminated in favor of workstations with low dividers, permitting all employees to have access to views and daylight.

In addition, the project team protected the indoor environment by specifying low-emitting materials for all paints, carpets, composite woods, furniture, and insulation.

Green Strategies

- **Visual Comfort and The Building Envelope**
  - Choose interior and exterior glazing to maximize daylight transmission
- **Visual Comfort and Interior Design**

- Design open floor plans to allow exterior daylight to penetrate to the interior
- Select only white to midrange finishes to maximize reflectance of light
- **Visual Comfort and Light Sources**
- Use electronic ballasts with fluorescent lighting
- **Ventilation and Filtration Systems**
  - Specify ventilation rates that meet or exceed ASHRAE Standard 62-1999
- **Building Commissioning for IEQ**
  - Commission the mechanical and electrical systems prior to occupancy
- **Maintenance for IEQ**
  - Design for easy access to HVAC components

CASE 24

PASSIVE HOUSE

Passive Progressive: A bamboo-clad passive house outside of Paris breaks free from local tradition.

Architects Milena Karanesheva and Mischa Witzmann's bamboo-clad passive house in Bessancourt, France, 20 miles northwest of Paris, has lured architectural tourists, locals, film crews, and friends of friends. They've come around to marvel at its presence in a town where 12th- and 13th-century structures along dense, narrow streets and courtyards trump modern design. As improbable as the house is, located between a historic district and small residences from the '70s and '80s, and as challenging as it was to build, it has helped promote the passive house ethos in a country that has been slower than others in Europe to adopt it.

When it was completed in 2009, the officially named Passive House was the second in France and the first in the Paris region. Since then, Karanesheva and Witzmann, wife and husband who founded their Paris-based firm Karawitz Architecture in 2005, have designed about seven passive houses. All except for two are in various stages of construction and completion. And in February, Karawitz was seeking a building permit for a coop apartment building in Paris that will use the passive house tenets.

The 1,900-square-foot, two-story bamboo Passive House is technically and programmatically straightforward, in large part because of strict local regulations and old civil codes, explains Karanesheva. They required a sloped roof and limited windows for intimacy and privacy. "We are modern architects—we are not from the 18th century. For us it was very important to make it contemporary," says Karanesheva. She and Witzmann accomplished that by abstracting the traditional form.

A nearly 2-foot-wide "spine" splits the simple rectangle in two. The south-facing section of the house, where most of the openings are, is twice the size of the north-facing section. The kitchen and living room face the south on the ground floor; three bedrooms and a play area face the south on the second floor. Bathrooms and a laundry room face the north. The spine opens at two points, serves as load-bearing support, and hides mechanicals. A metal lattice walkway on the southern facade of the second floor doubles as a balcony and supports window shutters.

After contemplating dozens of types of wood cladding, Karanesheva and Witzmann chose bamboo for its airy quality and irregularity. "As the house was compact, it was important that the skin be very light, that you could look through it," remarks Karanesheva. In Europe, there are few projects using bamboo, and cladding a home with the hollow stems gave it a more noble purpose. It was also less expensive than wood.

The relative simplicity of the house, however, belies the bureaucratic and technical struggles the architects endured to realize it. Karanesheva, who is Bulgarian, and Witzmann, who is Austrian and German, were familiar with the passive house concepts. The performance certification has roots in homes built across North America in the 1970s during the oil crisis, and was formalized in Germany in 1996, when Dr. Wolfgang Feist (see Feist's Physics, p. 21 in the January/February 2011 issue) founded the PassivHaus Institut. But when the architects searched for a client to finance their prototype in France, they were met with doubts about its functionality and sometimes laughter.

"It was hopeless," says Karanesheva. At the same time, their family needs were changing and they decided to build the house for themselves.

The site was an important factor—Karanesheva didn't want to rely on a car, so the house had to be near the local rail station and amenities. A well-oriented spot just behind a church from the 12th century was perfect, but a local decision-making body in charge of protecting monuments initially resisted Karawitz's design. Bamboo? Photovoltaics? Absolutely not. After many exchanges, the group's skepticism turned into support, but not without some setbacks along the way. (Now even the local mayor is a fan.)

Simultaneously, Karanesheva and Witzmann had to find carpenters who could conform to the precise air tightness specifications necessary for passive houses—a rarity in France, where most builders are masons. With a carpenter from Brittany and a Paris-based firm specializing in sustainable construction in place, the project became a success.

"We thought, 'Well, a house without heating could be a problem,'" says Karanesheva, but "I was surprised how comfortable it is." When it's sunny, the temperature in the house rises quickly, with only 0.48 air changes per hour and a heat recovery rate of 76 percent. The architects were in luck when it came to the triple-glazed windows as a local firm had just begun to supply them. While the ideal passive house should have less glazing, "our house has quite a lot of glazing proportional to the ground floor and envelope, but that's because we like it," comments Karanesheva.

The result is an elegant, modern take-off on the local barns of the Ile-de-France region, and a prototype against the odds. "It shows that it is possible, that costs are not higher than normal construction costs, and that it works," says Karanesheva.

CASE 25
SETAGAYA-KU FUKASAWA SYMBIOTIC HOUSING COMPLEX

Project Outline

A rebuilding initiative of post-war social housing asset for a sustainable future

The Setagaya Ward decided to dismantle the 39 municipally owned and dilapidated wooden detached houses, built in 1952 as a post-war policy drive on a site of 7,388m², and to replace them with a complex of five apartments of 70 dwelling units in total, associated with a variety of community facilities under the banner of "Environmentally Symbiotic Housing".

The goals of this initiative were 1) to help preserve the global environment, 2) to be in harmony with the local environment, and 3) to provide a comfortable and healthy residential environment, through this rebuilding process. Respecting and preserving the historical elements of the place including the rich greenery were the central planning agendas. It was required to enhance the quality of life on and off the site with least environmental loads, as well as to guarantee an increase of its affordable housing capacity. The new housing was, therefore, designed and built with deep consideration to the local natural conditions, and incorporated various passive day-lighting, heating, and cooling solutions.

The types of apartment were planned to create a social-mix, integrating custom-built units for disabled users and others for elderly residents into the ordinary social housing type around the central court. The rebuilt complex reached its 10th anniversary in April 2007, and has developed again into a close-knit community nowadays unusual in Tokyo through its maturing process.

The voluntary Residents' Association has been providing a forum for discussion and problem-solving, and also organized cleaning, recycling, and gardening rotas. The residents' prior involvement in the planning and running process of the complex helped enhance the level of their communal and environmental awareness.

As a governmental pilot project, this initiative has attracted attentions and debates locally, regionally, nationally, and even globally (World Habitat Award 2002).

Basic Information

[Location]Setagaya Ward, Tokyo
[Completion date] March, 1997
[Site area] 7,388 m²
[Total floor area] 6,200 m²
[Structure] Apartment 1: RC Rahmen Construction, Apartment 2–5: RC Wall Construction
[Floors] Block 1: 3–5 floors above ground, Blocks 2–5: 3 floors above ground (in part, 4 floors)

Awards

- 1st JIA Sustainable Architecture Award, Prize of Excellence (The Japan Institute of Architects, 2000)
- Selected Architectural Designs of the AIJ (The Architectural Institute of Japan, 2000)
- World Habitat Awards 2002, (United Nations + Building and Social Housing Foundation, and others)

CASE 26
VANKE CENTER

A Horizontal Skyscraper Greens the Land: Steven Holl fuses architecture and landscape to make one of the most sustainable buildings in China.

Three decades of breakneck economic development have made China one of the world's great polluters, but a new green ethos is beginning to take root in the Land of 1.3 Billion People. Not only is the Chinese government moving to reduce carbon dioxide emissions and encourage alternative energy production, but a growing number of Chinese companies are demonstrating a strong commitment to sustainable design. A leader of this movement is China Vanke, the country's largest residential developer and a company that has hired innovative architects from China and abroad to design a number of projects. Its founder and chairman, Wang Shi, has made a name for himself not only as an entrepreneur, but as a mountain climber (he has reached the summit of Mt. Everest twice) and dedicated environmentalist. So it is not surprising that Vanke wanted its headquarters in Shenzhen to embody the highest green values.

Designed by Steven Holl Architects, which completed its Linked Hybrid residential complex in Beijing in 2009 and is busy working on large-scale projects in Chengdu, Hangzhou, and Nanjing, the 1.14-million-square-foot Vanke headquarters hovers 50 feet above the ground—a "horizontal skyscraper" that is a bit longer (1,310 feet) than the Empire State Building is tall (1,250 feet). By raising the building off the land (on eight supporting structures clad in back-lit, translucent glass), the architects were able to turn almost the entire site, including the area under the building, into a park open to the public. And by planting the roof, they created about the same amount of green space on the site as had been there before. "Our aim was to use a private development to create a public park," states Steven Holl.

Holl and his Beijing-based partner Li Hu approached the project, which was one of the first LEED Platinum buildings in China, as a seamless combination of architecture and landscape. Built on reclaimed land that forms part of the city's stormwater management system, the complex—which includes condos, a hotel, and a conference center, in addition to offices—sits on a lagoon that functions as a bio-swale/retention pond connected to adjacent creeks. The architects redesigned a waterfront retaining wall as a planted estuary, establishing a restorative ecology that minimizes run-off, erosion, and environmental damage. (The LEED status applies only to the office portion, which was completed first.)

A series of courtyards, sunken gardens, ponds, and planted mounds creates a circulatory system that regulates and redistributes stormwater throughout the site. In areas where pavement was required, the architects specified permeable materials such as local river stones, gravel, open-joint stone pavers, grass-crete, and compressed sand pavers to absorb water and naturally filter it. "The landscape is really a machine for cleaning the water and tempering the climate," states Holl.

Because the building sits above the ground, breezes from the nearby South China Sea flow underneath it and cool it. The building creates temperate micro-climates in a part of the world known for hot, moist weather, explains Holl. Raising the structure also gives the spaces inside better views of the sea (to the south) and mountains (to the north). The building's long, narrow floor plate ensures that office workers inside can rely mostly on daylight for illumination. Large operable windows 6.6 feet wide reduce dependence on mechanical ventilation, especially during cooler months (November to March) when natural ventilation can take over 60 percent of the time, estimate engineers at Transsolar. Operable windows can also cut electrical energy consumption annually by about one-quarter or 5 kWh per square meter.

"Dealing with the hot and humid climate and the small daily temperature variation was the biggest challenge for us," states Peter Voit, the partner in charge for Transsolar. "But we did detailed calculations of shading performance and devised a system of fixed louvers and operable windows that achieves very comfortable conditions with natural ventilation during the winter season," explains Voit.

High-performance glass, with two low-e coatings and a custom-designed system of perforated aluminum louvers, protects the curtainwall from the full impact of the sun. To get the most protection while maximizing daylight and views, the architects designed a different elevation for each of the building's 26 faces—adjusting the amount of fixed and operable louvers and the size of the perforations in the louvers to the orientation of the sun. A computer-and-sensor-controlled system automatically tunes the operable louvers to the movement and intensity of the sun. When closed, the louvers reduce solar heat gain by 70 percent, while allowing 15 percent of daylight to filter through the perforations. By suspending the louvers beyond the glass face of the building, the architects created a convective stack effect that draws cool air from the underside of the structure while pulling hot air out from the top.

To reduce dependence on conventional energy sources, the architects installed 15,000 square feet of photovoltaic panels on the building's roof. They estimate that these solar cells will provide 12.5 percent of the headquarters' total electricity needs.

Throughout the project, Holl's team specified products made from renewable materials. For example, the architects used bamboo for doors, floors, and furniture, and carpet tiles with vinyl backing made from recycled carpet and manufacturing waste. All paints, finishes, and adhesives in the building have either few or no VOCs.

To conserve potable water, the building is equipped with low-flow, highly efficient plumbing fixtures and waterless urinals. In addition, dual-flush toilets use recycled graywater. Outdoors, rainwater filtered by the bio-swale system is used to irrigate the grounds.

Holl worked with engineers at the China Academy of Building Research to design an innovative structural system that combines a high-strength concrete frame with the kind of steel cable-stay technology most often used on bridges. The solution eliminated the need for large trusses that would have impaired views from office areas and disrupted interiors more than the angled cables that were used. These cables transmit the building's vertical load to key structural elements such as reinforced-concrete cores, walls, and columns and then to the foundation.

Like Holl's Linked Hybrid in Beijing, the Vanke headquarters combines different functions in one complex—an 86,000- square-foot conference center tucked into green-roofed mounds at its base, 214,000 square feet of hotel space, and 211,000 square feet of condominium apartments. Parking is mostly underground. Because the office, condo, and hotel functions all occupy one long building, the scheme offers flexibility in terms of the amount of space allocated to each segment.

While some people question China's commitment to sustainability, Holl says all of his Chinese clients have asked for the greenest buildings possible. "In other parts of the world, clients want to nickel-and-dime sustainability, questioning every expenditure," states the architect. "Chinese clients aren't thinking that way. They're thinking of building the future."

CASE 27
VICTOR CIVITA PARK

An Eco-park Rises from the Ash: In São Paulo, the transformation of a brownfield into green space creates a model for landscape reuse and management in Brazil.

What once served as a garbage incinerator now hosts the public for a variety of educational and leisure activities. Victor Civita Park occupies 3.1 acres in central São Paulo with the main objective of promoting and exhibiting sustainable design strategies, appropriate for a brownfield site that, after four decades of continuous activity, was deactivated in 1990.

In 2002, the city announced its intention to create a number of new parks in São Paulo, proposing this site as one of them. Establishing a partnership with Grupo Abril, a publishing house founded by Victor Civita, this public-private partnership became the first in Brazil involving urban parks. Hamilton Santos, director of Grupo Abril, remarked: "If we can transform an incinerator site into a green area, it means we can do the same with other neglected spaces." Thus the project has served as a cornerstone for sustainable development in the city.

In 2006, a series of chemical studies of the site's soil conditions indicated that contamination was too high for human occupation. The client then hired Levisky Arquitetos Associados, a local architecture firm to help. "When we started working on this project, there was no national legislation that would guide us on how to proceed," remarked Adriana Levisky, director of the firm. Therefore, the first, and probably smartest decision Levisky made was to insist that the project be limited by the original public-private partnership agreement, preserving its original goals. The design team contacted Brazilian architect Anna Dietzsch, who heads the São Paulo office of New York-based firm Davis Brody Bond Aedas, to help develop a formal solution. Instead of a conventional approach, Aedas suggested converting the incinerator building into exhibition space, the surrounding land into gardens, and creating a raised deck for access, an inventive solution that preserved the site, allowing it to serve as a learning lab for the public.

The architects decided to minimize intervention in the 12,500-square-foot incinerator building, exposing and preserving the brick walls and concrete structure. Renovated to serve as a museum of sustainability, the first floor of the facility is used for permanent exhibitions with the second floor not yet occupied. A 20,750-square-foot deck of recycled Brazilian hardwood floats three feet over the contaminated soil, serving as the main organizing principle of the park. In addition to creating a safe distance between the contaminated soil and visitors, elevating the structure also preserved the site's abundant rubber, eucalyptus, ficus, and fruit trees.

Transported from Brazilian rain forests, Ipê, Garapa, and Sucupira create the deck structure. The wood is so dense that it doesn't require weather treatment, and a gray patina developed over time serves as an added layer of protection. The elevated platform establishes a main linear pathway that crosses the site with a long diagonal. It also creates a central plaza, generating secondary paths of varying sizes and forms that are shaped into gathering areas, overlooks, and seating that invite public use. When reaching the sides, the horizontal planes of the deck undulate upwards becoming fences, overhangs, and exhibit panels that explain the systems used in the park. In places, a series of "windows" have been cut out of the ramp's vertical panels to allow viewing of the gardens.

In addition to existing trees, newly planted areas organized thematically recall fields of farmland in their arrangement. "I wanted the place to reflect agricultural concepts, with linear and geometrical patterns that farmers use to cultivate the land," Dietzsch explains. Following this idea, various regional fruits, vegetables, and bulbs are planted in alternating strips. These include plants used for biomass, medicinal purposes, transgenic plants, and a vertical hydroponic garden.

Contributing to the eco-theme of the park, water collection and reuse are other key objectives. Developed by the landscape architect Benedito Abbud to separate the contaminated soil from the new soil, "The Tec-Garden consists of an elevated system of plates that create an impermeable surface for planting. Above the plaques, a geotextile blanket is laid for the soil. Holes drilled into the plaques accommodate tubes that transport water in both directions, irrigating the plants," he explains. In addition, water from the restrooms is conducted underground to an ornamental pond adjacent to the museum where it is filtered for irrigation reuse.

Additional cultural and educational facilities include a covered amphitheater, renovation of an existing building for a 2,900-square-foot center for the elderly, and a 1,350-square-foot space where workshops on the subject of sustainability are held. Photovoltaics were originally planned, but cut from the program due to cost.

Part of the "Plan of 100 Parks for the City of São Paulo," the park's importance to the city is unparalleled. "It establishes a public place for cultural activities, so few in São Paulo," Mayor Gilberto Kassab affirms.

CASE 28

WWF AND ABU DUBAI'S MASDAR INITIATIVE UNVEIL PLAN FOR WORLD'S FIRST CARBON-NEUTRAL, WASTE-FREE, CAR-FREE CITY

Located near Abu Dhabi International Airport, Masdar City will be the world's first zero-carbon, zero-waste, car-free city, aiming to exceed the 10 sustainability principles of "One Planet Living^{TM}"–a global initiative launched by the Worldwide Fund for Nature and environmental consultancy BioRegional.

Masdar City's electricity will be generated by photovoltaic panels, while cooling will be provided via concentrated solar power. Water will be provided through a solar-powered desalination plant. Landscaping within the city and crops grown outside the city will be irrigated with grey water and treated waste water produced by the city's water treatment plant.

The city is part of the Masdar Initiative, Abu Dhabi's multi-faceted investment in the exploration, development and commercialisation of future energy sources and clean technology solutions. The six-square kilometre city, growing eventually to 1,500 businesses and 50,000 residents, will be home to international business and top minds in the field of sustainable and alternative energy.

A model of the Masdar City will be unveiled on January 21, at the World Future Energy Summit in Abu Dhabi. Ground breaks for the construction of the city in the first quarter of 2008.

Jean-Paul Jeanrenaud, Director of WWF International's One Planet Living initiative, said: "Today Abu Dhabi is embarking on a journey to become the global capital of the renewable energy revolution. Abu Dhabi is the first hydrocarbon-producing nation to have taken such a significant step towards sustainable living.

"Masdar is an example of the paradigm shift that is needed. The strategic vision of the Abu Dhabi government is a case study in global leadership. We hope that Masdar City will prove that sustainable living can be affordable and attractive in all aspects of human living—from businesses and manufacturing facilities to universities and private homes," Jeanreneaud continued.

Dr. Sultan Al Jaber, CEO of the Masdar Initiative, said: "Masdar City will question conventional patterns of urban development, and set new benchmarks for sustainability and environmentally friendly design—the students, faculty and businesses located in Masdar City will not only be able to witness innovation first-hand, but they will also participate in its development."

"We are pleased to be able to work with One Planet Living to make our vision a reality," he said.

Pooran Desai OBE, co-founder of BioRegional and Technical Director of the One Planet Living Communities programme, said Masdar would be the largest and the most advanced sustainable communities in the world.

"The vision of One Planet Living is a world where people everywhere can lead happy, healthy lives within their fair share of the Earth's resources. Masdar gives us a breathtaking insight into this positive, alternative future.

Masdar City Press Release, January 13, 2008.

"In realising the goal of a sustainable future, Masdar is committed to surpassing the One Planet Living Program's 10 Guiding Principles, covering issues that range from how waste is dealt with to the energy performance of the buildings."

The One Planet Living programme is based on 10 unique principles of sustainability. Masdar City will meet and exceed each of these, as detailed below.

These targets are to be achieved by the time the Masdar City is completed and fully functioning in 2015.

One Planet Living principle	Masdar Target
ZERO CARBON	100 per cent of energy supplied by renewable energy–Photovoltaics, concentrated solar power, wind, waste to energy and other technologies
ZERO WASTE	99 per cent diversion of waste from landfill (includes waste reduction measures, reuse of waste wherever possible, recycling, composting, waste to energy)
SUSTAINABLE TRANSPORT	Zero carbon emissions from transport within the city; implementation of measures to reduce the carbon cost of journeys to the city boundaries (through facilitating and encouraging the use of public transport, vehicle sharing, supporting low emissions vehicle initiatives)
SUSTAINABLE MATERIALS	Specifying high recycled materials content within building products; tracking and encouraging the reduction of embodied energy within materials and throughout the construction process; specifying the use of sustainable materials such as Forest Stewardship Council certified timber, bamboo and other products
SUSTAINABLE FOOD	Retail outlets to meet targets for supplying organic food and sustainable and or fair trade products
SUSTAINABLE WATER	Per capita water consumption to be at least 50 per cent less than the national average; all waste water to be re-used
HABITATS AND WILDLIFE	All valuable species to be conserved or relocated with positive mitigation targets
CULTURE AND HERITAGE	Architecture to integrate local values.
EQUITY AND FAIR TRADE	Fair wages and working conditions for all workers (including construction) as defined by international labour standards
HEALTH AND HAPPINESS	Facilities and events for every demographic group

REFERENCES FOR CASE STUDIES

American Institute of Architects. (2011). "Charles Hostler Student Center." Retrieved on September 22, 2011, from http://www.aiatopten.org/hpb/overview.cfm?ProjectID=1301

City of Los Angeles Department of Public Works—Bureau of Engineering. (n.d.). "Boyle Heights Youth Technology Center." Retrieved April 3, 2011, from http://eng.lacity.org/projects/sdip/boyleheights.htm

City of Portland. Bureau of Planning and Sustainability. "Portland University Epler Hall." (n.d.). Retrieved April 3, 2011, from http://www.portlandonline.com/bps/index.cfm?c=41947&a=112553

City of Portland. Bureau of Planning and Sustainability. "Sellwood House." (n.d.). Retrieved April 3, 2011, from http://www.portlandonline.com/bps/index.cfm?c=41703&a=121696

City of Santa Monica. (n.d.). "Anneberg Community Beach House." Retrieved April 3, 2011, from http://www.smgov.net/uploadedFiles/Departments/OSE/Categories/Green_Building/Annenberg-BeachHouse_CaseStudy2.pdf?n=7929

City of Santa Monica. (n.d.). "Colorado Court Project." Retrieved April 3, 2011, from http://www.smgov.net/Departments/OSE/Categories/Green_Building/Colorado_Court_Project.aspx

Google's Green Data Centers: Network POP Case Study. (2011). Retrieved June 16, 2011, from http://static.googleusercontent.com/external_content/untrusted_dlcp/www.google.com/en/us/corporate/datacenter/dc-best-practices-google.pdf

Japan Sustainable Building Database. (n.d.). "Setagaya-ku Fukasawa Symbiotic Housing Complex." Retrieved April 3, 2011, from http://www.ibec.or.jp/jsbd/F/index.htm

Martignoni, Jimena. (2010). "Victor Civita Park, São Paulo, Brazil: An Eco-park Rises from the Ash: In São Paulo, the transformation of a brownfield into green space creates a model for landscape reuse and management in Brazil." Greensource: McGraw-Hill Publication. Retrieved on September 22, 2011, from http://greensource.construction.com/green_building_projects/2010/1005_VictorCivitaPark.asp

Masdar City. (2008). "WWF and Abu Dubai's Masdar Initiative Unveils Plan for World's First Carbon-Neutral, Waster-Free, Car-Free City." Retrieved February 10, 2011, from http://www.masdarcity.ae/en/75/resource-centre/press-releases/?view=details&id=55

Pearson, Clifford A. (2011). "Case Study: Vanke Center, Shenzhen, China: A Horizontal Skyscraper Greens the Land: Steven Holl fuses architecture and landscape to make one of the most sustainable buildings in China." Greensource: McGraw-Hill Publications. Retrieved September 22, 2011, from http://greensource.construction.com/green_building_projects/2011/1104_Vanke_Center.asp

Raskin, Laura. (2011). "Case Study: Passive House, Bessancourt, France. Passive Progressive: A bamboo-clad passive house outside of Paris breaks free from local tradition." Greensource: McGraw-Hill Publications. Retrieved September 22, 2011, from http://greensource.construction.com/green_building_projects/2011/1104_Passive_House.asp

United States Department of Agriculture. (n.d.). "Mother Goose Farms." Retrieved April 3, 2011, from ftp://ftp-fc.sc.egov.usda.gov/WSI/pdffiles/Sustainable_Agriculture_Case_Study_1.pdf

United States Department of Energy. (2001). "Greening Project Status Report: The White House." Retrieved April 3, 2011, from http://www1.eere.energy.gov/femp/pdfs/greening_whitehouse.pdf

United States Environmental Protection Agency. (2007). "A Former California Brownfield Recycled." Retrieved April 3, 2011, from http://www.epa.gov/brownfields/success/emeryvilleca_cd_ss_final.pdf

United States Environmental Protection Agency. (n.d.). "GE & Universal

Studios Hollywood–The Treasure Hunt." Retrieved April 3, 2011, from http://epa.gov/lean/studies/lockheed.htm

United States Environmental Protection Agency. (2000). "Las Vegas Cleanup a Sure Thing." Retrieved April 3, 2011, from http://epa.gov/brownfields/success/ss_vegas.pdf

United States Environmental Protection Agency. (n.d.). "Lockheed Martin." Retrieved April 3, 2011, from http://epa.gov/lean/studies/treasure.htm

United States Environmental Protection Agency. (1998). "Old Town's New Look: Along the Waterfront, an Abandon Manufacturing Site Joins Two City Parks." Retrieved April 3, 2011, from http://epa.gov/brownfields/success/ss_oldtn.pdf

United States Environmental Protection Agency. (2000). "On the Road to Success: Rome, New York's Rome Business Park." Retrieved April 3, 2011, from http://epa.gov/brownfields/success/ss_rom2.pdf

United States Environmental Protection Agency. (2000). "Provo City Selling Itself for Redevelopment." Retrieved April 3, 2011, from http://epa.gov/brownfields/success/ss_prov2.pdf

United States Environmental Protection Agency. (2000). "Rising from the Depths in Naugatuck Valley: The Restoration and Reuse of Idle Land." Retrieved January 5, 2011, from http://www.epa.gov/brownfields/success/ss_naug.pdf

United States Environmental Protection Agency. (n.d.). "Robins U. S. Air Force Base." Retrieved April 3, 2011, from http://epa.gov/lean/studies/robins.htm

United States Environmental Protection Agency. (n.d.). "Village Farms of Buffalo, Inc." Retrieved April 3, 2011, from http://www.epa.gov/region02/superfund/brownfields/tomato.htm

United States Green Building Council. (2011). "Omicron AEC, Ltd., Head Office Renovation." Retrieved on September 22, 2011, from http://leedcasestudies.usgbc.org/overview.cfm?ProjectID=670

Yudelson, Jerry. (2010). *Green Existing Buildings*. New York: McGraw-Hill.

APPENDIX A

ASSOCIATIONS, PROFESSIONAL SOCIETIES AND MEMBER ORGANIZATIONS

American Association for the Advancement of Science (AAAS)
Center for Science, Technology and Sustainability
1200 New York Avenue, NW
Washington, DC 20005
http://www.aaas.org/

American Congress on Surveying and Mapping (ACSM)
6 Montgomery Village Avenue, Suite 403
Gaithersburg, MD 20879
http://www.acsm.net/

American Council on Renewable Energy
American Council On Renewable Energy
1600 K Street, NW
Suite 700
Washington, DC 20006
http://www.acore.org/

American Geological Institute
4220 King Street
Alexandria, VA 22302-1502
http://www.agiweb.org/

American Institute of Biological Sciences (AIBS)
1444 I St., NW, Ste. 200
Washington, DC 20005
http://www.aibs.org/home/index.html

American Meteorological Society
45 Beacon Street
Boston, MA 02108-3693
http://www.ametsoc.org/

American Wind Energy Association
1501 M Street, NW
Suite 1000
Washington, DC 20005
http://www.awea.org/

Association of American Geographer
1710 16th Street, NW
Washington, DC 20009-3198
http://www.aag.org/

Biomass Thermal Energy Council
1211 Connecticut Ave., NW
Suite 600
Washington, DC 20036
http://www.biomassthermal.org/

Clean Technology and Sustainable Industries Organization
3925 West Braker Lane
Austin, TX 78759
http://www.ct-si.org/

Ecological Society of America
1990 M Street, NW Suite 700
Washington, DC 20036
http://www.esa.org/

Environmental Entrepreneurs
Natural Resources Defense Council
40 West 20th Street
New York, NY 10011
http://www.e2.org/jsp/controller?cmd=liqmain

Environmental and Energy Study Institute
1112 16th Street, NW
Suite 300;
Washington, DC 20036-4819
http://www.eesi.org/

European Wind Energy Association
Rue d'Arlon 80
B-1040 Brussels
Belgium
http://www.ewea.org/

Geological Society of America
3300 Penrose Place
Boulder, CO 80301-1806
http://www.geosociety.org

Geothermal Energy Association
209 Pennsylvania Avenue, SE
Washington, DC 20003
http://www.geo-energy.org/

Greenpeace
702 H Street, NW
Suite 300
Washington, D.C. 20001
http://www.greenpeace.org/usa/en/

IEEE Geoscience and Remote Sensing Society
445 Hoes Lane
Piscataway, NJ 08854
http://www.grss-ieee.org/

International Association of Hydrogeologists
PO Box 4130
Goring, Reading, RG8 6BJ
United Kingdom
http://www.iah.org/

International Hydropower Association
Nine Sutton Court Road
Sutton
London
SM1 4SZ
United Kingdom
http://www.hydropower.org/index.asp

International Society of Biometeorology
P.O. Box 413
University of Wisconsin-Milwaukee
Milwaukee, WI 53201-0413
http://www.biometeorology.org/

National Audubon Society
225 Varick Street
New York, NY 10014
http://www.audubon.org/

National Association of Environmental Professionals (NAEP)
PO Box 460
Collingswood, NJ 08108
http://www.naep.org/

National Brownfield Association
1250 South Grove Avenue, Suite 200
Barrington, IL 60010
http://www.brownfieldassociation.org/

National Geographic Society
1145 17th Street, NW
Washington, D.C. 20036-4688
http://www.nationalgeographic.com/

National Hydropower Association
25 Massachusetts Ave., NW
Suite 450
Washington, DC 20001
http://hydro.org/

Nature Conservancy
4245 North Fairfax Drive, Suite 100
Arlington, VA 22203-1606
http://www.nature.org/

Renewable Fuels Association
425 Third Street, SW, Suite 1150
Washington, DC 20024
http://www.ethanolrfa.org/

Sierra Club
85 Second Street, 2nd Floor
San Francisco, CA 94105
http://www.sierraclub.org/

Soil and Water Conservation Society
945 SW Ankeny Road
Ankeny, Iowa 50023-9723
http://www.swcs.org/

Solar Energy Industries Association
575 7th Street, NW
Suite 400, Washington DC 20004
http://www.seia.org/

Union of Concerned Scientist
Two Brattle Sq.
Cambridge, MA 02138-3780
http://www.ucsusa.org/

United States Green Building Council
U.S. Green Building Council
2101 L Street, NW
Suite 500
Washington, DC 20037
http://www.usgbc.org/

Urban Land Institute
1025 Thomas Jefferson Street, NW, Suite 500 West
Washington DC 20007
http://ww.uli.org/

World Wind Energy Association
Charles-de-Gaulle-Str. 5
53113 Bonn
Germany
http://www.wwindea.org/home/index.php

INTERNATIONAL GOVERNMENT AGENCIES AND PROGRAMS

Australia—Department of Sustainability, Environment, Water, Population and Communities
GPO Box 787
Canberra ACT 2601
http://www.environment.gov.au/

Austrian Federal Environment Agency
Kongens Nytorv 6,
1050 Copenhagen K, Denmark
http://sdo.ew.eea.europa.eu/networks/
austrian-federal-environment-agency

Bangladesh—Ministry of Environment and Forests
Government of the People's Republic of
Bangladesh
Building # 6, Level # 13
Bangladesh Secretariat, Dhaka
http://www.moef.gov.bd/

Belgian Federal Department of the Environment
Pachecolaan 19 PB 5
Brussels, 1010
Belgium
http://www.envirolink.org/resource.html?itemid=
90325134857&catid=4

Brazilian Institute of Environment and Renewable Resources
SCEN Trecho 2 - Ed. Sede - Cx.
Postal n° 09566 - CEP
70818-900 – Brasília-DF
http://www.ibama.gov.br/

Brazilian Ministry of the Environment
Ministry of Environment
Esplanada dos Ministerios
Bloco B
70068-900 - Brasília - DF
http://www.mma.gov.br/sitio/en/

CSIRO Tropical Forest Research Centre
(Australia)
CSIRO Enquiries
Locked Bag 10
Clayton South VIC 3169
Australia
http://www.csiro.au/org/AboutCSE.html

Canada—Environment Canada
Environment Canada
Inquiry Centre
10 Wellington, 23rd Floor
Gatineau QC
K1A 0H3
http://www.ec.gc.ca/

China—Ministry of Environmental Protection of
the People's Republic of China
No.115 Xizhimennei
Nanxiaojie, Beijing (100035)
http://english.mep.gov.cn/

Czech Ministry of Environment
Ministry of the Environment of the Czech
republic
Vršovická 65
Praha 10
100 10
http://www.mzp.cz/en/

Danish Ministry of Environment and Energy
Miljøministeriets Informationscenter
Strandgade 29
1401 Copenhagen K
Denmark
http://www.mim.dk/eng/

Egypt—Ministry of State for Environmental Affairs
30 Misr Helwan El-Zyrae Road, Maadi
Cairo, Egypt
http://www.eeaa.gov.eg/English/main/about.asp

England and Wales—Environment Agency
National Customer Contact Centre
PO Box 544
Rotherham
S60 1BY
http://www.environment-agency.gov.uk/default.aspx

Ethopia—Ethopian Environmental Protection
Agency
http://www.epa.gov.et/default.aspx

France—Ministry of Ecology, Sustainable Development, Transport and Housing
Grande Arche
Tour Pascal A and B
92055 La Défense Cedex
http://www.developpement-durable.gouv.fr/

Germany—Federal Ministry for Environment,
Nature Conservation and Nuclear Safety
Stresemannstraße 128-130
10117 Berlin, Germany
http://www.bmu.de/english/aktuell/4152.php

Greece—Ministry of Environment, Energy and
Climate
17 Amaliados Street
Ampelokipoi, Athens 11523
http://www.minenv.gr/#

Hong Kong—Environmental Protection Agency
/F-34/F and 46/F-48/F Revenue Tower
5 Gloucester Road
Wan Chai, Hong Kong
http://www.epd.gov.hk/epd/eindex.html

Iceland—The Environment Agency of Iceland
Skulagata 4
IS 150 Reykjavík
Iceland
http://www.fisheries.is/management/institutes/
the-environment-agency-of-iceland/

India—Ministry of Environment and Forest
Government of India
Ministry of Environment and Forests
Paryavaran Bhavan
CGO Complex, Lodhi Road
New Delhi - 110 003
INDIA
http://moef.nic.in/index.php

Indonesia—Ministry of Forestry Republic of
Indonesia
Kementerian Kehutanan
Gedung Manggala Wanabakti Blok I Lt. 3
Jalan Gatot Subroto - Senayan - Jakarta - Indone-
sia - 10270
http://www.dephut.go.id/

Ireland—Environmental Protection Agency
EPA Headquarters
PO Box 3000
Johnstown Castle Estate
Co. Wexford
Ireland
http://www.epa.ie/

Israel—Ministry of Environmental Protection
P.O.B. 34033
Jerusalem 95464, Israel
http://www.sviva.gov.il/bin/
en.jsp?enPage=e_homePage

Italy—Government of Italy, Ministry of the
Environment and Territory
44, Via Cristoforo Colombo
00147 Rome
Italy
http://www.minambiente.it/home_it/index.
html?lang=it

Japan—Ministry of the Environment Government
of Japan
Godochosha No. 5, Kasumigaseki 1-2-2,
Chiyoda-ku, Tokyo 100-8975, Japan
http://www.env.go.jp/en/

Mexico—Secretariat of the Environment and
Natural Resources
Blvd. Adolfo Ruiz Cortines # 4209 Col.
Jardines
en la Montaña, México, D.F. C.P. 14210
http://www.semarnat.gob.mx/Pages/Inicio.aspx

Mexican Agency for Environment, Natural
Resources and Fisheries
1849 C Street, NW
Washington DC 20240
http://www.doi.gov/intl/agreements/Secretariat-
of-Environment-Natural-Resources-and-Fisher-
ies-Mexico.cfm

Native American Nations—Inter-Tribal Environmental Council
208 Allen Road
Tahlequah, OK 74464
http://www.itecmembers.org/

Netherlands—Ministry of Housing, Spatial Planning and the Environment
Plesmanweg 1-6
2597 JG Den Haag
http://english.verkeerenwaterstaat.nl/english/

New Zealand—Department of Conservation
Conservation House, Manners Street
Wellington, New Zealand
http://www.doc.govt.nz/

New Zealand—Ministry of the Environment
Environment House
23 Kate Sheppard Place
Thorndon
Wellington
New Zealand
http://www.mfe.govt.nz/index.html

Nigeria—Federal Ministry of the Environment
340 Indepence Way
Central Area F.C.T.
Abuja – Nigeria
http://environment.gov.ng/

Northern Ireland Environmental Agency
Clarence Court
10 - 18 Adelaide Street
Belfast
BT2 8GB
http://www.doeni.gov.uk/niea/

Norwegian Ministry of the Environment
Myntgata 2
Oslo
http://www.regjeringen.no/en/dep/
md.html?id=668

Norwegian Directorate for Nature Management
Tungasletta 2
PO Box 5672
Sluppen, N-7485 Trondheim
http://english.dirnat.no/

Pakistan—Ministry of Environment
M/o Environment,
LG&RD Complex, G-5/2
Islamabad
http://moenv.gov.pk/

Philippines—Department of Environment and
Natural Resources
DENR Building, Visayas Avenue,
Diliman, Quezon City
http://www.denr.gov.ph/

Polish Institute of Environmental Protection
Krucza 5/11d
00-548 Warszawa, Poland
http://www.ios.edu.pl/eng/welcome.html

Portugal—Ministry for Environment, Spatial
Planning and Regional Development
Praça do Comércio
1149-010 Lisbon
http://portal.min-agricultura.pt/portal/page/portal/
MADRP/PT

Russia—Ministry of Natural Resources and the
Environment of the Russian Federation
4/6, Bolshaya Gruzinskaya Str.
Moscow, Russia
http://www.mnr.gov.ru/english/

Taiwan—Republic of China—Environmental
Protection Administration
No. 1, Sec. 1, Zhonghua Rd.,
Zhongzheng District,
Taipei, Taiwan 110, R.O.C.
http://www.epa.gov.tw/EN/

Saudi Arabia—Saudi Environmental Society
Kingdom of Saudi Arabia – Jeddah
Morgan District
Omar Al Khuza'ee Street – Villa No. 6440
http://www.sens.org.sa

Scotland—Scottish Environmental Protection
Agency
SEPA Corporate Office
Erskine Court
Castle Business Park
STIRLING
FK9 4TR
http://www.sepa.org.uk/

South Africa—Department of Environmental
Affairs
315 Pretorius Street
Cnr Pretorius and Van der Walt Streets
Fedsure Forum Building
North Tower
2nd Floor (Departmental reception) OR
1st Floor (Departmental information center)
Pretoria, 0001
http://www.environment.gov.za/

South Korea—Ministry of the Environment
88 Gwanmoon-ro, Gwacheon-si, Gyeonggi-do,
427-729
Republic of Korea
http://eng.me.go.kr/main.do

South Vietnam—Ministry of Natural Resources
and the Environment
83 Nguyen Chi Thanh
Dong Da - Ha Noi
http://www.monre.gov.vn/v35/default.
aspx?tabid=673

Spain—Ministry of Environment and Rural and
Marine
Paseo Infanta Isabel,
1 - 28071
Madrid
http://www.marm.es/

Ukraine—Ministry of Environment and Natural
Resources of Ukraine
35, Urits'koho Str.
Kyiv, Ukraine 03035
http://www.menr.gov.ua/

United Kingdom—Department for Environment,
Food, and Rural Affairs
Defra
Nobel House
17 Smith Square
London
SW1P 3JR
http://www.defra.gov.uk/

NONPROFIT AND RESEARCH ORGANIZATIONS (DOMESTIC AND INTERNATIONAL)

American Institute of Architects
1735 New York Ave., NW
Washington, DC 20006-5292
http://architectfinder.aia.org/

American Wind Energy Association
1501 M Street, NW, Suite 1000
Washington, DC 20005
http://www.awea.org

Center for Alternative Technology
Machynlleth, Powys
SY20 9AZ,
UK
http://www.cat.org.uk/

Center for Ecological Sciences, India Institute of Science
Indian Institute of Science
Bangalore 560 012, INDIA
http://ces.iisc.ernet.in/

Centre for Atmospheric Science—University of Cambridge, UK
Cambridge University, Chemistry Department
Lensfield Road, Cambridge, CB2 1EW, UK
http://www.atm.ch.cam.ac.uk/

Climate Impact Centre—Macquarie University, Australia
Building E8C Room 153
Macquarie University NSW 2109
http://www.climatecore.mq.edu.au/

Climate Research Unit—University of East Anglia
University of East Anglia
Norwich NR4 7TJ, UK
http://www.cru.uea.ac.uk/

Conservation International
2011 Crystal Drive, Suite 500
Arlington, VA 22202
http://www.conservation.org/Pages/default.aspx

Consortium for International Earth Science Information Network (CIESIN)
61 Route 9W, PO Box 1000
Palisades, NY 10964
http://www.ciesin.org/

Consultative Group on International Agricultural Research
1818 H Street, NW
Washington, DC 20433
http://www.cgiar.org/

Co-op America
1612 K Street NW, Suite 600,
Washington DC 20006
http://www.greenamerica.org/

Earth Island Institute
2150 Allston Way, Suite 460
Berkeley, California 94704-1375
http://www.earthisland.org/

Earthwatch
114 Western Ave,
Boston, MA 02134
http://www.earthwatch.org/default.aspx

Ecotrust (Pacific Northwest)
721 NW 9th Avenue, Suite 200
Portland, Oregon 97209
http://www.ecotrust.org/wwri/

Environmental Defense Fund
257 Park Avenue South
New York, NY 10010
http://www.edf.org/home.cfm

Environmental Working Group (EWP)
1436 U Street. NW, Suite 100
Washington, DC 20009
http://www.ewg.org/

Forever Wild Tree Conservancy
Suite 101
5924 Liebig Avenue
Riverdale, N.Y. 10471-1610
http://www.envirolink.org/resource.
html?catid=5&itemid=705

Friends of the Earth (U.K.)
26-28 Underwood Street,
London, N1 7JQ.
http://www.foe.co.uk/

Friends of the Earth (U.S.)
1100 15th Street NW
11th Floor
Washington, DC 20005
http://www.foe.org/

Friends of the Environment Foundation
(Canada)
Regional Manager
220 Dundas Street
4th Floor
London, ON
N6A 1H3
http://www.fef.td.com/

Green Parties of North America
7059 Blair Road NW, Suite 104
Washington, DC 20012
http://www.gp.org/index.php

Green Rivers Environmental Education Network
(GREEN)
2555 W. 34th Avenue
Denver, CO 80211
http://www.earthforce.org/index.php?PID=1

Greenbelt Alliance (San Francisco Bay Area)
631 Howard Street, Suite 510
San Francisco, CA 94105
http://www.greenbelt.org/

Greenpeace International
702 H Street, NW
Suite 300
Washington, D.C. 20001
http://www.greenpeace.org/usa/en/

Institute for Ground Water Research (IGWR)
GPO Box 2100
Adelaide SA 5001
Australia
http://www.groundwater.com.au/

Institute of Ecosystem Studies (IES)
Cary Institute of Ecosystem Studies
Millbrook, New York 12545
http://www.ecostudies.org/

International Energy Association (IEA)
Greenhouse Gas Research and Development
Programme
Stoke Orchard
Cheltenham
Glos.
GL52 7RZ
UK
http://www.isdemo5.co.uk/

Institute of Environmental and Landscape Management - Godollo University (Hungary)
Städtisches Kaufhaus Leipzig
Neumarkt 9-19
04109 Leipzig
http://www.coach-bioenergy.eu/index.php/en/
about/63

International Institute for Industrial Environmental Economics - Lund University, Sweden
Lund University, P.O. Box 196,
22100 Lund, Sweden
http://www.iiiee.lu.se/

International Institute for Sustainable
Development
161 Portage Avenue East, 6th Floor
Winnipeg, Manitoba, Canada
R3B 0Y4
http://www.isdemo5.co.uk/

Lincoln Institute of Land Policy
113 Brattle Street
Cambridge, MA 02138-3400
http://lincolninst.edu/

McGill University Centre for Climate and Global
Change Research (CCGCR)
Room 945, Burnside Hall
805 Sherbrooke Street West
Montreal, Quebec H3A 2K6
http://www.mcgill.ca/meteo/

National Center for Appropriate Technology
3040 Continental Dr.
Butte, MT 59701
http://www.ncat.org/index.php

National Parks and Conservation Association
777 6th Street, NW
Suite 700 Washington, DC 20001
http://www.npca.org/

National Wildlife Federation
11100 Wildlife Center Dr,
Reston VA 20190
http://www.nwf.org/

Natural Resources Defense Council
40 West 20th Street
New York, NY 10011
http://www.nrdc.org/

NCAT Sustainable Agriculture Project—
(National Center for Appropriate Technology)
The NCAT Sustainable Agriculture Project
P.O. Box 3838
Butte, MT 59702
https://attra.ncat.org/index.php

Northwest Ecosystem Alliance
1208 Bay Street #201
Bellingham, WA 98225
http://www.conservationnw.org/

Palouse—Clearwater Environmental Institute
P.O. Box 8596
Moscow ID 83843
http://www.pcei.org/

Rainforest Action Network (RAN)
221 Pine Street, 5th Floor
San Francisco, CA 94104
http://ran.org/

Resource Renewal Institute
187 East Blithedale Avenue
Mill Valley, CA 94941
http://www.rri.org/index.php

Rocky Mountain Institute
2317 Snowmass Creek Road
Snowmass, Colorado 81654
http://www.rmi.org/rmi/

Partnership for Sustainable Communities
900 Fifth Avenue, Suite 201
San Rafael, CA 94901
http://www.p4sc.org/

School of Earth Sciences at Macquarie University
Macquarie University
Sydney NSW 2109
Australia
http://www.eps.mq.edu.au/

Sustainable Buildings Industry Council
1112 16th Street NW
Suite 240
Washington, DC 20036
http://www.sbicouncil.org/

Tellus Institute for Resource and Environmental
Strategies
11 Arlington Street
Boston, MA 02116-3411
http://www.tellus.org/

The 2050 Project
28 W. 25th Street
6th Floor
New York, NY 10010
http://p2050.com/

The Center for the Study of the Environment (CSE)
245 8th Ave. #270
New York, NY 10011
http://www.naturestudy.org/

The East-West Center Program on Environment/
The Asia Foundation
1601 East-West Road
Honolulu, Hawaii 96848
http://www.eastwestcenter.org/research/research-
program-overview/environmental-change-vulner-
ability-and-governance/

The International Council for Local Environmental Initiatives (ICLEI)
Kaiser-Friedrich-Str. 7
53113 Bonn
Germany
http://www.iclei.org/

The Nature Conservancy
4245 North Fairfax Drive, Suite 100
Arlington, VA 22203-1606
http://www.nature.org/aboutus/index.htm

The North American Institute (NAMI)
708 Paseo De Peralta
Santa Fe, NM 87501
http://www.isn.ethz.ch/isn/Digital-Library/IR-
Directory/Detail/?lng=en&ots627=fce62fe0-528d-
4884-9cdf-283c282cf0b2&ots736=cab359a3-
9328-19cc-a1d2-8023e646b22c&id=49486

The Sierra Club
85 Second Street, 2nd Floor
San Francisco, CA 94105
http://www.sierraclub.org/

The Trust for Public Land
101 Montgomery Street, Suite 900
San Francisco, CA 94104
http://www.tpl.org/?gclid=CJaH-9emyqo
CFSwZQgodwSN-yw

The Wilderness Society
1615 M St, NW
Washington, DC 20036
http://wilderness.org/content/about-us

UNESCO - Education for Sustainable Development (ED/PEQ/ESD)
Division for the Promotion of Quality Education
7 Place de Fontenoy
www.unesco.org/education/desd

United States Partnership for Education for Sustainable Development
Division for the Promotion of Quality Education
7 Place de Fontenoy
http://www.uspartnership.org/

University of Toronto Centre for Landscape Research
230 College Street
Toronto, Ontario, CANADA
M5T 1R2
http://www.clr.utoronto.ca/about.htm

Washington Environmental Industry Association
4301 Connecticut Avenue, NW, Suite 300
Washington, DC 20008
http://www.environmentalistseveryday.org/membership-solid-waste-industry-associations/about-eia-solid-waste-management/index.php

World Business Council for Sustainable Development
4, Chemin de Conches
1231 Conches
Geneva
Switzerland
http://www.wbcsd.org/

World Conservation Monitoring Centre
219 Huntingdon Road,
Cambridge
CB3 0DL.
http://www.unep-wcmc.org/about-us_17.html

World Resources Institute
10 G Street NE
Suite 800
Washington, DC 20002
http://www.wri.org/

World Wild Life Fund for Nature (WWF)
Av. du Mont-Blanc 1196 Gland
Switzerland
http://wwf.panda.org/

U.S. FEDERAL AGENCIES AND PROGRAMS

Agency for Toxic Substances and Disease Registry (ATSDR)
4770 Buford Hwy NE,
Atlanta, GA 30341
http://www.atsdr.cdc.gov/

Comprehensive Epidemiologic Data Resource (CEDR)
1000 Independence Avenue, SW
Washington, DC 20585-1290
https://www.orau.gov/cedr/

Data Assimilation Office (NASA-Goddard)
NASA Headquarters
Suite 5K39
Washington, DC 20546-0001
http://gmao.gsfc.nasa.gov/

Earth Resources Observation Systems (EROS)
Data Center
12201 Sunrise Valley Drive
Reston, VA 20192
http://eros.usgs.gov/

EPA Environmental Monitoring and Assessment Program (EMAP)
1200 Pennsylvania Avenue NW
Washington, DC 20004
http://www.epa.gov/emap2/

EPA Hazardous Substance Research Center
104 Ward Hall
Kansas State University
Manhattan, KS 66506-2502
http://www.engg.ksu.edu/chsr/

Goddard Institute for Space Science (GISS)
2880 Broadway
New York, NY 10025
http://www.giss.nasa.gov/

Index of U.S. Geological Survey Servers
12201 Sunrise Valley Drive
Reston, VA 20192
http://seamless.usgs.gov/

National Centers for Environmental Prediction (NCEP)
5200 Auth Road
Camp Springs, Maryland 20746
http://www.ncep.noaa.gov/

National Geophysical Data Center (NGDC)
325 Broadway
Boulder, CO 80305-3328
http://www.ngdc.noaa.gov/ngdc.html

The National Institute for Global Environmental
Change
Tulane University
605 Lindy Boggs Center
New Orleans, LA 70118
http://www.nigec.tulane.edu/

National Oceanographic and Atmospheric
Administration (NOAA)
1401 Constitution Avenue, NW
Room 5128
Washington, DC 20230
http://www.noaa.gov/

National Renewable Energy Laboratory
1617 Cole Blvd.
Golden, CO 80401-3305
http://www.nrel.gov/

NCAR Atmospheric Technology
Division (ATD)
3090 Center Green Drive
Boulder, CO 80301
http://www.eol.ucar.edu/

NOAA Environmental Information Services
1335 East-West Highway, SSMC1,
8th Floor Silver Spring, MD 20910
http://www.nesdis.noaa.gov/

NOAA Great Lakes Environmental Research
Laboratory
4840 S. State Rd.
Ann Arbor MI 48108-9719
http://www.glerl.noaa.gov/

NOAA National Oceanographic Data Center
(NODC)
SSMC3, 4th Floor
1315 East-West Highway
Silver Spring, MD 20910-3282
http://www.nodc.noaa.gov/

NOAA Pacific Marine Environmental
Laboratory
7600 Sand Point Way NE
Seattle, WA 98115
http://www.pmel.noaa.gov/

Oak Ridge National Laboratories (ORNL)—
Environmental Sciences Division
P.O. Box 2008
Oak Ridge, TN 37831
http://www.ornl.gov/

Program for Climate Model Diagnosis and Inter-
comparison (PCMDI)
7000 East Avenue
Bldg. 170, L-103
Livermore, CA 94550-9234
http://www-pcmdi.llnl.gov/

Smithsonian Institution Center for Earth and
Planetary Studies (CEPS)
PO Box 37012
National Air and Space Museum, MRC 315
Washington, DC 20013-7012
http://www.nasm.si.edu/ceps/

The National Institute for Global Environmental
Change
Suite 200 Lindy Boggs Center
Tulane University
New Orleans, LA 70118
http://www.nigec.tulane.edu/

U.S. Department of Agriculture
1400 Independence Ave., SW
Washington, DC 20250
http://www.usda.gov/

U.S. Department of Energy
1000 Independence Ave. SW
Washington DC 20585
http://energy.gov/

U.S. Department of Energy Biological and Environmental Research Program
1000 Independence Ave., SW
Washington, DC 20585
http://science.energy.gov/

U.S. Department of Energy Global Change
Research
1000 Independence Ave., SW
Washington, DC 20585
http://science.energy.gov/

U.S. Energy Information Administration
1000 Independence Ave., SW
Washington, DC 20585
http://www.eia.gov/

U.S. Environmental Protection Agency (EPA)
1200 Pennsylvania Avenue NW
Washington, DC 20004
http://www.epa.gov/

U.S. Geological Survey (USGS)
12201 Sunrise Valley Drive
Reston, VA 20192
http://topomaps.usgs.gov/

USDA-ARS National Soil Erosion Research
Laboratory
1400 Independence Ave.
Washington DC, 20250
http://www.ars.usda.gov/main/site_main.
htm?modecode=36-02-15-00

USDA-ARS Wind Erosion Research Unit
1515 College Avenue
Manhattan, KS 66502
http://www.weru.ksu.edu/

USGS Global Change Research Program
12201 Sunrise Valley Drive
Reston, VA 20192
http://geochange.er.usgs.gov/

U.S. National Biological Service (NBS)
800 North Capitol Street, NW
Suite 700
Washington DC, 20001
http://www.federalregister.gov/agencies/
national-biological-service

U.S. STATE GOVERNMENT AGENCIES

Alabama Department of Environmental Management
1400 Coliseum Boulevard
Montgomery, AL 36110-2400
http://www.adem.state.al.us/

Alaska Department of Environmental
Conservation
P.O. Box 111800
410 Willoughby Ave., Ste. 303
Juneau, AK 99811-1800
http://www.dec.state.ak.us/

Arkansas Basin River Forecast Center (ABRFC)
(NOAA/NWS)
10159 E. 11th Street, Suite 300
Tulsa, OK 74128-3050
http://www.srh.noaa.gov/abrfc/

Arkansas Department of Environmental Quality
5301 Northshore Drive
North Little Rock, AR 72118-5317
http://www.adeq.state.ar.us/

Arizona Department of Environmental Quality
1110 West Washington Street
Phoenix, Arizona 85007
http://www.azdeq.gov/

Arizona Salt River Project
1521 N. Project Drive
Tempe, AZ 85281-1298
https://www.srpnet.com/Default.aspx

California Environmental Protection Agency
P.O. Box 2815
Sacramento, CA
http://www.calepa.ca.gov/

California Environmental Resources Evaluation
System (CERES)
1416 Ninth Street, Suite 1311
Sacramento, CA 95814
http://ceres.ca.gov/

Colorado Department of Public Health and Environment/Office of Environment
4300 Cherry Creek Drive S. EDO A5
Denver, CO 80246-1530
http://www.cdphe.state.co.us/opp/index.html

Connecticut Department of Environmental Protection
79 Elm Street
Hartford, CT 06106-5127
http://www.ct.gov/dep/

Delaware Department of Natural Resources and
Environmental Control
655 S. Bay Road, Suite 5N
Dover, DE 19901
http://www.dnrec.delaware.gov/Pages/default.aspx

Florida Department of Environmental Protection
3900 Commonwealth Boulevard M.S. 49
Tallahassee, Florida 32399
http://www.dep.state.fl.us/

Georgia Department of Natural Resources
Environmental Protection Division
2 Martin Luther King Jr. Drive
Suite 1152, East Tower
Atlanta, GA 30334
http://www.gaepd.org/

Hawaii Department of Land and Natural
Resources
1151 Punchbowl St.
Honolulu, HI 96813
http://hawaii.gov/dlnr/

Idaho Department of Environmental Quality
1410 N. Hilton
Boise, ID 83706
http://www.deq.idaho.gov/

Illinois Environmental Protection Agency
1021 North Grand Avenue East
P.O. Box 19276
Springfield, Illinois 62794-9276
http://www.epa.state.il.us/

Illinois Natural Resources Information
Network
One Natural Resources Way
Springfield, IL 62702-1271
http://www.dnr.illinois.gov/Pages/default.aspx

Indiana Department of Natural Resources
402 West Washington Street
Indianapolis, IN 46204
http://www.in.gov/dnr/

Iowa Department of Natural Resources
502 E. 9th Street
Des Moines, IA 50319-0034
http://www.iowadnr.gov/

Kansas Department of Health and Environment
Curtis State Office Building
1000 SW Jackson
Topeka, Kansas 66612
http://www.kdheks.gov/

Kentucky Environmental Quality Commission
603 Wilkinson Boulevard
Frankfort, KY 40601
http://eqc.ky.gov/Pages/default.aspx

Louisiana Department of Environmental
Quality
602 N. Fifth Street
Baton Rouge, LA 70802
http://www.deq.louisiana.gov/portal/

Maine Department of Environmental Protection
17 State House Station
Augusta, Maine 04333-0017
http://www.maine.gov/dep/

Maryland Department of Natural Resources
580 Taylor Avenue
Annapolis, MD 21401
http://www.dnr.state.md.us/

Massachusetts Department of Environmental
Protection
1 Winter Street
Boston, MA 02108
http://www.mass.gov/dep/

Michigan Department of Natural Resources
Mason Building,
Sixth Floor,
P.O. Box 30028,
Lansing MI 48909
http://www.michigan.gov/dnr

Minnesota Department of Natural Resources
500 Lafayette Road
St. Paul, MN 55155-4040
http://www.dnr.state.mn.us/index.html

Mississippi Department of Environmental Quality
515 E. Amite St
Jackson, MS 39201
http://www.deq.state.ms.us/

Missouri Department of Conservation
2901 W. Truman Blvd.
Jefferson City, MO, 65102
http://mdc.mo.gov/

Montana Natural Resource Information System
1515 East 6th Avenue
PO BOX 201800
Helena, MT 59620-1800
http://nris.mt.gov/

Nebraska Department of Environmental Quality
1200 "N" Street, Suite 400
PO Box 98922
Lincoln, Nebraska 68509
http://www.deq.state.ne.us/

Nevada Division of Environmental Protection
901 South Stewart Street, Suite 4001
Carson City, Nevada 89701–5249
http://ndep.nv.gov/

New Hampshire Department of Environmental
Services
PO Box 95
Concord, NH 03302-0095
http://des.nh.gov/

New Jersey Department of Environmental
Protection
DEP Main Building
401 East State Street
Trenton, NJ 08608
http://www.state.nj.us/dep/

New Mexico Environment Department
1190 St. Francis Drive
Suite N4050
Santa Fe, New Mexico 87505
http://www.nmenv.state.nm.us/

New York State Department of Environmental
Conservation
625 Broadway
Albany, New York 12233-0001
http://www.dec.ny.gov/24.html

North Carolina Department of Environment and
Natural Resources
1601 Mail Service Center
Raleigh, NC 27699-1601
http://portal.ncdenr.org/web/guest

North Carolina Division of Forest Resources
Bladen Lakes State forest
4470 Hwy 242 N
Elizabethtown, NC 28337
http://www.dfr.state.nc.us/

North Dakota Department of Environmental
Health
North Dakota Department of Health
Environmental Health Apx-Section
918 East Divide Avenue
Bismarck, ND 58501-1947
http://www.ndhealth.gov/ehs/

Ohio Department of Natural Resources
045 Morse Road, Building G
Columbus OH 43229-6693
http://www.dnr.state.oh.us/

Ohio Environmental Protection Agency
50 West Town Street, Suite 700
Columbus, OH 43215
http://www.epa.state.oh.us/

Oklahoma Department of Environmental Quality
707 N Robinson
Oklahoma City, OK 73102
http://ww.deq.state.ok.us/

Oregon Department of Environmental Quality
DEQ Headquarters Office
811 SW 6th Avenue
Portland, OR 97204-1390
http://www.oregon.gov/

Oregon Department of Forestry
2600 State St.
Salem, Oregon 97310
http://www.oregon.gov/ODF/

Oregon Department of Fish and Wildlife
3406 Cherry Avenue N.E.
Salem, OR 97303
http://www.dfw.state.or.us/

Pennsylvania Environmental Protection Agency
Rachel Carson State Office Building
400 Market Street
Harrisburg, PA 17101
http://www.depweb.state.pa.us/

Puerto Rico Environmental Quality Board
Environmental Agencies Building A.
Cruz Matos
San Jose Industrial Park Construction
1375 Ponce de Leon Avenue
San Juan, PR 00926-2604
http://www.gobierno.pr/jca/inicio

Rhode Island Department of Environmental
Management
235 Promenade St.
Providence, RI 02908-5767
http://www.dem.ri.gov/

South Carolina Department of Natural Resources
1000 Assembly Street
Columbia, SC 29201
http://www.dnr.sc.gov/

South Dakota Department of Environment and
Natural Resources
523 E Capitol
Pierre, SD 57501
http://denr.sd.gov/

Tennessee Department of Environment and
Conservation
401 Church Street
L&C Tower
Nashville, TN 37243
http://www.tn.gov/environment/org/

Texas Natural Resource Conservation
Commission
101 South Main
Temple, TX 76501
http://www.tx.nrcs.usda.gov/

U.S. Virgin Islands Environmental Protection and
Department of Planning and Natural Resources
8100 Lindberg Bay, Ste. 61
St. Thomas, U.S. Virgin Islands 00802
http://www.dpnr.gov.vi/dep/home.htm

Utah Department of Environmental Quality
195 North 1950 West
Salt Lake City, Utah 84114-4810
http://www.deq.utah.gov/

Vermont Department of Environmental
Conservation
103 South Main Street
Waterbury, VT 05671-0401
http://www.anr.state.vt.us/dec/dec.htm

Virginia Department of Conservation and
Recreation
203 Governor Street
Richmond, VA 23219-2094
http://www.dcr.virginia.gov/

Washington State Department of Ecology
P.O. Box 47600
Olympia, WA 98504-7600
http://www.ecy.wa.gov/

Washington State Department of Natural
Resources
PO Box 470001111 Washington Street SE
Olympia, WA 98504-7000
http://www.dnr.wa.gov/Pages/default.aspx

West Virginia Department of Environmental
Protection
601 57th Street SE
Charleston, WV 25304
http://www.dep.wv.gov/

Wisconsin Department of Natural Resources
101 S. Webster Street
PO Box 7921
Madison, Wisconsin 53707-7921
http://dnr.wi.gov/

Wyoming Department of Environmental Quality
122 West 25th St, Herschler Building
Cheyenne, WY 82002
http://deq.state.wy.us/

APPENDIX B

JOURNALS ON ENVIRONMENTAL, ECONOMIC, TECHNOLOGICAL, AND SOCIAL ASPECTS OF SUSTAINABILITY

Agriculture, Ecosystems and Environment
Elsevier Ltd
PO Box 800
Oxford OX5 1DX
United Kingdom
http://www.elsevier.com/wps/find/journaldescription.cws_home/503298/description

Atmospheric Environment
Elsevier Ltd
PO Box 800
Oxford OX5 1DX
United Kingdom
http://www.elsevier.com/wps/find/journaldescription.cws_home/246/description

Air Quality, Atmosphere, and Health
Springer Science and Business Media
Van Godewijkstraat 30
Dordrecht, 3311 GX
The Netherlands
http://www.springerlink.com/

Archives of Environmental Contamination and Toxicology
Springer Science and Business Media
Van Godewijkstraat 30
Dordrecht, 3311 GX
The Netherlands
http://www.springerlink.com/

Australasian Journal of Environmental Management
Copyright Agency Limited (Distributor)
Level 15
233 Castlereagh Street
Sydney, NSW 2000
Australia

BioCycle
J.G. Press Inc.
P.O. Box 351
Emmaus, PA 18049
http://www.jgpress.com/biocycle.htm

Building and Environment
Elsevier Ltd
PO Box 800
Oxford OX5 1DX
United Kingdom
http://www.sciencedirect.com.proxy1.ncu.edu/science/journal/03601323

Business and Society
Sage Publications
90 Tottenham Court Road
London W1P 0LP
http://bas.sagepub.com/

Business and the Environment
Aspen Publishers Inc.
111 Eighth Avenue, 7th Floor
New York New York 10011
http://www.aspenpublishers.com

Business Strategy and the Environment
Wiley Periodicals Inc.
111 River Street
Hoboken, NJ 07030
http://www3.interscience.wiley.com/cgi-bin/jhome/5329

Carbon and Climate Law Review: CCLR
Lexxion Verlagsgesellschaft mbH
Güntzelstr. 63 · 10717 Berlin
http://www.lexxion.de/zeitschriften/fachzeitschriften-englisch/cclr.html

Computers, Environment and Urban Systems
Elsevier Data Protection Officer
Elsevier Limited
the Boulevard
Langford Lane
Kidlington
Oxford OX5 1GB
United Kingdom
http://www.elsevier.com/wps/find/journaldescription.cws_home/304/description

Corporate Environmental Strategy
Elsevier Ltd
PO Box 800
Oxford OX5 1DX
United Kingdom
http://www.sciencedirect.com/science/journal/10667938

Current Opinion in Environmental Sustainability
Elsevier Ltd
PO Box 800
Oxford OX5 1DX
United Kingdom
http://www.elsevier.com/wps/find/journaldescription.cws_home/718675/description

Ecotoxicology and Environmental Safety
Elsevier Ltd
PO Box 800
Oxford OX5 1DX
United Kingdom
http://www.elsevier.com/wps/find/journaldescription.cws_home/622819/description#description

Corporate Environmental Strategy (International Journal for Sustainable Business)
Elsevier Science
The Boulevard
Langford Lane
Kidlington
Oxford OX5 1GB
United Kingdom
http://www.sciencedirect.com/science/journal/10667938

Corporate Reputation Review
Palgrave Macmillan
Brunel Road
Houndmills, Basingstoke, RG21 6XS
UNITED KINGDOM
http://proquest.umi.com.ezproxy.socccd.edu/pqdweb?RQT=318&TS=1312751543&clientId=27898&VType=PQD&VName=PQD&VInst=PROD&PMID=49212&Tab=3

Corporate Social - Responsibility and Environmental Management
Wiley Periodicals Inc.
111 River Street
Hoboken, NJ 07030
http://www3.interscience.wiley.com/cgi-bin/jhome/90513547

Ecological Economics
Elsevier Ltd
PO Box 800
Oxford OX5 1DX
United Kingdom
http://www.elsevier.com/wps/find/journaldescription.cws_home/503305/description#description

EHS Today
Penton Business Media, Inc. and Penton Media, Inc.
249 West 17th Street
NEW YORK, NY 10011
http://www.acssi.com

Energy Policy
Elsevier Science Ltd.
The Boulevard
Langford Lane
Kidlington, Oxford OX5 1GB
England
http://www.elsevier.com/wps/find/journaldescription.cws_home/30414/description

Environment
Taylor and Francis Inc.
325 Chestnut St, Ste 800
Philadelphia, PA 19106
http://www.taylorandfrancis.com/

Environment and Development Economics
Cambridge University Press
The Edinburgh Building
Shaftesbury Road
Cambridge CB2 2RU
United Kingdom
http://uk.cambridge.org/journals/ede/

Environment International
Springer Science and Business Media
Van Godewijkstraat 30
Dordrecht, 3311 GX
The Netherlands
http://www.elsevier.com/wps/find/journaldescription.cws_home/326/description

Environment, Development and Sustainability
Springer Science and Business Media
Van Godewijkstraat 30
Dordrecht, 3311 GX
The Netherlands
http://www.springer.com/environment/sustainable+development/journal/10668

Environmental and Ecological Statistics
Springer Science and Business Media
Van Godewijkstraat 30
Dordrecht, 3311 GX
The Netherlands
http://www.springer.com/life+sciences/ecology/journal/10651

Environmental and Experimental Botany
Elsevier Science Ltd.
The Boulevard
Langford Lane
Kidlington, Oxford OX5 1GB
England
http://www.elsevier.com/wps/find/journaldescription.cws_home/267/description#description

Environmental and Resource Economics
Springer Science and Business Media
Van Godewijkstraat 30
Dordrecht, 3311 GX
The Netherlands
http://www.springer.com/economics/environmental/journal/10640

Environmental Design and Construction
2401 West Big Beaver Road
Suite 700
Troy Michigan 48084
http://www.bnpmedia.com

Environmental Economics and Policy Studies
Springer Science and Business Media B.V.
Van Godewijkstraat 30
Dordrecht 3311 GZ
Netherlands
http://www.springerlink.com/home/main.mpx

Environmental Forensics
Elsevier Science Ltd.
The Boulevard
Langford Lane
Kidlington, Oxford OX5 1GB
England
http://www.sciencedirect.com.proxy1.ncu.edu/science/journal/15275922

Environmental Hazards
Elsevier Science Ltd.
The Boulevard
Langford Lane
Kidlington, Oxford OX5 1GB
England
http://www.elsevier.com/wps/locate/issn/17477891

Environmental Impact Assessment Review
Elsevier Science Ltd.
The Boulevard
Langford Lane
Kidlington, Oxford OX5 1GB
England
http://www.elsevier.com/wps/find/journaldescription.cws_home/505718/description

Environmental Innovation and Societal Transitions
Elsevier Science Ltd.
The Boulevard
Langford Lane
Kidlington, Oxford OX5 1GB
England
http://www.elsevier.com/wps/find/journaldescription.cws_home/724359/description

Environmental Management
Springer Science and Business Media
Van Godewijkstraat 30
Dordrecht, 3311 GX
The Netherlands
http://www.springer.com/environment/environmental+management/journal/267

Environmental Manager
John Wiley and Sons, Inc.
111 River Street
Hoboken New Jersey 07030
http://onlinelibrary.wiley.com/

Environmental Modeling and Assessment
Springer Science and Business Media
Van Godewijkstraat 30
Dordrecht, 3311 GX
The Netherlands
http://www.springer.com/new+%26+forthcoming+titles+(default)/journal/10666

Environmental Modeling and Software
Elsevier Science Ltd.
The Boulevard
Langford Lane
Kidlington, Oxford OX5 1GB
England
http://www.elsevier.com/wps/find/journaldescription.cws_home/422921/description

Environmental Monitoring and Assessment
Springer Science and Business Media
Van Godewijkstraat 30
Dordrecht, 3311 GX
The Netherlands
http://www.springer.com/environment/monitoring+-+environmental+analysis/journal/10661

Environmental Policy and Governance
Wiley Periodicals Inc.
111 River Street
Hoboken, NJ 07030
http://www.interscience.wiley.com

Environmental Policy and Law
IOS Press
Nieuwe Hemweg 6B
Amsterdam 1013 BG
Netherlands
http://www.iospress.nl/

Environmental Pollution
Elsevier Science Ltd.
The Boulevard
Langford Lane
Kidlington, Oxford OX5 1GB
England
http://www.elsevier.com/wps/find/journaldescrip-
tion.cws_home/405856/description#description

Environmental Quality Management
John Wiley and Sons, Inc.
111 River Street
Hoboken New Jersey 07030-5774
http://onlinelibrary.wiley.com/

Environmental Research
Elsevier Science Ltd.
The Boulevard
Langford Lane
Kidlington, Oxford OX5 1GB
England
http://www.elsevier.com/wps/find/journaldescrip-
tion.cws_home/622821/description

Environmental Science and Technology
American Chemical Society
2540 Olentangy River Road
Columbus Ohio 43202-1505
http://www.crcpress.com/

Environmental Science and Pollution Research
International
Springer Science and Business Media
Van Godewijkstraat 30
Dordrecht, 3311 GX
The Netherlands
http://www.springer.com/environment/
journal/11356

Environmentalist
Springer Science and Business Media
Van Godewijkstraat 30
Dordrecht, 3311 GX
The Netherlands
http://www.springer.com/environment/
nature+conservation+-+biodiversity/
journal/10669

Ethics and the Environment
Indiana University Press
601 North Morton Street
Bloomington, IN 47404
http://inscribe.iupress.org

Global Environmental Change
Elsevier Science Ltd.
The Boulevard
Langford Lane
Kidlington, Oxford OX5 1GB
England
http://www.sciencedirect.com.proxy1.ncu.edu/
science/journal/09266917

Greener Management International: The Journal
of Corporate Environmental Strategy and
Practice
Greenleaf Publishing
Aizlewood Business Centre
Aizlewood's Mill
Nursery Street
Sheffield, S3 8GG
United Kingdom
http://www.greenleaf-publishing.com/default.
asp?ContentID=8

Green Futures
Overseas House,
19 - 23 Ironmonger Row,
London, EC1V 3QN.
http://www.forumforthefuture.org/greenfutures/
about-us

Impact Assessment and Project Appraisal
Beech Tree Publishing
10 Watford Close
Guildford, Surrey GU1 2EP
England
http://www.scipol.co.uk/iapahomel.html

Industrial Environment
Worldwide Videotex
PO Box 3273
Boynton Beach Florida 33424
http://www.wvpubs.com/

Interdisciplinary Environmental Review
4501 Forbes Blvd., Suite 200
Lanham, MD 20706
http://www.rowmanlittlefield.com/RL/Journals/
IER/Index.shtml

International Environmental Agreements: Politics, Law and Economics
Springer Science and Business Media
Van Godewijkstraat 30
Dordrecht, 3311 GX
The Netherlands
http://www.springer.com/law/environmental/journal/10784

International Journal of Climate Change Strategies and Management
Emerald Group Publishing, Limited
60/62 Toller Lane
Bradford, West Yorkshire BD8 9BY
England
http://www.emeraldinsight.com/products/journals/journals.htm?id=IJCCSM

International Journal of Environment and Pollution
Inderscience Enterprises Ltd.
110 Avenue Louis Casai
Case Postal 306
Geneva, CH1215
Switzerland
http://www.inderscience.com/browse/index.php?journalID=9&year=2011&vol=45&issue=1/2/3

International Journal of Environmental Technology and Management
Inderscience Enterprises Ltd.
110 Avenue Louis Casai
Case Postal 306
Geneva, CH1215
Switzerland
http://www.inderscience.com/browse/index.php?journalID=11

International Journal of Hygiene and Environmental Health
Elsevier Science Ltd.
The Boulevard
Langford Lane
Kidlington, Oxford OX5 1GB
England
http://www.elsevier.com/wps/find/journaldescription.cws_home/701771/description#description

International Journal of Sustainability in Higher Education
Emerald Group Publishing Limited
Howard House
Wagon Lane
Bingley BD16 1WA
United Kingdom
http://emeraldinsight.com/products/journals/journals.htm?id=ijshe

International Journal of Sustainable Development
Inderscience Enterprises Ltd.
110 Avenue Louis Casai
Case Postal 306
Geneva, CH1215
Switzerland
http://www.inderscience.com/browse/index.php?journalCODE=ijsd

International Journal of Sustainable Strategic Management (IJSSM)
Inderscience Enterprises Ltd.
110 Avenue Louis Casai
Case Postal 306
Geneva, CH1215
Switzerland
http://www.inderscience.com/browse/index.php?journalCODE=ijssm

International Journal of Sustainable Transportation
Taylor and Francis Ltd.
2 Park Square
Milton Park
Abingdon, Oxfordshire, OX14 4RN
United Kingdom
http://www.tandf.co.uk/journals/journal.asp?issn=1556-8318&linktype=offers

International Journal of Technology Management and Sustainable Development
Intellect Ltd.
The Mill
Parnall Road
Fishponds
Bristol BS16 3JG
United Kingdom
http://www.intellectbooks.co.uk/journals/view-journal,id=133/

Journal of Agricultural and Environmental Ethics
Springer Science and Business Media
Van Godewijkstraat 30
Dordrecht, 3311 GX
The Netherlands
http://www.springer.com/social+sciences/applied+ethics/journal/10806

Journal of Arid Environment
Elsevier Science Ltd.
The Boulevard
Langford Lane
Kidlington, Oxford OX5 1GB
England
http://www.elsevier.com/wps/find/journaldescription.cws_home/622855/description#description

Journal of Environment and Development
Sage Publications Inc.
2455 Teller Road
Thousand Oaks California 91320
http://www.sagepub.com

Journal of Environmental Economics and
Management
Elsevier Science Publishing Company, Inc.
P.O. Box 882
Madison Square Station
New York, NY 10159-0882
http://www.elsevier.com/wps/find/journaldescrip-
tion.cws_home/622870/description#description

Journal of Environmental Law and Practice
Carswell Publishing
One Corporate Plaza
2075 Kennedy Road
Scarborough, Ontario M1T 3V4
Canada
http://www.carswell.com/description.
asp?docid=299

Journal of Environmental Management
Elsevier Science Ltd.
The Boulevard
Langford Lane
Kidlington, Oxford OX5 1GB
England
http://www.elsevier.com/wps/find/journaldescrip-
tion.cws_home/622871/description

Journal of Environmental Management and
Tourism
ASERS Ltd
No 5, Sabba Stefanescu Street
Craiova, 200145
Romania
http://www.asers.eu/journals/jemt.html

Journal of Environmental Permitting
Wiley Periodicals Inc.
111 River Street
Hoboken, NJ 07030
http://www.interscience.wiley.com

Journal of Environmental Planning and
Management
Taylor and Francis Ltd.
2 Park Square
Milton Park
Abingdon, Oxfordshire, OX14 4RN
United Kingdom
http://www.tandf.co.uk/journals/CJEP

Journal of Environmental Protection
Scientific Research Publishing
5005 Paseo Segovia
Irvine, CA 92603-3334
http://www.scirp.org/journal/jep/

Journal of Environmental Psychology
Elsevier Science Publishing Company, Inc.
P.O. Box 882
Madison Square Station
New York, NY 10159-0882
http://www.elsevier.com/wps/find/
journaldescription.cws_home/622872/
description#description

Journal of Environmental Radioactivity
Elsevier Science Publishing Company, Inc.
P.O. Box 882
Madison Square Station
New York, NY 10159-0882
http://www.elsevier.com/wps/find/
journaldescription.cws_home/405861/
description#description

Journal of Environmental Regulation
Wiley Periodicals Inc.
111 River Street
Hoboken, NJ 07030
http://www.interscience.wiley.com

Journal of Environmental Sciences
Elsevier Science Publishing Company, Inc.
P.O. Box 882
Madison Square Station
New York, NY 10159-0882
http://www.elsevier.com/wps/find/
journaldescription.cws_home/709941/
description#description

Journal of Environmental Studies and Policy
Tata Energy Research Institute
India Habitat Centre
Lodi Road
New Delhi, 110 003
India
http://www.teriin.org/index.php

Journal of Green Building
College Publishing
12309 Lynwood Drive
Glen Allen, VA 23059
http://www.collegepublishing.us/journal.htm

Journal of Healthcare Management
Health Administration Press
1 N. Franklin Street
Suite 1700
Chicago, IL 60606
http://www.ache.org/pubs/jhmsub.cfm

Journal of Housing and the Built Environment
Springer Science and Business Media
Van Godewijkstraat 30
Dordrecht, 3311 GX
The Netherlands
http://www.springer.com/social+sciences/
population+studies/journal/10901

Journal of Hydro-environment Research
Elsevier Science Publishing Company, Inc.
P.O. Box 882
Madison Square Station
New York, NY 10159-0882
http://www.elsevier.com/wps/find/journalde-
scription.cws_home/711617/description

Journal of Industrial Ecology
John Wiley and Sons Inc.
111 River St. MS 4-02
Hoboken, NJ 07030-5774
http://onlinelibrary.wiley.com/journal/10.1111/
(ISSN)1530-9290

Journal of Organizational Change
Management
Howard House
Wagon Lane
Bingley BD16 1WA
United Kingdom
http://www.emeraldinsight.com/products/jour-
nals/journals.htm?id=jocm

Journal of Sustainable Development
Canadian Center of Science and Education
4915 Bathurst St. Unit 209-309
Toronto, Ontario M2R 1X9
Canada
http://www.ccsenet.org/journal/index.php/jsd

Journal of Sustainable Product Design
Springer Science and Business Media
Van Godewijkstraat 30
Dordrecht, 3311 GX
The Netherlands
http://www.springer.com/engineering/
mechanical+eng/journal/10970

Journal of Sustainable Tourism
Routledge
4 Park Square
Milton Park
Abingdon OX14 4RN
United Kingdom
http://www.tandf.co.uk/journals/rsus

Land Economics
University of Wisconsin Press
1930 Monroe St
3rd Floor
Madison, WI 53711
http://le.uwpress.org/

Land Lines
Lincoln Institute of Land Policy
113 Brattle Street
Cambridge, MA 02138-3400
http://lincolninst.edu/

Marine Environmental Research
Elsevier Science Publishing Company, Inc.
P.O. Box 882
Madison Square Station
New York, NY 10159-0882
http://www.elsevier.com/wps/find/journaldescrip-
tion.cws_home/405865/description

Mitigation and Adaptation Strategies for Global
Change
Springer Science and Business Media
Van Godewijkstraat 30
Dordrecht, 3311 GX
The Netherlands
http://www.springer.com/earth+sciences+and
+geography/meteorology+%26+climatology/
journal/11027

Mutation Research/Environmental Mutagenesis
and Related Subject
Elsevier Science Publishing Company, Inc.
P.O. Box 882
Madison Square Station
New York, NY 10159-0882
http://www.elsevier.com/wps/find/journaldescrip-
tion.cws_home/522820/description#description

Mutation Research/Genetic Toxicology and Envi-
ronmental Mutagenesis
Elsevier Science Publishing Company, Inc.
P.O. Box 882
Madison Square Station
New York, NY 10159-0882
http://www.elsevier.com/wps/find/journaldescrip-
tion.cws_home/522820/description#description

Organization and Environment
Sage Publications Inc.
2455 Teller Road
Thousand Oaks California 91320
http://www.sagepub.com

Pollution Engineering
BNP Media
2401 W. Big Beaver Rd.
Suite 700
Troy, MI 48084
http://www.pollutionengineering.com/

Population and Environment
Springer Science and Business Media B.V.
Van Godewijkstraat 30
Dordrecht 3311 GZ
Netherlands
http://www.springerlink.com/

Population Ecology
Springer Science and Business Media
Van Godewijkstraat 30
Dordrecht, 3311 GX
The Netherlands
http://www.springerlink.com/content/103139/

Procedia Environmental Sciences
Elsevier Science Publishing Company, Inc.
P.O. Box 882
Madison Square Station
New York, NY 10159-0882
http://www.elsevier.com/wps/find/journaldescrip-
tion.cws_home/719992/description

Process Safety and Environmental Protection
Elsevier Science Publishing Company, Inc.
P.O. Box 882
Madison Square Station
New York, NY 10159-0882
http://www.elsevier.com/wps/find/journaldescrip-
tion.cws_home/713889/description

Remote Sensing of Environment
Elsevier Science Publishing Company, Inc.
P.O. Box 882
Madison Square Station
New York, NY 10159-0882
http://www.elsevier.com/wps/find/
journaldescription.cws_home/505733/
description#description

Review of European Community and International Environmental Law
John Wiley and Sons Inc.
111 River St. MS 4-02
Hoboken, NJ 07030-5774
http://www.wiley.com/WileyCDA/Section/
id-403426.html

Reviews in Environmental Science and
Biotechnology
Springer
233 Spring Street
New York, NY 10013
http://www.springer.com/environment/envi-
ronmental+engineering+and+physics/
journal/11157

Science of the Total Environment
Elsevier Science Publishing Company, Inc.
P.O. Box 882
Madison Square Station
New York, NY 10159-0882
http://www.elsevier.com/wps/find/journaldescrip-
tion.cws_home/503360/description

Society and Natural Resources
4 Park Square
Milton Park
Abingdon
Oxfordshire
OX14 4RN, UK
http://www.tandf.co.uk/journals/tf/08941920.html

Sustainable Development
John Wiley and Sons Inc.
111 River St. MS 4-02
Hoboken, NJ 07030-5774
http://onlinelibrary.wiley.com/journal/10.1002/
(ISSN)1099-1719

Sustainable Communities Magazine
Partnership for Sustainable Communities
900 Fifth Avenue, Suite 201
San Rafael, CA 94901
http://www.p4sc.org/

Sustainable Facility
BNP Media
2401 West Big Beaver Road
Suite 700
Troy Michigan 48084
http://www.sustainablefacility.com

The Environmentalist
Elsevier Science Publishing Company, Inc.
P.O. Box 882
Madison Square Station
New York, NY 10159-0882
http://www.sciencedirect.com/science/
journal/02511088

The International Journal of Environmental
Studies
4 Park Square
Milton Park
Abingdon
Oxfordshire
OX14 4RN, UK
http://www.tandf.co.uk/journals/titles/00207233.
html

The Journal of Material Cycles and Waste
Management
Springer
233 Spring Street
New York, NY 10013
http://www.springer.com/environment/
pollution+and+remediation/journal/10163

Transportation Research Part D: Transport and
Environment
Elsevier Science Publishing Company, Inc.
P.O. Box 882
Madison Square Station
New York, NY 10159-0882
http://www.elsevier.com/wps/find/journaldescrip-
tion.cws_home/31153/description#description

Urban Land
Springer
233 Spring Street
New York, NY 10013
http://www.springer.com/earth+scienc-
es+and+geography/geography/
book/978-3-540-43845-8

UrbanLand
Urban Land Institute
1025 Thomas Jefferson Street, NW, Suite 500
West
Washington DC 20007
http://urbanland.uli.org/

Waste Age
Penton Business Media, Inc. and Penton Media,
Inc.
249 West 17th Street
New York, NY 10011
http://www.wasteage.com

Waste Management and Research
Sage Publications Inc.
2455 Teller Road
Thousand Oaks California 91320
http://www.sagepub.com/journals/Journal201691

Water and Environmental Journal
Turret Rai Plc.
Uxbridge, Middlesex
United Kingdom
http://www.dmgworldmedia.com/

Water Engineering and Management
California State University, Long Beach
1250 Bellflower Blvd
Long Beach, California 90840
http://www.csulb.edu/colleges/coe/cecem/views/
programs/cert/wem_cert.shtml

Water, Air and Soil Pollution
Springer
233 Spring Street
New York, NY 10013
http://www.springer.com/environment/
journal/11270